"Michael Wilkins's work on discipleshi[p] ... it is fitting to publish a book honoring [his work on dis]cipleship. We are treated here to a survey of what discipleship [in] the New Testament from experts in the field, and we also see some of the wider dimensions of discipleship in this important work. All those wanting to understand discipleship will find this to be a valuable resource."

—Thomas R. Schreiner,
James Buchanan Harrison Professor of New Testament Interpretation,
The Southern Baptist Theological Seminary

"The aim of the contributors to the Michael Wilkins Festschrift is 'to serve contemporary believers' by 'providing an in-depth examination of the concept of discipleship across the New Testament and by explaining how the concept interfaces with important areas of the Christian life—the mind, the soul, and the local church.' The eminently readable volume has achieved this goal in a comprehensive and consistent manner, and thus is itself an act of discipleship which should provoke readers in the church and in the academy to assess how we read the biblical texts and how we shall live in the church and in the world."

—Eckhard J. Schnabel,
Mary F. Rockefeller Distinguished Professor of New Testament,
Gordon-Conwell Theological Seminary

"Of all the terms the Divine Son could have used and did in fact use to refer to humanity's relationship with himself, time and time again he returned to the language of 'disciple.' And yet, over the course of church history, the concept of 'disciple' and the way of discipleship to Jesus has often been neglected, misunderstood, and subjected to distortion. No living scholar has done more to reclaim Jesus and the Gospel writers' intended meaning of 'disciple' than Michael Wilkins. This book not only pays tribute to Michael's scholarly legacy but is at its best when the authors stand on the shoulders of Michael's work. Goodrich and Strauss are to be commended for corralling a compelling group of contributors. I keep up on the scholarly literature related to discipleship and there was not one chapter in this book that I was not eager to read. Indeed, a careful reading of this book would do much to reestablish a vision of what it is to be a disciple of Jesus, learning from him how to live life in his Father's kingdom by the Spirit."

—Steven L. Porter,
Professor of Theology and Philosophy,
Biola University

"John Goodrich and Mark Strauss have assembled an impressive roster of scholars who have addressed a vital but often neglected topic in both the church and in the academy. It is only right that this important collection of studies on discipleship is dedicated to Professor Michael Wilkins, whose excellent work on discipleship is widely recognized and appreciated. Rich with insight, *Following Jesus Christ* represents a major advance in this essential area of study."

— Craig A. Evans,
John Bisagno Distinguished Professor of Christian Beginnings,
Houston Baptist University

FOLLOWING JESUS CHRIST

The New Testament Message of Discipleship for Today

A Volume in Honor of Michael J. Wilkins

John K. Goodrich and Mark L. Strauss

EDITORS

Kregel
Academic

Following Jesus Christ: The New Testament Message of Discipleship for Today

Published by Kregel Academic, an imprint of Kregel Publications, 2450 Oak Industrial Dr. NE, Grand Rapids, MI 49505-6020.

The Hebrew font used in this book is NewJerusalemU and the Greek font GraecaU is available from www.linguistsoftware.com/lgku.htm, +1-425-775-1130.

ISBN 978–0–8254–4499–9

Printed in the United States of America

19 20 21 22 23 / 5 4 3 2 1

For Mike Wilkins
Teacher, friend, disciple

Table of Contents

Part 2—Discipleship Today

Contributors

Clinton E. Arnold (PhD, University of Aberdeen) is Dean and Professor of New Testament Language and Literature at Talbot School of Theology. He is a former President of the Evangelical Theological Society and is author of *Ephesians: Power and Magic* (Cambridge University Press), *The Colossian Syncretism* (Mohr Siebeck/Baker), and *Powers of Darkness* (IVP). He is also editor of the Zondervan Exegetical Commentary on the New Testament series, for which he wrote the volume on *Ephesians*.

Craig L. Blomberg (PhD, University of Aberdeen) is Distinguished Professor of New Testament at Denver Seminary. He is the author of *Matthew* (B&H), *1 Corinthians* (Zondervan), and *James* (Zondervan), as well as many other academic books, including *Jesus and the Gospels* (B&H), *From Pentecost to Patmos* (B&H), *A Handbook of New Testament Exegesis* (Baker), *The Historical Reliability of the Gospels* (IVP), and *Christians in an Age of Wealth* (Zondervan).

Darrell L. Bock (PhD, University of Aberdeen) is Executive Director of Cultural Engagement and Senior Research Professor of New Testament Studies at Dallas Theological Seminary. He is a Humboldt Scholar, a former President of the Evangelical Theological Society, and the author of more than thirty books, including *Luke* (Baker), *Acts* (Baker), and *A Theology of Luke and Acts* (Zondervan).

Tod E. Bolsinger (PhD, Fuller Theological Seminary) is Vice President and Chief of Leadership Formation, and Associate Professor of Leadership Formation at Fuller Theological Seminary. He is formerly Senior Pastor of San Clemente Presbyterian Church, as well as author of *It Takes a Church to Raise a Christian* (Brazos), *Show Time* (Baker), and *Canoeing the Mountains* (IVP).

David E. Briones (PhD, University of Durham) is Associate Professor of New Testament at Westminster Theological Seminary. He is coeditor of *Paul and Seneca in Dialogue* (Brill), as well as author of *Paul's Financial Policy: A Socio-Theological Approach* (Bloomsbury) and articles in such journals as *New Testament Studies*, *Journal for the Study of the New Testament*, and *Catholic Biblical Quarterly*.

Jeannine K. Brown (PhD, Luther Seminary) is Professor of New Testament at Bethel Seminary, San Diego. She is the author of *The Disciples in Narrative Perspective* (SBL/Brill), *Matthew* (Baker), *Matthew* (Eerdmans), *Scripture as Communication* (Baker), and *Becoming Whole and Holy* (Baker). She is also coeditor of the *Dictionary of Jesus and the Gospels* (2nd ed., IVP).

Robert L. Cavin (PhD, University of Durham) is Lead Teaching and Ministries Pastor at Northpark Community Church, Valencia, California. He is the author of *New Existence and Righteous Living: Colossians and 1 Peter in Conversation with 4QInstruction and the Hodayot* (de Gruyter).

Ben R. Crenshaw is a graduate of Denver Seminary, where he earned degrees in both New Testament Biblical Studies and Apologetics & Ethics, and served as research assistant to Craig L. Blomberg. Currently he is a PhD student in Politics at the Van Andel Graduate School of Statesmanship at Hillsdale College.

Buist M. Fanning (D.Phil., University of Oxford) is retired Senior Professor of New Testament Studies at Dallas Theological Seminary. He is coeditor of *Interpreting the New Testament Text* (Crossway), as well as author of *Verbal Aspect in New Testament Greek* (Oxford University Press) and essays in numerous books, including *Four Views on the Warning Passages in Hebrews* (Kregel).

John K. Goodrich (PhD, University of Durham) is Program Head and Associate Professor of Bible at Moody Bible Institute. He is coeditor of *Paul and the Apocalyptic Imagination* (Fortress), *Reading Romans in Context* (Zondervan), and *Reading Mark in Context* (Zondervan), as well as author of *Paul as an Administrator of God in 1 Corinthians* (Cambridge University Press).

Joseph H. Hellerman (PhD, University of California, Los Angeles) is Professor of New Testament Language and Literature at Talbot School of Theology. He is Team Pastor at Oceanside Christian Fellowship, Manhattan Beach, California, as well as author of six books, including *Reconstructing Honor in Roman Philippi* (Cambridge University Press), *Philippians* (B&H), and *Embracing Shared Ministry* (Kregel).

Moyer V. Hubbard (D.Phil., University of Oxford) is Chair and Professor of New Testament Language and Literature at Talbot School of Theology. He is the author of *New Creation in Paul's Letters and Thought* (Cambridge University Press), *Christianity in the Greco-Roman World* (Baker), and *2 Corinthians* (Baker).

Karen H. Jobes (PhD, Westminster Theological Seminary) is Gerald F. Hawthorne Professor Emerita of New Testament Greek & Exegesis at Wheaton College. She is the author of *Esther* (Zondervan); *1 Peter* (Baker); *1, 2, & 3 John* (Zondervan); *Letters to the Church* (Zondervan); and *Invitation to the Septuagint* (Baker). She is also editor of *Discovering the Septuagint* (Baker) and the Bringing the Bible to Life series (Zondervan).

Edward (Mickey) W. Klink III (PhD, University of St. Andrews) is Senior Pastor of Hope Evangelical Free Church, Roscoe, Illinois. He is the editor of *The Audience of the Gospels* (T&T Clark), as well as author of *The Sheep of the Fold* (Cambridge University Press), *Introducing Biblical Theology* (Zondervan), and *John* (Zondervan).

Andreas J. Köstenberger (PhD, Trinity Evangelical Divinity School) is Senior Research Professor at Midwestern Baptist Theological Seminary. He has authored, edited, or translated more than twenty books, including *John* (Baker), *Encountering John* (Baker), and *Commentary on 1–2 Timothy and Titus* (B&H). He is also editor of the Biblical Theology of the New Testament series (Zondervan), for which he wrote *A Theology of John's Gospel and Letters*.

Scot McKnight (PhD, University of Nottingham) is Julius R. Mantey Chair of New Testament at Northern Seminary. He is a prolific author, whose commentaries include the volumes on *Colossians*, *Philemon*, and *James* for the New International Commentary on the New Testament series, as well as *Sermon on the Mount* in The Story of God Bible Commentary series (Zondervan), for which he serves as New Testament general editor.

J. P. Moreland (PhD, University of Southern California) is Distinguished Professor of Philosophy at Talbot School of Theology. He has authored, edited, or contributed to more than thirty-five books, including *Kingdom Triangle* (Zondervan), *Jesus under Fire* (Zondervan), *Scaling the Secular City* (Baker), *Love Your God with All Your Mind* (NavPress), and *Philosophical Foundations for a Christian Worldview* (IVP).

Victor S. Rhee (PhD Dallas Theological Seminary) is Professor of New Testament Language and Literature at Talbot School of Theology. He is the author of *Faith in Hebrews* (Peter Lang), as well as several articles in *The New Interpreter's Dictionary of the Bible* (Abingdon) and such journals as the *Journal of Biblical Literature*, *Bibliotheca Sacra*, and *Journal of the Evangelical Theological Society*.

Mark L. Strauss (PhD, University of Aberdeen) is University Professor of New Testament at Bethel Seminary. He is the author of *The Davidic Messiah in Luke-Acts* (Sheffield Academic); *How to Read the Bible in Changing Times* (Baker); *Four Portraits, One Jesus* (Zondervan); *Distorting Scripture?* (IVP); and *Mark* (Zondervan). He is also New Testament general editor for the Teach the Text Commentary Series (Baker).

Judy Ten Elshof (PhD, Fuller Theological Seminary) is Professor of Christian Ministry and Leadership at Talbot School of Theology and Professor of Spirituality and Marriage & Family at Talbot's Institute for Spiritual Formation, where she is also Associate Director of the Center for Spiritual Renewal. She is editor of *Women and Men in Ministry* (Moody) and author of numerous essays and articles on topics relating to spiritual formation and soul care.

Benjamin R. Wilson (PhD, University of Cambridge) is Assistant Professor of Bible at Moody Bible Institute. He is the author of *The Saving Cross of the Suffering Christ: The Death of Jesus in Lukan Soteriology* (de Gruyter) and articles in such journals as *New Testament Studies*, *Catholic Biblical Quarterly*, *Neotestementica*, and *Journal for the Evangelical Theological Society*.

Abbreviations

AB	Anchor Bible
ABD	*Anchor Bible Dictionary*
BBR	*Bulletin for Biblical Research*
BDAG	A Greek-English Lexicon of the New Testament and Other Early Christian Literature
BECNT	Baker Exegetical Commentary on the New Testament
BHGNT	Baylor Handbook on the Greek New Testament
BNTC	Black's New Testament Commentary
BSA	*Annual of the British School at Athens*
BSac	*Bibliotheca Sacra*
BTCP	Biblical Theology for Christian Proclamation
BTL	Biblical Theology for Life
BTNT	Biblical Theology of the New Testament
BWANT	Beiträge zur Wissenschaft vom Alten und Neuen Testament
BZNW	Beihefte zur Zeitschrift für die Neutestamentliche Wissenschaft
CBQ	*Catholic Biblical Quarterly*
CBQMS	Catholic Biblical Quarterly Monograph Series
CBR	*Currents in Biblical Research*
ConcJ	*Concordia Journal*
CSB	Christian Standard Bible
CTR	*Criswell Theological Review*
EDNT	*Exegetical Dictionary of the New Testament*
ESV	English Standard Version
EuroJTh	*European Journal of Theology*
EvQ	*Evangelical Quarterly*
ExpTim	*Expository Times*
FRLANT	Forschungen zur Religion und Literatur des Alten und Neuen Testaments
HCSB	Holman Christian Standard Bible
HNTC	Holman New Testament Commentary
HTR	*Harvard Theological Review*
ICC	The International Critical Commentary
IVPNTC	IVP New Testament Commentary
JBL	*Journal of Biblical Literature*
JETS	*Journal of the Evangelical Theological Society*
JR	*Journal of Religion*
JSNT	*Journal for the Study of the New Testament*
JSNTSup	Journal for the Study of the New Testament Supplemental Series
JSOT	*Journal for the Study of the Old Testament*
JTI	*Journal of Theological Interpretation*

KJV	King James Version
LNTS	Library of New Testament Studies
LXX	Septuagint
NASB	New American Standard Bible
NCBC	New Cambridge Bible Commentary
NET	New English Translation
NICNT	New International Commentary on the New Testament
NIGTC	New International Greek Testament Commentary
NIV	New International Version
NIVAC	NIV Application Commentary
NLT	New Living Translation
NovT	*Novum Testamentum*
NovTSup	Supplements to the Novum Testamentum
NRSV	New Revised Standard Version
NSBT	New Studies in Biblical Theology
NTS	*New Testament Studies*
PNTC	Pelican New Testament Commentaries
RevExp	*Review & Expositor*
SBLAB	Society of Biblical Literature Academia Biblica
SBLDS	Society of Biblical Literature Dissertation Series
SHBC	Smyth & Helwys Bible Commentary
SJT	*Scottish Journal of Theology*
SNTSMS	Society for New Testament Studies Monograph Series
SNTW	Studies of the New Testament and Its World
SP	Sacra Pagina
StBibLit	Studies in Biblical Literature
SWBA	The Social World of Biblical Antiquity
TDNT	*Theological Dictionary of the New Testament*
THNTC	Two Horizons New Testament Commentary
TJ	*Trinity Journal*
TNTC	Tyndale New Testament Commentaries
TynBul	*Tyndale Bulletin*
WBC	Word Biblical Commentary
WTJ	Westminster Theological Journal
WUNT	*Wissenschaftliche Untersuchungen zum Neuen Testamente*
ZECNT	*Zondervan Exegetical Commentary on the New Testament*
ZNW	*Zeitschrift für die Neutestamentliche Wissenschaft*

Preface

This book has been several years in the making and would not have to come to fruition without the assistance of many. Special thanks are due to Clint Arnold for his counsel early in the planning stages, as well as to the team at Kregel Academic, notably Dennis Hillman and Shawn Vander Lugt, for their patience and professionalism. We are also grateful to David Kim for compiling the indices, and of course to the book's contributors for their insightful essays.

This volume is the product of a team of scholars who share a passion for its primary subject matter (discipleship) as well as a deep appreciation for the leadership, scholarship, and friendship of Dr. Michael J. Wilkins, to whom the contributors dedicate this volume on the occasion of his seventieth birthday. If the book accomplishes anything, we hope that it will contribute to the church's understanding of what it means to follow Jesus Christ in the twenty-first century. And if it accomplishes that, then we know Mike will have been appropriately honored. For there is nothing Mike himself is more committed to than following in the footsteps of Jesus his master and equipping others to do the same.

Mike has long devoted himself to the cause of Christian discipleship. Born August 7, 1949, in Southern California, Mike began to follow Christ upon his return from the war in Vietnam, receiving Jesus as Lord and Savior on December 31, 1971. Shortly afterward, Mike enrolled at Biola College, where he earned a bachelor's degree in psychology and social science (1974), followed by a master of divinity at Talbot Theological Seminary (1977) and a doctor of philosophy in New Testament Theology at Fuller Theological Seminary (1986). Both his master's thesis and doctoral dissertation concentrated on discipleship in select portions of the New Testament—the latter written under the supervision of celebrated New Testament scholars Ralph P. Martin and Donald A. Hagner, and examined by Jack Dean Kingsbury of Union Theological Seminary, Virginia. A revision of Mike's dissertation was published as *The Concept of Disciple in Matthew's Gospel: As Reflected in the Use of the Term Μαθητής* (1988) in Brill's prestigious Supplements to Novum Testamentum series. The volume has enjoyed a long shelf life, with a second edition released initially by Baker Books (1995) and later again by Wipf & Stock Publishers (2015).

For Mike, however, discipleship is not merely a pet research topic or a convenient pathway towards an academic qualification. Discipleship is for him the very purpose and goal of life. Thus, Mike's career has been punctuated by positions and achievements that do not often appear on the CV of the traditional university professor. The target audience of his scholarship, for example, has not exclusively or even primarily been theologians and professional exegetes, but folks from all walks of life who are fellow travelers on the journey of personal transformation into the image of our Lord Jesus. In addition to the technical monograph that was borne out of his doctoral studies, Mike has authored numerous books and essays on discipleship that seek to encourage and educate pastors, students, and ordinary lay people—including *Following the Master: A Biblical Theology of Discipleship* (which Mike affectionately calls "the fruit of [his] academic, professional, and personal walk with Jesus" [xiii]), and *In His Image: Reflecting Christ in Everyday Life* (which Mike describes as "a very personal book" in which he shares "[his] own experience of the Christian life" [10]). He also wrote the volume on *Matthew* for the NIV Application Commentary series, a thousand-page tome that was recognized as a finalist for the 2005 ECPA Gold Medallion Award. In the commentary, Mike skillfully guides the specialist and nonspecialist alike through what he calls the first evangelist's "manual on discipleship" (21). Yet this is a project that has not only shaped its readers, but whose undertaking proved to be transformative for Mike himself, as he candidly shares in the preface:

> As I have walked with Jesus in his first-century historical setting through Matthew's meticulous written reflections, as I have been instructed through Matthew's theological intentions for his community, and as I have opened myself to allow Matthew's insights to Jesus's identity and mission to penetrate my heart, soul, mind, and strength, I have been changed. The experience of writing this commentary has been one of the most deeply enriching spiritual experiences of my life. (13)

Ever mindful of his walk with Christ and the encouragement his own journey might offer to others, one wonders if it is even possible for Mike to write a book impersonally or dispassionately.

Mike also has significant experience working on the front lines of congregational ministry. He has served as senior pastor of churches in Carlsbad (1977–1980) and in Cayucos (1981–1983), California. He was also for a number of years a part-time pastor at San Clemente Presbyterian

Church (1984–2000), where he continues to serve in a lay capacity. An avid surfer, it is hardly surprising that Mike, together with his dear wife Lynne, has invested more than four decades to shepherding the locals in some of Southern California's finest beach communities.

Arguably the bulk of Mike's ministry contributions, however, have centered on the campus of his alma mater, Biola University. Appointed as a faculty member in 1983, Mike has been instrumental in teaching students and mentoring colleagues for more than thirty-five years. During his impressive tenure at Biola, Mike has served as chairman of the university's undergraduate Biblical and Theological Studies department (1985–1987), as chairman of the graduate department of New Testament Language and Literature (1987–2000), as Dean of the Faculty of Talbot School of Theology (1992–2013), and most recently as Distinguished Professor of New Testament Language and Literature (2008–present). Mike is the recipient of numerous institutional awards not only for teaching and scholarship, but also for mentoring and leadership. Frankly, it would be difficult to quantify—and nearly impossible to exaggerate—the impact of his institutional service on the professional development of his colleagues and the ethos of the wider Biola community. What is clear is that Mike approaches his appointment at Talbot not simply as professor or administrator, but as a disciple seeking to foster the spiritual growth of other disciples.

Discipleship is indeed Mike's vocation, the Great Commission his passion. While his ministry is sure to continue on for many years ahead, he has already left an indelible mark on countless local churches, university campuses, scholastic societies, and individual lives. The contributors to this volume are but a few of those whom he has blessed through friendship and faithful service in the Lord. It is therefore our great privilege to present this volume to Mike as an expression of our profound gratitude and respect. "The harvest is plentiful, but the laborers are few" (Matt. 9:37, ESV). Thank you, dear friend, for your labor.

The editors
May 20, 2019
Southern California

Following Jesus Christ Today

John K. Goodrich and Mark L. Strauss

> We confess that, although our Church is orthodox as far as her doctrine of grace is concerned, we are no longer sure that we are members of a Church which follows its Lord. We must therefore attempt to recover a true understanding of the mutual relation between grace and discipleship. The issue can no longer be evaded. It is becoming clearer every day that the most urgent problem besetting our Church is this: How can we live the Christian life in the modern world?
>
> —Dietrich Bonhoeffer, *The Cost of Discipleship*[1]

Written at the dawn of the Second World War, Bonhoeffer's *The Cost of Discipleship* famously and relentlessly chided the antinomianism that pervaded German Protestantism after the Nazis co-opted the German national church. Bonhoeffer's solution, to resuscitate the notion and necessity of personal discipleship, was simple yet costly: simple, because the solution was so obviously biblical; costly, because of the ethical demand discipleship places on the individual—a cost Bonhoeffer himself paid in full when, as a result of his intense political activism, he was arrested and executed by Hitler's cruel regime. "Suffering," as Bonhoeffer came to know all too well, "is the badge of true discipleship."[2]

Eighty years have passed since the publication of Bonhoeffer's classic book, yet its message remains equally relevant today. Indeed, *The Cost of Discipleship* is, in many respects, a timeless work whose refrain must be repeated in each and every generation. For while many themes within

---

1 Dietrich Bonhoeffer, *The Cost of Discipleship*. (trans. R. H. Fuller, New York: Touchstone, 1995), 55; originally published as *Nachfolge* (Munich: Chr. Kaiser, 1937).
2 Bonhoeffer, *The Cost of Discipleship*, 91.

theological discourse are considered to be of first importance, none can claim to be of greater significance to the overall message of the New Testament than *discipleship*—the process of being called by and conformed to Jesus Christ. Engagement in this process is Jesus's fundamental commission to his church (Matt. 28:18–20). Indeed, the entire New Testament bears witness to this vocation and seeks to foster precisely this relationship between wayward humanity and its redeemer and Lord. Not only that, but it is the right conceptualization of discipleship that ties together so much of daily Christian practice. As Richard Longenecker maintains, "The concept of discipleship lies at the heart of all Christian thought, life, and ministry."[3]

Unfortunately, the language of discipleship has, once again, fallen out of favor in western Christianity, and as a result confusion has shrouded the term. Discipleship, to some, connotes a special level or calling of Christian living. For others, discipleship is inherently tethered to spiritual growth programs and curricula. And to others, especially those directly impacted by increased secularism in the West, the term is associated with—well, nothing at all. As Dallas Willard lamented in a 2005 *Christianity Today* interview, "*Discipleship* as a term has lost its content, and this is one reason why it has been moved aside."[4] Willard elaborated on this semantic development in his book *The Great Omission*: "Discipleship on the theological right has come to mean preparation for soul winning, under the direction of parachurch efforts that had discipleship farmed out to them because the local church really wasn't doing it. On the left, discipleship has come to mean some form of social activity or social service, from serving soup lines to political protest to . . . whatever. The term 'discipleship' has currently been ruined so far as any solid psychological and biblical content is concerned."[5]

The same was recently concluded by the Barna Research Group in a massive study on discipleship commissioned by the Navigators.

> We asked a random sample of Christians—including practicing and non-practicing Christians—what words or phrases they use to describe "the process of growing spiritually." The

---

3 Richard N. Longenecker, "Preface," in *Patterns of Discipleship in the New Testament* (ed. R. N. Longenecker, Grand Rapids: Eerdmans, 1996), ix–x, at ix.

4 Agnieszka Tennant, "The Making of the Christian: Richard J. Foster and Dallas Willard on the Difference between Discipleship and Spiritual Formation," *Christianity Today*, September 16, 2005, https://www.christianitytoday.com/ct/2005/october/9.42.html.

5 Dallas Willard, *The Great Omission: Reclaiming Jesus's Essential Teachings on Discipleship* (New York: HarperSanFrancisco, 2006), 53.

most preferred term was "becoming more Christlike" (selected by 43% of respondents), followed by "spiritual growth" (31%), and "spiritual journey" (28%). The term "discipleship" ranked fourth on the list and was only selected by fewer than one in five Christians (18%). . . . Among those who did not select the term "discipleship," we asked if the word still has relevance to their Christian experience. Surprisingly, only one-quarter of these respondents said "discipleship" is very relevant. The implication is that while spiritual growth is very important to tens of millions, the language and terminology surrounding discipleship seems to be undergoing a change, with other phrases coming to be used more frequently than the term "discipleship" itself.[6]

Of course, a number of factors are responsible for these results. They are due, in the first place, to the sporadic usage of explicit discipleship terminology within the Bible itself. As a glance through any ordinary Bible concordance will quickly demonstrate, the term "disciple" is basically absent from the Old Testament as well as from the New Testament epistles. It is hardly a surprise, then, that even careful students of Scripture will be left without a clear sense of the term once they venture outside the Gospels and Acts.

Beyond this, discipleship to many is an antiquated concept that is difficult to contemporize. This challenge has only become more acute in the wake of the recent cultural revolution underway in the Western world. In his 2015 book *Prepare*, Paul Nyquist, then president of Moody Bible Institute, reflected soberly on the rapid societal progress many believers have witnessed firsthand in the United States: "Insulated in our Christian subculture bubble and disconnected from the secular world, many of us have been largely unaware of society's movements. But events this past year awakened us. With our eyes wide open, we realize America's changed. . . . [T]he culture war is over—and we lost."[7]

The continued and speedy movement of western culture away from its Judeo-Christian heritage has had incalculable effects on the lives of

6 https://www.barna.com/research/new-research-on-the-state-of-discipleship. For the study's published results, see *The State of Discipleship: A Barna Report Produced in Partnership with The Navigators* (Ventura, CA: Barna Group, 2015). See also the follow-up volume by Preston Sprinkle, *Go: Returning to the Front Lines of Faith* (Colorado Springs: NavPress, 2016).
7 J. Paul Nyquist, *Prepare: Living Your Faith in an Increasingly Hostile Culture* (Chicago: Moody Publishers, 2015), 22.

twenty-first-century believers. There is no denying that the so-called culture war has impacted not only central areas of Christian life and practice but also aspects of Christian identity and purpose as well. Indeed, as the world continues to change, so does the vocabulary of the modern church, as well as its appreciation for the Bible's central topics. The notion of discipleship is one such causality.

All of the above, however, are poor reasons to allow the language of discipleship to slip further into disuse. Not only does the *concept* of discipleship pervade the New Testament (even where the term itself is absent), but we cannot afford, as Willard feared, to lose or misunderstand the *content* of a term so central to the message and mission of the church. If the language of discipleship is forfeited to other terms, then we will undoubtedly lose focus on how believers ought to relate to their Lord—including all that is involved in maintaining and nurturing that relationship. As Bonhoeffer observed long ago, "Christianity without discipleship is always Christianity without Christ."[8] It is high time, then, to reclaim the notion of discipleship for the twenty-first-century church, to recalibrate our awareness of its presence in the Bible, and to remind ourselves of its implications for daily living.[9]

This books aims to serve contemporary believers in just this way, by providing an in-depth examination of the concept of discipleship across the New Testament and by explaining how the concept interfaces with important areas of the Christian life—the mind, the soul, and the local church. Our goal in this volume is neither to offer a new one-size-fits-all definition of discipleship, nor is it to leave the concept so open-ended that just about any meaning will do. Rather, while recognizing the unity and diversity of the New Testament witness to the topic, this book seeks to provide an exposition of discipleship from each book of the New Testament and to explore its relevance for today.

---

8 Dietrich Bonhoeffer, *The Cost of Discipleship*, 59.

9 Curiously, limited academic study has focused on discipleship directly. Especially in recent years, very little has been written on discipleship that is both comprehensive and accessible, and even less has been published that brings together both exegetical rigor and pastoral reflection. See, e.g., Fernando F. Segovia, ed., *Discipleship in the New Testament* (Philadelphia: Fortress, 1985); James D. G. Dunn, *Jesus's Call to Discipleship,* Understanding Jesus Today Series (Cambridge: Cambridge University Press, 1992); N. T. Wright, *Following Jesus: Biblical Reflections on Discipleship* (Grand Rapids: Eerdmans, 1995; 2nd ed. 2014); Richard N. Longenecker, ed., *Patterns of Discipleship in the New Testament* (Grand Rapids: Eerdmans, 1996); Andrew Ryder, S.C.J., *Following Christ: Models of Discipleship in the New Testament* (Franklin, WI: Sheed and Ward, 1999); Jonathan Lunde, *Following Jesus, the Servant King: A Biblical Theology of Covenantal Discipleship* (Grand Rapids: Zondervan, 2010).

Before proceeding, it is important to offer a working definition of what we mean by *discipleship*. For this we will rely on the prior work of Michael J. Wilkins, undoubtedly the most important voice on the academic study of discipleship in the past generation. Wilkins has contributed much to this discussion through several notable publications of varying levels of technicality.[10] In his most comprehensive analysis, he defined discipleship as follows:

> In common parlance, *discipleship* and *discipling* today relate to the ongoing life of the disciple. *Discipleship* is the ongoing process of growth as a disciple. *Discipling* implies the responsibility of disciples helping one another to grow as disciples. Therefore, discipleship and discipling can be narrowly understood as a technical discussion of the historical master-disciple relationship, but these terms can also be understood in a broader way as Christian experience—that is, the self-understanding of the early Christian believers as believers: what such a way of life requires, implies, and entails. Thus, when we speak of Christian discipleship and discipling we are speaking of what it means to grow as a Christian in every area of life. Since *disciple* is a common referent for *Christian*, discipleship and discipling imply the process of becoming like Jesus Christ. Discipleship and discipling mean living a fully human life in this world in union with Jesus Christ and growing in conformity to his image.[11]

Wilkins's excellent definition requires no substantive revision. His words are just as reliable now as when they were first penned. Wilkins's exegetical analysis is also still important, selective though it is. Nonetheless, the present volume seeks to build on Wilkins's distinguished scholarship, by bringing together leading evangelical thinkers to examine afresh the New Testament message of discipleship and its relevance for today.

Part 1, by way of seventeen exegetical essays, surveys the varied presentation of discipleship across multiple New Testament books and

---

10 See especially Michael J. Wilkins, "The Concept of Disciple in Matthew's Gospel: As Reflected in the Use of the Term Μαθητής," NovTSup 59 (Leiden: Brill, 1988), republished as *Discipleship in the Ancient World and Matthew's Gospel* (2nd ed., Grand Rapids; Baker, 1995); ibid., *Following the Master: A Biblical Theology of Discipleship* (Grand Rapids: Zondervan, 1992); ibid., *In His Image: Reflecting Christ in Everyday Life* (Colorado Springs: NavPress, 1997).

11 Wilkins, *Following the Master*, 41–42.

corpora. The authors of these essays are specialists in these various biblical texts. The three chapters in Part 2 approach discipleship from the perspective of other disciplines, exploring how it converges with important areas of contemporary theological and ministerial reflection. Authored by leading evangelical scholars with expertise in philosophy, psychology, and practical theology, these chapters discuss the principal challenges of, as well as propose essential strategies for, making and growing disciples in our contemporary context.

It is our hope that this volume will serve students, pastors, and scholars of the next generation in a way similar to how Bonhoeffer's book has served Christians for the past eighty years and the way Wilkins's work served the last generation of readers—namely, by clarifying what it means to follow Jesus Christ while living in a world that is growing increasingly hostile to those who do.

PART 1

The New Testament
Message of Discipleship

CHAPTER 1

Living Out Justice, Mercy, and Loyalty: Discipleship in Matthew's Gospel

Jeannine K. Brown

MATTHEW'S THEOLOGICAL MESSAGE

Matthew communicates that Israel's God is inaugurating the kingdom in Jesus the Messiah. Jesus teaches that the arrival of God's reign involves the restoration of justice, mercy, peace, and wholeness (5:7–10); and Jesus enacts this vision in his compassionate ministry of healing for Israel (in Galilee; chs 8–9, 12, 14–15). Matthew portrays Jesus as Messiah (1:1; 16:16), as God's very presence (1:23), and as Israel's representative (chs. 3–4). As the embodiment of faithful Israel, he stands in for his people; and in his death and resurrection he brings forgiveness and life to them (1:21; 26:28; 27:53) and ushers in these gifts for all the nations (28:19).

Understandably, Matthew's focus is on Jesus and therefore on Christology. In addition to the Christological contours already mentioned, which each have discipleship implications, Jesus is also characterized as Torah embodied and as Isaiah's servant of Yahweh. Jesus not only obeys God's law and is its consummate teacher; he is Torah enfleshed (11:2, 19, 28–30). As his followers pursue relationship with him and loyalty to him, they are on the path to covenant faithfulness through their obedience to Jesus's own commands (see 28:19–20). In this way, they will find that Jesus's yoke is easy to carry. As servant of the Lord, Jesus acts as a ransom for his people, thereby providing the consummate example of service for them (20:28). In these and in many other ways, Matthew's Christology points toward his view of discipleship. "Matthew's Gospel envisions and shapes its readers toward faith and obedience; they are to be true followers of Jesus and his teachings."[1]

---

1 Jeannine K. Brown, *Matthew* (Teach the Text New Testament Commentary Series, Grand Rapids: Baker, 2015), 1. I use narrative-critical methodology in this chapter as the basis for my analysis of discipleship themes; see Jeannine K. Brown, "Narrative Criticism," in *Dictionary of Jesus and the Gospels* (2nd ed.; eds. J. B. Green, J. K. Brown, N. Perrin, Downers Grove, IL: InterVarsity Press, 2013), 619–24.

THE CONTOURS OF DISCIPLESHIP IN MATTHEW[2]

A. The Relational Basis of Discipleship

Although Matthew's emphasis, in terms of sheer amount of teaching, is upon expectations or obligations for disciples, there is a strong basis of covenantal relationship for these expectations. Early in his Gospel, Matthew affirms that Jesus is "Emmanuel," God's presence with Israel (1:23). He confirms this theme at the very end of the narrative, when Jesus promises to be *with his followers* to the very end of the age (28:20). This inclusio (or bookend) accents the centrality of this theme for his understanding of Jesus's relationship to those who follow him. The theme is echoed in Matthew's Community Discourse (ch. 18), where Jesus's words about his church are the focus. At a key hinge of the chapter, Jesus promises to be "in the midst" (ἐν μέσῳ) of his people as they together live out values of protection of the most vulnerable and lavish forgiveness (18:20).[3] This subtle but crucial motif of "Jesus with us" provides a firm anchor for the relational basis of Matthew's vision of discipleship. The person of Jesus is at the center of the life of discipleship.

We can also see this relational emphasis in the first major teaching block of Matthew's Gospel—the Sermon on the Mount. While the Sermon certainly focuses on covenant obligation in the time of the kingdom's arrival (e.g., 5:20; 6:1; on the use of δικαιοσύνη, see below), there are important indications that in this inaugural sermon Jesus is communicating that *God is the one who initiates restoration and redemption*, placing the focus of covenant faithfulness on relational responsiveness (rather than on only legal obligation). This is clear if we seek to understand the Jewish background to Matthew, especially related to how the Torah was understood as a gift for Israel to know how to live in relationship with their redeeming God (see Exod. 19:1–6; 20:2).[4]

The way the sermon begins also signals that God is initiator of restoration, and that Jesus's followers are to respond in faithfulness. The first four Beatitudes announce blessing upon those most experiencing the underside of life—the (spiritually) impoverished (5:3), those whose deep losses cause them to mourn (5:4), people of lowest status (5:5), and those

---

2 Some of the material in this chapter is based conceptually on my work in Jeannine K. Brown and Kyle Roberts, *Matthew*, Two Horizons New Testament Commentary Series (Grand Rapids: Eerdmans, 2018), chapter 13, "Thinking Theologically with Matthew: Discipleship."
3 All translations are my own and are from Brown and Roberts, *Matthew*.
4 Peter T. Vogt, *Interpreting the Pentateuch: An Exegetical Handbook* (Grand Rapids: Kregel, 2009), 81.

who are "starved for justice" (5:6).[5] Jesus is able to announce blessing upon the most unlikely candidates because God's kingdom is arriving with its anticipated reversals and God is bringing mercy and justice to the earth (6:10). It is from this place of restoration that Jesus offers the second set of blessings on those who commit to joining God's work of restoration by showing mercy (5:7), pursuing wholeness and integrity (5:8), working for peace (5:9), and being willing to experience persecution for bringing justice to those who need it (5:10).[6] Besides the opening blessings, we could also note that the theology proper of the sermon points to a God who is indiscriminate in love and so "complete and whole" (5:45–48). This is a God who is quick to hear and answer prayer and lavishes good things on those who ask (6:7–8; 7:9–11). All of this provides a significant covenantal (i.e., relational) basis for discipleship in Matthew.

B. *How* Matthew Communicates Discipleship

Before considering our central question of what discipleship looks like in Matthew, it will be helpful first to explore briefly how Matthew communicates discipleship, or, if you will, *how Matthew shapes disciples*. Matthew, as he tells the Jesus story, draws on several narrative devices to shape his ideal or implied reader, or the reader who "fulfills the goals of the text."[7] And "the implied reader represents (or stands in for) a community who lives out the call to follow Jesus faithfully, empowered by the presence of Jesus in their midst."[8] In particular, the narrative devices of *characterization*—of Jesus, of the disciples, and of others who respond to Jesus in various ways—and *dialogue*, most often in Jesus's teachings, prove foundational to Matthew's vision for discipleship.

One of the most obvious ways Matthew inculcates discipleship is through his focus on *Jesus's teachings*. For the evangelist, the words of Jesus are to shape the reader and hearer toward authentic discipleship. And the teachings of Jesus in Matthew are gathered together primarily in the five great discourses of chapters 5–7, 10, 13, 18, and 24–25. These five discourses shape the reader to live out Matthean discipleship. In the Sermon on the Mount, the reader is shaped to pursue covenant faithfulness in light of the

---

5 For this reading of the Beatitudes, see Mark Allan Powell, "Matthew's Beatitudes: Reversals and Rewards of the Kingdom," *CBQ* 58 (1996): 460–79; and Brown, *Matthew*, 52–55.

6 Powell, "Matthew's Beatitudes."

7 Jeannine K. Brown, *The Disciples in Narrative Perspective: The Portrayal and Function of the Matthean Disciples*, SBLAB 9 (Atlanta: Scholars Press, 2002), 123.

8 Brown and Roberts, *Matthew*, 336.

arriving kingdom (5:1–7:29). In the second discourse, the reader is guided to emulate Jesus's mission which has focused on enacting God's reign (cf. 4:23; 9:35), even if persecution ensues (10:1–11:1). Matthew's reader is encouraged to respond in faith to the kingdom as an "already" reality, as well as something that is "not yet" (13:1–53). In the fourth discourse, the reader is directed away from status preoccupation and toward care for the marginalized ("little ones"), protection of the purity of the community, and lavish forgiveness (18:1–35). Finally, the fifth discourse focuses the attention of the reader on the importance of living in ways that are prepared, faithful, merciful, and just in the face of the future realities of the temple's destruction and the reappearing of the Son of Man (24:1–25:46).[9] When, after his resurrection, Jesus directs his followers to "disciple the nations" (28:19) by "teaching them to obey all that I have commanded you" (28:20), it is these five great discourses that come most quickly to the reader's mind.

Another important way Matthew highlights discipleship is by pointing to *what Jesus does*, since Jesus is the exemplar for disciples to follow. When Jesus, after arriving in Jerusalem, teaches about the qualities of justice, mercy, and covenant loyalty (23:23), the reader already knows what these virtues look like since Jesus himself has lived them out. In the earlier narrative, Jesus has shown mercy to the many from Israel who have come seeking healing (8:1–4, 9:1–8, 18–34; 12:22–23; 14:34–36; 15:29–30; 17:14–20; 19:1–2). And his Galilean ministry has been described as characterized by justice (12:18, 20). In all this, Jesus acts as the Servant of the Lord from Isaiah, who brings justice and mercy to the nations through his embodiment of Israel's vocation (12:18–21).[10] And while Jesus is certainly unique in certain facets of his ministry—as in his representative death that brings about restoration and life, the shape of his life is to be a template for the lives of those who would follow him. As Howell puts it, as Jesus does, so "disciples must do."[11] Kierkegaard speaks eloquently of the importance of Jesus's example for discipleship:

> Christ came to the world with the purpose of saving the world, also with the purpose—this in turn is implicit in the first purpose—of being the *prototype,* of leaving footprints, for the

---

9 For my reading of the shape of these five discourses, see Brown, *Matthew.*

10 Jeannine K. Brown, "Matthew's Christology and Isaiah's Servant: A Fresh Look at a Perennial Issue," in *Treasures New and Old: Essays in Honor of Donald A. Hagner* (eds. C. S. and C. B. Kvidahl, Wilmore, KY: Glossa House, 2017), 93–106.

11 David B. Howell, *Matthew's Inclusive Story: A Study in the Narrative Rhetoric of the First Gospel,* JSNTSup 42 (Sheffield: JSOT Press, 1990), 259.

person who wants to join him, who then might become an *imitator*; this indeed corresponds to "footprints."[12]

Besides Jesus, other characters in the narrative become foils or examples for those who follow Jesus, showing positive or negative aspects of discipleship. The Jewish leaders, and particularly the Pharisees, provide a significance contrast to Matthean discipleship, as they are portrayed as hypocritical rather than people of integrity (15:1–9; 23:13–36; cf. 6:1–18). They and others are "examples of what not to do" in discipleship.[13] On the positive side, various seekers who come to Jesus for healing are characterized by *faith* (e.g., 8:10; 9:2, 22, 29; 15:28), including some Gentiles who exhibit *great faith* (8:5–13; 15:21–28). Other positive discipleship qualities that are highlighted in various characters and that the reader is to emulate include *faithfulness to Jesus* (the women at the cross and tomb; 27:55–56; 28:1) and *worship of Jesus* (the Magi; 2:1–12).

The twelve disciples fall somewhere in between these foils and models; they are portrayed as those who leave all to follow Jesus (4:18–22; 9:9), yet still struggle to understand (e.g., 16:8) and fully trust Jesus (8:26; 14:31; 16:8; 17:20). Given that the Twelve are those who follow Jesus most closely in his public ministry, they are the most likely candidates for an exploration of discipleship. Yet they exhibit a mixed portrayal in Matthew, and so they function as exemplars at some points and foils at others.[14] Or as Kingsbury has framed it, they provide for the reader both a point of identification and a place for distancing.

> Because the disciples possess conflicting traits, the reader is invited, depending on the attitude Matthew as narrator or Jesus takes toward them on any given occasion, to identify with them or to distance himself or herself from them. It is through such granting or withholding of approval on cue, therefore, that the

---

12 Søren Kierkegaard, *Practice in Christianity* (Princeton, NJ: Princeton University Press, 1991), 238. While Kierkegaard is not expressly focused on Matthew, his words capture the both/and of Matthew's Christology for discipleship: Jesus is both redeemer and example.
13 Terence L. Donaldson, "Guiding Readers—Making Disciples: Discipleship in Matthew's Narrative Strategy," in *Patterns of Discipleship in the New Testament* (ed. R. N. Longenecker, Grand Rapids: Eerdmans, 1996), 30–49, at 43. We could also observe how Herod the tetrarch (14:5) and the chief priests and elders (21:26) fear of responses of the crowds. Matthew contrasts this kind of fear of others with the discipleship qualities of trust in God and willingness to brook opposition (e.g., 10:16–20, 26–31).
14 Warren Carter, *Matthew: Storyteller, Interpreter, Evangelist* (Peabody, MA: Hendrickson, 1996), 243.

reader becomes schooled in the values that govern the life of discipleship in Matthew's story.[15]

C. *What* Matthew Communicates about Discipleship

Given the story Matthew tells about Jesus, who gathers twelve apostles to him (10:1), we can highlight *following* as the central discipleship metaphor or activity. This image of journeying with Jesus has a strong relational cast to it, especially as we consider language used in the passion narrative to suggest the relational reality of Jesus "with" his disciples (e.g., 26:18, 29, 36) and the expectation that they are "with" him (26:38).[16] In fact, Peter's denials that he has been "with Jesus" (μετὰ Ἰησοῦ; 26:69, 71) appear to be a fundamental negation of the essence of his call to follow Jesus (4:18–22; cf. 10:1).

Since Matthew's basis for discipleship is thoroughly relational, it is important to lay accent on the call to "follow *Jesus*." In other words, the emphasis is more so on the person than the action of following, although I would suggest that for Matthew these fit together hand in glove. This relational kind of following—or the following of the person of Jesus—comes through clearly in chapter 11, where Jesus takes on the persona of Wisdom and invites people to take on his comfortable and sustainable yoke. Much like Wisdom in various Jewish texts (e.g., Prov. 8:22–31; Sir 24:19; 51:26–27), Jesus gives an invitation to come to him and put on his "yoke." The yoke image was used in Judaism for living within the Torah's covenantal obligations. In 11:29, Jesus describes his "yoke"—his teaching—as "easy" and "light." And Matthew portrays Jesus as the embodiment of Wisdom (see 11:2, 19); as Jesus speaks with the voice of Wisdom (11:28), the relational nature of discipleship derived from the personification of Wisdom in these various Jewish texts is retained and heightened. For Matthew, Torah and Wisdom are now a person—they find their climactic expression in the Messiah.[17]

1. Discipleship as Allegiance to Jesus and the Kingdom

Under the aegis of following Jesus, Matthew draws on a variety of images, terms, and concepts to communicate the contours of discipleship. A key concept is that following Jesus is an act of allegiance (4:19; 10:24–25).

15 Jack D. Kingsbury, *Matthew as Story* (2nd ed., Philadelphia: Fortress, 1988), 14.
16 For the theme of Jesus being with his disciples and the expectation that they are to be with him in Matthew's passion narrative, see David E. Garland, *Reading Matthew: A Literary and Theological Commentary* (Macon, GA: Smyth and Helwys, 2001), 255.
17 For this Christological motif, see Brown, *Matthew*, 126–27.

Disciples in the Jewish world of the first century approached a rabbi to become a follower. As a disciple, they would learn from the rabbi and imitate him. The most important relationship a disciple would have was with their teacher (e.g., 10:24–25). Disciples of Jesus, the Messiah–Teacher (see 23:8–10), were expected to attach their loyalty to him; as such, the heart of Christian discipleship is allegiance.[18]

Following Jesus is an act of covenantal loyalty, sustained by trust in Jesus's compassion and authority and by faithfulness to him and his ways (23:23). Exemplary faith, ironically, is not the purview of the Twelve, who struggle to trust that Jesus can do what he has promised to do and are characterized as those of "little faith" (6:30; 8:26; 14:31; 16:8: 17:20).[19] Instead, a number of minor characters demonstrate commendable and even, at times, exemplary faith (e.g., 8:2, 10; 9:2, 22, 29; 15:28). For Matthew, pursuing faithfulness (or allegiance) to Jesus is lived out through a distinctive set of values. Being loyal to Jesus means cutting ties of allegiance with one's possessions (6:19–24; 19:21–24) and differentiating oneself from the opinions of others (21:25–26, 46) and even from one's family (10:34–37) and home. Following Jesus is a journey of displacement in the service of mission, as Matthew highlights Jesus beginning his life as refugee (2:13–15) and committing to an itinerant (homeless) existence, which his disciples are to emulate (8:18–20).[20]

Allegiance to Jesus in Matthew correlates with allegiance to God and God's reign—or the "kingdom of heaven" (ἡ βασιλεία τῶν οὐρανῶν), as the evangelist most often refers to it (e.g., 4:17). This focus is captured well in Jesus's words from the Sermon on the Mount: "pursue above all else [God's] kingdom and promised redemption [δικαιοσύνη]" (6:33).[21] In Matthew, out of this allegiance to God as king practices of piety organically emerge—practices like prayer, longing, fasting, and a posture of readiness. The Lord's Prayer provides a model of praying for the kingdom's arrival. Each of its first three petitions accent the desire for God's kingdom to arrive fully in this world:

---

18 Brown and Roberts, *Matthew*, 338. See Michael J. Wilkins, *Discipleship in the Ancient World and Matthew's Gospel* (2nd ed., Grand Rapids: Baker, 1995).

19 Donald J. Verseput, "The Faith of the Reader and the Narrative of Matthew 13:53–16:20," *JSNT* 46 (1992): 3–24; Brown, *Disciples in Narrative Perspective*, 101–07.

20 See Ched Myers and Matthew Colwell, *Our God Is Undocumented: Biblical Faith and Immigrant Justice* (Maryknoll, NY: Orbis, 2012); and Robert J. Myles, *The Homeless Jesus in the Gospel of Matthew*, SWBA, Second Series 10 (Sheffield: Sheffield Phoenix Press, 2014).

21 For this understanding of δικαιοσύνη at 6:33, see Brown and Roberts, *Matthew*, 72–75.

May your name be recognized as holy,

May your kingdom come,

May your will be done, as in heaven so also on earth (6:9b–10).

Disciples are oriented toward the coming reign of God, and they long for the consummation of God's restoration of all things. Disciples also are encouraged to pray for their daily needs, knowing that God is good and is attentive to their prayers (6:8; 7:11). A sign of authentic and whole discipleship is prayer for one's enemies; by doing so, Jesus's followers show themselves to be imitators of their God (5:48).

Matthew also highlights fasting as a practice that fits the discipleship pattern of longing and praying for the coming of God's kingdom.[22] Just as Jesus's teachings presume that his followers will pray ("when you pray;" 6:5), so he assumes they will fast ("when you fast"; 6:16), although Jesus also teaches that his followers will not fast until he goes away (9:14–17). While it might seem from a contemporary perspective that giving to the poor (the other act of piety included in 6:1–18) fits better under discipleship carried out toward our neighbor (below), these three obligations are often connected together in Judaism (e.g., Tobit 12:8). Anderson highlights the petitionary focus of all three: "fasting was frequently joined to intercessory prayer because it functioned as a means of persuading God to attend to one's cause. . . . Almsgiving has a similar role to play in quickening God's affection and mercy toward a supplicant."[23]

Being prepared or ready is another discipleship motif that connects with allegiance to Jesus and the coming kingdom. This motif comes to the fore later in Matthew, especially in the Eschatological Discourse (Matt. 24–25; see 24:36–41, 42–44; 25:13, 19). Jesus calls his followers to be prepared for his "reappearing" (παρουσία)—an expectation, like prayer and fasting, that is tied to Jesus and to the kingdom, since Jesus's reappearing coincides with the consummation of God's reign at the "end of the age" (24:3). Instead of trying to determine the precise timing of that final day, disciples are to always be prepared by living faithfully and expectantly (25:1–30).

True worship is also a part of a disciple's allegiance to Jesus and to the kingdom. And, while Jesus points his followers to authentic worship

---

22 Each of these practices are to be done for God alone and not to gain praise from people (6:1–6, 16–18).

23 Gary A. Anderson, *Charity: The Place of the Poor in the Biblical Tradition* (New Haven, CT: Yale University Press, 2013), 144.

of Israel's God (e.g., 4:10), Matthew indicates that this will involve worship of Jesus himself.[24] The term προσκυνέω can connote either showing great reverence or an act of worship (in either case often accompanied by bowing low before someone), and on Matthew's *plot level* the former connotation often makes a great deal of sense (e.g., 8:2; 9:18; 15:25; 20:20). Yet Matthew in his communication with his audience (the narrative's *discourse level*)[25] lays accent on προσκυνέω, by using it in reference to Jesus eight times (more than the combined total for Mark, Luke, and John) and by using it to begin and conclude his Gospel: the magi worship Jesus (2:2, 11) and the followers of Jesus—both women and men—worship him (28:9, 17, respectively). Another important moment of worship tied to discipleship occurs when the twelve see Jesus's mastery over the water and the wind (14:22–33): "Then those in the boat worshipped him and said, 'Truly, you are God's son'" (14:33).

A presupposition for each of these orientations or practices of allegiance is an adequate understanding of Jesus, his mission, and what he expects of his followers. The portrayal of the twelve disciples contributes to the Matthean theme of understanding, albeit more often than not as a foil to ideal discipleship.[26] The disciples are at their best when they leave everything to follow Jesus early in the Gospel narrative (4:18–22; 9:9) and rightly identify and respond to Jesus as Messiah (e.g., worshipping him at 14:33; confessing his identity as Messiah at 16:16). They are less able to trust and understand Jesus and the wide scope of his authority (e.g., 8:26; 16:8; 17:20). As Verseput suggests, the "little faith" of the Matthean disciples involves "the unjustified incapacity of the disciple[s] to grasp and rely upon Jesus's inexhaustible power."[27] And the twelve engage in an ongoing struggle to understand Jesus's mission to "give his life a ransom for many" (20:28) and his call to them to "take up their cross and follow [Jesus]" (16:24). That is, they do not comprehend adequately how their own mission and

---

24 On the potential tension of this dual worship focus, see Joshua E. Leim, "Worshiping the Father, Worshiping the Son: Cultic Language and the Identity of God in the Gospel of Matthew," *JTI* 9 (2015): 65–84.

25 The discourse level of a narrative is a heuristic for understanding the (implied) author's interaction with the (implied) reader or *how* the story is told. "On the discourse level, rhetorical devices of various sorts, thematic presentation, and point of view are used to communicate" with the reader; Jeannine K. Brown, *Scripture as Communication: Introducing Biblical Hermeneutics* (Grand Rapids: Baker Academic, 2007), 157.

26 For an extended exploration of the portrayal of the disciples in Matthew and its function, see Brown, *Disciples in Narrative Perspective.*

27 Verseput, "The Faith of the Reader," 23.

destiny is to be patterned from his (e.g., 18:1; 19:30; 20:20–23). From the view across the whole of Matthew, "the disciples are consistently portrayed as prone to misunderstand and as wavering in their faith."[28]

Yet this portrait of the Twelve does not, on its own, define discipleship in Matthew. Instead, readers are drawn to emulate the disciples when they respond appropriately to Jesus and to distance themselves from the disciples when they misconstrue Jesus and his expectations for them. In this way, Matthew's reader is schooled in discipleship *to understand what the Twelve do not*—that Jesus is the Messiah who comes not to use his authority for his own gain but in his mission of service and restoration, and that all who follow this Messiah must follow this same pattern of service (see below). Matthew's characterization of the disciples then functions as *"an incentive to the implied reader toward ideal discipleship."*[29]

2. Discipleship as Covenantal Loyalty and Service to Others

Turning from what we might think of as "vertical" discipleship to covenantal loyalty expressed toward others, a number of central metaphors and terms invigorate Matthew's portrait of "horizontal discipleship." I will explore this horizontal area of discipleship under the rubrics of sibling relationships, the servant motif drawn from Isaiah, and the three Torah values highlighted at Matthew 23:23: justice, mercy, and faithfulness.

Disciples as Siblings. A primary discipleship metaphor in Matthew, as well as in the New Testament more generally, is that of siblings, as brothers and sisters (ἀδελφοί). The evangelist in 12:45–50 accents this theme after narrating that Jesus's (physical) mother and siblings come to see him (12:46):[30] "whoever does the will of my Father who is in heaven, this person is my brother and sister and mother" (12:50). This familial emphasis creates a vision of the disciple as a child of God (e.g., 5:9). And as Pattarumadathil suggests, "in the gospel of Matthew discipleship is viewed as a process of becoming children of God."[31]

---

28 Brown, *Disciples in Narrative Perspective*, 120.

29 Brown, *Disciples in Narrative Perspective*, 130 (italics in original).

30 Much of Matthew's use of ἀδελφός fits in the category of physical siblings; see 1:2, 11; 4:18, 21; 10:2, 21; 13:55; 14:3; 17:1; 19:29; 20:24: 22:24. See 5:47 for a debatable instance.

31 Henry Pattarumadathil, *Your Father in Heaven: Discipleship in Matthew as a Process of Becoming Children of God* (Roma: Pontificio Istituto Biblico, 2008), 203. See Jeannine K. Brown, "Disciple, Discipleship, N.T.," in *Encyclopedia of the Bible and its Reception* (Berlin: de Gruyter, 2013), 6:887–89, at 888.

The language of ἀδελφός to reference fellow members of the faith community has already been used earlier in Matthew, in the Sermon on the Mount. The focus there is to avoid anger and hypocritical judgment of a brother or sister (5:22–24; 7:3–5). The metaphorical use of ἀδελφός provides a centerpiece for the Community Discourse, where restoration of an erring brother or sister is a high priority (18:15) and forgiveness from the heart is to be lavished on them (18:21, 35). Earlier in the Community Discourse, believers are commended to eschew pursuit of status (18:1–5) and instead to care for those who are most vulnerable and who exist on the margins of the community (18:6–14). These "little ones" (μικρός) may be low in status from a human perspective, but they are of great worth to God (18:10, 14) and so to God's people. As Matthew moves from "little ones" to its superlative "least of these," the importance of believers caring for their faith siblings who are on the margins only increases (25:40).

The image of disciples as brothers and sisters emerges most fully into a familial constellation in 23:8–12. Jesus turns from a critique of status-preoccupied scribes and Pharisees (23:5–7)—Israel's teachers—to a vision of the believing community as a spiritual family with a single father—Yahweh—and a single "master teacher" (καθηγητής)—the Messiah.[32] As for the rest, they "are all sisters and brothers" (23:8); i.e., "they are all equal."[33] This vision for community, in which status distinctions like "rabbi" and "father" are withheld from community members, is strikingly egalitarian within Matthew's context in which the *paterfamilias* held absolute household authority.[34] As Bauckham notes, "Among the new relationships Jesus establishes in the community of his disciples, the renewed Israel, fatherhood is pointedly excluded . . . because it represents hierarchical authority in the family."[35]

---

32 For a discussion of Matthew's use of this *hapax*, in part, to highlight status themes, see Brown and Roberts, *Matthew*, 207; and Samuel Byrskog, *Jesus the Only Teacher: Didactic Authority and Transmission in Ancient Israel, Ancient Judaism and the Matthean Community* (Stockholm: Almqvist & Wiksell International, 1994), 288–89. Matthew's final use of ἀδελφός at 28:10 highlights how Jesus himself can be understood as a "brother" to his disciples: "go and report to *my brothers* that they should go to Galilee" (referring to the Eleven at this point in the story).

33 Pattarumadathil, *Your Father in Heaven*, 207.

34 See Michael H. Crosby, *House of Disciples: Church, Economics, and Justice in Matthew* (Eugene, OR: Wipf & Stock, 1988) 105–08.

35 Richard Bauckham, "Egalitarianism and Hierarchy in the Bible," in *God and the Crisis of Freedom: Biblical and Contemporary Perspectives* (Louisville: Westminster John Knox, 2002), 116–27, at 123.

Matthew 20:1–28 also highlights the counter-cultural egalitarian values of the faith community. The parable of the first and last workers in a vineyard (20:1–15) turns on the response of the first-hour workers to the equal payment for disparate amounts of work: "These last ones worked only one hour, and you have made them equal to us, we who have borne the burden of a full day and the sun's burning heat" (20:12). In the aphorism that brackets the parable, Jesus forbids status presumption among his followers (19:30; 20:16; cf. 23:12). Then in 20:20–28, Matthew identifies discipleship with service instead of status, and provides Jesus's own example as the Isaianic servant (see below) as the basis for this kind of discipleship.

> Jesus overturns expectations of what the Messiah would be— from a conquering, imperialist political ruler to a servant of humanity and humble harbinger of the *peaceful* kingdom of God (20:28). Those who follow him into the peaceful kingdom he announces and brings are called to renounce status ambitions to become least and last (20:25–27; 23:8–12).[36]

Discipleship as Servanthood. Another Matthean metaphor for discipleship is service. Given that in the first-century world, servants and slaves were part of the household, this metaphor, like the sibling analogy, fits within the constellation of family or household.[37] A central passage for this metaphor comes in Jesus's teaching in Matt. 20:25–28, arising from the request for highest ranking positions in the kingdom from among Jesus's disciples (20:20–23). Jesus presses against such status preoccupation:

> You know that the Gentile rulers lord it over people and those in high positions exercise their authority over them. It should not be this way for you. Instead, whichever one of you wants to become great must be a servant [διάκονος] to the others, and whichever one of you wants to be first must be a slave [δοῦλος]—just as the son of man did not come to be served but to serve [διακονέω] and to give his life as a ransom for many.

Two important considerations emerge from this passage. First, the theme of service is directly tied to the metaphor of being a servant or a

---

36 Brown and Roberts, *Matthew*, 335.
37 Warren Carter, *Households and Discipleship: A Study of Matthew 19–20*, JSNTSup 103 (Sheffield: JSOT, 1994).

slave (20:24–25; reiterated at 23:11), and this metaphor operates within the sphere of status categories in the first-century world. Much like Jesus calls his disciples to emulate the low status of a child (18:1–5), so here Jesus evokes the role of servants and slaves to indicate that authentic discipleship requires disavowing status preoccupation to pursue caring for and serving others in the believing community (and beyond).[38] Within Matthew's storyline, discipleship as service is exemplified by a number of the story's characters. At 8:15, when Jesus heals Peter's mother-in-law, she begins "serving" (διακονέω) Jesus. Similarly, Matthew highlights "many women" who watch Jesus being crucified and then notes that "these women had followed [ἀκολουθέω] Jesus from Galilee and had served [διακονέω] him" (27:55). The pairing of discipleship language ("followed") with service at 27:55 suggests that Matthew is using διακονέω language thoughtfully to evoke discipleship themes, both here and at 8:15. The importance of serving for discipleship is confirmed in the parable of the sheep and the goats, where those who had ignored "the least of these" wonder when they had seen Jesus in need and not "served" (διακονέω) him (25:44).

Second, servanthood matters for discipleship because servanthood is crucial for Matthew's Christology. According to 20:28, Jesus's service of giving his life "as a ransom for many" is the basis or comparison for the call to disciples to take on the position of a servant or slave (20:26–27). The motif of Jesus as servant arises from Matthew's deliberate use of Isaiah's servant of the Lord figure across his Gospel (4:17; 8:17; 12:18–21; 17:5; 20:28; 26:28 and various echoes in the passion narrative).[39] The longest citation from Isaiah's servant passages comes in the citation of Isaiah 42:1–4 in Matthew 12:18–21, where Jesus's ministry of justice and compassion for Israel and, by extension, for the nations is identified with the mission of Isaiah's "servant" (παῖς; Matt. 12:18 from Isa. 42:1). Just as Jesus has not come to be served but to serve (20:28), so those who follow him are to become servants of one another and agents of justice and mercy. As Cooper concludes, "following Jesus ultimately has to be following Jesus *in the pattern of the Servant.*"[40]

Discipleship Centered on Justice, Mercy, and Loyalty (23:23). In addition to these familial/household metaphors for discipleship of siblings and

---

38 See Brown, *Matthew*, 209.
39 For a fuller discussion, see Brown, "Matthew's Christology and Isaiah's Servant."
40 Ben Cooper, *Incorporated Servanthood: Commitment and Discipleship in the Gospel of Matthew*, LNTS 490 (London: Bloomsbury, 2013), 255.

servants, Matthew draws on a number of central values for his portrait of the ideal disciple. To frame this final set of reflections on Matthean discipleship, we will focus on the cluster of values or virtues addressed in Matthew 23:23, which Jesus refers to as the "weightier matters of the law" and delineates as "justice and mercy and loyalty" (κρίσις, ἔλεος, and πίστις, respectively).[41] We will explore each in turn from across Matthew's narrative.

The importance of justice for discipleship begins with its centrality for Christology: pursuit of justice characterizes Jesus's ministry across the Gospel. Jesus expresses his deep concern for those on the underside of justice from his earliest teachings in Matthew; the fourth beatitude pronounces (unexpected) blessing on those who are hungry and thirsty for justice (5:6; δικαιοσύνη).[42] And in his summary of Jesus's ministry of teaching and healing (chs 5–9), Matthew portrays Jesus as burdened by the crowds who are "distressed and discarded, like sheep without a shepherd" (9:36). Throughout Jesus's ministry in Galilee, Jesus proves to be an able shepherd, enacting justice by healing and feeding these crowds (8:1–9:38; 14:13–15:39). Matthew's perspective of Jesus as the bringer of justice is clarified further in 12:18–21, in his application of Isaiah 42:1–4 to Jesus's Galilean ministry. Justice is highlighted in this passage and contributes to the portrait of Jesus as a Messiah whose ministry will result in "justice [κρίσις] [being made] victorious" at the end (12:20).

Following this christological pattern, Matthew commends the pursuit of justice as a key discipleship trait, which is not at all surprising given the centrality of justice in the Old Testament law and prophets (e.g., Exod. 23:1–9; Mic. 6:8 [see above]; Matt. 23:23). Justice as a discipleship motif emerges in Jesus's teachings, beginning with the blessing he announces to those are "persecuted because of justice" (δικαιοσύνη; 5:10a), presumably persecuted because they have committed themselves to participate in the establishment of God's justice in this world.[43] Although persecuted, they are blessed because "the kingdom of heaven belongs to them" (5:10b). At Jesus's final teaching moment in Matthew,

---

41   There is an allusion here to Micah 6:8 LXX, where Yahweh's expectations for Israel involve "doing justice [κρίμα] and loving mercy [ἔλεος] and being ready to walk with the Lord your God" (i.e., being loyal to God; my translation).

42   For the sense of "justice" for δικαιοσύνη in the Beatitudes, see Jeannine K. Brown, "Justice, Righteousness," in *Dictionary of Jesus and the Gospels,* 2nd ed., eds. J. B. Green, J. K. Brown, N. Perrin (Downers Grove, IL: InterVarsity Press, 2013), 463–67, at 465.

43   Powell, "Matthew's Beatitudes," 474.

the theme of justice recurs in combination with the practice of mercy (Matt. 25:31–46). Mercy and justice combine in actions of solidarity done by the "just" (δίκαιος; 25:37, 45) on behalf of "the least of these" (ἐλάχιστος; 25:40, 46), including feeding the hungry, welcoming the outsider, and visiting those in prison (25:37–39). This passage "picks up and develops the stress in chap. 23 [v. 23] on the weightier matters of the law"—justice, mercy, and loyalty.[44]

Mercy, like justice, is both a virtue that is to mark a disciple (23:23) and a central trait of Jesus himself: Jesus is a compassionate Messiah. He expresses his willingness to heal a leper (8:3); and Matthew indicates that Jesus is moved to compassion at the cries for mercy (ἐλεέω) from two men who are blind (9:27) and a Canaanite woman who pleads for the welfare of her demon-possessed daughter (15:22). Matthew employs language that accents Jesus as full of mercy across his public ministry (σπλαγχνίζομαι at 9:36; 14:14; 15:32; 20:34).

Jesus commends practices of mercy for his followers as well (as at 23:23). He pronounces blessing to those who are merciful (5:7), and twice draws on Hosea 6:6 to emphasize that God's priority is mercy above sacrifice (i.e., purity or Sabbath regulations; 9:13; 12:7), without negating the importance of the Torah's stipulations on either. And in 25:31–46, care for the "least of these" involves acts of mercy and solidarity toward those who are on the lowest rungs of society (25:31–46; see also the motif of Jesus's concern for "little ones" at 10:40–42; 18:6–14). Merciful practices for Matthew include the prioritization of forgiveness. Forgiveness as a communal quality is a divine imperative (6:12–14), and lavish forgiveness is a signal of authentic, merciful community (18:21–35; see 18:27).

Loyalty (and love) is the third Torah value of prominence for Matthean discipleship (23:23). As with justice and mercy, this virtue is christological as well as important for Matthew's pattern of discipleship. The loyalty and faithfulness of Jesus is intimated in God's words of commendation at Jesus's baptism (3:17) and transfiguration (17:5): "This is my son, the one I love; with *him I am well pleased*." This expression of divine pleasure with Jesus is immediately followed by the temptation narrative, in which Matthew highlights Jesus as faithful son in his time of testing in the wilderness (4:1–11). This portrait directly contrasts with Israel in their wilderness wanderings, as the trio of citations from Deuteronomy make clear. The comparison of

---

44 Dan O. Via, Jr., "Ethical Responsibility and Human Wholeness in Matthew 25:31–46," *HTR* 80 (1987): 79–100, at 84.

unfaithful son to faithful son has already begun at 2:15 (cf. with Hos. 11:1–2). As Donaldson summarizes, "Like Israel of old, Jesus has been called by God out of Egypt to a life of humble obedience; like Israel, this calling was put to the test in the wilderness. The hope of the story is that, unlike Israel, Jesus will remain faithful where Israel was disobedient."[45] That hope is realized most especially in the passion narrative, where Matthew recapitulates Jesus as faithful to his mission to "give his life" (20:28) in the face of significant temptation to turn back from his God-given vocation (see 16:22–23; 26:36–46, 53; 27:40, 42).

In line with this christological pattern, disciples are to pursue the virtue of loyalty (πίστις; 23:23): loyalty to Jesus and the kingdom (discussed above) and loyalty toward others. Jesus draws from the requirements of the Torah to express how his disciples are to pursue covenant loyalty toward others (e.g., 5:17–48; 19:17–21). And in their relationships, Jesus's followers are to live in such a way that their inner and outer lives are consonant—they are to live with integrity (5:8; 5:43–48). They are to "be complete and whole as [their] Father in heaven is complete and whole" (τέλειος; 5:48).[46] As they do this, they will pursue the greatest virtue—love.

In reality, love provides the culmination of the discipleship values of justice, mercy, and loyalty. Love in Matthew includes love for God (22:36–38; see also 6:24), love for neighbor (22:39–40), and love of enemy (5:43–48). The latter finds its basis in God's own commitments and actions toward all peoples (5:44–45):

> But I say to you, love your enemies and pray for those who persecute you, in order that you might be children of your Father in heaven. For he causes his sun to rise on the evil and the good and sends rain on the just and the unjust.

While enemy love has its antecedents in the Torah (e.g., Exod. 23:4–5), Matthew presses this ethic further and farther. "By commanding love of even enemy, Matthew presses boundary categories, since love of enemy and neighbor exhausts all human categories; with enemy added to neighbor, there is no one left *not* to love."[47]

---

45 Terence L. Donaldson, "The Vindicated Son: A Narrative Approach to Matthean Christology," in *Contours of Christology in the New Testament,* ed. R. N. Longenecker (Grand Rapids: Eerdmans, 2005), 100–21, at 116.

46 Brown and Roberts, *Matthew,* 346: "The contrasting picture in Matthew is well represented by the 'hypocrite,' whose inner and outer lives are at odds with one another (e.g., 6:1–18; 15:7; 23:13–33)."

47 Brown and Roberts, *Matthew,* 346–47.

Discipleship as Mission. A final discipleship category to address is Matthew's focus on mission. As Jesus has been living out the mission of God to announce the "gospel of the kingdom" and begin to enact its arrival in his Galilean ministry (4:23–25). His death and resurrection have accomplished redemption and life for his people. Now, his disciples are called to live missionally as their Messiah has. Living missionally involves pursuing people with this good news of the kingdom ("fish for people," 4:19; see 10:1–8). Disciples of Jesus are to "disciple [μαθητεύω] all the nations" (28:19); in other words, they are to do what Jesus has done as he has called, been with, and ministered with the Twelve. The final words of Matthew's Gospel form the famous commissioning of those who have followed Jesus and are to continue his mission in this world (28:18–20); and these words are deeply connected to all that has gone before in Matthew. Jesus's mission as servant for Israel and the nations now is shared with his disciples who are to serve all peoples by "baptizing them in the name of the Father and the Son and the Holy Spirit [and by] teaching them to obey everything that [Jesus has] commanded" (28:19–20a). Disciples of Jesus never pursue mission on their own, because it is Jesus's mission that they join and because Jesus goes with them: "And remember I am with you always, even to the end of the age" (28:20b). "Across Matthew, Jesus's mission is a holistic one that attends to physical, emotional, social, and spiritual needs of people. Mercy and justice, gospel proclamation and enactment—these are all woven into a holistic mission to disciple the nations into the ways of Jesus (28:19–20)."[48]

CONCLUSION

We have seen that Matthew attends to discipleship narratively—by drawing on what Jesus says and does, by using the story's other characters as either foils or exemplars for his readers, and by highlighting key metaphors, images, and values that are to captivate and come to characterized Jesus's disciples. Those who follow Jesus enter a family, led by Israel's God and the Messiah, in which they are equals—sisters and brothers, children of God. Disciples of Jesus are also emulators of Jesus as servant; they too serve others rather than pursuing status and honor for themselves. Jesus's followers are those who live missionally— they disciple others as they themselves have learned from Jesus. And

---

48 Brown and Roberts, *Matthew,* 264.

the values that characterize their life together—that they disciple others into—are justice, mercy, and covenantal loyalty. All this is possible because God has already covenanted with them in the Messiah and because Jesus promises his presence with his people "even to the end of the age."

CHAPTER 2

To Serve, Not to Be Served: Discipleship in Mark's Gospel

Mark L. Strauss

It is widely[1] acknowledged that discipleship is a major theme in Mark's Gospel,[2] second in importance only to Christology.[3] John Donahue writes, "While a work which begins with the statement 'the good news of Jesus, Messiah, Son of God' (Mark 1:1) has an obvious Christological thrust, with the sayings and deeds of Jesus in the forefront, the story of the disciples occupies a strong second position."[4] Elizabeth Struthers Malbon similarly writes: "Discipleship—that is, following Jesus—has been recognized as a central theme or motif in the Gospel of Mark."[5]

The structure of Mark's narrative indicates the importance of discipleship. Jesus begins his public ministry announcing that the kingdom of God has come near and calling for repentance and a response of faith in

---

1 This essay is joyfully dedicated to a friend and colleague, Michael J. Wilkins, who practices what he preaches when it comes to discipleship. Mike in fact gave me my first opportunity at college-level teaching way back in 1987 as a young ThM candidate. Then, through a variety of circumstances (and a story too long to tell), he was instrumental in my receiving a position in New Testament at Bethel Seminary San Diego—a place I've called home for twenty-five years. This kind of mentoring is just part of Mike's DNA.

2 Important works on discipleship in Mark include: Robert P. Meye, *Jesus and the Twelve: Discipleship and Revelation in Mark's Gospel* (Grand Rapids: Eerdmans, 1968); R. Tannehill, "The Disciples in Mark: The Function of a Narrative Role," *JR* 57 (1977): 386–405; Ernest Best, *Following Jesus: Discipleship in the Gospel of Mark*, JSNTSup 4 (Sheffield: JSOT Press, 1981); Augustine Stock, *Call to Discipleship: A Literary Study of Mark's Gospel* (Wilmington, DE: Glazier, 1982); D. N. Sweetland, *Our Journey with Jesus: Discipleship according to Mark* (Wilmington, DE: Glazier, 1987); Suzanne Watts Henderson, *Christology and Discipleship in the Gospel of Mark*, SNTSMS 135 (Cambridge: Cambridge University Press, 2006); David E. Garland, *A Theology of Mark's Gospel: Good News about Jesus the Messiah, the Son of God*, BTNT (Grand Rapids: Zondervan, 2015), 388–454.

3 A third theological theme held to be central for Mark is eschatology. See especially Willi Marxsen, *Mark the Evangelist: Studies on the Redaction History of the Gospel* (Nashville: Abingdon, 1969). Though a groundbreaking redaction-critical study, Marxsen's claim that Mark's narrative was a call to the Jerusalem church to escape the Jewish war by fleeing to Galilee where the Lord would return to meet them is no longer widely held.

4 John R. Donahue, *The Theology and Setting of Discipleship in the Gospel of Mark*, Pere Marquette Theology Lecture 1983 (Milwaukee: Marquette University Press, 1983), 2.

5 E. S. Malbon, "Fallible Followers: Women and Men in the Gospel of Mark," *Semeia* 28 (1983): 29–48, at 29.

the good news (1:15). The first thing Jesus does after defining his ministry is to call disciples, starting with the four fisherman brothers (1:16–20).[6] From this point on the disciples are Jesus's constant companions and participants in his ministry (1:29, 36; 2:15, 16, 18, 23–24; 3:7, 9, 20; 4:34, 35, 38; etc.).

If these early passages suggest the importance of the disciples and discipleship in Mark's Gospel, the second half of the book confirms this emphasis. Following Peter's confession (8:29), the midpoint of Mark's narrative, Jesus repeatedly teaches on the role of a true disciple and the humility and perseverance necessary for followers of Jesus the Messiah. Though developed through a narrative, rather than in an epistolary or didactic genre, Mark's Gospel functions as a handbook on Christian discipleship.

While these early passages confirm the importance of the disciples as thematic characters and discipleship as a key theological theme in Mark's Gospel, as the narrative progresses they are more often presented as a negative model to be avoided than a positive model to be emulated.

THE NARRATIVE ROLE OF THE DISCIPLES IN MARK'S GOSPEL

A. The Positive Position and Role of the Disciples

In important ways, the disciples are protagonists and positive examples in Mark—at least in the early parts of the Gospel. In a narrative where sides are starkly drawn between the purpose of God and the destructive work of Satan, the disciples are clearly on the side of Jesus and the kingdom of God. When Jesus calls Peter and Andrew, they drop everything and follow him. James and John, too, respond immediately to Jesus's call, even leaving their own father Zebedee behind in the boat (1:16–20). Levi the tax collector follows suit, leaving behind his lucrative occupation as a tax collector to follow Jesus (2:13–14). While the primary point here is the authority of Jesus in calling disciples, a secondary one is the immediate and obedient response by the disciples—an example for all followers of Jesus.

From this point on, the disciples are a fundamental part of Jesus's ministry. Jesus comes to their defense when they are criticized for not fasting (2:18–22) and are accused by the scribes of working on the Sabbath (2:23-28). He appoints the Twelve as his "apostles" (3:13–18; 6:3) and trusts them enough to send them out to expand his own ministry of preaching,

---

6 Sweetland, *Journey with Jesus*, 13–14.

healing, and exorcism (6:6–13). And they are successful: "They went out and preached that people should repent, and they cast out many demons and anointed many sick people with oil and healed them"[7] (6:12–13).

The importance of the disciples is also indicated by the number twelve (3:14, 16; 4:10; 6:7; 9:35; 10:32; 11:11), which almost certainly signifies that they represent the restored remnant of the tribes of Israel. This identification finds support in Mark's Beelzebul controversy (3:22–30), which follows the appointment of the Twelve (3:13–19), where the religious leaders may be seen to represent illegitimate shepherds over Israel in contrast to the Twelve, the true reconstituted Israel (3:14). Two contextual indicators support this conclusion. First, 3:20–35 is one of Mark's famous intercalations, where one episode interrupts another and the two mutually interpret one another. The Beelzebul controversy (3:23–30) is "sandwiched" between the beginning and end of the attempt by Jesus's family to bring him home. Just as Jesus's own family think he's crazy, so his own people (as represented by these leaders) think he's demon-possessed. When Jesus says, "Whoever does God's will is my brother and sister and mother" (3:34), the implied reader would immediately think of the Twelve who have followed God's will by responding positively to Jesus's kingdom proclamation. A second piece of evidence for this contrast is Mark's identification of Jesus's challengers as those γραμματεῖς "who came down from Jerusalem" (3:22). They are presented as official representatives of the Jewish leadership in Jerusalem and so stand in contrast to the restored remnant represented by the Twelve.

In short, the Beelzebul controversy (3:20–30) together with Jesus's identification of his true family as "those who do God's will" (3:34– 35) serve as positive representations of the disciples. While his own family (3:21) and the leaders of his own nation (3:22) reject him and so are on the "outside" (3:32), the Twelve are Jesus's true family—"insiders" because they are doing God's will. Immediately after this, Jesus begins teaching in parables, the purpose of which is to reveal "the secret of the kingdom of God" to those on the inside (4:11), but to blind the eyes of "those on the outside" (4:12; citing Isa. 6:9–10). Whatever role the disciples will subsequently play, at this point they are clearly "insiders"—faithful followers of Jesus and protagonists in the Markan narrative.

Individual disciples are also portrayed as faithful followers of Jesus. Peter is the first human character in the Gospel to recognize that Jesus is

---

7 All translations are the author's own unless otherwise noted.

the Messiah, and his confession of this in 8:29 is an important climax for the first half of Mark's Gospel. At the Last Supper, when Jesus predicts his abandonment by the disciples, Peter insists he will never fall away, and would die before he disowns Jesus (14:31). James and John demonstrate similar loyalty. Although the implied reader rightfully views their attempt to gain the best seats in the kingdom on Jesus's right and left (10:35–45) as a negative and prideful request, in one sense it is a positive one. Like Peter, these two have come to believe that Jesus is the Messiah who will successfully establish his royal throne (and so will need advisers like them!). Mark 10:37 could be called *their* confession that Jesus is the Messiah.

B. The Negative Portrayal of the Disciples

Despite the disciples' positive position and status as followers of and representatives for Jesus and the kingdom of God, in Mark's narrative theology they ultimately function as a negative example and a foil for the ideal model of a disciple, which is Jesus himself.

Mark is fond of structuring his narrative around patterns of three, and these triads are consistently related to the failures of the disciples. For example, the disciples take three boat trips in Mark, and in each they exhibit a lack of faith and are rebuked by Jesus. Following these three boat trips, Jesus three times predicts his own death. Each "passion prediction" is followed by an act of pride or self-interest on the part of the disciples, after which Jesus teaches on self-sacrificial servant leadership. A third triad of failures occurs in the Garden of Gethsemane. Jesus repeatedly tells the disciples to keep watch and pray (14:34, 38), but each time he returns to find them sleeping. Finally, as Jesus predicted, three times Peter denies that he knows Jesus. It will be useful to survey each of these triads.

Three Boat Trips. The first boat trip follows Jesus's teaching in parables and involves a storm on the Sea of Galilee (4:33–41). When a furious squall arises, the disciples fear for their lives. Jesus, however, is asleep on a cushion in the stern of the boat. Jesus's ability to sleep through the storm may be meant to indicate his exhaustion, and so his humanity. Or, it may indicate his complete trust in God through life's storms. When the disciples cry out, "Teacher, don't you care if we die?" Jesus stands up, rebukes the wind, and with a command calms the storm. There are strong implications of deity here, since the Hebrew Scriptures speak of God's mastery over the storm: "You . . . stilled the roaring of the seas, the roaring of their waves" (Ps. 65:5–7; cf. 89:9; 107:23–29). Jesus then rebukes the disciples, "Why are you so afraid? Do you still have no faith?" (4:40). Having "no faith" is a serious charge. Matthew and Luke soften Jesus's words. Matthew has, "You of little faith, why are you so afraid?" (8:26), and Luke, "Where is your faith?" (8:25).

The second boat trip occurs following the feeding of the five thousand (6:45–56). After the miracle, Jesus sends his disciples ahead of him to Bethsaida by boat while he goes up to a mountain to pray. That evening, when the boat is in the middle of the lake and the disciples are straining against the wind, Mark says that Jesus "went out to them, walking on the sea" (6:48). This action, too, has implications of deity, since God alone makes a path through the sea (Ps. 77:19; Isa. 43:16; 51:10). Furthermore, Jesus's intention to "pass by them" may be intentional theophanic language, meant to echo God's manifestation to Moses in Exodus 33:18–23 and to Elijah in 1 Kings 19:10––12.[8]

While Jesus's criticism of the disciples is relatively mild here, telling them only to have courage and not to be afraid, the narrator provides a stronger critique: "They were completely amazed, for they had not understood about the loaves; their hearts were hardened [ἦν αὐτῶν ἡ καρδία πεπωρωμένη]" (6:51–52). "Hard hearts" in Scripture means obstinate rebellion against God's will. Pharaoh's hard heart results in his unwillingness to let his Hebrew subjects leave Egypt, provoking God's judgment in the plagues and ultimately the death of the Egyptian firstborn (Exod. 7:3, 13, 22; 8:15, 32; 9:12; 10:1). More foreboding in the present context is the fact that the religious leaders have similarly demonstrated "hard hearts" (πωρώσει τῆς καρδίας) when they sought to trap Jesus earlier (3:5; cf. 10:5). Are the disciples going the way of Jesus's enemies?

The third boat trip is the journey to Dalmanutha and back following the second feeding miracle (8:9–21). Jesus warns the disciples against "the leaven of the Pharisees and the leaven of Herod" (8:15). Though leaven can be a neutral image, it is more often a negative one, referring to the permeating power of sin.[9] Here the leaven most likely refers to rejection of Jesus's proclamation of the kingdom of God—one of the few things the Pharisees and the Herodians would have agreed upon. The disciples are clueless and

---

8 So W. L. Lane, *The Gospel according to Mark*, NICNT (Grand Rapids: Eerdmans, 1974), 236; Garland, *A Theology of Mark's Gospel*, 263–64; Joel Marcus, *Mark 1–8: A New Translation with Introduction and Commentary*, AB 27 (New York: Doubleday, 2000): 426; Robert H. Stein, *Mark*, BECNT (Grand Rapids: Baker, 2008), 325; Adela Yarbro Collins, *Mark*, Hermeneia (Minneapolis: Fortress, 2007), 334.

9 The removal of leaven from the home was originally related to the haste Israel needed in their departure from Egypt (Exod. 12:39). Yet it came to be associated with permeating power of sin (Matt. 16:6, 7, 8; 1 Cor. 5:6; Gal. 5:9).

think that Jesus is referring to their failure to bring bread on the trip. Jesus rebukes them for missing his point: "Why are you talking about having no bread? Do you still not see or understand? Are your hearts hardened? Do you have eyes but fail to see, and ears but fail to hear?" (8:17–18, NIV). Again the reference to a lack of understanding and hard hearts recalls the attitude of the religious leaders (3:5; 10:5). Also Jesus's words, "Do you have eyes . . . ?"[10] are ominously similar to Mark 4:12 (quoting Isaiah 6:9–10), where the religious leaders were similarly described as blind and deaf to the meaning of Jesus's kingdom parables. Again Mark seems to be saying that the disciples are perilously close to going the way of Jesus's opponents and falling into unbelief. The blundering disciples are far from ideal models of Christian discipleship.

Three Passion Predictions. The second set of triads that highlights the failure of the disciples involves a pattern of three cycles. In each, (1) Jesus predicts his suffering and death, (2) the disciples respond with pride or self-interest, and (3) Jesus teaches on humility and servant leadership. The first of these is the key, central passage and turning point in Mark's Gospel (8:27–37). Having demonstrated his messianic authority by means of miracles and authoritative teaching, Jesus now withdraws with his disciples to the region of Caesarea Philippi. On the way he asks them who people say that he is. Their answer: "Some say John the Baptist; others Elijah; still others, one of the prophets." This provokes a second question: "But what about you? . . . Who do you say I am?" Peter responds for the rest, "You are the Messiah" (8:27–29).

Peter has obviously reached the right conclusion. As the narrator announced in the first line of the book, Jesus is the Messiah (1:1), Israel's promised Savior. Yet Jesus now makes the shocking revelation that the Messiah is going be rejected by the Jewish leaders and killed. Peter is appalled by this defeatist language. Taking Jesus aside, he rebukes him. Jesus, in turn, rebukes Peter right back: "Get behind me, Satan! . . . You do not have in mind the concerns of God, but merely human concerns" (8:33, NIV). Jesus's identification of Peter as Satan is shocking and reveals the severity of Peter's error. For Jesus to avoid the cross would play directly into Satan's hands by superseding God's plan to deal with humanity's sin through Jesus's atoning death on the cross (10:45). This is not only a satanic response but also a "merely human" one. As fallen people, the typical human response is to seek immediate position, power, and security.

---

10 Probably an allusion to Jeremiah 5:21 and Ezekiel 12:2.

Peter wants to see Jesus conquer the Romans and cannot yet fathom the greater goal of Jesus's atoning sacrifice for sins.

Jesus follows with teaching on discipleship. "Whoever wants to be my disciple must deny himself and take up his cross and follow me" (8:34). Taking up your cross does not mean a willingness to bear a heavy burden, but rather a willingness to suffer martyrdom. Those condemned to crucifixion would be forced to carry their crossbeam (*patibulum*) to the place of crucifixion. Such sacrifice, however, will result in eternal life. In a paradoxical play on words, Jesus says that whoever wishes to save their (physical) life (ψυχή) will lose it (= eternal life). But whoever willingly gives up their (physical) life (ψυχή) will save it (= gain eternal life).[11] What benefit is it to gain the whole world (in the present life), yet forfeit your life/soul (ψυχή) (in the age to come).

The second passion prediction is followed by another failure on the part of the disciples and another lesson on discipleship from Jesus (9:30–37). Jesus again teaches his disciples that "the Son of Man is going to be delivered into human hands. They will kill him, and after three days he will rise" (9:31). The disciples demonstrate spiritual dullness, first, by their lack of understanding and fear of asking Jesus any further questions (9:32). Then, when Jesus asks them about their discussion on the road, they remain silent, since they were arguing about who among them was the greatest (9:33–34). Spiritual ignorance is made worse by pride and self-aggrandizement. Jesus responds by teaching that discipleship involves humility: "If anyone wants to be first they must be last and servant of all" (9:35).

Jesus illustrates this humility by welcoming a child into their midst and teaching that "Whoever welcomes one of these little children in my name welcomes me; and whoever welcomes me does not welcome me but the one who sent me" (9:37, NIV). In a society where social status was, for the most part, fixed and inviolable and where children were viewed as having little or no status, Jesus calls his followers to lower their own position and treat the lowliest member of society as their equals.[12] To welcome them is to welcome Jesus himself, which is equivalent to welcoming the one who sent him—God himself. This is radical teaching, shattering society's values of social position and authoritarian leadership.

---

11 R. T. France, *The Gospel of Mark*, NIGTC (Grand Rapids: Eerdmans, 2002), 340–41.

12 On the status of children in the Greco-Roman world, see T. Wiedemann, *Adults and Children in the Roman Empire* (London: Routledge, 1989); and B. Rawson, ed., *The Family in Ancient Rome* (Ithaca, NY: Cornell University Press, 1986).

The third passion prediction repeats the threefold pattern (10:32–45). Jesus predicts his death but the disciples miss the point and again demonstrate pride and self-centeredness. This time it is the request by James and John that they be rewarded with the best seats in the kingdom on Jesus's right and left (10:35–37). The other disciples respond with indignation—no doubt because they wanted these coveted positions of honor for themselves! A third time Jesus gathers the disciples and teaches them about servant leadership. Although the leaders of this world rule with power and oppression, this is not how Jesus's followers are to lead: "Not so with you. Instead, whoever wants to become great among you must be your servant, and whoever wants to be first must be slave of all" (10:43–44). The model for this servant attitude is Jesus himself: "For even the Son of Man did not come to be served, but to serve, and to give his life as a ransom for many" (10:45).[13]

Mark 10:45 has rightly been seen as a key literary and theological climax in Mark's narrative, and the epitome of his Christology. Structurally, it is the climactic third cycle in a narrative full of triads. It also occurs just before Jesus arrives in Jerusalem, where he will fulfill the messianic task. In light of what Jesus says about the power and glory of the "Son of Man" in 13:26 and 14:62, there is little doubt that the title here alludes to the glorious messianic figure of Daniel 7:13–14, who appears before the Ancient of Days and is given all authority, glory, and sovereign power and is worshipped by all nations and peoples. Jesus says that "even the Son of Man"—who will reign over the universe at God's right hand—has come as a lowly servant to humbly accomplish God's will. If this is the case, his followers should respond with the same kind of self-sacrificial attitude and actions. Victory and vindication come through humility and self-sacrifice.

Three Failures in Gethsemane. The next important triad in Mark's Gospel occurs in Gethsemane, following Jesus's last meal with his disciples. At the Last Supper, Jesus predicted that all the disciples would fail him. "One of the Twelve"—a member of his closest followers—would betray him (14:18–21); all the disciples would "fall away" (14:27); despite his bravado, Peter would deny he knew Jesus (14:29–31). In Gethsemane, Jesus tells all the disciples to "sit here while I pray"; then he takes Peter, James, and John further, telling them to "stay here and keep watch" (14:34) and to "watch and pray so that you will not fall into temptation" (14:38). Yet true to form,

---

13 See Best, *Following Jesus,* 12, 127–128; Sweetland, *Journey,* 69.

the disciples fail and three times Jesus returns to find them sleeping. On the third, he announces the arrival of the betrayer (14:42).

This failure and unfaithfulness by the disciples contrasts sharply with Jesus's response to the situation. Although he is in emotional agony—"deeply distressed and troubled" (14:33) and "overwhelmed with sorrow to the point of death" (14:34)—he remains faithful to God's plan. Although he prays that, if possible, God would "take this cup from me," nevertheless he accepts God's will: "Yet not what I will, but what you will" (14:36). Again, the model of true discipleship comes not from Jesus's disciples, but from Jesus himself.

Three Denials in the Courtyard. A final triad pointing to the disciples' failures in Mark's Gospel is Peter's threefold denial of Jesus. After Jesus's arrest, he is taken under guard to the high priest and a gathering of the Sanhedrin. Here we likely have another one of Mark's intercalations. The account of Peter's denial begins with his arrival in the courtyard of the high priest (14:54) but is then interrupted by the insertion (intercalation) of the account of Jesus's trial (14:55–65), resuming again in 14:66–72. While in most cases in Mark, the intercalated episode repeats and emphasizes the theme of the episode it interrupts (3:20–35; 5:21–43; 6:12–30; 11:12–25), in this case it presents a contrasting theme.[14] Jesus faithfully proclaims his identity as the Messiah and Son of God before the Sanhedrin, but Peter denies his own identity as a disciple of the Messiah. Peter's failure is starkly emphasized when the rooster crows and Peter breaks down weeping (14:72).

In summary, consistently in Mark's Gospel Jesus's disciples appear not as examples to be emulated, but as failures to be avoided. Jesus alone represents the true and faithful disciple, who takes up his cross and so remains faithful to God's purpose.

C. Mark's Purpose with Reference to the Failures of the Disciples

While Mark's negative portrait of the disciples seems beyond dispute, scholars debate his narrative purpose behind this presentation. T. J. Weeden claimed Mark's purpose was to combat a false Christology, which was being promoted by false teachers who had infiltrated his community. The heretics claimed Jesus was a "divine man," a heavenly figure with supernatural powers—powers all Christians should claim. They replaced

---

14 For a discussion of various ways to interpret intercalations, with this perspective as the consensus, see Geoffrey David Miller, "An Intercalation Revisited: Christology, Discipleship, and Dramatic Irony in Mark 6.6b–30," *JSNT* 35 (2012): 176–95, at 178.

the true theology of the cross (*theologia crucis*) with a theology of glory (*theologia gloriae*). In his Gospel, this heresy is represented by the disciples' view of Jesus's messiahship. The disciples move progressively from *imperceptivity* to *misconception* to *outright rejection* of Jesus's messianic role, with no restoration in the end.[15] In Weeden's view, the emphasis on Jesus's authority and miracles in the first half of the Gospel is corrected in the second half by Jesus's emphasis on his suffering role.

Werner Kelber agrees with Weeden's negative view of the disciples, but takes it in a different direction. In his view the heresy represented by the disciples is not so much christological as eschatological. According to Kelber, Mark wrote after the destruction of Jerusalem and is supporting a Galilean-based community in opposition to a Jerusalem-based one. The Jerusalem group claimed that the destruction of Jerusalem was a sign of the return of Christ. The disciples in the Gospel represent this Jerusalem-based group. Mark counters through the discourse of Jesus in Mark 13, seeking to show that Jesus's return is still future and will take place in Galilee, not Jerusalem.[16]

The problem with all views that treat the disciples as unreconciled or believe that Mark stands in opposition to the original apostles is Jesus's own words in the Gospel. Although Jesus predicts the failure of the disciples, he also predicts their restoration. "You will all fall away," he says, but then "after I have risen, I will go ahead of you into Galilee" (14:27–28). The angel at the tomb says the same thing: Jesus "is going ahead of you into Galilee. There you will see him. Just as he told you" (16:7). From Mark's perspective, the resurrection appearances and the restoration of the disciples are facts of history. Jesus also says in the Olivet Discourse that the disciples will preach the gospel to all nations through the empowerment of the Holy Spirit and will suffer persecution for Jesus's name (13:9–11). These are not things that Mark would say about heretics. The implied author clearly expects the disciples to be restored. A better explanation of Mark's narrative purpose with reference to the disciples is that he contrasts their failures with Jesus's success and so illustrates the true suffering role of the Messiah and the nature of authentic discipleship.[17]

15 T. J. Weeden, *Mark—Traditions in Conflict* (Philadelphia: Fortress, 1971); idem, "The Heresy That Necessitated Mark's Gospel," ZNW 59 (1968): 145–58.
16 W. H. Kelber, *The Kingdom in Mark: A New Place and a New Time* (Philadelphia: Fortress, 1974), 138. Richard A. Horsley, *Hearing the Whole Story: The Politics of Plot in Mark's Gospel* (Louisville: Westminster John Knox, 2001), similarly sees Mark's Gospel as a polemic against the Jerusalem elite (in favor of Galilean villagers).
17 So Tannehill, "Disciples in Mark," 402; Best, *Following Jesus,* 12; Sweetland, *Journey,* 84; Stock, *Call to Discipleship,* 204–05.

MINOR CHARACTERS AND DISCIPLESHIP IN MARK'S GOSPEL

While studies of the Markan theme of discipleship have focused primarily on the role of the Twelve, other characters also play a significant role in Mark's theology of discipleship. Joel Williams counts twenty-two passages in Mark's Gospel where so-called "minor characters" emerge from the crowd.[18]

A few of the minor characters in Mark represent negative models. The people of Jesus's hometown miss out on kingdom blessings because of their lack of faith (6:1–6).[19] The rich man who asks Jesus what he must do to inherit eternal life is ultimately unwilling to trade his earthly wealth for treasures in heaven and to follow Jesus (10:17–31). The women at the tomb cannot (yet) comprehend the announcement of the resurrection and flee from the tomb, "trembling and bewildered" (16:8).

While a few represent negative models, most of the minor characters in Mark are positive examples of faith. A number of these come to Jesus as suppliants and receive healing because of their faith. A woman with a chronic blood disease secretly touches Jesus, believing she will be healed, and is rewarded because of her faith (5:25–34). Jairus, a synagogue leader, receives his daughter back from the dead after Jesus encourages him, "Don't be afraid; just believe" (5:36). A demon-possessed boy with epileptic-like symptoms is healed after his father responds to Jesus's call to faith, "I believe; help my unbelief!" (9:24). A blind man named Bartimaeus is healed because of his persistent faith, after repeatedly pleading with Jesus, "Son of David, have mercy on me" (10:46–52).

Other minor characters not seeking healing are praised by Jesus for their words or actions. A scribe who answers Jesus wisely is said by Jesus to be "not far from the kingdom of God" (12:34). A widow's sacrificial gift to the temple receives Jesus's commendation, since she gave all that she had despite her poverty (12:41–44). A woman who anoints Jesus's head with expensive perfume receives his commendation for her sacrificial act on his behalf (14:1–9). Wherever the gospel is preached her act will be remembered (14:9).

Most striking are demonstrations of faith by those who are outsiders. Levi, a despised tax collector, responds to Jesus's call by leaving behind his lucrative trade and following Jesus (2:13–17). A Syro-Phoenician woman,

---

18 Joel F. Williams, "Discipleship and Minor Characters in Mark's Gospel," *BSac* 153 (1996): 332–43, at 333; idem, *Other Followers of Jesus: Minor Characters as Major Figures in Mark's Gospel*, JSNTSup 102 (Sheffield: JSOT Press, 1994).

19 Crowds that act in unison are viewed as characters by literary critics.

while at first rebuffed by Jesus, receives healing for her demon-possessed daughter when she persists in faith (7:24–30). Her insistence, that "even the dogs under the table eat the children's crumbs," shows remarkable insight that God's plan for Israel's salvation extends also to the Gentiles. Finally, while Jesus's own people reject him and his own disciples abandon him, the Roman centurion at the cross recognizes that "truly this man was the Son of God" (15:39). Remarkably, a Gentile outsider is the first human character in Mark's narrative to recognize that *through his suffering* Jesus reveals himself to be the Messiah and Son of God.

MARK'S THEOLOGY OF DISCIPLESHIP

Having surveyed the role of the disciples and other characters in Mark's Gospel, we can draw conclusions concerning Mark's theology of discipleship.

A. The Cost of Discipleship

The cost of discipleship is high. It means giving up everything to follow Jesus.[20] Simon and Andrew leave their nets—and their livelihood—behind to follow him (1:18). James and John leave their father Zebedee in the boat (1:20). Levi leaves his tax booth and his occupation (2:14). By contrast, a rich man fails the test of discipleship because he is unwilling to leave his riches behind (10:21–22). Peter sums it up when he says, "We have left everything to follow you!" (10:28). Leaving everything does not mean simply abandoning other relationships or commitments. Mark knows that Peter is married (1:29–31), and there is no suggestion that he abandoned his wife and family (cf. 1 Cor. 9:5). What it means is that all of a person's resources and relationships are dedicated first to Jesus and the kingdom.

Total commitment means that our whole life belongs to God. Salvation costs us nothing; it is a free gift by faith alone (1:15, "Repent and *believe* the good news"). But at the same time it costs us everything. As noted earlier, in his first discourse on discipleship (8:34–9:1) Jesus says that discipleship involves self denial and taking up one's cross (8:34). Since carrying a cross was the prelude to crucifixion, Jesus is saying that discipleship requires the commitment of one's very life, even to the point of martyrdom. And an unwillingness to give up one's physical "life" (ψυχή)

---

20 See Garland, *A Theology of Mark's Gospel,* 438–54.

results in the loss of true spiritual "life" (ψυχή), that is, eternal life (8:35). This saying also sets Jesus apart as the ultimate model of discipleship, since he alone in Mark's Gospel takes up the cross.

B. The Rewards for Discipleship

If the cost of discipleship is great, the rewards are greater. The ultimate reward is eternal life, the greatest gain anyone can experience. Jesus says, "What good is it for someone to gain the whole world, yet forfeit their soul? Or what can anyone give in exchange for their soul?" (8:36–37). The reward of "life" brings with it "treasures in heaven" (10:21) and entrance into the kingdom of God. Yet participation in the kingdom (= God's sovereign reign) does not wait to begin until the afterlife. Jesus invites his followers to enter the kingdom now and to experience the rewards of salvation in the present. When Peter reminds Jesus that he and the other disciples have left everything to follow him, Jesus points out that:

> Truly I tell you . . . no one who has left home or brothers or sisters or mother or father or children or fields for me and the gospel will fail to receive a hundred times as much in this present age: homes, brothers, sisters, mothers, children and fields—along with persecutions—and in the age to come eternal life. (10:29–32)

While eternal life and treasures in heaven are the ultimate gift from God, in the present discipleship means entrance into the new family of God. This means not only new family relationships around the world (brothers, sisters, mothers, fathers, children), but also all the resources that belong to that family. It also means membership in a family that is at odds with the present world system and experiencing increasing persecution and suffering (cf. 10:32; 13:9–13).

Jesus's teaching here would have been shocking in its first-century Greco-Roman context, where loyalty to family, clan, and tribe superseded all other relationships. Jesus teaches instead a radical new ethic of spiritual relationships. This theme appeared already earlier in Mark's narrative. When Jesus's family comes to take charge of him, concerned about his mental health, Jesus is told that his mother and brothers and sisters were outside looking for him. Jesus shockingly responds, "Who are my mother and my brothers?" Gesturing toward his disciples around him he adds, "Whoever does God's will is my brother and sister and mother" (3:33–35).

Jesus's teaching here has profound implications not only for Mark's community in the first century, but also for the present-day church. Christians in the wealthy Western economies and in Asia have a family commitment and responsibility to their brothers and sisters worldwide, especially those facing suffering and persecution. Our resources should be viewed as their resources to be used for the benefit of the people of God and the advancement of the gospel.

C. The Attitude of the Disciple

Finally, the attitude of the disciple of Jesus Christ should be one of humility and servanthood. When Jesus teaches his disciples about leadership, the repeated theme is the upside-down values of the kingdom of God. Anyone who wants to be first must be the very last and the servant of all (9:35). Whoever welcomes a lowly child welcomes Jesus himself (9:36–37). Many who are first will be last, and the last first (10:31). To become great you must become a servant, and to be first you must become a slave (10:43). In a society marked by hierarchy, elitism, social status, and strict reciprocity for favors, Jesus calls on his followers to welcome and exalt the lowest members of society, to become slaves instead of rulers, to live a sacrificial life for the good of others, and not to expect to be paid back for your good deeds. Discipleship means a life lived for others, "For even the Son of Man did not come to be served, but to serve, and to give his life as a ransom for many" (10:45).

CHAPTER 3

Following Jesus by Engaging the World: Discipleship in Luke's Gospel

Darrell L. Bock

Jesus's teaching on discipleship in Luke appears in an array of fascinating contexts.[1] We tend to think of discipleship as a relationship that takes place between an individual and God. However, in some scenes in Luke, Jesus teaches about discipleship by modeling what it means to follow him and by engaging in mission. What we find in those scenes is an interpersonal element in discipleship that is often overlooked. In such contexts it is Jesus's associations with others that drives what he teaches or shows about being a disciple, and the nature of those associations is surprising, reflecting his values about mission. Most discipleship programs today focus on what Jesus *says*, but what Jesus *shows* also has much to teach us about discipleship. That "showing discipleship" is the focus of this article. It reflects a direction often not addressed in discipleship teaching.

Our guide is where Luke uses the term "disciple" in a passage, so we can see what these passages demonstrate about what Jesus is doing. We proceed mostly in narrative order. This study focuses first on some key events where Jesus teaches by example. Then we look at the remainder of the disciple passages in Luke and examine discipleship principles for today.

EXAMPLE EVENTS WHERE DISCIPLES ARE PRESENT

Many of the passages about disciples in Luke treat scenes where they accompany Jesus or are reacting to events he has generated. As a whole these passages suggest that discipleship is both caught as well as taught. Such a teaching method assumes close personal time in real life, not just discussion of what discipleship looks like. That personal dimension to discipleship is an important element in producing disciples.

---

1 The following is an expansion of the section on disciples and discipleship in my *A Theology of Luke and Acts* (Grand Rapids: Zondervan, 2012), 315–23. In this version I develop the idea what discipleship is, something Mike Wilkins's life does beautifully. All Scripture translations are NIV unless otherwise noted.

A. Disciples and Their Association with Sinners

Interestingly, the first appearance of the term "disciple" involves a complaint that the Pharisees and scribes make about Jesus's associations with outsiders that taught the disciples and others (Luke 5:30). These disciples are placed in the middle of a controversy account. The dispute asks about the kind of associations disciples should pursue in life and ministry. In a sense, this is a discipleship text leading into other passages that develop the thought of engaging sinners, because they show both what Jesus taught about following him in mission as well as what he did, even in the midst of controversy. Jesus pursued association with sinners because his mission was to call sinners to repent, like a physician who provides a cure to the sick (Luke 5:32). His life also showed the same point. What Jesus said, he did. So disciples are not just operating in-house. They are to carry out the mission of outreach that Jesus called his disciples to undertake. That requires taking the initiative in relationships with those outside the church.

As a result, we see Jesus engaged with folks like the sinful woman in Luke 7:36–50 or Zacchaeus in Luke 19:1–10. He travels into the Gentile Decapolis region in Luke 8:26–39. The Pharisees grumble about these relationships (Luke 15:1), but Jesus understands why he pursues them. He is seeking the lost.

B. Disciples and Practices of Piety: Fasting and Prayer

Another lesson displayed in controversy has to do with the practices of Jesus's disciples. It shows up in the very next passage, in Luke 5:33–39. The expression of religious faith by Jesus and his disciples is unlike that of John the Baptist's followers or the Pharisees. They do not fast or offer public prayers (Luke 5:33), practices well established in Second Temple Judaism. By grouping the Pharisees' disciples and John's disciples, Luke makes clear that an issue of the larger Jewish community is at stake. That issue applied to Jesus's time as well as to the early church, since the way of Jesus would be a new way. Jesus comes out of Judaism, but his way of piety goes in a distinct direction with different values. In our more secular age, it is easy to underestimate the importance of such practices. A look at their importance at the time shows how widely and highly regarded such community practices were. It is often not appreciated how frequent and important fasting was seen to be. Once we see what is at stake, then we can see just how distinctive Jesus's approach to piety was.

As noted, fasting was an important aspect of spiritual activity during this period. It was seen as a central part of walking with God. To be a follower of God in this era meant taking fasting seriously. Yet Jesus seemed dismissive of it. To appreciate the contrast, let's see how pervasive fasting was and why. The Old Testament discusses fasts for specific occasions (Lev. 16:29–34; 23:26–32; Num. 29:7–11).[2] Individual fasts were taken for differing reasons: Some fasted in hope of God's deliverance (2 Sam. 12:16–20; 1 Kings 21:27; Pss. 35:13; 69:10 [69:11 MT]), while others hoped to turn aside calamity (Judg. 20:26; 1 Sam. 7:6; 1 Kings 21:9; 2 Chron. 20:3–4; Jer. 36:6, 9). By combining prayer and fasting, the participants hoped that God would answer, since fasting often accompanied confession and intercession (Ezra 8:21, 23; Neh. 1:4; Jer. 14:12). The one who fasted reflected a mourner's mood (1 Kings 21:27; Esther 4:3; Isa. 58:5; Dan. 9:3; Joel 2:12–13). The usual fast lasted one morning and evening (Judg. 20:26; 1 Sam. 14:24; 2 Sam. 1:12). More severe were the three-day fast (Esther 4:16) and the weeklong fast (1 Sam. 31:13), where food was forbidden only during the day (2 Sam. 3:35). The three-week fast described in Dan 10:2–3 belongs to this latter type of severe fast. Needless to say, such fasting had an influence on the body (Ps. 109:24).

Fasting extended beyond an individual act. National fasts occurred on the Day of Atonement and the four-day memorial to recall Jerusalem's fall. Thus, fasting held a high place in Judaism's psyche. It occurred frequently and had great significance. In fact, fasting prepared one for all kinds of activity in Judaism. Many apocalyptic materials mention that fasting preceded their visions (2 Esdras [= 4 Ezra] 5:13, 19–20; 2 Bar. 9.2; 12.5). A vow often was confirmed with a fast, as was the case for the Jews who had conspired to kill Paul (Acts 23:12, 14). Fasting was often regarded as a virtue (T. Jos. 3.4–5; 4.8; 10.1). It even was regarded in some circles as meritorious (1 En. 108.7–9; Philo, *Special Laws* 2.32 [197]). Only here and there do voices warn that fasting without actual turning from sin is useless (Sir 34:31). The zealous fasted twice a week, usually on Monday and Thursday. Didache 8.1 shows that some in early Christianity took up this practice. Fasting was not permitted on Sabbaths and festival days (Jdt 8:6; Jub. 50.10, 12). Clearly, this activity had a major role in first-century religious life, so one can see why Jesus's lack of emphasis raised questions about his piety and practice. Surely the thought was that a disciple seeking to please God would care deeply about such practices.

---

2 Frederick Danker, *Jesus and the New Age according to St. Luke* (St. Louis: Clayton, 1972), 127; Johannes Behm, "νῆστις, νηστεύω, νηστεία," in *TDNT*, eds. G. Kittel and G. Friedrich; trans. G. Bromley (Grand Rapids; Eerdmans, 1967), IV:928–29.

So when Luke focuses on Jesus's unusual approach to prayer and fasting, the issue is not on the periphery of religion. Jesus is seemingly minimizing a central act of great piety minimized. Luke alone mentions prayer with fasting, probably because the two activities went together. One fasted in order to spend focused time with God. The remark concerns a serious issue in ancient Jewish spiritual life.

Still, Jesus defends his disciples' seemingly irreligious practice in Luke 5:33–39.[3] Despite the role of such practices in Second Temple Judaism, Jesus teaches the arrival of the new era as something new and fresh, something that could not be patched on to what was old (5:36). This is new wine (5:37–39). Those who like the old wine will not want the new. Jesus is highlighting that such practices are done not for display or to gain attention from others, but are to represent sincere, not rote, engagement. There will come a time, Jesus says, when such acts will be appropriate, but not while the bridegroom is with them (i.e., in a time of presence and celebration).[4] In the Sermon on the Mount (in a portion Luke does not include), Jesus notes that prayer and fasting must not be done in public to draw attention to one's practice (Matt. 6:1–8, 16–18). So in the larger context of Jesus's teaching from Matthew he shows disciples that the practices of piety are not done for public attention. Acts of discipleship are never done for show, so that the attention is drawn to the disciple. They are done for and before God. The issue is not the act itself but the heart that comes with it. In an era in which the rite had almost taken on the form of a ritual, Jesus was redirecting disciples to think about the heart and the new era's emphasis on the heart. Luke's version of this scene is making the same point. A new era brings a fresh assessment of how we look at pious practices.

C. Disciples and Practices of Piety: Sabbath

A third lesson that involves disciples in controversy concerns the Sabbath (Luke 6:1–5). Here the Pharisees complain about the disciples plucking grain on the day of rest. This complaint is not unlike the previous controversy. The charge is that Jesus's disciples ignore standard public piety, only here the complaint is about a commandment. This charge is an escalation of previous concerns.

Jesus replies in two ways. First, Jesus points to the precedent of Scripture with the example of David and his men eating forbidden bread (Luke

---

3 Darrell L. Bock, *Luke 1:1–9:50*, BECNT (Grand Rapids: Baker, 1994), 515–16.
4 This might allude to the Messiah (Matt. 25:1, 5, 6, 10; John 3:29).

6:3–4). Second, he makes the even more controversial point that he is Lord of the Sabbath (Luke 6:5). The first reply makes the point that the Sabbath is not designed to be excessively restrictive. Again, the heart is in view. Is the issue the holy day or what the holy day is for? Jesus argues that the example shows the day was never designed to be restrict caring for people or their needs. The second argues that Jesus has the authority to decide what is right for the Sabbath. This is a claim to extensive authority for the Sabbath is a part of the Ten Commandments, is in the Torah, and is modeled on God's rest on the seventh day of the creation. As Mark 2:27 says explicitly, "The Sabbath was made for man, not man for the Sabbath." This shows Jesus's authority over what the Sabbath is and that its design was not to impede people from functioning daily with basic needs. This teaching makes Jesus the teacher and leader of how piety is seen and defined. Piety includes caring about how people are treated. Behind reflecting on God is considering how that impacts how we treat others (Luke 1:16–17; 3:10–14). The one who follows and learns as a disciple follows and learns from Jesus. This is why a careful study of the Gospels for both what Jesus says *and* does is important. Jesus teaches by example, as his own exhortation about coming not to be served but to serve also shows (Luke 22:24–27).

OVERVIEW OF LUCAN DISCIPLESHIP THEMES

There are other discipleship texts beyond these opening, disciple event texts. Jesus teaches the disciples in an array of areas. We now survey these texts where the term "disciple" appears, mostly in narrative order so how they fit in the movement of Luke can also be appreciated. They surface a variety of concerns. Here we see the movement into and about discipleship in action. Narrative not only discusses; it shows its themes descriptively in activity. That is what we have in this section. The key theme is that discipleship is about trusting God in a hostile world, while relating well to God's mission and others. Discipleship is not as much what we know as much as what we do and how we do it. Discipleship is not so much about how we behave among other believers but how we engage with a needy world. Discipleship is not designed to turn us inward but outward.

A. Discipleship as Leadership Development: The Choice of the Twelve

Jesus built leadership from within his larger group of disciples, since he chose Twelve out from among them (Luke 6:13). This was not a kind of favoritism, but a genuine program of leadership development in which some specifically were asked to lead. It shows us that disciples can have different roles and callings within what God asks of them. Some have more responsibility than others. Without visible leaders, the movement of the church becomes too random, uncoordinated, and decentralized.

B. The Ethics of Disciples: Love and Meeting Needs

The Sermon on the Plain records the ethical core of love the disciples should have (6:20). Here Jesus stresses a love superior to what one normally finds in the world among sinners, as he issues a call to love one's enemies. The disciple is to be different from a world that loves only friends or those who love back. Relationally, a disciple is to be exceptional in not keeping score. The example given is God's care for the unrighteous. Such love shows one to be a child of God in action. Note how this is primarily seen in how one relates to those outside the faith. Real discipleship is seen in the activity one undertakes outside of the church. One could well suggest this is the opposite of what one often thinks about discipleship. We often argue it is about developing the edification of the believer, which is true. However, that maturity is designed to better equip the disciples to engage.

Disciples show who they are. They do not just talk about it. They don't act to draw attention to themselves or to what they do, but their actions are a reflection of their genuine character. They just do it. This kind of love also means not judging but being accountable in a healthy way. Being accountable and not judging means one looks to oneself for faults before dealing with others. It means owning your own junk so that you deal with it before God. A disciple is careful as to the teaching he or she follows and builds on the rock of Jesus's teaching (6:20–49). No disciple is greater than his teacher, so the model of teaching matters (6:40). This ability to be self-critical before God and others in a healthy way is a sign of maturity. In this context, a disciple as a learner shows he or she is still learning.

The disciples witness Jesus's miraculous acts. In seeing this, it is easy to be drawn to the miracle and forget what Jesus is doing. He is actively ministering to people's needs and serving them. He is showing God's care and love for people. He is modeling what a disciple should be doing. For example, they are with him when he raises the widow of Nain's son (Luke 7:11). Others also witness this when John's disciples report to John what Jesus is doing (7:18). This leads John to ask for confirmation that Jesus truly is the one to come. Jesus's actions in healing the blind, lame, deaf, and others are the evidence he gives to answer the question positively (7:22–23). Ministry to people on the fringe, often invisible people, shows God cares for all. If God cares for those we forget, he cares for all. We model the heart of God when we do the same as he did in ministry. So, again, discipleship is seen as changing our hearts so that we are in a better position to minister to all.

C. Disciples Are Receptive, Responsive Learners

The disciples ask Jesus to teach them when they ask for an interpretation of the parable of the sower. Jesus points to the different kinds of reactions the word of the kingdom generates, depending on a person's heart (Luke 8:9). So the disciples learn that Satan grabs the word before some have a chance. Others have a short-lived faith but persecution causes them to fall away, while the concerns and riches of life choke the word in the lives of still others. Finally, there are those who with an honest and good heart hold fast to the word and bear fruit with patience. Disciples are to have the heart of the good soil, but they also are to appreciate the variety of responses they will face in mission. Some of those responses will be disappointing. However, the one who bears fruit from the word receives that word and embraces it. They are continually shaped by the perspectives the word brings to them.

D. Disciples Appreciate Jesus's Power and Person

Jesus's power is displayed to the disciples when he calms the storm (Luke 8:22), causing them to ask, "Who is this? He commands even the winds and the water, and they obey him" (8:25). The disciples witness Jesus's authority, an authority like God's ability to control the seas (Ps. 107:27–29). Another display of Jesus's ability to provide is the multiplication of the loaves and fish, which the disciples witness (Luke 9:16). They are to learn to trust Jesus's power and sovereign presence.

With his disciples alone, Jesus asks who people say he is (Luke 9:18). The disciples answer that the crowds wonder if he is some sort of prophet. Peter, however, speaks for the disciples and proclaims Jesus as "God's Messiah" (9:20). Jesus is not simply one among many. These disciples, who have spent time with Jesus, appreciate that he has a unique role in God's program. They have seen his power and care. Initially it is his power that is attractive about him. Jesus will have a lesson for them that goes in a direction different than being focused only on his power. Still, the starting point for the disciples is that they understand the uniqueness of Jesus and why drawing near to him is central for developing spiritually.

E. The Disciples' Willingness to Face Suffering

Jesus tells the disciples that he will suffer. This is completely a surprise to them. If Jesus suffers, so will they as his followers. The disciples too must be prepared to take up their cross daily and lose their lives to gain them, not being ashamed of the Son of Man (Luke 9:23–27). This unit is one of three major teaching sections on being a disciple in Luke (also 9:58–62; 14:25–35). One could focus on these three sections, but in the flow of the narrative there is a mixture of teaching and showing what discipleship is. While Jesus has been showing them what disciples are, now and again he stops and comments on what he is showing them.

Jesus repeats the idea of suffering to come when he notes that the Son of Man is going to be betrayed (9:43–44). Here is the kind of Messiah Jesus will be—one who serves and suffers. In teaching this, Jesus is also revealing to the disciples their path. When suffering for faith comes to disciples, it is something they should be prepared for and should not catch them out as something surprising. It is not something they should complain about or fear. God knows what they are facing. This theme is important as Jesus is preparing disciples for facing the world. It is all too easy to react out of fear, turn inward, or complain about the suffering and rejection believers often face. Jesus is preparing them to move past those options, to be prepared for it, and to trust God for what that may require.

F. The Demands of Discipleship: The Mission, the Use of Power, and Rejection

Jesus explicitly tells his mission to Zacchaeus, and to those who protest Jesus's staying with him. He says that the Son of Man came to seek and save the lost (19:10). Despite Jesus's power, he comes to serve. Disciples who follow Jesus are to walk in a similar direction. Disciples are to share in the enablement Jesus brings and the mission he presents to them. Disciples are formed so they can engage. A discipleship that is strictly inward and for the church is not discipleship at all.

It is important to note how many passages about disciples in Luke point to mission, encouraging us to relate to those who appear distant from God or irrelevant to society. In a kind of last-testament statement later in Luke, Jesus tells the disciples that he has not been a figure of power with them, but one who serves as an example (22:24–27). This theme runs throughout the gospel. Jesus shows who matters to him and points to who should matter for disciples. All people count.

At this point in Luke's Gospel, the disciples still have much to learn, for they fail to exorcise a demon from a boy (Luke 9:40) and respond poorly to the rejection by some in Samaria. They want to bring judgment immediately rather than continuing to witness in the face of rejection (9:54). The disciples James and John want to rain fire down from heaven. Jesus just moves on after rebuking them. Discipleship is not about power, but about faith, service, and suffering rejection without paying back in kind. Events and examples continue to focus on these ideas so distinct from the exercise of power. When Jesus shows what discipleship is, he is constantly reminding them it leads into engagement with and an invitation to those outside. Judgment is God's business, while pointing the way for outsiders to walk with God is the call of the disciple.

Jesus goes on to a new teaching block. He teaches them that disciples must be ready for such rejection, since the Son of Man has no place to put his head (Luke 9:57). Luke 9:58–62 is our second key teaching block on being a disciple in Luke that reinforces the idea that disciples will meet resistance, and that they are not be surprised when they do. Here Jesus speaks to what he has already shown. Discipleship in the context of such rejection allows nothing to get in the way, not even family obligations or longing for attachment to the world. This is our first detailed take on how difficult discipleship can be. What will living as a disciple look like? What will it demand from the Jesus-follower? Jesus warns those who want to sign on about what lies ahead. It will demand everything, as it is a priority of life.

Jesus makes three key points. The first incident involves a volunteer who commits to follow Jesus wherever he goes (Luke 9:57–58). We know nothing about this man or how he came to this decision. Since his declaration is so open-ended, Jesus responds with equal openness about what such a commitment means. In the parallel (Matt. 8:18–19), the man offers to be Jesus's student and follow him, since there he calls Jesus "teacher" (διδάσκαλε). But, of course, Jesus wants more than a student. Students of Judaism lived with their teachers in order to learn the Torah, but what Jesus offers is a more compelling and dangerous course (Luke 6:40).[5] It

---

5 Alfred Plummer, *St Luke*, ICC (Edinburgh: T&T Clark, 1986), 265; E. Earle Ellis, *Gospel of Luke* (Grand Rapids: Eerdmans, 1974), 153.

is a reorientation of life, involving suffering and perhaps death. If one is to go wherever Jesus goes, one must be ready for rejection (9:51–56). Jesus's claims challenge commonly held views. People often do not receive challenge well. Jesus provokes us to grow. Disciples will face that kind of challenging reception and yet go to outsiders anyway. "Join me if you will," Jesus is saying, "but be prepared."

Jesus describes what disciples can expect when he is their example. His situation is worse than that of a common animal: Foxes and birds have places to stay, but the Son of Man has no home (Luke 9:58). Bultmann argues that the Son-of-Man reference is generic and applies to people in general, but this contradicts the conception of Scripture that God loves and cares for people more than he does other creatures.[6] Most people have homes, so the reference must be to Jesus.[7] "Homelessness" has been Jesus's fate from his birth.[8] A disciple of Jesus must realize that following him means living as a stranger in the world, as an exiled member of the kingdom of God, because a choice for Jesus is a choice rejected by many in the world. So despite the world marginalizing us, we go into it with eyes wide open, serving and giving as we invite people into God's grace— not because they deserve it, but because disciples are called to reflect the very graciousness that is the heart of the gospel.

Jesus then asks a second man to follow him (Luke 9:59a). Unlike Levi (Luke 5:28), who immediately left all to follow Jesus, this man comes up with a reason not to follow, at least initially: He wants to take time to bury his father (Luke 9:59b). The request seems reasonable, as this responsibility was one of the most important a family member in Judaism could perform (Tobit 4:3–4; 12:12). Jesus's teaching often has a surprising twist to portray emphatically what God desires (Luke 9:60). The twist in this passage causes the reader to reflect on Jesus's reply.

Proper burial was a major concern in ancient culture. That cultic purity was regarded as less important than burying the dead shows that burying the dead was a Jewish ethical priority.[9] The language of the request follows 1 Kings 19:19–21, where Elisha asked Elijah for permission to kiss his parents goodbye. Sirach 38:16 expresses the sentiment of this would-be disciple: "My child, let your tears fall for the dead. . . . Lay out

---

6 Rudolph Bultmann, *History of the Synoptic Tradition* (New York: Harper & Row, 1963), 28, n. 3.

7 I. Howard Marshall, *The Gospel of Luke*, NIGTC (Grand Rapids: Eerdmans, 1978), 410.

8 Martin Hengel, "φάτνη," in *TDNT*, eds. G. Kittel and G. Friedrich; trans. G. Bromley (Grand Rapids: Eerdmans, 1973), IX:55.

9 Ellis, *Gospel of Luke*, 153.

the body with due ceremony, and do not neglect the burial" (NRSV). So in refusing this man's request, Jesus describes a demand that is greater than this important familial responsibility, rooted in the commandment to honor one's parents. In fact, the remark may point to Jesus's bringing in the new era. Priorities that go beyond the Ten Commandments suggests the presence of messianic authority.[10] The new Moses has come. Following Jesus is top priority, and disciples are to share that priority list.

Is the remark, "Let the dead bury their own dead" (Luke 9:60) as harsh as it seems, or is the father already dead and awaiting burial? Arndt argues that the man is asking to wait until his father has passed away—whenever that may be.[11] If that is the request, then discipleship is delayed indefinitely and the rebuke seems more reasonable. Adherents of this view note that ἀκολούθει ("follow") is a present imperative that means "be my follower." They also argue that it is unlikely that a man with a dead father awaiting burial would be out traveling about town. Those who prepared a body for a funeral were unclean for a week and therefore would not be out in public, except for the funeral (so Luke 7:12; cf. Num. 19:11). If this view is correct, the son wants to postpone devoting himself to Jesus until basic familial duties are behind him, putting commitment to family ahead of service to the kingdom. Jesus's response shows that his call has priority.

However, the parallel Luke 14:25–27 makes a similar point with hyperbolic language. More important, the request is parallel to 9:61–62, where an immediate request is in view. Plummer also seems to reject Arndt's explanation, though he allows that perhaps the father is very ill.[12] Rejecting this "down the road" option regards the effort to press the present imperative as unlikely and argues more correctly that Jesus's reply about burial becomes unnecessary if a later burial were in view. The demand appears much too urgent for this view. So in the second request, Jesus highlights the urgency of the demands of discipleship. Following God is a first priority, even coming above family commitments. Following Jesus first of all is the call of every Jesus-follower.

The pericope closes with a third figure volunteering to follow Jesus (Luke 9:61). He also wishes to introduce a proviso before starting. He asks for the right to tell his family that he is leaving and to bid them farewell (Luke 9:61). Only Luke includes this third scene, while the previous two examples have a parallel (Matt. 8:19–22).

---

10 Ben Witherington, *The Christology of Jesus* (Minneapolis: Fortress, 1990), 139–40.

11 William Arndt, *The Gospel according to St. Luke* (St. Louis: Concordia, 1956), 277.

12 Plummer, *St Luke*, 266.

Again, the request seems reasonable. It parallels Elisha's response to Elijah's call (1 Kings 19:19–21), a passage that also had some conceptual parallelism to the previous request to Jesus.[13] Elisha, an Old Testament "disciple," asks to kiss his mother and father before joining the prophet, and Elijah grants that request. As in other Lucan texts, the story of Elijah supplies the background (cf. Luke 1:15–17; 4:25–27; 7:27; 9:30–32, 54). It may well be that the nature of Jesus's response is purposefully contrastive to this Old Testament text, which suggests a greater urgency in the present situation because this is a greater era in God's program. As with the first man, this volunteer indicates he will follow Jesus. And Jesus similarly replies in terms of what that volunteer's commitment really requires. One cannot follow after two things at the same time. Following Jesus means making him the compass of one's life. It is easy to miss what discipleship demands. Jesus makes sure this commitment is clear from the very start.[14] There is no bait and switch with Jesus. He teaches disciples about the absolute priority of discipleship from the start of his discourse on it.

Jesus's reply is a warning, since he sees a danger in the request (Luke 9:62). One may follow him initially, only to long for the old life later. Such looking back does not promote spiritual health. If one is going to follow Jesus, one needs to keep following him and not look back. Jesus's reply here is not so much a refusal as it is a remark designed to lead into reflection about an ongoing, long-term commitment.[15]

Looking back is a picture of regret for a choice now being pursued. The nation of Israel looked back after the exodus (Exod. 16:3). Lot's wife looked back after departing Sodom (Gen. 19:26; cf. Luke 17:32). Once we commit to Jesus, we are to hold fast our confession. If one confesses Jesus, only to renounce permanently that confession later, then the apparent confession is false, and one's position is as perilous after the "departure" as before the profession (Matt. 7:21–23; 22:11–13; Luke 13:25–27; 1 Cor. 15:2; Col. 1:21–23; cf. the warnings in Hebrews 6:4–6; 10:19–25).

Perhaps in the desire to bid farewell, the heart never leaves the attachment to old values and the old way of life. It is this lack of a clean break against which Jesus warns here. To follow Jesus means not to look back to the way life was before one came to follow him. Good service to God and his program requires undivided loyalty. Alliance to Jesus means a

---

13 Marshall, *Luke*, 412.
14 Karl Heinrich Rengstorf, "μαθητής," in *TDNT*, IV:450.
15 Arndt, *Luke*, 278.

break with the world.[16] Discipleship is not an emotional decision of one moment, but a walk of life.[17]

In sum, putting Luke 9:58–62 all together shows how Jesus presents discipleship as a full vocation. Nothing else comes ahead of it. In it we have a calling that overshadows all other identities and callings.

G. Discipleship and Dependence in a Challenging World

Discipleship and mission combine again in the next reference to disciples. Where there is genuine discipleship, there is mission. This connection pops up now and again in the development of the narrative, having appeared initially in Luke 5:27–32. Jesus is grateful for his disciples as they engage in mission. So he prays to the Father with gratitude that God has revealed himself to them and tells the disciples they are blessed for having seen what prophets and kings had longed to see (Luke 10:24–25).

Having heard Jesus urge dependence on God, the disciples sense the importance of developing their walk with God. The disciples are learning and ask Jesus to teach them to pray. He gives them a corporate prayer that affirms God's uniqueness, submission to his will, an acknowledgment of daily needs, and a prayer for spiritual protection (Luke 11:1–4).[18] We call this prayer the Lord's Prayer, but it really is the disciples' prayer, and the placement of the apostrophe is important. It is intercession we make for and with one another. The disciples' prayer is intercession that communicates complete dependence on God in every key sphere of life: material matters, spiritual matters, and with a humble attitude that is forgiving as God has forgiven us. It also shows how disciples recognize they are a team, not just individual followers. The agenda they have is a shared one.

In contrast to such shared dependence is the hypocrisy of the Pharisees, about which Jesus warns the disciples (Luke 12:1). In this section of Luke where Jesus is journeying to Jerusalem to meet his divine destiny, Jesus is preparing his disciples for his absence in a world that will treat them as it did him. Acceptance and seeking the approval of others are things to avoid. Understanding that the world will push back against disciples is important. The disciples need to be prepared for it. They also need to develop how they will face such push back. Worry is not to preoccupy them.

---

16 Ellis, *Luke*, 154.

17 Karl Ludwig Schmidt, "βασιλεία," in *TDNT*, I:588; Bock, *Luke 9:51–24:53*, 977–83.

18 I discuss this prayer in detail in Bock, *Luke 9:51–24:53*, 1045–56.

These disciples can trust the Father to provide whatever they need, just as he does for the birds and wild flowers (Luke 12:22–31). They are not alone, and what their heart pursues will show where their treasure is. So they should be watchful, knowing they are accountable for the gifts God has given them, something Peter asks Jesus to explain (12:35–48, esp. v. 41). In doing so, Jesus calls them to faithfulness. As Jesus heads to the cross, he builds into the disciples a call to trust and depend on God for what lies ahead, no matter how difficult.

H. Discipleship and Counting the Cost

This brings us to the third and final major block of direct teaching on discipleship (with 9:23–27; 9:58–62). It also is the longest block, as it involves Luke 14:25–35. As we have seen, these blocks are interspersed with how Jesus modeled discipleship by what he did. They are key commentary on his actions. The first unit stressed the cost of discipleship. The second treated discipleship as a primary vocation for all. This last block highlights counting the cost of discipleship.

Discipleship demands counting the cost and even loving God over family (Luke 14:26), a point that reinforces what was said in Luke 9:58–62. Again, Jesus notes that one must be ready to carry one's cross (14:27), echoing Luke 9:23–27, so that our three blocks of discipleship teaching end up being linked together in this final block of direct teaching. This verse stresses the process of discipleship in carrying the cross, not the decision to enter into it. This emphasis is indicated because βαστάζει ("bears") and ἔρχεται ("comes") are both present tense: "whoever is not bearing and is not coming after me." Βαστάζω means "to carry an object" or "to bear a burden" (Luke 7:14; 10:4; 11:27; 22:10; Acts 3:2; 9:15; 15:10).[19] The picture of bearing underscores how this is an ongoing burden.

Counting the cost is a picture Jesus uses to describe discipleship in Luke 14:28–30. Jesus describes starting a building and not finishing it as a negative example not to follow. Before building, the wise person assesses the expense and effort required to finish the job. One does not build the tower, despite its benefits, until one knows it is affordable and can be brought to completion. The wise decision involves reflection, not reaction. Sitting and calculating the cost mean a reasoned assessment. So, Jesus suggests, it should be with discipleship: One should assess whether

---

19 Friedrich Büchsel, "βαστάζω," in *TDNT*, I:596; Bock, *Luke 9:51–24:53*, 1286.

one is ready to take on the personal commitment and sacrifice required to follow Jesus. Jesus wants people to appreciate what they are getting into when they agree to be a follower of his.

Danker cites a similar teaching from Epictetus 3.15.10–13, a portion of which says, "Look these drawbacks over carefully, and then, if you think best, approach philosophy, that is, if you are willing at the price of these things to secure tranquility, freedom, and repose." The object for Epictetus is different, but the attitude is similar.[20] Jesus's teaching is in common with the moral exhortations of the day, but the object that draws is very different, namely the work of grace and enablement from God. A decision to pledge allegiance to Jesus is life-changing and is to be entered into with sober reflection.[21]

A second picture about discipleship points to the picture of settling differences with a stronger king in Luke 14:31–32. This second parable differs slightly from the first in that the builder makes up his own mind whether to start a project; in the second, a decision is forced on the king by a stronger power. Both pictures are important and show the slight difference between the parables of 14:28–30 and 14:31–32. The first pictures coming to Jesus; the second deals with contemplating the option of following after him or being opposed to God. First, consider what discipleship will cost. Second, consider what refusing the "more powerful one" will mean. Can you enter battle against him? In short, consider the cost of entry and the benefits of allying with the one who carries the power. As you consider your options, imagine what it is like to be in a battle against God. It is better to sue for peace.

I. Obstacles to Discipleship: Overdependence on Possessions and Delay in the Full Arrival of Promise

This discipleship also includes the renunciation of possessions, which means that God is more important than what we have and own (Luke 14:33). Here Luke raises a common obstacle to the full pursuit of discipleship, namely how possessions can distort how we see life and others.

The theme of how to handle possessions appears again in Luke 16. Disciples must be careful with how they handle resources, doing so generously as the unjust steward did when he was facing being fired (Luke

---

20 Danker, *Jesus and the New Age*, 273.
21 Bock, *Luke 9:51–24:53*, 1287–89.

16:1–13). Jesus warns the disciples not to be a stumbling block to the little ones of the kingdom (17:1–2). He notes they will long to see the days of the Son of Man, but they will not yet come (17:22). That day will come suddenly, but only after Jesus is rejected. There are a variety of issues for disciples to cope with: the distraction of possessions, the spiritual responsibility of being a good example, and the longing for God to complete what he has started. Nonetheless, one is to move ahead.

J. Discipleship Means Regarding All as Valuable and Having Open Hands with Resources

Jesus rebukes the disciples when they try to prohibit little children being brought to him; he insists that the kingdom is made up of such little ones like these (Luke 18:15–17). The picture is one of simple trust and dependence. It also reminds the disciples that everyone is important, as children had no status in the ancient world. Jesus challenges what the culture had taught them about people and their value. A disciple relates to the world differently than to the disciple.

In the warning to the young rich man to give all and follow Jesus is a picture of the primary commitment one is to have to Jesus (Luke 18:18–30). The exchange Jesus has with Zacchaeus stands in contrast to the young rich man. Zacchaeus shows an open hand with regard to his wealth through repentance. He makes restitution for his defrauding others and is commended for it. So Zacchaeus is not asked to sell all (Luke 19:1–10). The difference in the two hearts is a difference God sees. Zacchaeus is one example of a rich person who repents and is praised for how he ends up using his resources.

K. Discipleship Means Learning by How Jesus Faced Rejection: Service in the Midst of Rejection

Having come to Jerusalem, Jesus now faces his death in a manner that left an impression on the disciples. After sending two disciples (Luke 19:29) to prepare for Jesus's entrance into Jerusalem and to procure an animal for him to ride, Jesus enters the city to the praise of his disciples. They cry out in the language of Psalm 118 about the king, the one who comes in the name of the Lord (Luke 19:37–38). When the Pharisees ask that Jesus rebuke his disciples (19:39), he refuses. The disciples know who Jesus is and that he fits in God's plan, but exactly how that will work comes with some shocks and surprises along the way. However, the disciples are learning as they proclaim Jesus in the midst of the skepticism of their audience.

As the pressure of rejection in Jerusalem mounts, Jesus tells his disciples to beware of the scribes who like attention but are full of hypocrisy, taking advantage of those in need (Luke 20:45–47). Jesus's disciples are not to follow the scribes' example. It is not popularity that counts, but faithfulness. Those scribal leaders stand in contrast to a poor woman who gives everything she has by giving a mere two lepta. By doing so as a poor woman, she gives her very life (21:1–4). That is the example disciples are to follow. They also should understand that examples to follow can come in surprising packages and from surprising places. Faithfulness can reside on any corner.

Although things sometimes seem chaotic, God's plan is advancing. The disciples can trust in this. So Jesus tells the disciples about the destruction of the temple and the return of the Son of Man, not by giving its exact timing but by telling them what will come with it. He assures them that their redemption is drawing near as they persevere (Luke 21:5–37). They will need to be strong, but the Spirit will help them when they are examined by those who have arrested them. This promise is also something we see realized in the book of Acts. Persecution will come, but so will enablement in the midst of the pressure. Jesus does not leave without resources the disciples who will feel the pressure of rejection.

Jesus gathers his disciples for a special meal (Luke 22:11), where he expounds on his upcoming death using the picture of the exodus and Passover as a means of speaking of the new deliverance of the new covenant. He also calls them to serve and promises them a role in the judgment to come (22:7–30). Jesus wants the disciples to think less about rank and more about service. Once again Jesus is subverting cultural norms and expectations.

There will be failure as well, for even Peter will deny Jesus. They must understand that Jesus is numbered among the sinners, and that they will need to fend for themselves (22:31–38). They will need to be strong in the face of opposition.

So the disciples follow Jesus to the Mount of Olives (Luke 22:37), and there they fail again, for they are sleeping when he told them to be on watch (22:45). Peter also fails as predicted, denying Jesus three times (22:54–62). This group is well-meaning, but they need what Jesus will provide, the Spirit of God.

L. Discipleship Means Resting in God's Enablement

In Luke 24, we see the initially disappointed disciples struggle to believe the report of the women about the empty tomb. They are still processing what has taken place in Jerusalem (as the Emmaus disciples also show). Only appearances by Jesus reverse their sense of despair; he reminds them of what he and the Scriptures have taught. Jesus then gives them a commission to go into the world with the message of repentance after they have been clothed with the Spirit of power from on high. This is precisely what discipleship has prepared them for and equipped them to be: witnesses in a needy world. Jesus has taught them well about what to expect. Now they need the enablement to undertake the journey, and God promises to supply that as well. They can anticipate opposition, but they will not be alone. He has told them what they need: humble, dependent trust and reliance on the provision of the Spirit (Luke 24:49). He has shown them what discipleship looks like with his life. He has shown them that the way to glory is through the path that leads to and through the cross. He has shown them that discipleship is not about turning inward but preparing for the commission he has given them to go into the world.

CONCLUSION

So we see Jesus opening the disciples up to a different way of living. Ultimately discipleship has two concerns: (1) our priority to walk with God in the midst of a sometimes hostile world; and (2) reaching out to that world in love and service as a reflection of the life of Jesus and the call of the disciple's mission. Some might translate that into (1) love for God and (2) love for neighbor. That sounds like a summary of the Great Commandment. Discipleship is about how to get there, representing God and drawing on what he provides by grace in order to honor him and carry out his call. The disciple is to be a vessel for reconciling others to him. Discipleship in the end is quite a challenge, especially when it calls constantly for things like faith, humility, service, selflessness, sacrifice, and being different from the world around us.

What this means is that faith is not so much about ritual as it is relational. Discipleship is not merely a set of teaching ideas. It is shown, not just discussed. It is not just for the church, but to build the church by reaching out. Because our relationship with God matters, people made in his image matter, as does honoring him by how we live. Because truth matters, being different matters, as we seek to be faithful to God. Our service can help people to appreciate the difference by showing we care and by displaying lives that are lived by standards distinct from the world—including a love that includes those who reject them. The faithfulness shows a different way to live. Disciples will surely sometimes fail in this faithfulness, but its presence, even to some degree, points to a distinctive way of life and engagement that mirrors God. God so loved the world that he gave his only Son. In other words, God so loved the world that he gave. Disciples are to do the same. We who follow him are also called to give as a reflection of him. The Son of Man came to serve. We who have learned from him should do no less.

CHAPTER 4

Come and See: Discipleship in John's Gospel

Edward W. Klink III

The Gospel of John reveals its purpose at the end of the Gospel, the goal it was written to achieve: that every reader would believe in the person of Jesus and participate in the life that he provides (20:31). This purpose is clearly oriented toward discipleship, directing people toward the Father through the Son and in the Spirit. No reading of the Fourth Gospel should miss this missional and ministerial intention of the narrative.[1]

In biblical scholarship, however, the theme of discipleship has not been given due attention in the Gospel of John. More than thirty years ago Culpepper suggested that the theme of discipleship in the Gospel of Mark, specifically the portrayal of the disciples' failure, garnered all the attention so as to miss or simply ignore the same theme in John.[2] Even Brown acknowledges that "discipleship is the primary category in John," yet his own legion of work fails to examine the theme further.[3] In the past two decades several studies, whether in part or in whole, have been more intentional in addressing the theme of discipleship.[4] These studies have not only been guided by a plethora of definitions regarding "discipleship," but they have also reflected a variety of methodological approaches. The variety of studies, for example, are guided by different sorts of questions: What is the nature of discipleship in John? How does John present the disciples? Whom do the disciples represent? Or even, what is the function of the disciples in the narrative of John? Of course,

---

1 All Scripture translations are the author's own unless otherwise noted.

2 R. Alan Culpepper, *Anatomy of the Fourth Gospel: A Study in Literary Design* (Philadelphia: Fortress, 1983), 115. A similar statement regarding Johannine scholarship was made just a few years later by Fernando F. Segovia, "'Peace I Leave with You; My Peace I Give to You': Discipleship in the Fourth Gospel," in *Discipleship in the New Testament*, ed. F. F. Segovia (Philadelphia: Fortress, 1985), 77: "the question of discipleship per se has been largely by-passed."

3 Raymond E. Brown, *The Community of the Beloved Disciple: The Life, Loves, and Hates of an Individual Church in New Testament Times* (Mahwah, NJ: Paulist, 1979), 84.

4 For a helpful overview of examinations of discipleship in John from 1970–2000, see Rekha M. Chennattu, *Johannine Discipleship as a Covenant Relationship* (Peabody, MA: Hendrickson, 2006), 1–22.

if the goal is to answer these questions in the context of the "Johannine community," the conclusions will be very different than if the goal is to determine how John prescribes discipleship for the living and contemporary Christian faith.[5] This essay's examination of discipleship in John will not simply locate the meaning of discipleship in the original context,[6] but will assume that John, as part of Christian Scripture, addresses discipleship for the life of the Christian and the mission of the church.[7]

Based on the above methodology, this essay will argue that the theme of discipleship in John is not merely descriptive through the historical and literary characters in the Gospel, but is prescribed for the reader through the narrative's overall rhetorical strategy. This strategy does two things. First, it invites and guides the reader through *the process of discipleship*. By using the key themes in the Gospel—follow, believe, and remain—John invites the reader how to become a disciple of Jesus Christ. Second, the Gospel's strategy teaches and explains to the reader *the properties of discipleship*. By explaining key aspects of discipleship—position

---

5   For an analysis of the difference between the original, extended, and contemporary audiences of John, see Edward W. Klink III, "Audience," in *How John Works: Storytelling in the Fourth Gospel*, eds. D. Estes and R. Sheridan (Atlanta: SBL, 2016), 241–57, esp. 241–45.

6   What is probably a more common approach in biblical studies is to treat the theme of discipleship primarily as a historical category of analysis and not a theological one. For example, Andreas J. Köstenberger, *A Theology of John's Gospel and Letters: the Word, the Christ, the Son of God*, BTNT (Grand Rapids: Zondervan, 2009), in a nice treatment on discipleship in John, explains that his approach employs a "hermeneutical triad": (1) theology: the reality of God and his revelation in Scripture; (2) literature: the texts containing revelation that need interpretation; and (3) history: the reality of history, which is real history but also "salvation history" (42). While acknowledging that all three are necessary, he claims the last two (literature and history) are "foundational," with theology "occupying the apex" (42). By "foundational" it can be assumed he means literary and historical analyses are the basis or groundwork of meaning, the thing needed to set up or establish meaning, for "apex" is the peak, what one arrives to as a "summit." Further proof of Köstenberger's understanding is when he makes this claim: "it must be remembered that *texts* do not have a theology; *people*—authors—do" (44, emphasis original). Yet his book is in a series called "Biblical Theology of the New Testament," without any mention of the "New Testament authors." While we can agree with what Köstenberger is trying to affirm—a theology that does not abandon history and authors, and language and literature, what he denies is the significant role theology must play from the start of any methodological work done in Scripture. Theology is not simply a flag one flies at the top of one's (historical and literary) conclusions, once the research has already been done. Theology is not just a *topic*; it is also a *tool*, and a necessary one. A true hermeneutical "triad," not a "dyad," will make theology as foundational as literature and history. Our analysis of discipleship in John is not limited to the biblical descriptions of the historical disciples, but should also include the biblical prescriptions of discipleship, since from its inception God intended Scripture to guide and direct all his disciples, not merely the Twelve but even the holy catholic church.

7   For a fuller explanation of such a method, see Edward W. Klink III, *John*, ZECNT 4 (Grand Rapids: Zondervan, 2016), 21–41, esp. 31–33.

in the person of Christ, partnership in the service of Christ, participation in the life of God, and presentation of the love of God—John exhorts the reader to experience the fullness of God and the Christian life. After examining both the process and properties of discipleship in John, we will draw some overall conclusions at the end of the essay.

THE PROCESS OF DISCIPLESHIP

The Gospel of John is an invitation to its readers, guiding them to "come and see" the person and work of Jesus Christ. This invitation is arguably given in three progressive stages or steps of coming and seeing Jesus: follow, believe, and remain. While there is no space here to defend these three or their progression, our concern is be attentive to the narrative itself, the emphasis it places on these three stages, and their progressive connection to Jesus Christ.

A. Follow

From the very beginning of the Gospel, the narrative is directing the reader to Jesus Christ. A brief overview of these opening pericopae of John is needed to explain the narrative's "directing." From the opening words of the prologue (1:1–18), the reader is directed to see how Jesus is not only the continuation and focal point of the biblical story, but also the focus of God's personal engagement and work in the world. For example, its opening language, "in the beginning," is not merely an echo of Genesis 1, but serves conceptually to situate the rest of the Gospel within the whole Bible's biblical-theological framework. "The opening phrase is directing the action from the past into the present, focusing its attention on its subject matter about whom this biography speaks."[8] The subject matter is Jesus, in whom the entire story of Scripture and personal and ministerial work of God are finding climactic expression.

In the very next pericope (1:19–34), the reader is directed to see how Jesus is the focal point of all religious activity and piety. If the narrator did the directing in the first pericope of the Gospel, in this pericope it is John the Baptist—a qualifier never stated in the Gospel (John hereafter), one sent by God for this very purpose: as a witness to the light (1:6–8). The narrator sets the context for John's role with the opening phrase, "Now this is the witness of John" (1:19), which

---

8 Klink, *John*, 86.

transitions away from the narrator's own witness. The questions asked of John by religious establishment from Jerusalem, as well as all the negative answers given by John (1:19–22), magnify Jesus's person and work for religious purposes.

Even more, the dialogue between John and the religious establishment in this pericope communicates two important things about Jesus's religious and ministerial role. The first is about his person: Jesus is the primary *minister* of God. John clearly denies that he is the primary minister, but the options presented by the religious leaders (Elijah, the Prophet) reveal that the minister of Jesus will fulfill and eclipse any others (1:21)—something the rest of the Gospel will make clear. When John presents Jesus, again by negation ("I am not worthy to untie," 1:27) and not by name, he establishes Jesus's office as the primary office of God and religion.

The second important thing is his work: Jesus performs the primary *ministry* of God. In what is intended to be the very same unit of text, the narrative transitions from John's negatives to a significant positive: "Behold, the Lamb of God" (1:29). The depiction of Jesus as the Lamb of God who takes away the world's sin makes clear that Jesus's ministry is international (not just for Israel); it is universal (it is not just for this generation—"*the* lamb," not "*a* lamb"); and it is *the* supreme purifying and religious act of God. The affirming presence of the Spirit (1:32–33)— making the scene fully Trinitarian!—declares to the reader that the ministry of Jesus is the ultimate and final religious act of God.

Finally, the third pericope in the Gospel (1:35–51), and fittingly the last in chapter 1,[9] directs the reader to Jesus specifically as the one to "follow," the one to whom everything and everyone points. It is no longer the narrator explicitly or John (the Baptist) doing the pointing, for after the opening two-part introduction Jesus offers his own personal invitation to the reader. This invitation, however, is mediated by the disciples, who become in the Fourth Gospel a model for the reader (e.g., 20:24–31), with the Beloved Disciple serving as the primary model for the reader—the ideal reader. "The aim of the author is to make the reader a disciple. . . . The reader models the Beloved Disciple by receiving his testimony [as author] . . . and by responding according to the rhetorical strategy of the narrative's witness."[10]

---

9 This is not to say the "original" author has a "chapter 1" in mind. Our reading of the Gospel is simply interpreting that the narrative's first three pericopae serve as a developing introduction and invitation to Jesus. It just also helpfully happens that all are located in the first chapter of the Gospel of John in what is now the received form of the canonical text.
10 See Klink, *John*, 923.

The rhetorical strategy of the narrative can be seen in several of its details. An easily missed detail is how John's announcement is repeated (1:36). The repetition is not an editorial mistake, but serves here as a formal introduction to Jesus in his first appearance in the Gospel and reiterates that he is the one to "follow." The very fact that the narrative describes him as "walking by" means the disciples were now to begin following. Probably the most important detail occurs in the various inter-actions between Jesus and the first disciples. In these interactions, Jesus invites the disciples formally to become followers, first with the statement "come and see" to the two disciples (1:39); then with the implicit invita-tion and claiming of Peter by giving him a new name (1:42); followed by the formal invitation to Philip, "follow me" (1:43); and finally the theo-logically loaded inclusion of Nathanael regarding the things to be seen through Jesus (1:47–51).

While each of these examples could be explained in much greater de-tail, the rhetorically strategic point of the narrative is to direct the reader to see how *discipleship involves following Jesus*. Discipleship has a starting point, a place of entering into a relationship, even without full knowledge and understanding. If Jesus is who the narrator says he is (1:1–18), who John says he is (1:19–34), and whom Jesus himself claims to be (1:35–51), then he is worth coming and seeing (1:39, 46), following (1:43), even staying with (1:38–39). "Entry into the relationship of a disciple is not only the result but also the beginning of seeing what is to be seen in Jesus."[11] A disciple is one who follows the primary minister and ministry of God, which the Gospel declares emphatically to be Jesus Christ. John and Jesus declare this to be true and invite such following, as does the narrator, who serves as a witness to Jesus for the reader, thereby inviting all potential disciples to follow Jesus.

B. Believe

The Gospel explains its goal at the end of the Gospel proper: "these things have been written in order that you may believe" (20:31). It is with these words that the Gospel's rhetorical strategy is centered upon belief. The Gospel (as Scripture) was written to facilitate belief in its reader. Unsurprisingly, the term "belief" is a central term in the Gospel of John, used a total of ninety-eight times, which towers above the use of the term

---

11   Karl Barth, *Witness to the Word: A Commentary on John 1*, ed. W. Fürst; trans. G. W. Bromi-ley (Grand Rapids: Eerdmans, 1986 [repr. Eugene, OR: Wipf & Stock, 2003]), 153.

by other New Testament authors (even more than Paul—fifty-four times). While "follow" was strategically placed at the Gospel's beginning, "believe" is a theme spread throughout the entire narrative. The important connection between the invitation to "believe" and discipleship is made clear in several ways in John.

First, the invitation to believe is given definition at the very beginning of the Gospel when the narrator explains that belief in Jesus is the means by which a person must "receive him" (1:12). This belief, however, is belief "in [Jesus's] name"—an important distinctive. The concept of a "name" in the ancient world was not merely a label but comprised the character of a person. When, for example, the psalmist spoke of the name of God (Ps. 20:1), he did not have in mind simply the uttering of the name; he was speaking of all that "God" means. Those "who believe in [Jesus's] name" (1:12) believe in the totality of his person and work (cf. 3:36; 4:21).

Receiving Jesus (and coming to Jesus) by means of belief is further explained by the motif of eating and drinking in John 6. To believe in Jesus is to eat him. Just as Jesus uses the metaphor of "bread" to describe what he offers to the world, so he uses the metaphor of "eating" to describe what it means to "come" and to "believe" (see 6:32–58). It is important to note that "eating" is not intended to swallow the semantic meaning of "believe," but to contribute to the reader's understanding of what the term actually entails. Amidst all the debate regarding Jesus's instruction to eat his flesh and drink his blood, one thing should not be missed: the centrality of the cross. To eat and drink Jesus is to believe in the work and power of his death on the cross.

Second, to believe is to fulfill the duty of the Christian. When Jesus is questioned about what "works of God" must be performed by the religious person (6:28), Jesus explains that "This is the work of God: to believe in the one he has sent" (6:29). Any work for God must involve faith in his Son. The duties and responsibilities of humanity are entirely eclipsed by this one task of trusting in the person and work of the Son. The real, religious "work" to be done is performed by the Son himself—which the disciple receives by faith. By framing the singular task of the Christian as belief, and after noting that "believe" in 6:29 is in the present tense, it can be said that believing in Jesus is less an *act* of faith and more a *life* of faith. Certainly *belief is inclusive of propositions, but it is also reflected in properties of discipleship that display a certain kind of existence*, a set of properties that we will explain below.

Finally, it is worth noting how frequently the Gospel calls the reader to see how belief is facilitated through various witnesses. A primary witness is the Word himself, who is a witness to the Father (12:44) and was sent to reveal him (1:18). But even besides Jesus, the primary witness, the Gospel describes the significant role of many secondary witnesses. In 1:7, for example, John is a witness to Jesus. Another example is in 17:20, where in Jesus's prayer to the Father for disciples who will receive the witness of his disciples, the apostles. This is even more clearly seen in the Thomas pericope (20:24–31), in which Jesus uses Thomas to show how the apostolic proclamation of the Gospel is to be received, that is, "believed."[12] In light of this apostolic witness, it is no surprise that the Gospel itself is such a witness that calls for belief (see 19:35; 20:30–31). The Fourth Gospel does not merely explain discipleship, it was written specifically to make disciples by witnessing to Jesus Christ and exhorting the reader to believe in him.

C. Remain

The Fourth Gospel not only exhorts the reader or disciples to follow and believe in Jesus, but also to remain in him. The term "remain" is one of the central terms in the Gospel: The Father "remains" in the Son (14:10), the Spirit "remains" upon Jesus (1:32–33), and believers "remain" in Christ and he in them (15:4). To "remain" can be explained as having several aspects.

An important explanation of the term "remain" is given in 6:56, where it is depicted as a co-participatory existence, where the "being" of the believer is determined or regulated by Jesus.[13] In this way, "remain" serves to depict an intimate relationship that exists between Jesus and his disciples. Jesus later uses language of mutual indwelling and even interpenetration to describe not only the relationship between the Father and the Son, but also to Son and his disciples: "I am in my Father, and you are in me, and I am in you" (14:20). To give a biblical example of this co-participatory existence, mutual indwelling, or what it means to "remain," the apostle Paul considers himself to have shared so deeply in Christ that the crucifixion of Christ was in a real way also his death, with his life being lived (empowered) by Christ in him (Gal. 2:20). To "remain," then, speaks

---

12 For a detailed explanation, see Klink, *John*, 875–81.
13 C. K. Barrett, *The Gospel according to John: An Introduction with Commentary and Notes on the Greek Text*, 2nd ed. (Philadelphia: Westminster, 1978), 300.

about a kind of "existence" between Jesus and the disciple, to participate in an intimate relationship to God through Christ.

The Gospel gives another sense in 8:31, where the term "remain" carries the sense of "presence." In a lengthy dialogue with the religious leaders, Jesus declares, "If you remain in my word, you are truly my disciples." In this context the term "remain" communicates the sense of a permanent residing in a specific location. To remain is not only to share in the being of Christ, it is to be located in him. In the verse quoted above, to remain "in my word," based upon the rest of the Gospel, means to remain in the Word or in the person and work of Jesus Christ. It "is taking personal and permanent residence in the spiritual presence of God mediated through the Son and . . . to be empowered and facilitated by the Spirit."[14] In this sense, then, to "remain" is to be with Christ and to have Christ be with you (by the Spirit).

But the clearest and longest explanation of "remain" in the Gospel is in 15:1–17. In the middle of his "farewell discourse," Jesus uses the imagery of a vine and a branch to depict the co-participatory existence of Jesus and his disciples. In 15:2, Jesus makes clear that the branches are "in me," that is, in the vine. As the next few verses explain, connection to the vine is essential for the branches' existence and productivity (15:4–7). Even more, the branches are expected to be fruitful, otherwise they are removed. There is no possibility that the branch is attached but dormant; a branch that remains in the vine is a cared-for and productive branch.

What may be most significant about Jesus's teaching in John 15 is that it is not only the disciple who is commanded to remain in Jesus, but Jesus also promises to remain in the disciple. This is most clearly stated in 15:4, after which Jesus explains the benefits of "remaining": the bearing of much fruit (15:4–5), the avoidance of being removed from the vine and burned (15:6), a ministerial authority that aligns with God's workings (15:7), the glorification of the Father (15:8), and the experience of the love and joy of Christ (15:9–11).

In the larger context of the Gospel of John, to "remain" is to dwell in the house of God, to "tabernacle" with God through Christ and by the Spirit, even if a more perfect and fuller dwelling is still to come (cf. 14:2). And this command is matched by a promise that if we remain in Christ, he pledges to "remain" with us. Ultimately, *to remain is to exist in the grace and love of God*, and it is the mark of true belief and a true disciple.

---

14 Klink, *John*, 414.

Summary: The argument of this essay is that the rhetorical strategy of the Gospel reveals a three-stage *process of discipleship* by which someone follows, believes, and remains in Jesus. As much as these stages or steps are not mutually exclusive, the Gospel defines them in such a way that they can be given a sequence of sorts, by which they cumulatively define the process by which a person becomes a disciples of Jesus. The Gospel's invitation to the reader takes great care not only to show to whom a disciple must come and see, but even how a disciple must come. Like Andrew, the brother of Peter, the narrator is bringing the reader to Jesus (1:42).

THE PROPERTIES OF DISCIPLESHIP

The Gospel of John's concern to direct a disciple to Jesus is matched by its concern to define the nature of discipleship. According to John, discipleship is not simply a process but also a set of properties; it can be described not merely as an act of faith but as a life of faith. This description is arguably provided in four related aspects of discipleship: position in the person of Christ, partnership in the service of Christ, participation in the life of God, and presentation of the love of God. While there is no space here to defend these four aspects over and against other themes that can be found in John, our contention is that these four aspects summarize the nature of discipleship in John.

A. Position in the Person of Christ

The first property of a disciple in John is their *position in God through Christ*, and this is clearly presented in the Gospel by the depiction from enslavement to sin and death to freedom in Christ. The term "freedom" in John (cf. 8:33, 36) is not best defined by Stoic or rabbinic definitions, but by being contrasted with sin (8:34), which suggests that the "freedom" about which Jesus speaks is equivalent to salvation. The truth, which centers upon the person and work of Jesus, is liberating (8:32). Again, this liberation is not philosophical or rooted in politics but is a spiritual freedom. Nor is this kind of freedom based on the original freedom of humanity, the authentic self of man, but a freedom that belongs entirely to God.[15] It is the kind of liberation that can only come from a birth "from above" (3:3); it is liberation that flows out of the eschatological birth "from water and spirit" (3:5).[16]

---

15 Rudolf Bultmann, *The Gospel of John: A Commentary*, eds. R. W. N. Hoare and J. K. Riches; trans. G. R. Beasley-Murray (Philadelphia, Westminster, 1971), 436.
16 Klink, *John*, 414.

The notable feature of Christian freedom, according to Jesus, is that it is freedom from an enslavement to sin (8:34). When Jesus's Jewish interlocutors hear Jesus speak of becoming "free," they immediately protest claiming that as the elect seed of Abraham, they have never been enslaved to anyone, and thus have no need to "become" free (8:33). But Jesus offers a counter-challenge by explaining that slavery is defined not by a person's "seed" (heritage) but by a person's sin (hamartiology). In a sense, Jesus demands his opponents define their "freedom" not only by means of their relation to Abraham but also by their relation to Adam—and now to the Second Adam. In this way, while the Jewish people are distinct from the world according to their Abrahamic nature, they are identical to the world according to their Adamic (human) nature. They, too, are enslaved to sin (8:34). The very law of God that made them a unique people in the world should have also revealed to them their similarity to the world; it should have been through the law that they became "conscious of [their] sin" (Rom. 3:20).

An important distinction needs to be made between the biblical depiction of freedom and the contemporary use of the term.[17] The Old Testament understood freedom in very concrete terms. The emphasis on freedom offered by the exodus narrative and beyond was not, surprisingly, freedom from slavery. The Bible expects slavery in the sense that all people will serve something (cf. Rom. 6). Freedom in the Bible is not a contrast between freedom and slavery but between an inappropriate master (Pharaoh, sin) and an appropriate master—God (cf. Exod. 9:14). It was freedom *for* something more than freedom *from* something. The freedom about which the exodus is the paradigmatic instance is liberation from degrading bondage, for the endless service of the God who remembers his covenant, redeems from exile and oppression, and gives commandments through which the people of God are sanctified. This is the biblical notion of freedom about which Jesus speaks.

This explains why Jesus moves from "freedom" to "sonship" in 8:35–36. Freedom in John—in Scripture as a whole—is not simply *from* something but *to* something. The disciple of Jesus is invited not only to leave something but to join something. A slave is an outsider, a mere tool, but a son is a member, an heir and, in the case of this Gospel, a "child of God" (1:12). The language of "son" (or "sonship") in 8:35 is not intended to be gender-exclusive, but to declare that it is a freedom that belongs entirely

---

17 Helpful here is Richard Bauckham, *God and the Crisis of Freedom: Biblical and Contemporary Perspectives* (Louisville: Westminster John Knox, 2002).

to the Son, and thus to all his disciples. It is a freedom that belongs to the Son and that only he can give. It is a freedom that is unknown not only to the world but even to the descendants of Abraham—a freedom from the tyranny of sin.[18] In this sense, the freedom that Jesus offers also includes liberation from enslavement to self-interest and the devil; it is *a freedom that turns slaves into sons and daughters* and those of the household of the devil into eternal members of the household of the Father (1:12).

B. Partnership in the Service of Christ

The second property of a disciple in John is *participation in the service of Christ*. The disciple of Jesus not only becomes a member of the household of God, but also commits oneself to the family business. In the Fourth Gospel there are two aspects of the family business that can be describes simply as Christian service, both of which are communicated in key moments in the ministry of Jesus.

The first is the foot washing scene in 13:1–20, where Jesus washes the disciples' feet. The act of foot washing is significant in a couple ways. One is that footwashing was preparatory.[19] The act of "foot washing serves to prepare one for a specific task, experience, or relationship."[20] Thus, when Jesus washes his disciples' feet, he is not simply communicating something about himself and his ministry; he is also communicating something about them and their ministry of service. By washing the disciples' feet, Jesus prepares them for the service to which they are about to be assigned because of his death and resurrection—his ultimate act of service. Jesus makes this explicit in 13:15: "I have given an example to you in order that you might do just as I did to you." The word "example" can also be translated as "model" or "pattern."[21] In this context the term should not be understood too narrowly but as depicting something like "a rule of life."[22]

The footwashing is preparation for service, the initiation of Christian discipleship. This service is performed not only to one another, but also as

---

18 Hoskyns, *Fourth Gospel*, 339.

19 See Mark Thiessen Nation, "Washing Feet: Preparation for Service," in *The Blackwell Companion to Christian Ethics*, eds. Stanley Hauerwas and Samuel Wells (Malden, MA: Blackwell, 2004), 441–51.

20 John Christopher Thomas, *Footwashing in John 13 and the Johannine Community*, JSNTSup 61 (Sheffield: Sheffield Academic Press, 1991), 59.

21 BDAG 1037.

22 Herman N. Ridderbos, *The Gospel of John: A Theological Commentary*, trans. J. Vriend (Grand Rapids: Eerdmans, 1997), 463.

part of the mission of God to the world, heralding the new covenant and the gospel of Jesus Christ. And since Christ was superior in every way to those whose feet he washed, no Christian may ever claim to be so superior that he or she is above washing the feet of another (cf. Matt. 20:16). The footwashing scene depicts the readers anointing for service, in which we are assigned to "wash the feet" of one another, thereby adopting the role of the servant that was exemplified for us by the Servant. We are to be serving others in humility and with sacrifice as Christ served us: Again, we following the example of Christ: "We [serve] because he first [served] us" (cf. 1 John 4:19).

The second is the sending scene, when Jesus offers his Spirit (20:22), promises the church its authoritative ministry (20:23), and sends them into the world (20:21). Jesus makes a significant statement that summarizes the task of the disciple: "Just as the Father has sent me, I also send you" (20:21). With this statement Jesus declares that the disciples—and the church as a whole—are called to partner in the mission of God in a manner similar to the Son, albeit with an important difference: the Father sends the Son; the Son sends the disciples, which means the roles of the sent ones are also different.

It is important that the reader see the developing and logical progression of this scene in the immediate pericope and the larger context of the Gospel. The apostolic mission declared by Jesus in this context is rightly situated between the peace-creating crucifixion wounds of Jesus (20:20) and the Spirit-received command of Jesus (20:22). And in light of this verse, the giving of the Spirit that follows is not merely empowerment for the mission of God but a divine manifestation for partnership in it.[23] That is, the church partners in the missionary life of God by remaining in Christ (15:4) and receiving the Spirit (20:22). The service that Jesus performed to create disciples is what propels the kind of discipleship that is done in Jesus's name, by his Spirit, and as part of his mission.

C. Participation in the Life of God

The third property of a disciple in John is *participation in the life of God*. "Life" is an important term for the Gospel of John. It occurs thirty-six times in John, whereas no other New Testament writing uses it more than seventeen times (Revelation). Thus, more than twenty-five percent of all

---

23 Cf. Thomas R. Hatina, "John 20,22 in Its Eschatological Context: Promise of Fulfillment?" *Biblica* 74 (1993): 196–219 (218).

the uses of the term in the New Testament are found in this Gospel. The term is used in John to describe the multifaceted gift of God in regard to both human existence and participation in the life of God.

"Life" is given prominence at the beginning of the Gospel; it has its source and meaning in Jesus. "Life," according to 1:4, is not mediated through the Word but is "in" the Word. Jesus embodies life. John's prologue is made especially difficult with the use of such loaded terms, from which interpreters can find many interesting parallels.[24] In light of 1:1–3, it is quite logical to assume that "life" is in connection to creation and thus refers to physical life. Yet in the remainder of the Gospel the term is related specifically to salvation. While interpreters feel forced to decide between these two options for the use of the term in 1:4, to separate the connection between the Word (Jesus) and life in the context of the prologue is to create a false dichotomy between physical and spiritual realities—something that is foreign to the Gospel. In the context of the Gospel, the prologue's terse introduction of Jesus as "life" must be referring to life in the fullest of all its possible senses. Only in this way is an understanding given to passages which speak of the life Jesus brings (e.g., 10:10), a life rooted from the beginning and ultimately in God himself.[25]

It is in 14:6 that "life" is given further connection to Jesus's person and work. Jesus is "the life" in that he is the source through which Christian existence and participation in God are founded and given their origin. The Gospel has worked hard to explain how Jesus is the life: Jesus is life itself (1:4), is the one who has life in himself (5:26), and is the one who defines life even over death, for Jesus is "the resurrection and the life" (11:25). Since Jesus is "the life," as formally declared in 14:6, all the dichotomies are broken that have been created between life and death, this life and the life to come, the seen and the unseen.

Finally, the Gospel's purpose statement in 20:30–31 makes explicit the narrative's goal to invite the reader into the "life" offered and authored by Jesus Christ: "that . . . you may have life in his name" (20:31). Such language reflects the in-depth teaching about "life" throughout the Gospel. The "life" Jesus offers the reader is eternal life, an eschatological life in which the reader is invited to participate in the cosmological realities to which the Gospel has been pointing. This life is both provided by Jesus and grounded in him. What Jesus offers therefore is all-embracing,

24 Ridderbos, *John*, 38.
25 Klink, *John*, 95.

extending beyond what any person can grasp about physical and spiritual life (even the afterlife). The "life" is rooted "in his name," that is, in the character of his person—his power, authority, and love (cf. 1:12). For the disciples of Jesus, to "have life" is to share in the very life of God.

D. Presentation of the Love of God

The fourth property of a disciple in John is *presentation of the love of God*. Nothing is more properly basic to disciples of Jesus than love—both received and given. The first occurrence of the term "love" is in the famous verse in 3:16, which occurs right after an important conflict with Nicodemus, who represents the world's challenge of God. In 3:16 the narrator offers a commentary on Jesus's encounter with Nicodemus, explaining that the intention of Jesus, and of God, is love. What does the narrator explain? Quite simply, that the motivation behind the words and actions of Jesus is God's love for the world. Everything Jesus does and says is rooted in the love of God. In this first occurrence of "love" in the Gospel, it is rather shocking that the object of God's love is "the world." Nowhere else in this Gospel or anywhere else in the New Testament is God explicitly said to "love" the world. In 3:16 the Gospel reveals the deeper intentions of God. What made God come? What made God embrace human weakness and suffering? What made God endure mockery and shame? The answer is, his love for the world! The disciple of Jesus is one who has received the love of God.

The disciple of Jesus, however, does not simply receive God's love, but presents his love to others. This is explained specifically by Jesus in 13:34–35, with what he calls a new or love commandment: "I give a new commandment to you: love one another. Just as I loved you, you also should love one another" (13:34). The content of this command is not entirely "new," for love was a fundamental rule in the life of the Old Testament people of God (cf. Lev. 19:18; Luke 10:25–27). Even more, Jesus has already initiated this command by means of the footwashing, which serves as the foundational example of the source and nature of this love (see 13:14–15). The newness of this love is not that it is an independent love, for Christian love is a subset of and is founded upon the love of God himself; it is "the response to the love of Jesus."[26] The love commandment finds its source in and emulates the love between the Father and the Son (cf. 8:29; 10:18; 12:49–50; 14:31; 15:10).

---

26 Bultmann, *John*, 529.

The presentation of God's love may be directed at other disciples, but according to 13:35 it will also serve to declare the existence of God's love to the rest of the world. Love becomes the character trait and identity marker of the people of God, but it also becomes the church's primary witness to the world about Christ. The love of God first expressed by Jesus has now "become flesh" in an even more expansive way and is to go out into every corner of the world through the body of Christ, the church. The plan of God had always been to share the love between the Father and the Son with the children of God and ultimately the world. The people of God are not only the recipients of the love of God but also become the expression of the love of God in the world. Quite simply: "We love because he first loved us" (1 John 4:19).

As much as the disciple of Jesus will show God's love to the church and the world, the primary object is always God himself. This is made clear in Jesus's final interaction with Peter, when Jesus asks in 21:15: "Do you love me more than these?" As Jesus has done elsewhere (see 12:7), Jesus makes love for others, even for brothers and sisters in Christ, a subset of a love for Christ. A disciple's love for God is not merely a result of his love; it is also a response to his love. And as much as a response to God's love is applied to the church and even the world, it is God for whom our love finds its truest and most desired source. That is why Jesus, after grounding Peter's discipleship in a love for him, immediately commands for its expression to be in the form of an obedient and sacrificial following of him. To follow Christ is to make one's own life a subset of the life of Christ. Just as the love of God was expressed by the cross, so the Christian's life is to be a cruciform expression of their love of God.

Summary: The argument of this essay is that the Gospel offers four *properties of discipleship*, or marks of a true disciple of Jesus. These properties are not mutually exclusive, and are admittedly categories that summarize a multifaceted dimension of discipleship and Christian existence; yet they serve to emphasize what could be called the passive (position and participation) and active (partnership and presentation) aspects of discipleship according to John.

CONCLUSION: READER, COME AND SEE

The purpose statement of the Gospel in 20:31 has long been debated regarding its intended strategy, made more difficult by the text-critical uncertainty regarding the verb "believe"—is it a present subjunctive that calls for "continued belief," or is it an aorist subjunctive that calls for "initiated belief"?[27] Too often interpreters feel forced to choose between these two options. This essay has suggested that such a decision is mistaken, itself a misreading of the Gospel's rhetorical strategy and narrative intention. The Gospel of John is doing both at once—*inviting* the reader through the process of discipleship and *instructing* the reader in the life of discipleship.

The stated purpose of the Gospel, and arguably its expressed intention inscribed throughout the narrative as a whole, is ultimately to invite *and* instruct the reader to live in, with, and for God in all things. In every way, then, this Gospel speaks about Jesus (and God) in a manner inclusive of the reader, not simply the first disciples. This was never only a story of something past; it has always been a story about the present—and even the future. To read the Gospel in any other way is a misinterpretation. And not to respond to the Gospel is a form of rebellion, a rejection of the living voice of God.

As significant as the purpose statement is for understanding the Gospel's intention and rhetorical strategy, the careful reader of the narrative is quickly grasped by the beauty and majesty of the Gospel's subject matter, the person and work of Jesus Christ. Like the earliest disciples, the reader of the Gospel is confronted by Jesus and asked, "What do you seek?" (1:38). Through the Fourth Gospel, Jesus questions the reader and invites him or her to believe in him and to have life in his name (20:31), that is, to become his disciple. Every reader of this Gospel, no matter their relationship to God or stage of their Christian walk, is beckoned to "come and see" (1:39, 46). In this Gospel, the Beloved Disciple comes alongside the reader and shares his testimony and life with the reader. Just as the Gospel begins with a disciple of Jesus (Andrew) seeking his brother (Peter) and leading him to Jesus (1:41), so the Gospel ends with a disciple of Jesus (the Beloved Disciple) leading a brother or sister (the reader) to Jesus. Ultimately, the mysterious identity of the Beloved Disciple is eclipsed in importance by his ministerial role as author of the Gospel, and it is the reader who becomes the referent of this mystery as he or she receives the Gospel's message, believes its subject matter, and lives as a disciple of Jesus Christ. And since all disciples are sent by Jesus, even the Beloved Disciple's text-based ministry is an extension of the love of God to the reader, an ongoing invitation to believe in Jesus Christ and receive life in his name.

---

27 The issue is not quite this simple. For further explanation, see Klink, *John*, 882–84.

CHAPTER 5

A Faith That Can Be Seen: Discipleship in Acts

Benjamin R. Wilson

The book of Acts tells the story of the church's expansion from a small group of disciples of Jesus in Jerusalem to a fledgling multiethnic movement of congregations spread throughout the Mediterranean world. As an account of church growth, the bulk of Acts is naturally oriented toward various visible facets of church life: the founding and expansion of new assemblies, the quality of the believers' community life together, the resolution of disputes within and threats without, and so forth. Accordingly, readers of Acts will find that Luke's account of the growth of the church has more to say about the public, communal, and relational dimensions of discipleship than about matters of individual spirituality. Put differently, one might say that in Acts we see more of what we tend to think of as the product rather than the process of Christian spirituality, at least in so far as the process entails the interior work of the Spirit in the life of the believer, which then manifests itself through our visible interactions with others. In Acts we gain only a glimpse of the precise mechanics of the personal transformation wrought by the interior work of the Holy Spirit, whereas we gaze mostly upon the visibly transformed lives of believers whose experience of salvation results in a dramatically altered way of living in the world.[1]

I would like to consider this portrait of discipleship in Acts from two vantage points in this essay: First, I will survey the language that is employed to refer to and describe disciples in Acts. Beyond the term "disciple," a diverse range of images is utilized to refer to the Christian community and the ongoing progression of the Christian life, and this imagery offers some insight into Luke's conception of discipleship. After surveying the terminology of Christian living in Acts, I will attempt in the second part of the essay to assess what Acts might say about the requirements of discipleship: What distinctive

---

1 All Scripture translations are the author's own unless otherwise noted.

qualities characterize those who are identified with the terminology and imagery of discipleship in Acts? Or, more simply, what makes a disciple a disciple in Acts?[2]

TERMINOLOGY OF DISCIPLESHIP IN ACTS

The way that we refer to ourselves and others will inevitably reveal facets of how we understand our own identity and the identity of those around us. When, for example, I tell a new acquaintance that I am a teacher, I disclose not just my occupation but also a whole range of implications about how and where I spend my time, the sorts of people with whom I am associated, and perhaps some of the values that inform my opinions and decisions. Thus, the descriptors that we use to refer to ourselves and to each other can be rather revealing, and our study of the nature of discipleship in Acts is likely to be enriched by a consideration of the various terms and images by which the Christian community is referenced and described within the narrative.[3]

A. Disciples

Acts is the lone book in the New Testament in which the term "disciple" is used to refer to members of the Christian movement who did not accompany Jesus on his itinerant ministry.[4] In the Gospels, the term "disciple" is employed with strict reference to that subgroup of Jesus-followers who quite literally followed Jesus throughout Galilee and Judea, having left behind their prior stations in life in response to

---

2 It is a privilege to contribute this essay in honor of Michael Wilkins. As a student at Talbot School of Theology, I never had Dr. Wilkins for a course, yet his influence at our school impacted me nonetheless, providing a model of dedicated service and principled leadership that has stuck with me ever since.

3 Our analysis will be limited to a brief survey of the most common descriptors that are employed to speak of Jesus-followers or groups of Jesus-followers in Acts. In actuality, a wide variety of labels appear in Acts with reference to the Christian community. Moreover, these diverse descriptors are employed from diverse vantage points, with the narrator, Christian spokespeople, and nonbelievers within the narrative all employing distinct ways of referring to and describing the Christian community. For more thorough considerations of this topic, see J. A. Fitzmyer, "The Designations of Christians in Acts and their Significance," in *To Advance the Gospel* (Grand Rapids: Eerdmans, 1998), 314; P. Trebilco, *Self-Designations and Group Identity in the New Testament* (Cambridge: Cambridge University Press, 2012); S. Walton, "Calling the Church Names: Learning about Christian Identity from Acts," *Perspectives in Religious Studies* 41 (2014): 223–41, at 223.

4 The term appears twenty-eight times in Acts, in the plural in every instance except Acts 16:1. The feminine μαθήτρια also appears in Acts 9:36.

Jesus's direct and individual call.[5] Elsewhere in the New Testament, the concept that we in contemporary parlance typically refer to as discipleship is described with alternative terms and images. Only in Acts, then, is "disciple" actually employed with reference to followers of Jesus post-Pentecost.

In terms of what this unique way of speaking might tell us about Luke's conception of discipleship, the usage of "disciple" in Acts serves to underscore the continuity between the ministry of Jesus and the ongoing life of the Christian community after Jesus's resurrection and ascension.[6] Most of the disciples in Acts had never encountered Jesus during his earthly ministry, and yet their lifestyle conforms to the way of living prescribed for Jesus's disciples during his itinerant ministry, particularly in their self-denial and acceptance of hostility arising from their allegiance to Jesus.[7] If Jesus taught his original disciples that they must deny themselves and take up their cross and follow him (Luke 9:23), the disciples in Acts are shown at various points to faithfully embody this teaching (Acts 9:1; 19:9), and they are similarly assured that "through many tribulations we must enter the kingdom of God" (Acts 14:22).[8] Thus, the "disciples" of Jesus in Acts show themselves to be followers of Jesus in a manner similar to his original disciples, and Jesus's instruction about the nature of discipleship is shown to be authoritative for the church in Luke's own day.[9]

---

5 See J. A. Fitzmyer, "Discipleship in the Lucan Writings," in *Luke the Theologian: Aspects of His Teaching* (New York: Paulist, 1989), 119–20.

6 Trebilco, *Self-Designations*, 227.

7 On the continuities between the ministry of Jesus and the experience of the church in Acts, see C. K. Barrett, "Theologia Crucis–in Acts," in *Theologia Crucis—Signum Crucis*, eds. C. Andresen and G. Klein (Tübingen: Mohr, 1979), 79–80; R. F. O'Toole, "Parallels between Jesus and His Disciples in Luke-Acts: A Further Study," *Biblische Zeitschrift* 27 (1983): 195–212; R. N. Longenecker, "Taking up the Cross Daily: Discipleship in Luke-Acts," in *Patterns of Discipleship in the New Testament*, ed. R. N. Longenecker (Grand Rapids: Eerdmans, 1996), 52–53; D. J. Horton, *Death and Resurrection: The Shape and Function of a Literary Motif in the Book of Acts* (Eugene, OR: Pickwick, 2009), 40–80; and C. K. Rowe, *World Upside Down: Reading Acts in the Graeco-Roman Age* (Oxford: Oxford University Press, 2009), 173.

8 See R. P. Martin, "Salvation and Discipleship in Luke's Gospel," *Interpretation* 30 (1976): 366–80.

9 The term "disciple" also serves a practical narrative function in Acts, providing Luke with language to refer to both Gentile and Jewish followers of Jesus without distinction before the standing of the Gentiles within the Christian community has been settled in the narrative. By contrast, Gentile Christians are only called "brothers" after the Jerusalem council in Acts 15. See Trebilco, *Self-Designations*, 229.

B. Believers

At many points in Acts, the members of the Christian community are designated as "believers."[10] This designation is vocalized occasionally by Christian speakers within the story of Acts (11:17; 21:20; 22:19), but most often it is the narrator himself who refers to Christians as "believers" (2:44; 4:32; 5:14; 11:21; 15:5; 18:27; 19:18).[11] Especially noteworthy are passages where this designation is used to distinguish members of the Christian community from some other group.[12] In Acts 15:5, for instance, the narrator refers to "some believers from the sect of the Pharisees." In 21:20, James speaks of "many myriads of those who have believed among the Jews." In 22:19, Paul recalls how he had traveled throughout the synagogues persecuting "those who believed" in Jesus. Similarly, in 18:27 and 19:18, Gentile "believers" are distinguished from non-Christian Gentiles in Corinth and Ephesus. Such passages establish belief as a distinctive feature of Christian identity, distinguishing followers of Jesus from the unbelieving world around them. This is in keeping with the way in which belief is presented as the proper response to the apostolic proclamation.[13] For Luke, belief is an indispensable condition of Christian identity, such that whatever else may be said of Christians, it will certainly be the case that such people are marked by their belief in the substance of the apostolic *kerygma*—so much so that at times the commitments of discipleship are summarized by Luke simply as "the faith" (Acts 6:5; 13:8; 14:22; 16:5). Believing, quite simply, is a *sine qua non* of discipleship in Acts.

C. Brothers and Sisters

The most commonly used designation for Christians in Acts is the term ἀδελφοί, which can usually be translated most accurately as "brothers and sisters."[14] The term appears fifty-seven times in Acts and entails a wide range of referents: Jewish non-Christians refer to each other (Acts 3:22) and to Jewish Christians (Acts 2:37; 13:15) with such kinship terminology, and the designation is also used by Jewish Christians to refer to

---

10 Participial forms from the verb πιστεύω appear as designations and descriptors for the Christian community throughout the narrative, and substantival usages of the adjective πιστός occur with reference to Christians in Acts 10:45; 16:1, 15.
11 The designation is never used by non-Christian characters within Acts to refer to Christians.
12 See Trebilco, *Self-Designations*, 105.
13 See Acts 4:4; 5:14; 8:12; 10:43; 13:39; 14:1; 15:7; 16:31; 17:34; 18:8; 19:4.
14 Walton, "Calling the Church Names," 225.

non-Christian (Acts 13:46) and Christian Jews (Acts 15:7).[15] The pivotal shift in usage, however, occurs at the Jerusalem council in Acts 15, where for the first time the language of kinship is used by Jewish Christians to refer to Gentile Christians, and the letter from the council to the churches abroad is addressed "to the brothers and sisters from the Gentiles through-out Antioch and Syria and Cilicia" (15:23). The narrator carefully avoids applying the language of kinship as a designation for Gentile Christians up to this point in the narrative, with the result that readers are left with a striking sense of the significance of the council as a watershed moment in the growth of the early church and its understanding of the position of Gentile Christians within the people of God.

The designation of Christians as "brothers and sisters" is likely root-ed in the teaching of Jesus (cf. Mark 3:31–35) and parallels the way in which the language of kinship is employed within the Old Testament for Israelites to refer to one another.[16] Given that kinship terminology is the single most commonly used designation for Christians in Acts, it would appear that the early church conceived of itself in familial terms. This is surely significant for our understanding of the Lukan outlook toward discipleship. If in Acts the believers are shown to relate to one anoth-er primarily as brothers and sisters, then discipleship to Christ must entail a range of social obligations and relational commitments to fel-low disciples in keeping with the expectations of kinship ties in ancient Mediterranean culture.[17] This, in fact, is what we see unfold in Acts, as the early church extends benevolence, exhibits hospitality, and exercises accountability in ways which correspond to the norms of kinship bonds in antiquity. Thus, the frequent designation of believers as "brothers and sisters" in Acts provides a helpful insight into the expectations of disci-pleship in the early church.

D. Witnesses

Some Christians in Acts are also designated as "witnesses" at numer-ous points in the narrative. When used with reference to believers, the noun μάρτυς is employed solely to refer to Christians who either were present for Jesus's earthly ministry or experienced encounters with the risen Christ, the lone exception being the usage in Acts 22:20, where

---

15 Trebilco, *Self-Designations,* 50.
16 Walton, "Calling the Church Names," 225–26.
17 On the structure of ancient Mediterranean families, see J. H. Hellerman, *The Ancient Church as Family* (Minneapolis: Fortress, 2001), 27–58.

Stephen is identified by Paul as the Lord's witness.[18] Most often, the resurrection of Jesus is the primary object of witness (2:32; 3:15; 5:32; 10:41; 13:31), though in Acts 10:39 Peter speaks of himself as a witness to the earthly ministry of Jesus, and in Acts 22:15 and 26:16, Paul describes how he was appointed as a witness of what he had seen and heard in his Damascus road encounter. In addition to the uses of the noun μάρτυς as a designation for Christians, verbal forms from the same root are also employed regularly within Acts to describe the evangelistic activity of figures such as Peter and Paul.[19] Hence, the act of witness is shown to be a central function of the preeminent leaders within the early church.

Because the terminology of witness is confined primarily to Christian spokespeople who had uniquely experienced the earthly ministry of Jesus and his resurrection appearances, one might wonder the extent to which Luke intends for his Christian readership to conceive of themselves as witnesses as well. However, the terminology of witness does also appear with reference to Barnabas (Acts 14:3) and Stephen (22:20), and Paul's sermon to the Ephesian elders in Acts 20:18–35 presents Paul's ministry as an example to follow.[20] It would therefore seem that believers in Luke's day and ours are to see themselves as witnesses, though in a different way from the original witnesses in Acts.[21] Whereas the original witnesses testified to their firsthand experience of the earthly ministry of Jesus and his resurrection, later witnesses testify to that which the original witnesses proclaimed. Readers of Acts are invited first to receive the testimony of the witnesses within the narrative, then to act as witnesses to that testimony themselves, making it known in their own day and setting.[22]

E. The Way

At six points in Acts, the Christian movement is referred to as "the Way" (Acts 9:2; 19:9, 23; 22:4; 24:14, 22).[23] This designation is employed both by the narrator and by Paul in direct speech (22:4; 24:14), and the

---

18 In Acts 6:13 and 7:58, the noun is used with reference to non-Christians within the narrative.
19 Cf. Acts 2:40; 8:25; 10:42; 14:3; 18:5; 20:21, 24; 23:11; 26:22; 28:23.
20 On the speech of Paul at Miletus, see S. Walton, *Leadership and Lifestyle: The Portrait of Paul in the Miletus Speech and 1 Thessalonians*, SNTSMS 108 (Cambridge: Cambridge University Press, 2000).
21 See P. G. Bolt, "Mission and Witness," in *Witness to the Gospel: The Theology of Acts,* eds. I. H. Marshall and D. Peterson (Grand Rapids: Eerdmans, 1998), 191–214, esp. 210–14.
22 See also Fitzmyer, "Designations," 315–16.
23 Trebilco also considers the usages in 18:25–26 as additional occurrences of the designation (see *Self-Designations,* 248).

use of this terminology as a designation within the early Christian movement is unique to Acts. Motifs of journey and travel are prominent within in Luke-Acts, as Luke's Gospel contains a lengthy journey section (Luke 9:51–18:31), and significant events throughout Luke's two volumes tend to happen in transit: the appearance of the resurrected Jesus to the men on the road to Emmaus; the encounter of Philip and the Ethiopian eunuch on the road to Gaza; and the confrontation of Saul on the road to Damascus. The road is a significant setting for spiritual encounter within Luke's narrative. As such, the designation of the Christian movement as "the Way" naturally resonates with one of the prominent motifs in Luke's narrative, perhaps conveying that the Christian life itself is a journey along a path (i.e., the pattern of Jesus's example) toward a destination (i.e., salvation).[24] Thus, this imagery may speak to the developmental nature of Christian discipleship.[25]

F. Saints

Acts occasionally employs the designation "holy ones" or "saints" (ἅγιος) to refer to Jewish Christians in Judea. In Acts 9:13, and in Paul's retelling of the same situation in 26:10, the Christians in Jerusalem and Judea whom Saul persecuted prior to his conversion are called "saints." In Acts 9:32 and 41, the Jewish Christian believers in Lydda and Joppa are likewise designated in this way. The designation of new-covenant believers as "saints" may speak to the continuity between the early Christian movement and the Old Testament conception of God's people as a holy nation.[26] However, in the Old Testament, the term "saints" as a designation appears almost always with reference to heavenly beings and is employed with clear reference to humans at only a few places in the Psalms (Ps. 34:10; 73:3 LXX; 82:4–5 LXX).[27] With the coming of the Messiah, "the Holy One of God," the people of God under the new covenant are now rightly conceived as "holy ones" in a new way. Thus,

---

24 This motif in early Christianity may be rooted in Isaiah 40:3, "A voice cries: 'In the wilderness prepare the way of the LORD; make straight in the desert a highway for our God.'" This passage is central to the ministry of John the Baptist (cf. Luke 3:4–6), and the Isaianic passage is interpreted within the gospels to find its fulfillment in the ministry of Jesus. See Walton, "Calling the Church Names," 237–38.

25 On the theme of progressive maturation in Luke-Acts, see C. H. Talbert, "Discipleship in Luke-Acts," in Discipleship in the New Testament, ed. F. F. Segovia (Philadelphia: Fortress, 1985), 62–75, esp. 66.

26 D. Seccombe, "The New People of God," in Witness to the Gospel, 349–72, esp. 372.

27 Trebilco, Self-Designations, 122–23.

the New Testament usage of the term is distinctive, though for Luke it appears to be limited to a very particular time and place within early Christianity.

G. Other Significant Designations

Aside from the above designations, Christians in Acts are also referenced corporately in a couple of additional ways: At numerous points, groups of Christians are referred to as the assembly/church (ἐκκλησία). Most often this designation is used with reference to actual local gatherings of Christians, though in Acts 9:31 a broader reference to all believers within the regions of Judea and Samaria would seem to be in mind; and in Acts 20:28, the designation refers to all believers in all places.[28] The designation is also used in the Old Testament to refer to the assembly of Israel, so that again this designation conveys a continuity between the Christian movement and God's people in the Old Testament. Finally, the term "Christian" appears in Acts 11:26 and 26:28, where it seems to be a designation used only by outsiders to refer to those who were followers of Jesus.[29] That outsiders could speak of the believers with a distinct designation shows that the church was differentiated from other religious organizations, such as the synagogue, from a very early stage in the growth of the Christian movement.[30]

REQUIREMENTS OF DISCIPLESHIP IN ACTS

Our survey of the terminology of discipleship has shown that following Jesus entails a variety of responsibilities and commitments in Acts. Indeed, the picture of discipleship which we see emerging in Acts corresponds rather fittingly to the startling challenge of Jesus in Luke's gospel: "Any one of you who does not renounce all that belongs to him cannot be my disciple" (Luke 14:33).[31] For in Acts we find that followers of Jesus consistently exhibit an all-encompassing pattern of believing and feeling and acting that flows out of their commitment to the lordship of Christ.[32] Our exploration of the requirements of discipleship will begin with this foundational commitment to the lordship of Christ, and then explore

---

28 See Walton, "Calling the Church Names," 232–34.
29 On the negative connotations of this designation, see Rowe, *World Upside Down,* 126–31.
30 Trebilco, *Self-Designations,* 296.
31 Martin, "Salvation and Discipleship," 380.
32 See Rowe, *World Upside Down,* 116.

some of the ways in which this commitment generates a distinctive way of living for followers of Jesus.

A. The Lordship of Christ

In a poignant moment at the climax of his speech at Pentecost, Peter exhorts his Jerusalem audience, "Let all the house of Israel therefore know for certain that *God has made him both Lord and Christ, this Jesus whom you crucified*" (Acts 2:36). This confession, restated in various ways as the central refrain of the believers throughout the remainder of the narrative, is not intended within the context of Acts primarily as an abstract ontological affirmation about the second person of the trinity.[33] Rather, Peter's climactic declaration is asserted as a daring claim about the progression of the biblical narrative and the position of Jesus within it. With the resurrection of Jesus, a new age of salvation history has arrived (cf. Acts 2:17–21; 3:23–26; 13:38–39), such that Jews and Gentiles alike are called to recognize the arrival of this new epoch and reorient their lives accordingly (cf. Acts 2:38; 3:19–22; 10:42–43; 17:30–31). This is the essence of repentance in Acts: to begin speaking and acting in light of the resurrection of Jesus as God's eschatological people who await the consummation of God's work in Jesus, the crucified and resurrected Messiah who is Lord of all (cf. Acts 10:36).[34]

The activity of Jesus's disciples and the life of the church depicted in Acts are but the outworking of this central conviction about the place of Jesus and his followers within the unfolding biblical narrative. In this way, the narrative of Acts forms its readers as disciples by showing them their place in the biblical story.[35] Discipleship in Acts is therefore first and foremost a matter of internalizing the apostolic kerygma of Jesus's exaltation as Messiah and Lord, such that the apostolic story becomes the paradigm that shapes how we think and feel and act in every area of life.

---

33 The logic of Peter's sermon, however, does exert a "trinitarian pressure" upon its audience. See C. K. Rowe, "Acts 2.36 and the Continuity of Lukan Christology," *NTS* 53 (2007): 37–56.
34 In the sermons to Jewish audiences in Jerusalem, the call to repentance relates specifically to their past opposition to Jesus (Acts 2:38; 3:19). Elsewhere, repentance is still a consistent refrain in the church's proclamation, and its precise character depends upon the specific setting of the call to transformed living (Acts 8:22; 11:18; 17:30). At its core, the call to repentance is simply an exhortation for people to turn from their old ways of living in light of the revelation of Christ's lordship that has come through the resurrection and ascension of Jesus and his present work in the church through the Holy Spirit.
35 See J. B. Green, "Doing Repentance: The Formation of Disciples in the Acts of the Apostles," *Ex Auditu* (2002): 6–14.

This ongoing act of believing in Jesus will inevitably result in a distinctive way of relating to others and carrying oneself in the world, a Spirit-empowered transformation that surely encompasses all of life.[36] Within the narrative of Acts, however, we can identify four practices that stand out as key elements of faithful discipleship.

B. A Universal Mission

The assertion that Jesus is the Lord of all is a universal claim that in Acts contains no exception clauses or loopholes. The lordship of the Messiah is not confined to a particular people or place. Rather, its scope is universal, and God now calls "all people everywhere to repent" before the one he has established by the resurrection as the judge over all the world (Acts 17:30–31). The universal ministry of the Messiah necessarily generates a universal mission for the men and women who are his followers, and Acts shows the disciples of Jesus embarking upon an aggressive, ongoing campaign to declare the lordship of the Messiah among the nations, in keeping with Jesus's promise that the disciples would be his witnesses "to the end of the earth" (Acts 1:8).[37]

In fact, the universal mission of the church in Acts is perhaps the Christian movement's most striking and peculiar feature, a trait of Christian self-understanding that was unprecedented in the other social and religious movements of antiquity. As Rowe observes, "Unlike anything else we know of in the ancient world, the Christian mission actively envisioned its target audience as anyone or everyone."[38] Acts depicts a church whose energy and resources are uniquely devoted to its own expansion, with considerable effort given to strategic evangelistic outreach across the Mediterranean world.

Here we must correct a common misconception about the expansion of the church in Acts. It is often suggested that the church in Acts only reluctantly spreads beyond its original setting in Jerusalem, as though the Christian movement would never have moved beyond the confines of the holy city had it not been for the forced migration prompted through the persecution of Stephen. It is true that encounters with persecution do at times

---

36 Hence, Paul conceives of diametric oppositions when he ponders the difference between a life of discipleship and one's prior existence apart from Christ: those who become disciples have had their eyes opened, so that they have turned from darkness to light and from the power of Satan to the power of God (Acts 26:18).

37 See E. J. Schnabel, *Early Christian Mission* (Downers Grove, IL: IVP, 2004), 436–43.

38 Rowe, *World Upside Down*, 125.

propel the church toward expansion at points in Acts, and certainly Luke stresses the Lord's initiative in his accounts of the gospel breaking into new frontiers (Acts 8:26–40; 10:1–11:18; 16:6–10).[39] Still, the reality is that most of the missionary initiatives in Acts do not arise as the result of persecution or in spite of the church's reluctance. Instead, the missionary work of the church in Acts is depicted within the overall narrative as a fitting expression of the church's sense of calling to bear witness to the nations. Of course this is particularly clear in the example of Paul, who speaks forthrightly about his commission to proclaim the gospel to the nations (cf. Acts 13:47; 22:15, 21; 26:16–17). But some hints of a missionary self-understanding of the church are also evident from the very beginning with the Jerusalem apostles, for at Pentecost we find Peter speaking of the promise of salvation "for all who are far away, whom the Lord our God calls to himself" (Acts 2:39), and at the temple in Acts 3 Peter looks forward to the expansion of Abrahamic blessing to all nations of the earth (cf. Acts 3:25–26).[40] Discipleship in Acts is thus always a life of mission, and following Jesus consists largely in bearing witness to his lordship among the nations.

C. Prayer

The ambitious scope of the church's mission naturally forms the church into a community that is utterly dependent upon God for its vitality, and so the practice of prayer is another key element of faithful discipleship in Acts.[41] Hence, prior to the outpouring of the Holy Spirit, the disciples in Jerusalem were devoting themselves to prayer (Acts 1:14), and prayer is also one of the defining practices of the church post-Pentecost (2:42). The Jerusalem apostles prioritize the work of prayer, delegating the care for widows to others in order to remain devoted to prayer and the ministry of the word (6:4). Throughout the narrative, again and again the church turns to God in prayer for boldness

---

39 In the case of the first Gentile conversion in Acts 10, one can certainly detect a hesitancy in Peter about the encounter with Cornelius. However, I would suggest that Peter's apparent reluctance has less to do with reservations about a Gentile mission *per se* and more to do with a couple of specific concerns: (1) confusion about the terms under which the mission was to be conducted and under which the Gentiles were to be integrated into the fellowship of the church, and (2) discomfort over the specific circumstances by which the Lord had arranged for Peter and Cornelius to encounter one another. See Benjamin R. Wilson, "Jew-Gentile Relations and the Geographic Movement of Acts 10:1–11:18," *CBQ* 80 (2018): 81–96.
40 In addition, the appointment of a twelfth apostle to replace Judas can also be seen as an indication of the Jerusalem church's sense of commission. See Schnabel, *Early Christian Mission*, 394–95.
41 See Fitzmyer, "Discipleship," 137; and Green, "Doing Repentance," 17.

(4:29–31), empowerment (6:6; 13:2–3; 14:23), and deliverance (12:5), and significant events and advances in mission are frequently preceded or accompanied by references to prayer (8:15; 9:40; 10:2, 4, 9; 16:25; 28:8). In short, discipleship in Acts is marked by constant reliance upon God in prayer.

Most of the time Luke simply summarizes the prayers of the church through indirect speech, but in Acts 4:24–30 a prayer is recorded that gives us a more detailed portrait of the community in prayer. The context is one of opposition, as the church has just received a report of the threats against it from the Jerusalem authorities (Acts 4:23). The response of the church to this opposition is to turn to God in prayer.

The supplication of the church begins with an affirmation of the Lord's sovereignty over all of creation: "Sovereign Lord, who made the heaven and the earth and the sea and everything in them" (Acts 4:24). In light of this conviction in the Lord's sovereignty, the recent opposition to Jesus and his present work in the church can be seen as vain striving, and so the prayer progresses, "'Why did the Gentiles rage, and the peoples plot in vain? The kings of the earth set themselves, and the rulers were gathered together, against the Lord and against his Anointed'—for truly in this city there were gathered together against your holy servant Jesus, whom you anointed, both Herod and Pontius Pilate, along with the Gentiles and the peoples of Israel, to do whatever your hand and your plan had predestined to take place" (Acts 4:25–28; citing Ps. 2:1–2). Here the disciples draw upon Psalm 2:1–2 to interpret the hostility against Jesus as futile opposition that only serves to accomplish what the Lord has foreordained. Finally, having affirmed the sovereign Lord's authority and control over the opposition they are presently encountering, the disciples pray for boldness and empowerment in their mission: "And now, Lord, look upon their threats and grant to your servants to continue to speak your word with all boldness, while you stretch out your hand to heal, and signs and wonders are performed through the name of your holy servant Jesus" (Acts 4:29–30).

The outcome of the prayer is recorded at the end of the passage: "And when they had prayed, the place in which they were gathered together was shaken, and they were all filled with the Holy Spirit and continued to speak the word of God with boldness" (Acts 4:31). In this manner, the prayers of the church are shown to be central to the church's ongoing health and growth. Our mission is not an easy one, and we cannot fulfill it apart from the Lord's empowerment and blessing. Thus, to bear faithful witness amidst the opposition that gospel ministry will inevitably evoke, disciples must remain ever-reliant upon the Lord in prayer.

D. Personal Conformity to the Pattern of Jesus's Lifestyle

A third key element of faithful discipleship in Acts is the conformity of one's lifestyle to the pattern of Jesus's personal example.[42] This can be seen most especially in the willingness of the disciples in Acts to endure opposition for the sake of their allegiance to the Lord, by which believers are shown to follow Jesus in their sufferings. Indeed, prior to his arrest and crucifixion, Jesus had taught his disciples that their mission would be conducted from a posture of vulnerability (Luke 9:3–6; 10:2–16; 22:35–38), and in Acts the disciples are seen to experience what Jesus had anticipated. Just as Jesus remained faithful in the midst of his trials, the disciples steadfastly endure hardship with unflinching devotion to the Lord (cf. Acts 4:19–20; 5:29–32), attesting that they can do no other than to bear witness to Jesus the Messiah.

The martyrdom of Stephen is a particularly poignant instance of conformity to Jesus's example, for Luke has crafted his narrative of Stephen's death to parallel the death of Jesus in many ways. Just like Jesus at the crucifixion, Stephen prays for his persecutors:

> And falling to his knees he cried out with a loud voice, "Lord, do not hold this sin against them." And when he had said this, he fell asleep. (Acts 7:60)

> And Jesus said, "Father, forgive them, for they know not what they do." (Luke 23:34)

Additionally, both Stephen and Jesus offer up their spirits at the moment of their deaths, though Stephen offers his spirit to the "Lord Jesus," whereas Jesus offers his spirit to the Father:

> And as they were stoning Stephen, he called out, "Lord Jesus, receive my spirit." (Acts 7:59)

> Then Jesus, calling out with a loud voice, said, "Father, into your hands I commit my spirit!" And having said this he breathed his last. (Luke 23:46)

Moreover, even small contextual details from the two events are shown to share similarities: The passages which describe the martyrdom

---

42 See O'Toole, "Parallels," 207–09.

of Stephen and the death of Jesus both include references to garments (Acts 7:58; cf. Luke 23:34b); Both passages entail what might be considered atmospheric anomalies, since Stephen gazes into heaven to see Jesus standing in regal authority (Acts 7:55–56), And the sun is darkened at the death of Jesus (Luke 23:44–45).[43] These contextual similarities and the resemblances in behavior between Stephen and Jesus leave readers with the impression that Stephen's experience as a disciple has fittingly conformed to the experience of his Lord.

Again and again, the accounts of the church's suffering in Acts are narrated in such a way as to make the parallels between the experience of the church and Jesus quite obvious, and readers are thereby left with a clear sense that the church's experience will conform to the pattern of Jesus's own destiny of suffering and vindication. As Paul and Barnabas exhort the congregations they had planted in the course of their first missionary journey, "Through many tribulations we must enter the kingdom of God" (Acts 14:22). Discipleship in Acts involves the willingness to deny oneself and bear one's cross, in keeping with Jesus's instruction about discipleship in Luke's Gospel (cf. Luke 9:23).

E. Familial Relations in the Community of Believers

Finally, discipleship in Acts is a communal enterprise, and it is by no means coincidental that the most common way by which disciples refer to one another in Acts is with the language of kinship. Those who come to faith in Jesus as the Messiah and Lord are integrated into a fellowship whose members treat one another according to the norms and expectations of a family.

The familial quality of the early church can be seen especially in its distinctive patterns of generosity and hospitality: In Acts 2:44–45 and 4:32–35, we learn that the earliest believers in Jerusalem held everything in common and shared their possessions in such a way as to ensure than none were in need. When the Greek-speaking widows in the Jerusalem church were being neglected in the distribution of resources, the church moved quickly to address the problem, showing a sense of familial obligation to care for the practical needs of the widows (Acts 6:1–7). Yes, the pooling of resources in Jerusalem is depicted as a voluntary action (cf. Acts 5:4), and the practice does not seem to have been carried out in

---

43 See J. Delobel, "Luke 23:34a: A Perpetual Text-Critical Crux," in *Sayings of Jesus: Canonical and Non-Canonical*, eds. W. L. Petersen, et al. (Leiden: Brill, 1997), 25–36, at 34–35.

precisely the same way elsewhere in Acts. However, the spirit of familial generosity reflected in the early Jerusalem community does find expression throughout Acts. When the church in Antioch, for example, learns of impending economic hardship for the churches in Judea, a collection is taken to be sent to the Jerusalem elders (Acts 11:28–30). Similarly, Acts is replete with examples of hospitality among believers. Indeed, the very nature of the early Christian movement as a network of house churches necessitated that hospitality was built into the structural fabric of the church (Acts 2:46), and the missionary orientation of the movement relied upon hospitality for traveling evangelists such as Paul and his companions. Such generosity and hospitality was natural for the early church, for disciples conceived of their bond to one another in terms of the bond between siblings, which was the most foundational relationship in ancient familial systems.[44]

The familial quality of the church's fellowship also becomes apparent in the face of opposition and hostility. When Paul faces the prospect of persecution and physical violence, fellow believers come to his aid and offer helpful protection and escape (Acts 9:24–25, 30). When Peter is imprisoned, the church prays earnestly for him (Acts 12:5). Likewise, during Paul's lengthy imprisonment, the church ministers to his practical needs (Acts 24:23; 27:3). As Jesus had taught his disciples that they were members of a new surrogate family in the faith (Luke 8:19–21), the book of Acts depicts familial relations within the community of believers as a key element of discipleship.

CONCLUSION

What makes a disciple a disciple in Acts? We have seen that the contours of discipleship in Acts flow from the foundational conviction that the unfolding biblical narrative has come to a climactic moment in Jesus, the crucified and resurrected Messiah who now stands in a position of heavenly authority as Lord of all. As Christians orient their lives by faith in response to the revelation of Christ's lordship, they embrace a universal mission to the nations. Recognizing their utter dependence upon God for such a mission, they are formed to be people of prayer. In the course of their mission, disciples accept suffering and self-denial in conformity to the example of their Lord, and they exercise hospitality and generosity toward each other as brothers and sisters in the family of God.

---

44 Hellerman, *The Ancient Church as Family,* 35–37.

The various designations by which Christians are called in Acts reflect facets of this picture of discipleship, demonstrating that the early Christians addressed one another in ways consistent with the reality of their transformed existence in Christ. In this way, we see that in Acts discipleship is nothing less than a thoroughly distinctive way of living, right down to the very language that we use to speak of ourselves and our shared experience as followers of Jesus.

CHAPTER 6 ▬▬▬▬▬▬▬▬▬▬▬

The Challenge of Allegiance in the Roman Empire: Discipleship in Romans and Galatians

Scot McKnight

As a college student with the fire of zeal in my belly, a mind saturated with Bible, and a hope that the church would become what it was called to be, I was convinced the church needed something I had. I'm not so embarrassed these days by ignorant zeal as I am by my incomprehension of God's grace. Zeal has its place—and I had it—and the theologian that satisfied me most was one not all my fellow evangelicals (at that time) thought acceptable. His name was Dietrich Bonhoeffer, his book was *The Cost of Discipleship*,[1] and the theme that struck to my heart and set my zeal ablaze was "cheap grace." I didn't know how to make it real for ordinary lay folks or for the youth group I, along with my wife Kris, was then pastoring, but what I knew was that the word "discipleship" was the fire in my heart.

I tried Ray Stedman's concept of body life, and we worked on the fruit of the Spirit,[2] but behind those two attempts was my desire to make Bonhoeffer's clear vision for "costly" grace more prominent in both our evangelism and our church education programs. Before I had my feet under me, Kris and I moved to Chicagoland, I entered Trinity Evangelical Divinity School, and my zeal shifted only slightly. It was still fired by Bonhoeffer, but I became intoxicated with the Gospel of Matthew, thanks to a course by Grant Osborne and a general course on the Synoptic Gospels by Walter Liefeld. And then Kris and I were off to England, to the University of Nottingham, where I began a doctoral program under Professor James D. G. Dunn. My topic? Matthew's missionary discourse

---

1 Dietrich Bonhoeffer, *Discipleship,* Dietrich Bonhoeffer Works 4 (Minneapolis: Fortress, 2001); idem., *Ethics*, eds. I. Tödt and C. J. Green, Dietrich Bonhoeffer Works 6 (Minneapolis: Fortress, 2005).
2 Ray Stedman, *Body Life: The Book That Inspired a Return to the Church's Real Meaning and Mission,* rev. ed. (Grand Rapids: Discovery House, 1996).

(9:36–11:1). I defended my thesis in 1986 (it was never published), I became a professor at Trinity, and very early in my career Mike Wilkins's book *The Concept of Disciple in Matthew's Gospel* appeared. I devoured it, absorbed it, and with it enhanced a course I was occasionally teaching called "Jesus's Teachings on Discipleship."[3]

A few years afterward, Mike published the sort of book I was aiming for, called *Following the Master*.[4] I never wrote that book, though many years later I put together some of my ideas on discipleship in a book called *One.Life*.[5] But to this day I look to Mike's two books, with the original academic study now freshly updated in a second edition, as the benchmark for understanding Jesus's summons to follow him. A recent book carrying on this same thematic emphasis is Matthew Bates's provocatively titled but biblically rich study, *Salvation by Allegiance Alone*.[6] In one way or another, with his own important nuances, Mike Wilkins has been in the middle of this deep concern about the church's holiness, obedience, and devotion.

Between those early professor years and today I have swung from an irritation with the apostle Paul, because he ignored my pet themes in Matthew's Gospel about discipleship and kingdom, to a love of Paul for his gift of taking Jesus into the Roman Empire with themes so deeply rooted in Jesus's message of discipleship that he can make them sing a new song in a new land.[7] It is with appreciation of Mike's work and my memory of engaging him in so many of my classes and writings that I offer to him this piece on how Paul understood discipleship in Romans and Galatians. I shall emphasize the former, with the latter brought in as a harmonious voice. While I love the niceties of biblical theology that focus on each New Testament letter's distinct emphases—discipleship in Galatians vs. discipleship in Romans vs. discipleship in Colossians, etc.—I am persuaded Paul was a coherent thinker, that his letters mesh well in spite of their contextual distinctives, and that Romans itself is

---

3 Michael J. Wilkins, *The Concept of Disciple in Matthew's Gospel: As Reflected in the Use of the Term Μαθητής*, NovTSup 59 (Leiden: Brill, 1988); republished as *Discipleship in the Ancient World and Matthew's Gospel*, 2nd ed. (Grand Rapids: Baker, 1995).

4 Michael J. Wilkins, *Following the Master: A Biblical Theology of Discipleship* (Grand Rapids: Zondervan, 1992).

5 Scot McKnight, *One.Life: Jesus Calls, We Follow* (Grand Rapids: Zondervan, 2010).

6 Matthew W. Bates, *Salvation by Allegiance Alone: Rethinking Faith, Works, and the Gospel of Jesus the King* (Grand Rapids: Baker Academic, 2017).

7 Notice how Wilkins opens his chapter on discipleship in the Epistles: Wilkins, *Following the Master*, 291–94. I agree completely with his take on the presence of discipleship teachings (consistent with Jesus's own teachings) in the letters of Paul.

in many ways Paul's major letter. The overlap between Romans and Galatians is substantive enough to provide more synthesis than analytical difference in what follows.

ROMANS AND DISCIPLESHIP: HOW TO READ ROMANS

Romans, considered by many to be the archetypal early Christian writing and the fount of much of Western Christian theology, has been read one way, and there is nothing wrong with that.[8] How so? We read it from Romans 1:1 to the end of chapter 16, though some today think Romans 16 is suspect (I'm unconvinced by their suspicions).[9] The problem with reading Romans this way, which is how Phoebe (16:1–2) would have read the letter to the five or more house churches in Rome (16:3–16),[10] is that by the time one gets to Romans 12 the reader is numbed into a stupor by the intensity of the theology and the swiftness of Paul's rhetorical moves. After all, Romans would have been considered a letter well beyond limits in the first century.

What I mean is this: If one reads Romans from front to back, one will see Romans 1–11 as theology (more or less) and Romans 12–16 as practice, ethics, morality, or Christian living. Put differently, chapters 12–16 become the "application" of Paul's theology in the earlier chapters. Here's the problem, however: When read this way, Romans 1–11 becomes abstract systematic thinking, pure theology, or even pure philosophy—and for some today, pure political thinking. I'll put the problem another way: When the various segments in Romans 1–11 are divorced from the pastoral project in Romans 12–16, Romans ceases to be what it is—pastoral theology—and becomes what it is not—in effect,

---

8 In what follows I am touching on what I argue in Scot McKnight, *Reading Romans Backwards: A Gospel of Peace in the Midst of Empire* (Waco, TX: Baylor University of Press, 2019). I must also mention several important studies on Romans that have shaped my own thinking:: Mark Reasoner, *Romans in Full Circle: A History of Interpretation* (Louisville: Westminster John Knox, 2005); Ernst Käsemann, *Commentary on Romans* (Grand Rapids: Eerdmans, 1980); N. T. Wright, "The Letter to the Romans," in *The New Interpreter's Bible*, vol. 12 (Nashville: Abingdon, 2002), 393–770; James D. G. Dunn, *Romans*, 2 vols., WBC 38 (Nashville: Thomas Nelson, 1988); Robert Jewett, *Romans: A Commentary*, Hermeneia (Minneapolis: Fortress, 2006); James D. G. Dunn, *The Theology of Paul the Apostle* (Grand Rapids: Eerdmans, 1998); N. T. Wright, *Paul and the Faithfulness of God*, 2 vols. (Minneapolis: Fortress, 2013); E. P. Sanders, *Paul: The Apostle's Life, Letters, and Thought* (Fortress, 2015).
9 All citations from the Bible are from the NIV 2011.
10 On Phoebe, see Jewett, *Romans*, 942–48. On the public performance of letters, see William D. Shiell, *Delivering from Memory: The Effect of Performance on the Early Christian Audience* (Eugene, OR: Pickwick, 2011).

two letters, one of pure theology and one of pure practice. This is a serious mistake and leads to a profound misapprehension of what Romans 1–11 are actually doing. They are not simply setting up something different in the final chapters but are a piece with the final chapters. Romans 1–11 is pastoral theology just as much as is Romans 12–16.

I propose, then, that we learn to read Romans backwards—that is, begin with Romans 12–16 and only then read chapters 9–11, and then read chapters 1–8 (or even 5–8, and then 1–4)! Of course this is backwards, but it may be the only way to recapture Romans as pastoral theology and recapture what the audience—the "strong" and the "weak" of Romans 14–15—actually heard as Phoebe read this letter aloud to each house church. This, it must be admitted, is only a temporary measure until we regain our footings in this most marvelous of letters. This backwards reading of Romans will bring into sharper focus the overlap between Romans and Galatians. We don't have space here to work our way all the way from end to beginning in Romans, so I will focus on the end to give a taste of what can be known if one then learned to read Romans backwards.

THE HOUSE CHURCHES OF ROME

To make a complex story short—and Peter Lampe's amazing *From Paul to Valentinus* is the place to go for a full study of this information—the following are some social realities of the Roman house churches.[11] First, there were at least five of them, and they were led by the house church of Prisca and Aquila (16:3–5a); then come the house churches connected to Aristobulus (16:10), Narcissus (16:11), Asyncritus and others (16:14), and that of Philologus, Julia, and others (16:15).[12]

Second, if Peter Oakes is anywhere near being accurate, and many think he is, there would be a maximum of forty persons per house church, and probably at best half of that, so we are looking at somewhere between one and two hundred Christians in Rome at the time of this letter.[13]

Third, Paul knows perhaps as many as a quarter of the Christians in Rome, so any theory that Paul is writing to unknowns is deeply mistaken. He provides too much insider information about Christians in Rome for us to think this is a letter to churches that know nothing of Paul. Prisca

---

11 Peter Lampe, *From Paul to Valentinus: Christians at Rome in the First Two Centuries*, ed. M. D. Johnson; trans. M. Steinhauser (Minneapolis: Fortress, 2003).

12 For great synthesis, see Jewett, *Romans*, 949–74.

13 Peter Oakes, *Reading Romans in Pompeii: Paul's Letter at Ground Level* (Minneapolis: Fortress, 2009).

and Aquila, after all, had spent considerable of time with Paul already, participating with him in both Corinth and Ephesus.

Fourth, there is a mixture of Jewish and Gentile believers in the Roman house churches, though the percentages are not knowable. There are at least seven Jewish names in Romans 16: Mary [Miriam, Mariam], Andronicus, Junia, Aquila and probably Prisca, Herodion, and Rufus (of Mark 15:21 fame) and his mother. There are only three Latin names (Ampliatus, Julia, Urbanus); the rest are Greek names.

Fifth, many of the Christians in Rome are either slaves or freed slaves, and many too are immigrants from other parts of the empire.

Sixth—and I'll let this one remain a loose end—there is a clear focus on women, at least some of whom are leaders, in the Roman house churches: Prisca, Mary, Junia,[14] Tryphaena and Tryphosa (perhaps sisters), Persis, Rufus's mother, Julia, Nereus's sister, as well as the sisters in the household of Asyncritus.[15]

Seventh, earliest Christianity in Rome was Jewish, and it is well-nigh certain they were in the middle of the problems that provoked Claudius to cut the knees out from under them by exiling those deemed problem-makers (Acts 18:2). This is how an early Roman historian described it: "Since the Jews constantly made disturbances at the instigation of Chrestus, he expelled them from Rome" (Suetonius, *Claudius* 25.4).[16] His "Jews" were probably our "Jewish Christians." In the middle of this group of Jewish Christians were Prisca and Aquila. When Nero relaxed Claudius's decree, some of those exiled returned.

Finally, I believe we can know some more quotidian realities that unmask some deep realities about the Roman house churches. Twisting north to south through Rome is the Tiber River and west of the Forum and south of the Vatican (a first-century term also) was the port area of the Tiber called the Trastevere. Christians in house churches were located here in the first century. South and slightly east of the Forum, on a main road through the heart of first-century Rome called Via Appia, was another area where Christians lived and gathered. Between the two, in an area called the Aventine, was a third location, but the evidence is not as abundant for the Aventine. North and slightly west of the Forum was Mars Field and along its eastern side is the Via Lata/Flaminia, yet another

---

14   Eldon Jay Epp, *Junia: The First Woman Apostle* (Minneapolis: Fortress, 2005).
15   For discussion, Susan Mathew, *Women in the Greetings of Romans 16.1–16: A Study of Mutuality and Women's Ministry in the Letter to the Romans*, LNTS 471 (London: T&T Clark, 2014).
16   Translation from Loeb Classical Library.

area where Christians lived. These areas are connected, as we might expect, with Jewish settlements and synagogue gatherings. These locations were dense with an (over)population of mostly poor and immigrants; the areas were unhealthy lowlands as well. The Trastavere in particular was composed of workers connected to the harbor and trade and transportation like sailing. Trade would create shopkeepers and those who tanned skins (with their putrid odors). As home to travelers, the Trastevere was filled with foreign religious shrines and adherents. What we know of the area along the Via Appia was that it was filled with transportation vehicles, with workers and porters, as well as with craftsmen. The Aventine hill, however, was mixed with upper-class Romans and their slaves and workers. Mars Field is more or less the same as the Aventine population.

All of this to say: The Christians of Rome were poor, but there were probably also some with connections to some high-status individuals. Their homes were often apartments (tenements) and not villas, though there were some villas in each of these areas. These homes were the location for business and were therefore public spaces. If we think they sealed off their public space for Sunday morning worship, we need to think again.

Whenever I work my way through this kind of information, and I do so both in classes and public speaking as well, I come to this conclusion: This isn't my father's church. Nor is it mine. And it probably isn't yours. There's very little in the USA anything like this, and one has to think more of public spaces where Christians might gather to approximate a first-century Roman house church. It is in such a context that Phoebe read this long, long, long letter to the Roman house churches.

What is not so dissimilar, unfortunately, is tension among and between Christians. In Galatia there is a problem between Jewish and Gentile Christians over how much law the Gentile converts are to observe, with the Jewish Christians clearly playing a dominant, even coercive role. Jews were pleading with the Gentiles to Judaize; that is, the Gentiles were converting the whole way by observing the Torah and having themselves circumcised.[17] Turnabout is (un)fair play, for in Rome the coercive side is the "strong," and we have every reason to believe that the strong are more or less Gentile believers who know freedom from the law. On the

---

17 There are many intense discussions but a consensus is that only a Gentile can Judaize; a Jew doesn't "Judaize" a Gentile. Rather, some Jewish believers were "proselytizing" Gentiles to the effect that some Gentile believers were Judaizing. On this discussion, see now Michael F. Bird, *An Anomalous Jew: Paul among Jews, Greeks, and Romans* (Grand Rapids: Eerdmans, 2016), 196–99. On Galatians, for now see James D. G. Dunn, *The Epistle to the Galatians*, BNTC (Peabody, MA: Hendrickson, 1993); and Scot McKnight, *Galatians*, NIVAC (Grand Rapids: Zondervan, 1995).

other hand, the weak are Jewish believers who want to observe food laws, Sabbath, and circumcision, both as an expression of their Jewish heritage as well as their messianic faith.[18] In other words, the situations in Galatia and Rome are in some important ways mirror social realities to one another. We cannot read Romans apart from the "strong and weak" context, nor can we read Galatians apart from their mirror reality of a different expressions of the strong and weak and the weak and strong! The approach to discipleship in both letters takes form in the context of social tensions between Jewish and Gentile believers.

Why is Paul so focused on the social tensions? The answer to that question is found in Paul's mission. Which is what? Paul, on his own terms over and over in his letters (e.g., Gal. 1:15–16) and appearing in Luke's own record (e.g., Acts 22:21), is that he was called from his conversion to a mission to the Gentiles, and thus his mission was to establish churches in the Roman Empire composed of both Jewish and Gentile believers. His was not a mission simply to get individuals saved but also to establish brand new communities, starting in synagogues and branching on their own, in which there would be a fellowship of "differents" rather than "likes" or the "sames." Hence, at the heart of his mission was a fellowship of Jews and Gentiles, slave and free, males and females (Gal. 3:28; 1 Cor. 12:13; Col. 3:11). Paul's favorite term for this group, surprising to some, is not "church" but "brothers [and sisters]," or what many today are calling "siblings." This siblingship is created by new birth (2 Cor. 5:17; Rom. 8:29).

It is in this context of social realities at work in Rome and Galatia that the teachings of the apostle Paul on discipleship demonstrate an almost "one term fits all" to where the Christian life begins. I turn now to that one term.

DISCIPLESHIP IN ROME AND GALATIA AS LOVE

What would the Christians have heard when Phoebe read that letter, and when whoever read Galatians? What did Paul expect of them as Christians in the heart of the empire or in the heart of Asia Minor? What, in other words, did discipleship look like for the Roman and Galatian Christians?

In one word: love. It all begins here; if discipleship doesn't begin here, it doesn't begin where Paul begins. We may forget how reducible the Christian life is to love only if we forget Jesus and the actual words of

---

18 For full discussion, see Mark Reasoner, *The Strong and the Weak: Romans 14.1–15.13 in Context*, SNTSMS 103 (Cambridge: Cambridge University Press, 1999).

Paul. Love is the right relation with God, with Jesus in following him,[19] with self, and with others (believers and nonbelievers). Christian identity, then, is fundamentally relational, and that identity at the core is a relation with Jesus as Savior and Lord, which means discipleship in Paul begins with union with Christ.[20] This leads us then to the centrality of love in discipleship.

We can begin with Jesus, in what I have called the Jesus Creed, where in Mark 12:29–31 Jesus reduces, by way of synthesis and intensification, the entire Torah to loving God and loving others. Matthew, of course, "edits" the concluding word to say, "All the Law and the Prophets hang on [or "from"] these two commandments" (Matt. 22:40). Whether it is Mark's grading of commands in "There is no commandment greater than these" or Matthew's more hermeneutical expression about all commands depending on love of God and love of others isn't the issue. What is the issue is that Jesus thinks love of God and love of others is capable of expressing the entire Torah for the people of God.[21]

We are then not surprised Paul carries this Jesus Creed theme into his ethical vision for disciples. In Galatians, he says, "For in Christ Jesus neither circumcision nor uncircumcision has any value. The only thing that counts is faith expressing itself through love" (Gal. 5:6). A paragraph later he says, "You, my brothers and sisters, were called to be free. But do not use your freedom to indulge the flesh; rather, serve one another humbly in love. For the entire law is fulfilled in keeping this one command: 'Love your neighbor as yourself'" (5:13–14). This is a quotation of Jesus more than a simple discovery of a reinforcing text in Leviticus 19:18. This is why, when Paul lists the fruit of the Spirit, he makes love the top item: "But the fruit of the Spirit is love, joy, peace, forbearance, kindness, goodness, faithfulness" (Gal. 5:22). We are only a stone's throw away from 1 Corinthians 13, but we need to turn to Romans.

By all accounts, the Roman house churches have mired themselves in contention. The terms Paul uses are "strong" and "weak," and the situation

---

19 I expand on the Christological shape of the ethics of Jesus in Scot McKnight, *The Sermon on the Mount*, Story of God Bible Commentary (Grand Rapids: Zondervan, 2013).

20 Constantine Campbell, *Paul and Union with Christ: An Exegetical and Theological Study* (Grand Rapids: Zondervan, 2012).

21 Scot McKnight, *The Jesus Creed: Loving God, Loving Others* (Brewster, MA: Paraclete, 2014). For a more academic study, see Scot McKnight, "Few and Far Between: The Life of a Creed," in *Earliest Christianity within the Boundaries of Judaism: Essays in Honor of Bruce Chilton*, ed. A. J. Avery-Peck, et al. (Leiden: Brill, 2016), 168–86. For an older study on love, see Leon Lamb Morris, *Testaments of Love: A Study of Love in the Bible* (Grand Rapids: Eerdmans, 1981).

is thick: This is not just about Torah and *halakah* (later rulings that make Torah more concrete for a specific situation), not just about Jewish Romans returning to Rome after driving out Jews and Jewish Christians for their disturbances, and it is not just about taxation under Claudius and Nero. It's all of these and probably more, but the dominant idea Paul teaches for the strong and the weak is love. Notice these words right up front in his teachings in Romans 12: "Love must be sincere. Hate what is evil; cling to what is good. Be devoted to one another in love. Honor one another above yourselves" (12:9–10). Then we hear yet another echo of the Jesus Creed in the next chapter:

> Let no debt remain outstanding, except the continuing debt to love one another, for whoever loves others has fulfilled the law. The commandments, "You shall not commit adultery," "You shall not murder," "You shall not steal," "You shall not covet," and whatever other command there may be, are summed up in this one command: "Love your neighbor as yourself." Love does no harm to a neighbor. Therefore love is the fulfillment of the law. (13:8–10)

We cannot pause to prove this at length, but these lines from Paul I have quoted in this section all can be summarized as saying what Jesus said and surely do echo the teachings of Jesus[22]: Spiritual maturity and the core expectation for Christians in Rome and in Galatia remains one and the same. The Christians are to love God with every globule of their being, which is expressed by Paul in other terms (Rom. 12:1–2), and they are to love their neighbors in a way that turns them from sparring partners of the strong and weak into genuinely loving siblings in Christ.

In other contexts, I have defended an explication of what love means.[23] A brief summary is all that can be done here. First, as a matter of hermeneutics, we need to avoid English dictionaries if we want to define the word "love," and the point needs to be emphasized because those dictionaries describe how people today understand love and because we don't define words in the Bible by looking at English dictionaries. I emphasize

---

22 Michael B. Thompson, *Clothed with Christ: The Example and Teaching of Jesus in Romans 12.1–15.13*, JSNTSup 59 (Sheffield: Sheffield Academic Press, 1991).

23 I have mentioned this in a number of contexts, but see now Scot McKnight, *A Fellowship of Differents: Showing the World God's Design for Life Together* (Grand Rapids: Zondervan, 2015), 51–63; and Jon D. Levenson, *The Love of God: Divine Gift, Human Gratitude, and Mutual Faithfulness in Judaism* (Princeton, NJ: Princeton University Press, 2016). I take the term "affective" from Levenson's own examination.

this because it is routinely disregarded, even by Bible scholars and pastors. Second, to define love we must watch God love in the Bible, and that means the sooner we get our minds off of churches and our fellow Christians, the better. That is, God is love and love is defined by how God loves, not by how we (fumble and fail in) love.

These two points are now followed by four. (1) Love, when defined by God's kind of love, begins with a rugged commitment or a covenant (בְּרִית), a covenant that is affective or even erotic (חשק) (Deut. 7:7). (2) Love is a rugged affective commitment of presence, seen most visibly in the glory of God attending the temple, in Jesus being Immanuel, in the Holy Spirit as God's παράκλητος (counselor) with us, and in Revelation 21:3's announcement of God's final eternal presence. (3) Love is a rugged affective commitment of presence and advocacy in that our God is one who says Israel will be his people and he will be their God (Exod. 6:7), which is a way of saying, "I've got your back because I am your warrior." (4) Finally, love is a rugged affective commitment of presence and advocacy that has direction: God is holy, so his people are to be holy; God is loving, so his people are to be loving. God's commitment of presence has a corollary of transformation. We call this at times in discipleship language "Christlikeness,"[24] and no text in the New Testament can be clearer than 2 Corinthians 3:18: "And we all, who with unveiled faces contemplate the Lord's glory, are being transformed into his image with ever-increasing glory, which comes from the Lord, who is the Spirit."

If this is love, what a challenge Paul has for the Galatians and Romans: In their social realities of intense tensions between Jewish and Gentile believers, Paul is calling them to love one another as the first and foremost virtue. That means he is calling each side to put down their swords and make a rugged affective commitment to one another—which sounds like a great idea until it is realized it means embodied presence with one another (eating together, living together, praying together, worshiping together, standing with one another against the Roman way of status and power), advocating for one another (Jewish believers for Gentile believers; Gentile

---

24 There are three ways this is expressed today: Christlikeness, cruciformity, and Christoformity. On Christlikeness, we are all indebted to Dallas Willard, *Renovation of the Heart: Putting on the Character of Christ* (Colorado Springs: NavPress, 2002). On cruciformity, see Michael J. Gorman, *Cruciformity: Paul's Narrative Spirituality of the Cross* (Grand Rapids: Eerdmans, 2001); idem, *Inhabiting the Cruciform God: Kenosis, Justification, and Theosis in Paul's Narrative Soteriology* (Grand Rapids: Eerdmans, 2009); idem, *Becoming the Gospel: Paul, Participation, and Mission* (Grand Rapids: Eerdmans, 2015). On Christoformity, see occasional uses of this term in Dunn, *The Theology of Paul the Apostle*, 625–712.

believers for Jewish believers), and living with one another in such a manner that each is helping the other become more and more Christlike. This is what Paul told the Romans, and what he told them was to love one another by imitating the way of Jesus himself.

> We who are strong ought to bear with the failings of the weak and not to please ourselves. Each of us should please our neighbors for their good, to build them up. For even Christ did not please himself but, as it is written: "The insults of those who insult you have fallen on me." For everything that was written in the past was written to teach us, so that through the endurance taught in the Scriptures and the encouragement they provide we might have hope. May the God who gives endurance and encouragement give you the same attitude of mind toward each other that Christ Jesus had, so that with one mind and one voice you may glorify the God and Father of our Lord Jesus Christ. Accept one another, then, just as Christ accepted you, in order to bring praise to God. (Rom. 15:1–7)

DISCIPLESHIP IS ABOUT RELATIONS

Everything about discipleship in both Galatians and Romans makes sense from this starting point of love (of God and others), and it alone explains why so much of the teachings on discipleship are so pervasively *relational* in manifestations. Speaking phenomenologically, the only way to talk about love is to talk about two: God and a human, and human with another human (or with other humans). Love is not the virtue of the solitary hermit, and this might explain why in modern spiritual formation discussions those who most emphasize the Roman Catholic tradition emerging from the monastics have little to nothing to say about love. (I'll avoid dropping names in a footnote.) Any reading of Galatians 5–6 or Romans 12–16 that seeks for behaviors of a disciple yields interrelational virtues. Freedom, which is a major idea in Galatians and needs to be a hermeneutical filter for reading from Galatians 1:1 on, is not simply an inner sense but a way of life with respect to God and others (5:1) and comes to living expression in "But do not use your freedom to indulge the flesh; rather, serve one another humbly in love" (5:13). Paul is concerned at Galatia with tensions in the church (5:15), which he sees as relational manifestations of the flesh (5:16–17, 19–21), and he advocates with them for healthy relations with one another (5:22–25). One could go on, but the point is clear.

So also in Romans. A disciple, if I simply skip through these chapters, is about surrendering one's entire body to God (12:1–2). In relation with siblings in Christ, it is about body life (12:3–8) and relational virtues like love (12:9, 10) and hospitality (12:13). In relation to outsiders, it is about blessing persecutors (12:14), living in harmony (12:16) and peace (12:18), and feeding the hungry (12:20). Noticeably in Romans there is a movement from love of one another and love of nonbelievers to extending such love into proper living with respect to Rome's jealous powers: They are to be "subject" and to pay taxes and to be good people of public good (13:1–7). This leads Paul immediately once again to love (13:8–10).

I haven't emphasized this but I want to: this focus on love comes from Jesus's own Jesus Creed (Mark 12:29–31). The *epitome of discipleship* for an apostle, for a teacher, for a pastor is to be one who does what Jesus says, and in that doing *teaches what Jesus teaches*. Paul's emphasis on love, then, is a manifestation of his own disciple relation with Jesus.

DISCIPLESHIP IN THE SPIRIT

Love is the fundamental expression of the spiritually formed person for Paul in both Galatians and Romans, but love is not the result of habits as taught in Aristotle's famous *Nicomachean Ethics*, and neither is love restricted as it is in the classical world to one's (male, elite) friends (φίλοι).[25] If Paul's close coworkers appeared in Galatia or Rome as "friends," it is noticeable that Paul did not ever call any of his coworkers his φίλοι.[26] Not once, and there's a reason for this: Paul's relation to his coworkers and to all other disciples of Jesus is not defined by the classical understanding of friendship but by the Christian sense of *siblingship*.[27] They have a new ontology: they are in Christ, they are sons and daughters of God the Father, and they are now brothers and sisters in Christ.

The love they have now derives not from habits but from the Spirit of God.[28] Hence, in both Galatians and Romans love, is an act of the Spirit.

---

25 David Konstan, *Friendship in the Classical World* (New York: Cambridge University Press, 1997).

26 I have a chapter on this theme in a forthcoming book tentatively called *Pastor Paul*.

27 Reidar Aasgaard, *"My Beloved Brothers and Sisters!" Christian Siblingship in Paul*, JSNTSup 265 (London: T&T Clark, 2004); Paul Trebilco, *Self-Designations and Group Identity in the New Testament* (Cambridge: Cambridge University Press, 2012). For a wider scope, see Joseph H. Hellerman, *The Ancient Church as Family* (Minneapolis: Fortress, 2001); idem, *When the Church Was a Family: Recapturing Jesus's Vision for Authentic Christian Community* (Nashville: B&H Academic, 2009).

28 The benchmark study here remains (and will for a long time be) Gordon Fee, *God's Empowering Presence: The Holy Spirit in the Letters of Paul* (Peabody, MA: Hendrickson, 1994).

Notice these lines from Paul in Galatians:

> So I say, walk by the Spirit, and you will not gratify the desires of
> the flesh. For the flesh desires what is contrary to the Spirit, and
> the Spirit what is contrary to the flesh. They are in conflict with
> each other, so that you are not to do whatever you want. But if
> you are led by the Spirit, you are not under the law. (5:16–18)

> But the fruit of the Spirit is love, joy, peace, forbearance, kind-
> ness, goodness, faithfulness, gentleness and self-control. Against
> such things there is no law. Those who belong to Christ Jesus
> have crucified the flesh with its passions and desires. Since we
> live by the Spirit, let us keep in step with the Spirit. (5:22–25)

The Christian life begins in the Spirit, and it is sustained by the Spirit
(3:1–5, 14; 4:6; 5:5; 6:1, 8). Everything good in the Christian life, beginning with love, is the fruit of what the Spirit does in us and through us.
Put in other terms, it is about God's grace at work to make us children of
God and to empower us to live as children of God (1:6, 15; 2:9, 21; 5:4;
6:18). Grace in the Pauline vision of the Christian life is a gift of God to
us that transforms us into grace-agents of Christ as we live in the Spirit. Grace then is not so much "pure" and "solely" gift; grace is a power
unleashed by God's goodness to us who don't deserve it but who, once
invaded by God's grace, are transformed into agents of grace.[29]

Romans 12–16, too, brings these two themes forward: Spirit and
grace. I begin in the last section of Romans, and call to our attention a
most profound claim by Paul: "For the kingdom of God is not a matter
of eating and drinking, but of righteousness, peace and joy in the Holy
Spirit" (14:17). Paul's prayer is about their being filled with the Spirit (15:13), and his Gentile mission converts become sanctified by the
Spirit (15:16) because it is all done by God's Spirit (15:19). Noticeably,
he ties love to the Spirit in 15:30: "by the love of the Spirit." Obedience

---

A number of other studies deserve mention, including James D. G. Dunn, *Jesus and the Spirit:
A Study of the Religious and Charismatic Experience of Jesus and the First Christians as Reflected
in the New Testament* (Philadelphia: Westminster, 1975); Michael Green, *I Believe in the Holy
Spirit*, rev. ed. (Grand Rapids: Eerdmans, 2004); Clark H. Pinnock, *Flame of Love: A Theology
of the Holy Spirit* (Downers Grove, IL: IVP, 1999); John R. Levison, *Filled with the Spirit* (Grand
Rapids: Eerdmans, 2009); idem, *Inspired: The Holy Spirit and the Mind of Faith* (Grand Rapids:
Eerdmans, 2013); Craig S. Keener, *Spirit Hermeneutics: Reading Scripture in Light of Pentecost*
(Grand Rapids: Eerdmans, 2016); and idem, *The Mind of the Spirit: Paul's Approach to Trans-
formed Thinking* (Grand Rapids: Baker Academic, 2016).
29 John M. G. Barclay, *Paul and the Gift* (Grand Rapids: Eerdmans, 2015).

itself is a Spirit-prompted way of life (8:2, 4, 5–6). Every believer has the Spirit (8:9–16). That Spirit groans for full redemption in the direction of Christlikeness (8:23) and it prompts prayers we cannot even bring into words (8:26–27). The moment one talks about grace in Romans, one finds one idea: grace abounds from God into the redemption of a person, who through that grace and the Spirit are transformed into agents of grace and love and peace and reconciliation (1:5; 3:24; 4:16; 5:2, 15–21; 6:1, 14–17; 12:3–8).

Here we must back up to show how pastoral all this is. The issue for both Romans and Galatians is tension in the church between a stronger presence and a weaker presence, that is, between Jewish and Gentile believers. For Paul, the one-term-fits-all Christian ethic of discipleship is love, but love is not toleration, which leaves people as they are and where they are, but a rugged affective commitment of embodied presence, advocacy and mutual growth in Christlikeness. This kind of love only occurs through the power of the Spirit at work in us and through us. The aim of Paul's ethic in both communities is not so much personal intimacy with God but reconciled relations of love among all the siblings in each of the churches.

DISCIPLESHIP AND DIVISIONS

The relational focus of discipleship (and here I focus on Romans but I suspect Paul said or would say the same to Galatia) comes to focus when Paul proposes how to deal with divisions. My contention is that genuine disciples knock down divisions among the siblings in Christ. Christian discipleship takes place at the table, and by that I mean table fellowship among Christians in Rome and Galatia and, to my Anglican ears, at the table called now Eucharist. I will focus on one passage, Romans 14:13–23.

His working conclusion, a conclusion that came to Paul over time and as a result of many tensions in his mission churches, is found in verse 14: "I am convinced, being fully persuaded in the Lord Jesus, that nothing is unclean in itself." That line for the weak, and for any Jew with any earshot of Phoebe's reading, was nothing less than a denial of all that made Jews Jewish: Food laws were identifiers. What was once an identifier has ceased being so. Still, Paul knows the reality and the heritage of the weak, and he concedes ground to them. How so? It is to the strong that he gives this pastoral reminder at the end of the verse just cited: "But if anyone regards something as unclean, then for that person it is unclean." Paul, like the strong, believes all foods are *kosher*, like Jesus did (Mark 7:15, 19), but he values the weak's convictions enough to give them respect and time to assimilate to his teachings (14:1, 2, 22–23; 15:13).

This working conclusion for the strong is expressed more deeply in verse 17: "For the kingdom of God is not a matter of eating and drinking, but of righteousness, peace and joy in the Holy Spirit." For the strong, this means respecting the weak's convictions; it means not insisting on offering to the weak food that had been sacrificed to the idols and sold in the marketplace. What was to regulate access to the strong's household dining room in Rome was the will of God in Christ (righteousness), the reconciliation of Jew and Gentile (peace), and inner satisfaction that this is the way of Christ for the people of God (joy). All in the Holy Spirit! The kingdom of God in the New Testament is more than the redemptive dynamic unleashed by Christ in the new era. It is a social matrix of God as king, God's rule by way of redemption and governance: God's people, God's will, and God's space embodied by this people.[30] As food and drink consumed embody church unity, so kingdom is embodied in these virtues for the kingdom to be what it is. In other words, the kingdom wants to become a social reality called "church."

Paul's working conclusion, then, was that kingdom of God suspends food as a dividing line in the churches. Now that the kingdom has been inaugurated in the church, that which distinguished Jews from Gentiles is erased from the equation. Theology is one thing, reality is another, so Paul remains thoroughly pastoral. How so? "[B]ecause anyone who serves Christ in this way is pleasing to God and receives human approval" (14:18). To the strong he says: *If that weak person over there is one who serves Christ and eats kosher, you need to remind yourself that the weak are in God's favor and so also to be in your favor.* That is, Welcome them! (14:1).

What does this look like in practice? Five guidelines are offered. This is where Romans becomes Romans, that is, this is where Romans becomes pastoral theology. His first guideline for the strong is to welcome the weak to the table: *Avoid stumbling blocks* (14:13b, 15, 20–21). In Rome this would mean, to take an obvious example, the strong insisting the weak eat pork from the market. The impact of the insistence is a weak person failing in her faith. Paul is not worried that Christians will disagree, for he has already affirmed diversity of viewpoints when he said some eat and some don't, some observe days and others don't (14:3, 5–6). His worry is

---

30 I argue for these five themes for the kingdom in Scot McKnight, *Kingdom Conspiracy: Returning to the Radical Mission of the Local Church* (Grand Rapids: Brazos, 2014).

the destruction of the weak person's faith! Here are Paul's terms in a graduated incline of seriousness as the passage moves onward: "stumbling block," "obstacle," "distressed," and "destroy." When insisting on eating food and drink destroys the faith of the weak into abandoning Christ, the insister is the one who is wrong.

The second guideline for the strong is *love*. If the strong insist on the weak eating food offered to idols, Phoebe, now looking them in the eyes, says, "you are no longer acting in love" (14:15). I discussed love's meaning above and need not repeat it here except to say: When love is a rugged, affective commitment of presence and advocacy that are shaped for growth into Christlikeness, intentional offense is wrong. Love does not act like that.

The third guideline for the strong concerns the *public*: "Therefore [you strong] do not let what you know is good be spoken of as evil," or, as I would render it for this context, "be blasphemed" (14:16). Forcing Jewish believers to eat food offered to idols or flagrantly offending members of their own community has the ability to get them all in trouble with the Roman authorities. This appears again in verse 20: "Do not destroy the work of God for the sake of food." The work of God here must mean the kingdom redemptive house churches in Rome.

The fourth guideline for the strong is *pursuing peace and mutual upbuilding* (14:19). Instead of insisting on one's view as the only view, the Christians of the Roman house churches are to turn their minds away from themselves and their own passionate convictions toward peace among the brothers and sisters, which means empowering others to grow into Christlikeness. Peace here does not mean tolerance. Rather, peace means reconciliation and fellowship; and for the strong, it means welcoming the weak without turning meal time into derisive, divisive debate that results in despising the weak.

The fifth guideline is perhaps the most pastoral of all: *The strong are to respect the weak's faith condition* (14:22–23). Phoebe turns her eyes toward the strong in the room: "So whatever you believe about these things keep between yourself and God" (14:22a). She gives them one more line: a blessing for those whose approval of food does not result in condemning themselves by forcing others to conform. Turning to the weak in verse 23, she pastorally offers them another way: not to eat if they have doubts (14:23a). Faith in the sense of personal conviction and conscience comes to the fore: Whatever is not based on that kind of faith is sin. The churches of Rome are not to be places of coercion but of mutual growth and respect into Christoformity.

It should have been observed by now by the attentive reader that Paul is particularly focused on the strong in Rome, namely, those who have social status and who believe in freedom from the Torah and the halakic decisions that express that Torah. My view is that in Galatia Paul's focus is on the Jewish believers, whom I called above the strong-weak. That is, those whom he calls weak in Rome are the strong in Galatia. Why this different emphasis? The answer is a key to comprehending discipleship for the apostle Paul. He thinks those with the capacity and location to make changes for the sake of the gospel are the ones to take the first step. Those with power in Galatia—the Jewish believers—were to drop their knives and welcome the Gentile believers to the table *on the basis of faith and in the power of the Spirit to create unity in love.* Those with power in Rome—the Gentile believers and Jewish believers who had joined their side in theology and praxis—were to come down from their socially high pedestal, wash the feet of the Jewish (weak) believers, and welcome them to the table.

Simply put, for Paul the Christian life—one animated by the Spirit and expressing itself in love—can be reduced to yet one more term, for in this term the entire embodiment of the Christian life would be manifested and become the virtuous practice that would reshape their approach to outsiders. That one term is found in Romans 14:1: "Welcome!" In the context of the letter to the Romans, not to ignore the entire mission of Paul in the Roman world, this one action embodies what it means to follow Jesus.

CHAPTER 7

Bearing the Image of the Man from Heaven: Discipleship in 1 Corinthians

John K. Goodrich

The church in Corinth struggled as much as, if not more than, any of Paul's communities to grasp and embody the truth of the gospel.[1] It is therefore fitting that the Corinthians were on the receiving end of some of the most pointed criticisms issued to any of the apostle's early converts. One, for example, can hardly find a more stinging critique in Paul's letters than, "I was not able to speak to you as spiritual, but as fleshly, as infants in Christ" (1 Cor. 3:1).[2] Seeking to remedy the problem of spiritual immaturity among the Christians in Corinth, Paul in 1 Corinthians identifies an array of ecclesial and ethical issues in need of attention and instructs his readers how to grow as disciples of Jesus.

Over the course of the letter, Paul explains to the church what Christian maturation involves and what being disciples looks like in the exigencies of their first-century lives. As we shall see, 1 Corinthians, like all of Paul's letters, portrays discipleship as being called by and conformed to Jesus Christ.[3] There remain unique aspects, however, to the message of discipleship in this particular letter. What makes discipleship in 1 Corinthians distinctive is (1) the progressive and comprehensive manner in which spiritual transformation is presented over the course of its sixteen chapters, as well as (2) the specific and practical ways in which Paul describes what obeying Jesus looks like in the lives of the troubled Corinthian believers.

---

1 I wish to thank Mike Wilkins for his involvement in my own growth as a disciple. First as a professor, then as a friend, Mike has been generous with his time as he has gently guided me in matters both personal and professional. Since my first year in seminary, I have sought to follow in his steps on the path to becoming an academic committed above all to serving the church. I am forever grateful to have had such an exemplary model during some of my most formative years.

2 All Scripture translations are the author's own unless otherwise noted.

3 For a similar, yet more comprehensive definition of discipleship, see Michael J. Wilkins, *Following the Master: A Biblical Theology of Discipleship* (Grand Rapids: Zondervan, 1992), 41–42.

Scholars have long been fascinated by the structure and argumentation of 1 Corinthians, observing especially how the letter is bookended by discourses on Jesus's death and resurrection. For some, this arrangement is even the key to unlocking Paul's rhetorical strategy. As Matthew Malcolm argues:

> Paul assigns a pastorally conceived unity to the complex of problems in Corinth, and allows the pattern of his *kerygma* to give overall shape to his epistolary response. The Corinthians are conceived as exhibiting boastful, present-obsessed autonomy, and are summoned rather to find their identity and status in *Christ*, who remains especially known in the shame of the cross until the day that he will finally be revealed in resurrected glory. Thus the main body of the letter (1:10–15:58) proceeds from the *cross* to *resurrection*.[4]

Beyond this basic twofold arrangement, it is important to observe how Paul's kerygmatic rhetorical structure has a corresponding argumentative logic that follows the entire process of discipleship. What I mean is that, according to 1 Corinthians, discipleship involves God first calling a person into "fellowship with Christ" (1:1–9), which leads to the person's cognitive renewal centered on "the mind of Christ" (1:10–3:4), which empowers moral and behavioral transformation reflecting the self-giving and holiness of Christ (3:5–14:40), which finally culminates in resurrection into the risen bodily "image" of Christ (15:1–58).

In this essay, we will trace this argumentative progression, unpacking each of those steps in turn, and finally show that, according to 1 Corinthians, discipleship is a holistic process that involves nothing less than being summoned by and conformed to the Lord Jesus Christ in every aspect of one's being—including in mind, behavior, and body.

RECEIVING THE CALL TO FELLOWSHIP WITH CHRIST

Paul's portrait of discipleship in 1 Corinthians begins with the Lord calling people to become his committed followers.[5] The call issued by Christ, coming as it does through the gospel (1:17–18; 2:1–5; 15:11), is both effective and transformative, amounting to nothing less than an act

---

4 Matthew R. Malcolm, *Paul and the Rhetoric of Reversal in 1 Corinthians: The Impact of Paul's Gospel on His Macro-Rhetoric*, SNTSMS 155 (Cambridge: Cambridge University Press, 2013), 2 (original emphasis).

5 For καλέω as summons or invitation, see 1 Corinthians 10:27.

of (new) creation, or a "calling into being" (cf. Rom. 4:17; 1 Cor. 1:28).[6] As Ciampa and Rosner explain, "For Paul, the call to salvation, which occurs at conversion, is a summons which is irresistible; it is not like the gangster's 'offer you cannot refuse,' but like the wooing by a lover of his beloved."[7] The irresistible nature of this calling is plain from the beginning of 1 Corinthians, where Paul introduces himself as one "called to be an apostle of Christ Jesus *by the will of God*" (1:1). Paul, to be sure, considered himself to be "the least of the apostles, unworthy to be called an apostle," yet God in his grace called Paul into his service, appointing him to and empowering him for a lifetime of evangelistic ministry (15:9–10).

While Paul's calling was distinctive insofar as it involved an apostolic commission and a vision of the risen Christ (9:1; 15:8), he insisted that the Lord's calling itself is in no way restricted to him or to other church leaders. Rather, *all* Christians receive a call to follow Jesus, since "those who are called" (1:24) are exactly "those who believe" (1:21), and those who have received a "calling" (1:26) are precisely those who have been "chosen" (1:27–28). Paul therefore refers to all the Corinthian Christians as those "*called* [to be] saints" (1:2), and he regards this summons as having been extended to all believers everywhere—both Jews and Greeks (1:24; 7:18), slaves and free (7:21–22)—who "*call upon* the name of our Lord Jesus Christ" (1:2).

Importantly, answering the call to discipleship involves offering one's total allegiance to Jesus, as is implied when Paul declares, "For he who was called in the Lord as a slave is a freedman of the Lord. And the free person having been called is a slave of Christ" (7:22). Regardless of whatever additional social connotations are attached to being a freedman or slave of Christ (and there are many),[8] in either case—whether slave or free(d)—Paul implies that service obligations, similar to those of a slave to his master, pertain to being called by the Lord.[9]

The result of this calling, then, is entrance into a fully committed relationship to Jesus. In fact, Paul maintains that believers have been

---

6 Stephen J. Chester, *Conversion at Corinth: Perspectives on Conversion in Paul's Theology and the Corinthian Church* (London: T&T Clark, 2003), 77–81.

7 Roy E. Ciampa and Brian S. Rosner, *The First Letter to the Corinthians*, PNTC (Grand Rapids: Eerdmans, 2010), 67.

8 Cf. Murray J. Harris, *Slave of Christ: A New Testament Metaphor for Total Devotion to Christ*, NSBT (Downers Grove, IL: InterVarsity Press, 1999).

9 This much is also implied when Paul addresses the church as "you/they who belong to Christ" (ὑμεῖς Χριστοῦ/οἱ τοῦ Χριστοῦ, 3:23; 15:23) and speaks of God's eschatological mission as involving putting all things under subjection to Christ (15:27–28).

"called into fellowship with [God's] son" (1:9), which is to be understood not only relationally, but also positionally. That is, as a result of their calling, believers experience union and participation "in Christ Jesus"—"who became to us wisdom from God, righteousness and sanctification and redemption" (1:30).[10] In other words, calling, and therefore union with Christ, results in believers enjoying all the redemptive benefits produced by Christ's death and resurrection. And, as we shall see next, it is in and through this participation in the person and work of Christ that discipleship takes root and spiritual growth occurs, especially as a result of the cognitive transformation that this union, together with the Holy Spirit's accompanying work of sanctification, generates within the person.

POSSESSING THE MIND OF CHRIST

In the case of the Corinthian believers, their calling into fellowship with Christ failed to produce appropriate signs of moral transformation. This troubled Paul deeply. Although they were united to Christ at conversion and therefore should have been worthy to bear the label "mature" (τέλειοι, 2:6), Paul had to confront the Corinthian church for behaving as mere "infants in Christ" (νήπιοι ἐν Χριστῷ, 3:1). They had received the Spirit of God and so ought to have been counted among the "spiritual," yet they were still fleshly and walking according to a mere human way of existence (3:3). What was responsible for their stunted growth as followers of Jesus?

According to Paul's diagnosis, the Corinthians had failed to allow the truth of the gospel to impact their moral reasoning. For Paul, spiritual growth begins in the mind. Accordingly, when addressing the church's preoccupation with speaking in tongues, he charges them, "Brothers, do not be children in your thinking. Be infants in evil, but in your thinking be mature" (14:20). And it is because of the fundamental role the mind plays within the maturation process that Paul, before ever elucidating what it looks like for a disciple to undergo behavioral change, first shows in chapters 1–2 how transformed living is directed and empowered by transformed thinking. Indeed, being made into the likeness of Jesus begins as believers take possession of what Paul calls "the mind of Christ" (2:16). But what does this mindset involve?

---

10 Gordon D. Fee, *The First Epistle to the Corinthians*, NICNT, rev. ed. (Grand Rapids: Eerdmans, 2014), 44.

Throughout 2:6–16, Paul shows how the Holy Spirit impacts the mind of the believer, participating in nearly every aspect of one's cognitive processes. Indeed, for Paul it is strictly by means of the Spirit that "wisdom" is revealed (ἀπεκάλυψεν, 2:10), known (οἶδεν/οἶδα, 2:11–12), comprehended (γινώσκω, 2:11, 14), taught (διδακτοῖς, 2:13), interpreted (συγκρίνοντες, 2:13), accepted (δέχεται, 2:14), and discerned (ἀνακρίνεται, 2:14–15). Thus, within the immediate context of 2:6–16, the mind of Christ amounts, in the first place, to *Spirit-enabled insight into divine revelation.*[11]

Given, however, the broader discussion of wisdom in 1:18–3:4, as well as Paul's reference to cognitive transformation as the mind of *Christ*, it is important also to consider the christological dimension of this reality. "The mind of Christ," as Wendell Willis explains, "is an ethical outlook formed around [Paul's message of the cross], which is manifest in the proper attitudes and conduct among believers."[12] Willis's description is instructive, for it rightly underscores the cognitive effects that accompany conversion beyond mere mental assent to fundamental propositions, as well as beyond trusting in Christ for salvation. Both of those, of course, are crucial for following Jesus (cf. 15:1–11), but according to Paul, conversion also generates a new way of viewing the world and, along with it, a radical reversal of values—indeed, what some scholars have called a "conversion of the imagination,"[13] or what Paul elsewhere refers to as "the renewing of the mind" (Rom. 12:2).[14] Ceasing to regard the world "according to the flesh" (1 Cor. 1:26), Christians are able to know and value all things in accordance with their new epistemological vantage point, "in Christ" (1:30; cf. 2 Cor. 5:16–17; Phil. 2:1–11).

---

11 Richard B. Hays, *First Corinthians*, Interpretation (Louisville: John Knox, 1989), 47: "This formulation restates in more striking language what was already explained in verses 10–13."

12 Wendell Willis, "The 'Mind of Christ' in 1 Corinthians 2,16," *Biblica* 70 (1989): 110–22, at 121.

13 As Richard B. Hays explains, "Paul has taken the central event at the heart of the Christian story—the death of Jesus—and used it as the lens through which all human experience must be projected and thereby seen afresh. The cross becomes the starting point for an epistemological revolution, a *conversion of the imagination*. For anyone who grasps the paradoxical logic of this text, the world can never look the same again" ("Wisdom According to Paul," in *Where Shall Wisdom Be Found? Wisdom in the Bible, the Church and the Contemporary World*, ed. S. C. Barton [Edinburgh: T&T Clark, 1999], 111–23, at 113 [original emphasis]).

14 Cf. André Munzinger, *Discerning the Spirits: Theological and Ethical Hermeneutics in Paul*, SNTSMS 140, (Cambridge: Cambridge University Press, 2007); and Craig S. Keener, *The Mind of the Spirit: Paul's Approach to Transformed Thinking* (Grand Rapids: Baker Academic, 2016).

Paul illustrates this kind of transformed thinking as he commences the body of the letter, by highlighting the discrete reception given to the message of the cross by its respective auditors. He says, "For the message of the cross is foolishness to those who are perishing, but to us who are being saved it is the power of God" (1:18). What the apostle describes here is the curious reality that, for unbelievers ("those who are perishing"), the gospel seems empty and arbitrary, for it is the senseless story of how an ancient Jewish peasant with royal aspirations was betrayed by his own people and shamefully executed at the hands of imperial authorities (1:21–23; 2:6–8). But for believers ("those who are being saved"), that same message resonates in a quite dissimilar and counterintuitive way. For them, the cross symbolizes nothing less than divine power and wisdom (1:24; cf. 1:17; 2:4–5), for it represents the means by which God has managed to reconcile the world to himself through the purposeful, substitutionary, and norm-shattering death of his own son (2:1–4; 5:7; 8:11; 15:3).

The crucifixion of Jesus, then, while failing to be grasped rightly by unbelievers, is for Christians the truest expression of the divine character—indeed, it is, according to Michael Gorman, "the *definitive* theophany."[15] But one must have the mind of Christ in order to perceive the cross in this way, and as one looks upon the cross in this manner, one's view of the world begins to change as well. As Alexandra Brown remarks, "One who perceives what the cross reveals is dislocated from that world and relocated in God's new creation. While he still awaits the parousia and the final subjection of all things to God (1 Cor. 15:27–28), he now waits in the life-giving apocalyptic perception of God's present and future redemption. To wait here is to wait in a newly defined territory, from which one's view of the world (and thus one's way of living in the world) is totally transformed."[16]

Properly integrated, then, the gospel, union with Christ, and receipt of the Spirit together transform the believer's cognition, such that all of his or her values are recalibrated in accordance with the paradoxical wisdom revealed in Jesus's self-giving life and death. How, then, is Christian "maturity" (2:6), that is, a life informed and shaped by the mind of Christ,

---

15 Michael J. Gorman, *Inhabiting the Cruciform God: Kenosis, Justification, and Theosis in Paul's Narrative Soteriology* (Grand Rapids: Eerdmans, 2009), 34 (original emphasis).

16 Alexandra R. Brown, *The Cross and Human Transformation: Paul's Apocalyptic Word in 1 Corinthians* (Minneapolis: Fortress, 1995), 80. "The God of the cross is the one who gave life to the world through the death of his son and by that act made weakness into power, suffering into redemption, and folly into wisdom. When one sees that this God is the *source* of life (1:30), then *all* of life (cognitive and relational) comes into new perspective (3:22–23)" (147).

supposed to manifest in the conduct of a disciple? In 1 Corinthians, Paul presents two primary ways in which maturity takes expression: imitation and sanctification.[17]

IMITATING THE SELF-GIVING OF CHRIST

Having introduced the notion of the mind of Christ in 1:18–3:4, Paul at numerous moments throughout the remainder of the letter expounds on the practical outworking of transformed thinking. The primary way renewed cognition takes on flesh is through the disciple's imitation of the self-giving of Christ (11:1). "To have the mind of the Lord," as Richard Hays explains, "is to participate in the pattern of the cross (cf. Phil. 2:1–11), for the wisdom of God is manifest definitively in the death of Jesus."[18] Two passages in particular display how the sacrificial death of Jesus provides the pattern for Christian conduct—1 Corinthians 4:6–20 and 8:1–11:1.

A. 1 Corinthians 4:6–20

Paul's discourse in 4:6–20 takes its cue from the immediately preceding section in 3:5–4:5. In that earlier passage, Paul censures those believers who were boasting about wisdom and competitively aligning themselves with various church leaders. The apostle's principal solution is to demonstrate the harmony that exists between him, Apollos, and other teachers. His stated goal is for the Corinthians to "learn in us" (ἵνα ἐν ἡμῖν μάθητε) how to conduct themselves as a community, "that none of you may be puffed up in favor of one against another" (4:6).

Paul, however, does not then cease to draw on his own apostolic example in the development of the argument. Just as the analogies involving him and Apollos in 3:5–4:5 show the church how to conceptualize its *leadership*, so Paul proceeds to draw on his own lifestyle and experiences to illuminate the essential traits of Christian *discipleship*, contrasting as he does his own cruciform existence and that of his apostolic companions with the relative ease of life enjoyed by the Corinthians.

---

17 For additional marks and metaphors of maturation in Paul, see, e.g., James G. Samra, *Being Conformed to Christ in Community: A Study of Maturity, Maturation and the Local Church in the Undisputed Pauline Epistles*, LNTS 320 (T&T Clark, 2006), 54–72; and J. Paul Sampley, *Walking in Love: Moral Progress and Spiritual Growth with the Apostle Paul* (Minneapolis: Fortress, 2016), 93–102.

18 Hays, *First Corinthians*, 47.

> For I think that God has displayed us apostles as last, like those
> condemned to death, because we have become a spectacle to the
> world, to angels and to people. We are fools for Christ's sake,
> but you are wise in Christ. We are weak, but you are strong.
> You are honored, but we are dishonored. To the present hour we
> hunger, we thirst, we are poorly clothed, we are beaten, we are
> homeless, and we labor, working with our own hands. When
> abused, we bless; when persecuted, we endure; when slandered,
> we encourage. We have become as the scum of the world, and
> are until even now the refuse of all things. (4:9–13)

Paul's list of afflictions evokes a number of images, not least the Roman
triumph. But even in the absence of an explicit reference to the cross,
Paul is clearly portraying his circumstances as a kind of recapitulation of
the conditions of Jesus's own ministry. As Hays says, "Paul regards these
experiences not merely as misfortunes or trials to be surmounted but
as identifying marks of the authenticity of his apostleship, because they
manifest his conformity to Christ's sufferings."[19] Moreover, the problems
he is busy underscoring are that the Corinthians have misplaced values,
and that they themselves look nothing like the apostle who spiritually
birthed them. Indeed, with respect to lifestyle, there is no familial resem-
blance between him and the church whatsoever.

Paul therefore issues a direct call for the Corinthians, as his spiritual
children, to begin to emulate the cruciform lifestyle assumed by him and
his companions.

> I write these things not to shame you, but to admonish you
> as my beloved children. For though you have countless care-
> takers in Christ, you do not have many fathers. For I became
> your father in Christ Jesus, through the gospel. I therefore ex-
> hort you, become imitators of me. This is why I sent you Timo-
> thy, who is my beloved and faithful child in the Lord, and who
> will remind you of my ways in Christ, just as I teach them in
> every church everywhere. (4:14–17)

Here, Paul instructs the Corinthians believers to pattern their lives after him, as well as after Timothy who will channel the apostle's example.
Indeed, they are to "become imitators of [Paul]" (μιμηταί μου γίνεσθε,
4:16) and to recall "[his] ways in Christ" (τὰς ὁδούς μου τὰς ἐν Χριστῷ,

---

19 Hays, *First Corinthians*, 72.

4:17).[20] In this context, Paul is undoubtedly referring to the pattern of Christlike and cruciform ("in Christ") living which he himself embodies and about which he is in the practice of "teach[ing] in every church everywhere" (πανταχοῦ ἐν πασῃ ἐκκλησίᾳ διδάσκω, 4:17).[21]

B. 1 Corinthians 8:1–11:1

A similar and lengthier discourse surfaces in 8:1–11:1, which concludes in a way reminiscent of 4:16—"Become imitators of me, just as I am of Christ" (μιμηταί μου γίνεσθε καθὼς κἀγὼ Χριστοῦ, 11:1). This exhortation, coming as it does at the end of Paul's idol-food discussion, is best understood not only in the light of its immediate context (10:31–33), but also, as we shall see, in the light of the self-giving ethic outlined throughout chapters 8–10.

Paul concludes chapter 10 with a summary: "Therefore, whether you eat or you drink, or whatever you do, do all things for the glory of God. Be blameless to Jews and Greeks and to the church of God, just as I try to please everyone in everything I do, not seeking my own advantage, but that of the many, in order that they may be saved" (10:31–33). Paul's exhortation to imitate him in 11:1 has, as its point of reference, his aim "to please everyone in everything" for the purpose of encouraging and enabling spiritual growth. This abstract principle, however, has concrete correlates in chapters 8 and 9. There, Paul offers his readers multiple examples of surrendering rights, privileges, and opportunities for self-advancement in order to benefit and build up others.

Paul introduces at the start of chapter 8 the same topic that will conclude chapter 10—the relationship between diet and religion. "We know," he insists, "that an idol is nothing in the world, and that there is no God but one" (8:4). "Food," moreover, "will not commend us to God." Therefore, with respect to food offered to idols, "we are neither better nor worse off if

---

20   It is important to note that imitation does not unambiguously refer to discipleship. As Victor A. Copan explains, "Imitation is understood to be subsumed under discipleship but not in an exclusive way; that is, imitation is not restricted to discipleship, because it occurs in many different relational contexts" ("Μαθητής and Μιμητής: Exploring an Entangled Relationship," *BBR* 17 [2007]: 313–23, at 323).

21   This view goes against that of Linda L. Belleville, who believes "the Pauline exemplar is to be found in a common core of ethical teachings and norms of Christian practice that were routinely passed along to new congregations," including "retaining the place in life that one has been assigned," "appropriate head covering for women functioning in liturgical roles," "and carrying out worship in a fitting and orderly fashion" ("'Imitate Me, Just as I Imitate Christ': Discipleship in the Corinthian Correspondence," in *Patterns of Discipleship in the New Testament*, ed. R. N. Longenecker [Grand Rapids: Eerdmans, 1996], 120–42, at 123–24).

we do or do not eat it" (8:8). "Some people," however, "through former association with idols, eat as if it were really food offered to an idol, and their conscience, being weak, is defiled" (8:7; cf. 8:12). And it is because of the weak consciences of brothers and sisters in the Lord such as these that Paul instructs the Corinthians to "watch out that this right of yours"—that is, the right to eat whatever one wishes irrespective of its previous involvement in idol worship—"does not somehow become a stumbling block to the weak" (8:9). Such would be tantamount to destroying a brother or sister for whom Christ died (8:11), sinning against them (8:12a), and even sinning against Christ himself (8:12b). "Therefore," Paul announces, "if food causes my brother to stumble, I will never eat meat, in order that I might not cause my brother to stumble" (8:13). In the light of Paul's references to Christ's death on behalf of humanity (8:11), together with his own refusal to consume anything that might spiritually harm another believer (8:13), it should be clear that the apostle's subsequent call for the church to become imitators of him as he is of Christ takes as its first concrete point of reference this example of self-denying accommodation and other-regard.

Paul's second example of self-denial is taken from his apostolic financial policy in chapter 9.[22] The argument commences with seventeen rhetorical questions over the course of the first fourteen verses, questions that establish Paul's right to receive support for his preaching. He asks, "Do we not have the right to eat and drink? Do we not have the right to take along a believing sister as a wife, as also do the rest of the apostles and the brothers of the Lord and Cephas? Or, is it only Barnabas and I who do not have the right to refrain from work?" (9:4–6). To establish the point further, Paul draws parallels to the rights of soldiers, farmers, and shepherds (9:7). Finally, as a way of clinching the argument, he refers to the Mosaic Law (9:8–11) and then to Jesus himself, reasoning, "Do you not know that those servicing the temple eat the food from the temple, and those serving at the altar have a share in the alter? In the same way, the Lord commanded those who proclaim the gospel to live by the gospel" (9:13–14).[23]

"But," he then responds, "I have made no use of any of these rights, and I am not writing these things in order that it might be so with respect

---

22 Paul's policy is to refuse financial support from churches he is in the midst of founding (2 Cor. 11:7–10). But he was under no mandate to do so; he adopted this policy because it was in the best interest of his churches, indeed, because he loved them (11:11). He seeks to demonstrate as much in 1 Corinthians 9. Cf. David E. Briones, *Paul's Financial Policy: A Socio-Theological Approach*, LNTS 494 (London: Bloomsbury T&T Clark, 2013).

23 David G. Horrell, *Solidarity and Difference: A Contemporary Reading of Paul's Ethics* (London: T&T Clark, 2005), 214.

to me. For it would be better for me to die than for someone to nullify my ground for boasting" (9:15). In other words, when it comes to his preaching ministry, Paul is committed to "present[ing] the gospel free of charge, in order that [he] might not make full use of [his] right in the gospel" (9:15, 18). He sums up his modus operandi in 9:19–23.

> For though I am free from all, I have enslaved myself to all, in order that I might gain the more. To the Jews I became as a Jew, in order to gain Jews. To those under the law as one under the law (though not being myself under the law), in order that I might gain those under the law. To those without the law I became as one without the law (though not being without the law of God but under the law of Christ), in order that I might gain those without the law. To the weak I became weak, in order that I might gain the weak. I have become all things to all people, in order that by all means I might save some. (9:19–23)

Space prohibits a full exposition of this passage. It will suffice to say that, by refusing to exercise his apostolic right to receive financial support for the purpose of benefiting those whose spiritual condition would have otherwise been adversely affected, Paul sought to imitate the self-giving pattern established by Jesus Christ himself (hence, "the law of Christ," 9:21). For Jesus likewise enslaved himself in order to benefit others (cf. Phil. 2:6–11), and thus he stands as the paradigm for how his own disciples are to conduct themselves in relation to other people.[24]

To be sure, the cruciform model of self-giving for the benefit and up building of others, while not always explicitly linked to the example of Jesus, runs like a thread throughout 1 Corinthians. Paul believed there existed "jealousy," "strife," and "factions" among the Corinthians (1:10–11; 3:3; 11:18; 12:25), which were the primary symptoms of their immaturity (3:3). Other-regard, therefore, was the principal treatment Paul prescribed to heal the Corinthian conflicts. For example, when he exhorts the church at the start of the letter—"that all of you agree, and that there might not be divisions among you, but that you be restored in the

---

24 See, esp., Michael J. Gorman, *Cruciformity: Paul's Narrative Spirituality of the Cross* (Grand Rapids: Eerdmans, 2001); idem, *Inhabiting the Cruciform God*; and Horrell, *Solidary and Difference*, 204–45. For additional parallels between aspects of Jesus's life and teaching and those of Paul in 1 Corinthians, see Seyoon Kim, "*Imitatio Christi* (1 Corinthians 11:1): How Paul Imitates Jesus Christ in Dealing with Idol Food (1 Corinthians 8–10)," *BBR* 13 (2003): 193–226. See also Dustin W. Ellington, "Imitating Paul's Relationship to the Gospel: 1 Corinthians 8.1–11.1," *JSNT* 33 (2011): 303–15.

same mind and the same thought" (1:10)—the mindset he has in view is undoubtedly the mind of Christ. For it is through the application of such other-regard that the church would be able to eliminate boasting in and aligning with human leaders (3:18–23). Additionally, it is only through other-regard that the civil lawsuits between the believers in Corinth would be dropped (6:7–8). And it is only through other-regard that the selfishness apparent in the celebration of the Lord's Supper would dissipate (11:33). Finally, it is only through other-regard that boasting in spiritual gifts and self-promotion would cease, for the church would then begin to devote itself to building one another up in love (chs 12–14). Thus, by imitating the self-giving love of Jesus in their day-to-day activities with one another, Paul hoped the Corinthian church would eventually reach the status of maturity they had been called and equipped to achieve.

EMBODYING THE HOLINESS OF CHRIST

The second way Christian maturity ought to come to fruition, according to 1 Corinthians, is through personal and communal holiness. To be sanctified is to be made holy, while to be holy is to be without sin or contamination. Paul taught that being united to Christ should result in believers participating less and less in sinful behavior, which consequently means they should become more and more morally distinct from the unbelieving world around them.

Although Paul was not under the delusion that Christians in this life are capable of abstaining from sin entirely, his gospel teaches that Christ's death and resurrection cleanses those who are united to him. Indeed, according to the letter opening, Christians have been "sanctified in Christ Jesus," are "called saints/holy ones" (1:2), and will be reckoned as "blameless on the day of our Lord Jesus Christ" (1:8). Moreover, Paul insisted of the Corinthians, "You were washed, you were sanctified, you were justified in the name of the Lord Jesus Christ and by the Spirit of our God" (6:11). And it is because of the sanctifying work which Jesus accomplished for believers that disciples are called to live up to the holiness they already possess: "Do you not know that a little leaven leavens the whole lump? Clean out the old leaven, in order that you may be a new lump, *just as you are unleavened.* For Christ, our Passover lamb, has been sacrificed. Therefore, let us celebrate the festival, not with the old leaven, nor with the leaven of evil and wickedness, but with the unleavened bread of sincerity and truth" (5:6b–8).

In the subsequent chapter, Paul uses a quite different analogy, yet for the same purpose: "Do you not know that your bodies are members of Christ? Shall I therefore take the members of Christ and make them members of a prostitute? May it never be!" (6:15). Because the bodies of disciples have been united to the once crucified and now risen body of our Lord, it is incumbent upon them to put into practice the positional holiness they share as members of Christ's body, that is, by remaining pure in their bodily conduct.

With respect to bodily purity, what most alarmed the apostle in 1 Corinthians was the existence of sexually immoral behavior in the church. Paul reports how at least one believer in Corinth was involved in a kind of sexual immorality "not even present among pagans" (5:1). That is, one of the Corinthian men "has his father's wife"—a euphemism for sexual relations, which in this instance involved a form of incest. Paul therefore calls for the church to discipline this man by removing him from the fellowship (5:2, 5, 13) and by no longer associating with him (5:11). Paul's hope was that by purging this evil person from among them, the believing community might be cleansed (5:6–8) and the sexually immoral person, having been "handed over to Satan," might repent and thus have his "spirit saved on the day of the Lord" (5:5).[25]

The Corinthians may have also been in the practice of hiring prostitutes (6:15–16). Paul therefore reminds the church that their bodies, which actually belong to Christ's body, are not to be contaminated. Instead, the believer's physical body is to remain pure, especially because of the fact that God, through his Spirit, dwells within them as his temple, and because their bodies will eventually be raised to new life (6:14, 19). One's physical body, Paul reasons, belongs to the God who purchased it (6:19–20). And since God is the Lord of the body, it should be used for the Lord's purposes, not for immorality (6:14).

To be sure, Paul did not believe sex to be sinful. But sexual activity must be practiced within an appropriate relationship—namely, between a man and a woman within the parameters of a marriage covenant (6:9). Believers therefore have two morally acceptable options available to them: They should either remain celibate—and thus serve and please the Lord with an

---

25 Space does not permit us a discussion about the important role of the local church in the spiritual formation of individual believers. On this topic, see especially Tod E. Bolsinger, *It Takes a Church to Raise a Christian: How the Community of God Transforms Lives* (Grand Rapids: Baker, 2005); and Joseph H. Hellerman, *Why We Need the Church to Be More Like Jesus: Reflections about Community, Spiritual Formation, and the Story of Scripture* (Eugene, OR: Cascade, 2017).

undivided mind (7:32–35)—or they should marry in order to avoid burning with passion (7:2–5, 9, 36). In either case, whether married or celibate,
they ought to seek to show "undivided devotion to the Lord" (7:35).

Thus, while Paul believed that followers of Jesus should not remove
themselves from the world (5:9–10), he insisted that they exist as a countercultural community free from all evil (5:13). Their positional holiness
is not a license to participate in sinful behavior; instead, it is a divinely
granted provision that ought to inspire and empower the pursuit of bodily and behavioral sanctification.

BEARING THE RESURRECTED IMAGE OF CHRIST

The process of discipleship in 1 Corinthians culminates in the resurrection of the believer's body. Many definitions of discipleship center on the
relationship between Jesus and his followers during the latter's pre-mortem
existence and so exclude resurrection from the discipleship process. However, because biblical discipleship encompasses conformity to Jesus, we
cannot ignore how Paul, especially in 1 Corinthians, presents transformation into the bodily image of the resurrected Christ as the climax of a process also involving imitation of Jesus's sacrificial death (15:20, 30–32).

In 1 Corinthians 15, Paul explores various matters relating to the resurrection of Jesus and his followers, not least the nature of the glorified body
(15:35–49). In so doing, Paul explains how the body, when it dies and is
buried ("sown" into the ground), is of one kind of nature, and the same
body, following the resurrection, is of another kind entirely. Paul explains,
"It is sown in corruption; it is raised is immortality. It is sown in dishonor;
it is raised in glory. It is sown in weakness; it is raised in power. It is sown
a natural body; it is raised a spiritual body" (15:42–44). This evolution of
bodily modalities, however, is anything but arbitrary. The composition of
our bodies is merely a reflection of the federal head whose image we bear
(Adam or Christ), and our participation in their images is determined simply by the phase of cosmic redemption in which we find ourselves.

> The first man [Adam] was from earth, a man of dust; the sec-
> ond man [Christ] is from heaven. As was the man of dust, so
> also are those made of dust, and as is the man of heaven, so
> also are those who are of heaven. And just as we have borne the
> image of the man of dust, we shall also bear the image of the
> man of heaven [καὶ καθὼς ἐφορέσαμεν τὴν εἰκόνα τοῦ χοϊκοῦ,
> φορέσομεν καὶ τὴν εἰκόνα τοῦ ἐπουρανίου]. (15:47–49)

As long as believers persist in the present life, they will bear the bodily image of Adam—that is, our bodies will remain perishable and weak, and they will eventually die. But as surely as Jesus, the man from heaven, was raised with a heavenly body, one that is imperishable, powerful, and eternal, so too will his followers bear his bodily image when they are resurrected into his glory and likeness.

The promise of resurrection, then, provides a vital incentive for Christians to grow continually in their maturity as disciples. As Paul declares earlier in the letter, "God raised the Lord and will also raise us up by his power" (6:14). Because of that promise, Paul is able to admonish all disciples of the Lord Jesus to "be steadfast, immovable, always abounding in the work of the Lord, knowing that your labor in the Lord is not in vain" (15:58).

CONCLUSION

Our investigation into the concept of discipleship in 1 Corinthians has shown that the theme pervades the letter, undergirding much of Paul's argumentative logic. The apostle presents the discipleship process in 1 Corinthians in a progressive and comprehensive manner, beginning with God calling a person into "fellowship with Christ" (1:1–9), which leads to the person's cognitive renewal centered on "the mind of Christ" (1:10–3:4), which empowers moral and behavioral transformation reflecting the self-giving and holiness of Christ (3:5–14:40), which finally culminates in resurrection into the risen bodily image of Christ (15:1–58). According to 1 Corinthians, then, discipleship is a holistic process that involves being summoned to and becoming like the Lord Jesus Christ in nearly every way. Thus, cruciformity—a term often substituted for discipleship in modern theological discourse—is actually too narrow a concept to encompass all that is involved in becoming like Jesus within this particular letter. Following Jesus is far more comprehensive, involving not only conformity to the cross, but also becoming like Christ in mind, behavior, and body.[26]

Moreover, Paul highlights in 1 Corinthians several practical and noteworthy ways disciples ought to obey Jesus. Christians, for example, are called to unity and peace with one another, and this should be pursued by accommodating to the needs of others and by prioritizing the spiritual

---

26 For this and like terms, see Gorman, *Cruciformity*; idem, *Inhabiting the Cruciform God*; idem, *Becoming the Gospel: Paul, Participation, and Mission* (Grand Rapids: Eerdmans, 2015); and Ben C. Blackwell, *Christosis: Engaging Paul's Soteriology with His Patristic Interpreters* (Grand Rapids: Eerdmans, 2016).

well-being and growth of others over one's own advantage. Moreover, a truly mature community of disciples should be committed to personal and collective holiness, particularly sexual purity. It is noteworthy that Paul pays far more attention to sexual ethics in 1 Corinthians than in any of his other letters, suggesting that sexual immorality was an especially challenging issue in a metropolis like Corinth. Modern churches find themselves in a similar milieu and have much to gain from Paul's remarks here on human sexuality.

These, of course, are not the only important traits of Christian discipleship according to Paul, but they speak to the very specific shortcomings of the Corinthian church, a community not unlike many local congregations in existence today. What 1 Corinthians assures us, however, is that God in his grace has provided the church with the resources and incentives necessary for even "infants in Christ" (3:1) to grow in maturity as they learn to participate fully in the fellowship they share with God's Son (1:9).

CHAPTER 8

Everything We Do Is for Your Upbuilding: Discipleship in 2 Corinthians

Moyer V. Hubbard

According to Jesus, the call to discipleship is a summons to join him in suffering and dying for others: "If anyone wants to come after me they must deny themselves and take up their cross daily and follow me. For whoever wants to save their life will lose it, but whoever loses their life for me will save it" (Luke 9:24; cf. Mark 8:34–35; Matt. 16:24–25).[1] Paul's turbulent relationship with the believers in Corinth illustrate the application of this truth in his own life, as the Corinthians gave the apostle so many opportunities to take up his cross and lay down his life. Quite apart from the numerous problems Paul addressed in 1 Corinthians, in 2 Corinthians we find that the Corinthians are doubting his character (1:12–2:4), questioning his leadership (chs. 10–12), disparaging his preaching (10:10; 11:6), rejecting his ethical admonitions (12:20–21), and reneging on their promise to help with the collection (chs. 8–9). It is no wonder that Paul begins this letter by praising the God "who comforts us in all our troubles" (1:4) and by referencing the "suffering for Christ that abounds in our experience" (1:5). Equally illustrative of the truth of Jesus's words are the fact that Paul views these very hardships as mediating the "comfort that comes from God" (1:4) and the "encouragement that abounds through Christ" (1:5).

Paul's experience of suffering plays a central role in 2 Corinthians,[2] and this theme will figure prominently in this chapter. Yet other major themes in this letter are also explicitly linked with Paul's discipleship agenda, and it would be little overstatement to describe 2 Corinthians as an extended

---

1 All Scripture translations are the author's own unless otherwise noted.

2 A few of the more important studies include Erhardt Güttgemanns, *Der leidende Apostel und sein Herr: Studien zur paulinischen Christologie*, FRLANT 90 (Göttingen: Vandenhoeck & Ruprecht, 1966); Scott J. Hafemann, *Suffering and Ministry in the Spirit: Paul's Defense of his Ministry in II Corinthians 2:14–3:3* (Grand Rapids: Eerdmans, 1990); Daniel L. Akin, "Triumphalism, Suffering, and Spiritual Maturity: An Exposition of 2 Corinthians 12:1–10 in Its Literary, Theological, and Historical Context," *CTR* 4 (1989): 119–44. Frank Matera, "Apostolic Suffering and Resurrection Faith: Distinguishing Between Appearance and Reality (2 Cor. 4:7–5:10)," in *Resurrection in the New Testament*, eds. R. Bieringer, et al. (Leuven: Leuven University Press, 2002), 387–405.

exercise in discipleship. In the final chapters Paul identifies the purpose of this letter and the intention of his apostolic authority as "your upbuilding" (οἰκοδομή, 10:8; cf. 12:19; 13:10), which can be understood as a near-synonym for the process of discipleship. The final chapters also reveal Paul's estimation of the spiritual condition of the Corinthians, which he describes as being in need of "restoration" (κατάρτισις, 13:9; καταρτίζω, 13:11). Second Corinthians, then, is Paul's attempt to disciple, or "build up," a community whom he had earlier called "fleshly," "worldly," and "immature" (1 Cor. 3:1–4) and who were still in desperate need of maturity and spiritual repair—in other words, discipleship.

Paul's approach to this acute but multifaceted disorder in Corinth is complicated by the fact he has other pressing concerns to address. He needs to explain his own failure to return to Corinth as he promised (1:12–2:4). He needs to defend his *modus operandi* as an apostle (2:14–7:4)—engaging in manual labor (11:5–11), eschewing high-powered oratory (10:10; 11:6), and enduring public ridicule and hardship (6:3–10), to name a few. He needs to reinvigorate enthusiasm for the collection (chs 8–9). He needs to confront intruding missionaries who are undermining the gospel (chs 10–13). This is a daunting agenda. Behind each of these issues Paul discerns a deeply spiritual ailment, which he bluntly diagnoses as a superficial value system: "You look only at appearances" (10:7; cf. 5:12).[3] As Paul turns his attention to these critical matters, he also provides various prescriptions for the underlying problem, sometimes more discreetly, sometimes more directly.

My presentation will organize the material thematically, treating the subjects in (roughly) descending order of importance. While one might expect that this approach would result in an arrangement prioritizing "hardship" as the lead heading, the logic of Paul's argument requires that another topic precede it—as it is this topic, with Paul as exemplar, that provides the grounds for the apostle's extended reflection on his suffering and hardship in this letter.[4]

---

3 This expression could also be rendered, "Look at what is before your eyes" (ESV). Commentaries and translations are divided. In favor of the reading offered here (so, NIV, NET, NLT, NASB) is the larger social context of Corinth's superficial value system, and the likelihood that τὰ κατὰ πρόσωπον, "things according to the face," is an idiom referring to judging by outward appearance (Johannes P. Louw and Eugene Albert Nida, *Greek-English Lexicon of the New Testament: Based on Semantic Domains* [New York: United Bible Societies, 1996], 1:369 (31.31).

4 My analysis will treat 2 Corinthians as a literary unity, taking the canonical form of the letter as the basis for theological reflection. Throughout most of the twentieth century, a strong consensus of New Testament scholars has considered 2 Corinthians to be a composite document.

"WE COMMEND OURSELVES IN EVERY WAY" (6:4): DISCIPLESHIP THROUGH EXAMPLE

A. The Example of Paul

The motif of imitation is a well-studied subject in Paul's letters, with several monographs and numerous articles devoted to the topic.[5] This theme is particularly important in 1 Corinthians, where twice Paul exhorts the Corinthians, "Imitate me!" (1 Cor. 4:16; 11:1; cf. Phil. 3:17; 1 Thess. 1:6; 2 Thess. 3:7, 9). Its development in 2 Corinthians is more subtle and often overlooked,[6] as there is no direct appeal or reference to imitation in this letter. Rather, Paul punctuates each movement of his argument with poignant autobiographical refrains that call attention to his exemplary manner of conduct, and does so in such a way as to invite the Corinthians to model their behavior, perspectives, and values after his.[7] This material focuses primarily on Paul's willingness to endure hardship, but also includes his exercise of virtue (6:6–7), and his concern for those under his care (6:10; 11:28–29). Paul's autobiographical material always has a didactic function, and in 2 Corinthians Paul presents his own story as one that the Corinthians should aspire to emulate. The call to imitation, while never as direct and overt as in 1 Corinthians, becomes virtually explicit in 6:3–10, which begins with Paul's emphatic, "We commend ourselves in every way" (6:4), and continues with, "in great endurance, in afflictions, hardships, distresses, in beatings, imprisonments, riots, in

---

The major compositional theories focus on chapters 1–7, 8–9, and 10–13 as discrete literary units. These are considered either letter fragments or independent letters that have been combined to form the present canonical 2 Corinthians. The last twenty years, however, have seen a significant shift in opinion, especially as advanced rhetorical analysis of the letter has rendered its structural integrity more defensible. Particularly important are: J. D. H. Amador, "Revisiting 2 Corinthians: Rhetoric and the Case for Unity," *NTS* 46 (2000): 92–111; Fredrick J. Long, *Ancient Rhetoric and Paul's Apology: The Compositional Unity of 2 Corinthians*, SNTSMS 131 (Cambridge: Cambridge University Press, 2004); Ulrich Schmidt, "*Nicht vergeblich empfangen"! Eine Untersuchung zum Zweiten Korintherbrief als Beitrag zur Frage nach der paulinischen Einschätzung des Handels*, BWANT 162 (Stuttgart: Kohlhammer, 2004); and Ivar Vegge, *2 Corinthians—A Letter about Reconciliation: A Psychagogical, Epistolographical and Rhetorical Analysis*, WUNT 2/239 (Tübingen: Mohr Siebeck, 2008).

5   The classic scholarly study is by Elizabeth A. Castelli, *Imitating Paul: A Discourse of Power* (Louisville: Westminster/John Knox, 1991). More recent and less technical are Jim Reapsome's *The Imitation of Saint Paul: Examining Our Lives in Light of His Example* (Eugene, OR: Cascade, 2013), and Frank Matera's *The Spirituality of Saint Paul: A Call to Imitation* (New York: Paulist, 2017).

6   Castelli (*Imitating Paul*), for example, has no reference to 2 Corinthians in her study.

7   See Linda L. Belleville, "'Imitate Me Just as I Imitate Christ': Discipleship in the Corinthian Correspondence," in *Patterns of Discipleship in the New Testament*, ed. R. N. Longenecker (Grand Rapids: Eerdmans, 1996), 120–42.

toiling . . . in purity, understanding, patience . . . in unhypocritical love"
(6:4–7). This method of psychagogy (presenting oneself as a model to
emulate) and this pattern of argumentation (employing a hardship catalog to illustrate character) was especially prominent among Stoic and
Cynic philosophers, who regularly advertised their hardships as evidence
of their virtue.[8] This Stoic-Cynic trope was so common,[9] and this brand
of philosophy so popular, there is little chance that the Corinthians would
have missed Paul's point, especially after his explicit calls to imitation in
his earlier letter.

A fuller exploration of Paul's hardship catalogs will continue in the
next major section, which will focus on the intent of hardship in the life
of a disciple. What is important to note here is that Paul's hardship catalogs are not merely a demonstration of the apostle's character; they are
also an implicit call to imitation. And Paul not only presents himself as a
moral exemplar; he also offers the example of others whose character and
behavior Paul hopes will guide the conduct of the Corinthians.

B. The Example of Jesus

Paul's earlier appeals to the Corinthians to follow his example are each
connected to an avowal from Paul that he himself is following the example of Jesus: "Be imitators of me, as I also am of Christ" (1 Cor. 11:1); "I
urge you to imitate me. For this reason I am sending Timothy . . . who
will remind you of my ways in Christ, just as I teach everywhere in every church" (1 Cor. 4:16–17). Paul emphasizes that his way of life and
his teaching were in conscious dependence on Jesus and that this was
his pattern wherever he preached. Second Corinthians likewise presents
Christ as the model the believer should follow. Paul presents Christ's incarnation (8:9), his life (10:1), and his death (5:14–15) as paradigmatic
in key respects for the believer's actions and attitudes in the world.[10]

In 2 Corinthians 8:9 Paul draws upon analogy from the incarnation
to motivate the Corinthians toward a generous contribution to the collection for the poor in Jerusalem: "For you know the grace of our lord, how,

---

8   The most important study remains that of J. T. Fitzgerald, *Cracks in and Earthen Vessel: An
Examination of the Catalogues of Hardships in the Corinthian Correspondence*, SBLDS 99 (Atlanta:
Scholars, 1988). A more accessible discussion is available in Moyer V. Hubbard, *Christianity in
the Greco-Roman World: A Narrative Introduction* (Grand Rapids: Baker, 2010), 84–87, 100–02.
9   A wealth of primary source material is presented by Abraham J. Malherbe, *Moral Exhortation: A Sourcebook* (Philadelphia: Westminster, 1986).
10   This thesis is fully explored by Thomas Stegman, *The Character of Jesus: The Linchpin to
Paul's Argument in 2 Corinthians*, AB 158 (Rome: Pontificio Instituto Biblico, 2005).

although rich, he became poor in order that you might be made rich by his poverty." As Christ made himself poor to bless others, reasons Paul, so too should the Corinthians be willing to sacrifice for their brothers and sisters in Jerusalem. In 10:1, as Paul prepares to launch his blistering attack on the intruders who are causing such havoc in Corinth, he appeals to "the meekness and gentleness of Christ" in expressing his concern that he may have to deal boldly with those who continue their disobedience. Although almost parenthetical, this brief comment underscores Paul's desire to emulate the character and demeanor of the earthly Christ in all his interactions (cf. Matt. 5:5; 11:29; Mark 11:5–37). Finally, 2 Corinthians 5:14–15 speaks of the love of Christ, exemplified in his sacrificial death, which "compels" Paul in his ministry and teaches all believers to live for others, not for themselves. For Paul, Christ's incarnation modeled generosity, his life modeled gentleness, and his death modeled sacrificial love. Paul wants the Corinthians to fully appropriate Christ's example and to follow in his steps.

C. The Example of the Macedonians

Another important example that Paul puts before the Corinthians is their brothers and sisters in Macedonia. In the same way that Jesus's incarnation modeled sacrificial generosity (8:9), so too does the liberality of the churches in Macedonia, who gave "beyond their ability" (8:3) in their collection for the poor in Jerusalem. In this honor-shame oriented society, Paul understands that extolling the superb example of the Macedonians will likely stimulate the Corinthians to at least match their donation, especially as the Corinthians were better off than their brothers and sisters in Macedonia. In the opening verses of chapter 8, Paul highlights five specific characteristics of the Macedonian effort that he wants the Corinthians to see as exemplary:

1. They gave *sacrificially*: "In great affliction . . . from the depth of poverty . . . beyond their ability" (8:2–3).
2. They gave *joyfully*: "The abundance of their joy" (8:2).
3. They gave *generously*: "Their dire poverty abounded in the riches of their generosity" (8:2).
4. They gave *eagerly*: "[O]f their own accord they kept imploring us for the opportunity to share in this ministry to the saints" (8:4).
5. They gave *reverentially*: "And beyond our expectations, they first dedicated themselves to the Lord, and then to us through the will of God" (8:5).

For both Jesus and Paul, disciples need an example to follow. While Paul is clear that the first and primary example for the believer is Jesus (1 Cor. 11:1; 2 Cor. 8:9; Phil. 2:5–11), he also understands the importance of believers modeling Christ's example for each other: "Join in imitating me, and keep your eyes on those who walk according to the example you have in us" (Phil. 3:17).

"OUR MOMENTARY, LIGHT AFFLICTIONS" (4:17): DISCIPLESHIP THROUGH HARDSHIP

As noted earlier, Paul's theology of hardship finds it fullest expression in 2 Corinthians. The hardship catalogs of 4:7–12, 6:3–10, and 11:23–29 have received particular attention in the secondary literature, but the theme pervades 2 Corinthians, appearing in numerous contexts with various shades of meaning. The motif is crystallized in the word groups θλῖψις (affliction)[11] and πάθημα (suffering),[12] but these are mere umbrella terms encompassing a wide assortment of experiences—physical, psychological, and existential—recounted by Paul in this letter: persecution, beatings, slander, imprisonment, labor, travel, hunger, anxiety, and so on.

Perhaps the most memorable articulation of this motif is found in 2 Corinthians 4:17–18, "For our light and momentary afflictions are achieving for us an eternal weight of glory beyond all comparison, as we fix our gaze not on things that are seen, but on things that are unseen. For what is seen is transitory, but what is unseen is eternal." This passage stands out for two reasons. First, it is the only passage in 2 Corinthians that explicitly links present suffering with eschatological reward. In fact, it is one of the only passages in all of Paul's letters to do so (cf. Rom. 8:18). Second, these verses speak more directly than others to the perspectival change that hardship offers. Paul contends that present suffering is "momentary" and "light" compared to its enduring and eternal achievement and calls attention to the attendant transformation of perspective that accompanies faithfully persevering in difficulties.[13] The ability to discern the "invisible" spiritual reality appears to take shape in the crucible of hardship, as the following material explains.

---

11 This root occurs twelve times in 2 Corinthians, in verbal and nominal forms: 1:4 (2x), 6, 8; 2:4; 4:8, 17; 6:4; 7:4, 5; 8:2, 13.

12 This root occurs four times in chapter 1, in verbal and nominal forms: 1:5, 6 (2x), 7.

13 The connection between 4:17 and 4:18, which is one sentence in Greek, is obscure. I take the participial construction that opens verse 18 to be circumstantial, "*as we fix our gaze not on things that are seen.*" So Margret Thrall, *A Critical and Exegetical Commentary on the Second Epistle to the Corinthians*, ICC (Edinburgh: T&T Clark, 1994), 1:355.

A. Hardship as Dying and Rising with Jesus

If 2 Corinthians 4:17–18 represents the most memorable hardship text in this letter, 2 Corinthians 4:7–12 offers the most productive text for comprehending the significance Paul attaches to suffering and for evaluating the use of this motif in this letter. Paul begins with a hardship catalog that enumerates both adversity and deliverance in a rhetorical style highly characteristic of Stoic philosophers.[14] In each instance the expected negative result is unexpectedly truncated to emphasize God's "surpassing power" (4:7): "oppressed, but not crushed, confounded but not despairing, persecuted, but not abandoned, struck down, but not destroyed" (4:8–9). Strikingly, this suffering is then defined as "carrying around the death of Jesus in our body" (4:10). Consistent with this perception, the purpose of these afflictions is that "the life of Jesus" might also be expressed "in our bodies . . . in our mortal flesh" (4:10–11). "Life" (ζωή) in this context is obviously not biological life, but spiritual vitality which energizes and sustains the sufferer. Paul interprets the intense suffering he endures in his ministry as an ongoing experience of Christ's suffering and death, which, mysteriously, allows him deeper participation in the resurrection life of Jesus. More than this, it also allows him to mediate this resurrection life to those around him: "So, death works in us, but life in you" (4:12; cf. 1:6). This passage, then, both delineates the significance of hardship for the disciple of Christ while also providing a convenient rubric understanding its purpose. In terms of its significance, hardship experienced in service of the gospel replicates the suffering of Jesus and mediates his resurrection power. In terms of its purpose, this resurrection life that suffering produces has a redemptive, life-giving effect on both the sufferer and suffering community.[15]

B. The Suffering Community

We will begin with the salutary effects of hardship on the community of disciples, for the simple reason that this is where Paul begins in the introductory verses of this letter (1:3–7). Paul opens 2 Corinthians by praising "the God of all comfort" and observes that God comforts us in our affliction, "so that we can comfort others in affliction with the same

---

14 See Hubbard, *Christianity*, 100–02.

15 In dividing the material between passages related to the community and passages related to the individual, I do not intend to imply a strict separation with no overlap. Rather, it is more a matter of prominence in emphasis. Some texts speak more directly to the effects on the sufferer, others more directly to the effects on the community.

comfort we ourselves have received from God" (1:4). Sharing in the "sufferings of Christ" (1:5), which can be understood as distress issuing from
faithfulness to the gospel, brings about a commensurate participation in
"comfort through Christ" (1:5).[16] Paul reiterates the other-directed intent
of hardship in 1:7, where he observes that both his suffering and his
consolation in Christ produce comfort and endurance in others. Hardship, then, has its intended effect when it pulls suffering disciples out of
themselves and enables them to help others who are similarly suffering.

Hardship in obedience to Christ not only has the specific benefit of
allowing us to comfort fellow-sufferers; it also has the more general benefit
of mediating presence of the crucified Christ to the world—believers and
unbelievers. Paul communicates this truth through symbolism and metaphor as he portrays himself as a captive of war being led in Christ's triumphal procession (2:14–16).[17] The imagery in this passage is drawn from the
spectacle of the Roman triumph, an enormous parade through the heart of
Rome celebrating victory over a vanquished foe. The triumphal procession
showcased spoils taken from the enemy, eminent captives, as well as the
triumphing general with his army. Temples and shrines in the city would be
lit with incense, and all of Rome would turn out to embrace their conquering hero. Paul depicts his hardship-ridden apostolic ministry as the fragrant
incense along the parade route which "spreads the aroma knowledge of
him everywhere" (2:14). The apostle notes the differing affects that this
aroma has on the participants. To some, presumably the crowds and the
conquering army (= "those being saved," 2:15a), this was fragrance of "life"
(2:16); to others, presumably the captives (= "those perishing," 2:15b), this
was the aroma of certain "death" (2:16a). While the focus of the metaphor
shifts somewhat in the telling, Paul's meaning is clear enough. Paul's suffering in the service of the gospel mediates the presence of the crucified
Christ to those around him. Through his hardships Paul carries the "dying
of Jesus" in his body so that the "life of Jesus" might be mediated to others
(4:10–12).

Finally, Paul regards his suffering as proof to others that he is a genuine "servant of Christ/God" (11:23; 4:4). While the primary aim of Paul's

---

16 Kar Yong Lim offers a full scale treatment of this important passage in *The Sufferings of
Christ Are Abundant in Us (2 Corinthians 1:5): A Narrative-Dynamics Investigation of Paul's Sufferings in 2 Corinthians* (London: T&T Clark, 2009).

17 On this reading of 2:14–16 see Hafemann, *Suffering and Ministry*; Thrall, *II Corinthians*, 1:195; Ralph P. Martin, *2 Corinthians*, WBC, 2nd ed. (Grand Rapids: Zondervan, 2014),
185–86; and Christoph Heilig, *Paul's Triumph: Reassessing 2 Corinthians 2:14 in Its Literary and
Historical Context*, Biblical Tools and Studies 27 (Leuven: Peeters, 2017).

hardship catalogs is to offer an example for others to emulate, he also sees in them an additional benefit to the community in that the afflictions themselves authenticate" his claim to be a servant of Christ, especially in contrast to the intruders (11:23–27). From Paul's perspective, enduring afflictions for the sake of Christ was a badge of honor which helped the community distinguish between a true apostle (or disciple) of Christ from mere pretenders.

C. The Suffering Disciple

One of the most remarkable features of 2 Corinthians is how, at key moments in the letter, Paul places himself in the very center of the argument. In particular, this letter highlights the emotional turmoil the apostle experienced in the course of his dealings with the Corinthians. Paul describes his tears (2:4; 6:10), his fears (7:5–6; 12:20–21), his inner distress (1:6; 4:8; 6:4; 7:5), his downheartedness (7:6), his weakness, (11:30; 12:10: 13:4), his jealousy (11:2), his anger (11:29), and of course his joy (6:10; 7:4, 7) and his love (2:4; 5:14; 6:6, 11; 11:11; 12:15). At one point in the argument, Paul even pauses to comment on how open and vulnerable he is being in this letter: "O Corinthians, we have spoken frankly to you and opened wide our heart" (6:11). Nowhere is Paul's open-hearted candor more evident and more instructive than in 1:8–10 and 11:30–12:10, where Paul recounts the lessons that he personally learned through his own experience of hardship. The precise historical circumstances of each situation is unclear, but that is quite peripheral to Paul's point. Rather, Paul's purpose in relating these traumatic events is to reflect on areas of his own spiritual and character growth in order to foster the same in his readers.

1. The Affliction in Asia

In 1:8–10 Paul references an "affliction in Asia" which he describes as "incredibly severe, beyond our ability to endure, so that we despaired even of living" (1:8). He notes that he and his associates experienced this affliction as "a death sentence within us" (1:9). Similarly, God's rescue is described as "deliverance from so perilous a death [ἐκ τηλικούτου θανάτου]" (1:10). Although some have interpreted this event as emotional or psychological distress, it is more commonly taken as a period of severe persecution, which is a more natural interpretation of the language.[18] More relevant to Paul's point than the event itself is the intended consequence of the event: "But this happened that we might not rely on ourselves but on God, who raises the dead" (1:9, NIV). Although the apostle does not specify the mode of his self-reliance, we can reasonably conjecture that he might have been tempted to take confidence in his own intellect, energy, resources, and so on. Paul's candid admission of his own deficit and need for spiritual growth is striking. God's method of discipleship for Paul and his co-workers ("we," "us") was to bring them into such difficult circumstances that they had no choice but to rely on God and not themselves. This event becomes almost paradigmatic of God's dealing with Paul. We see this pattern of interaction virtually replicated in the next passage to be discussed, where Paul needs to unlearn what he has been taught about weakness and strength.

2. Paul's Thorn in the Flesh

One of the most enigmatic expressions in all of Paul's letters occurs in 2 Corinthians 12:7, where Paul refers to his "thorn in the flesh." The apostle does not privilege his readers with the meaning of this metaphor, except by way of another metaphor, "a messenger of Satan to torment me." While speculation abounds concerning the precise nature of this "thorn,"[19] the reference to its effect in Paul's "flesh" leads most commentaries to speculate it was some kind of chronic physical ailment.[20] For our purposes, identifying this thorn is unnecessary—Paul mentions it not to discuss its nature and form, but to comment on its intended effect.

This passage is situated in a context which finds Paul defending himself against the boasting and character assaults of his rivals. Paul is forced into doing a little boasting of his own, although this violates his most basic sense of propriety and decorum (11:1, 17, 23; 12:1,

---

18 E.g., Thrall, *II Corinthians*, 1: 116–17; Paul Barnett, *The Second Epistle to the Corinthians*, NICNT (Grand Rapids: Eerdmans, 1997), 83–85.

19 A full catalogue of interpretations is provided by Murray J. Harris, *The Second Epistle to the Corinthians*, NIGNT (Grand Rapids: Eerdmans, 2005), 858–59. Harris divides the interpretations into three broad categories: 1) spiritual or psychological anxiety (for example, guilt over his previous persecution of Christians); 2) opposition to Paul, be it opponents in general, or a specific situation or individual; 3) physical malady—migraines, vision problems, and malaria are sometimes specified.

20 E.g., Harris, *Second Epistle*, 859; Thrall, *II Corinthians*, 2:817–18; C. K. Barrett, *The Second Epistle to the Corinthians*, BNTC (London: Continuum, 1973), 314–16.

11). After countering his rivals' claims to superior religious pedigree and service (11:1–29), Paul turns to his preferred manner of boasting: to boast in situations that expose his weakness (11:30–12:10). Paul first narrates his humiliating flight from Damascus, escaping from King Aretas by being lowered from a basket though a window (11:30–33). Quite in contrast to this, in 12:1–10 Paul relates his "exhilarating ascent into the presence of God,"[21] his rapture to paradise where he saw and heard things beyond his ability to express (12:4). Paul's thorn in the flesh is given in direct response to these "surpassing revelations" so that Paul might not "become arrogant" (12:7). Paul's request that his affliction be taken away is denied (12:8), but he is granted insight into God's purpose in allowing it to continue: "My grace is sufficient for you, for my power is made perfect in weakness" (12:9, NIV). Paul understands this "thorn" to be emblematic of all his suffering, which he now summarizes under the label "weakness": "That is why, for Christ's sake, I delight in weaknesses, in insults, in hardships, in persecutions, in difficulties. For when I am weak, then I am strong" (12:10, NIV). Paul's realization that his suffering and hardships, which appear to many as "weakness," are actually a manifestation of Christ's strength and may be the single most important theological insight in 2 Corinthians. This profound revelation that hardship is the channel for Christ's power to flow through the suffering disciple further clarifies Paul's earlier, somewhat enigmatic idea that, as he is "given over to death for Jesus's sake," so too "life is revealed" even in his mortal body and to those he serves (4:10–12).

"CHASTISED, BUT NOT PUT TO DEATH" (6:9): DISCIPLESHIP THROUGH DISCIPLINE

Discipleship and discipline walk hand-in-hand, be it discipline in the sense of self-denial leading to self-mastery or discipline in the sense of a parent reprimanding the behavior of their child. First Corinthians features a notable example of the former, where Paul compares himself to an athlete who engages in rigorous self-discipline (πάντα ἐγκρατεύεται) and avers, "I pummel my body to make it obey me" (1 Cor. 9:24–27). Second Corinthians contains several significant examples of the latter, involving members of the Corinthian community and even Paul himself.

---

21 Harris, *Second Epistle*, 821.

A. God's Discipline of Paul

While Paul's hardships were certainly divinely intended opportunities for growth (cf. Rom. 5:3–5), the apostle also acknowledges that at least some of these afflictions were God's means of disciplining him, in the sense of fatherly chastisement for his own correction and improvement. In 6:9 Paul speaks of being "chastised, but not put to death," using the expression παιδεύω, a term he regularly uses for God's corrective punishment.[22] It is generally agreed that 2 Corinthians 6:9 echoes Psalm 117:18 [LXX], where the same terminology is used: "The Lord has chastened me severely [παιδεύων ἐπαίδευσέν με ὁ κύριος], but he has not given me over to death."[23] The Septuagint uses this verb frequently of God's restorative discipline,[24] which informs Paul's use here, and earlier in 1 Corinthians 11:32, "Now, when we are being judged by the Lord we are being chastised [παιδεύω] so that we are not condemned with the world." In the context of a hardship catalog, Paul's assertion that he and his coworkers are "chastised, but not put to death," indicates that Paul perceives a divine hand working through the human agents responsible for the affliction. As John Chrysostom observes, "[The apostles'] enemies, against their own will, did them service."[25]

B. Paul's Discipline of the Corinthians

As noted earlier, Paul identifies the general purpose of his interactions with the Corinthians as he prepares to sign off, just before issuing a stern warning regarding his impending visit: "Everything we are doing, beloved, is for your upbuilding" (12:19). In what immediately follows Paul expresses his grave concerns regarding the continuing sin and carnality in Corinth (12:20–21), and then warns them that he will spare no one when he returns (13:1–3), even if he has to deal "harshly" with the Corinthians using the authority God had given him (13:10). Paul tells the Corinthians that this authority was intended "to build up, and not to tear down" (13:10), but he also understands his responsibility to "tear down" any false pretension that is set up against the truth (10:5)

---

22 1 Cor. 11:32; 1 Tim. 1:20; 2 Tim. 2:25; Titus 2:12. BDAG, "παιδεύω" 2b, cites 2 Corinthians 6:9 under the gloss, "discipline with punishment."

23 On this interpretation see Hans Windisch, Der zweite Korintherbrief (Göttingen: Vandenhoeck & Ruprecht, 1924), 208–09; Harris, Second Epistle, 482–83; Thrall, II Corinthians, 1:465–66; Martin, 2 Corinthians, 344–45.

24 Lev. 26:18, 23, 28; Deut. 4:36; 8:5; 1 Sam. 26:10; Ps. 6:2; 37:2; Prov. 3:12.

25 Hom. 2 Cor. 12.4.

and flatly warns the Corinthians that he is "ready to punish any disobedience whenever your obedience is fulfilled" (10:6). Paul's purpose in this letter and the reason for his severe reprimands and strong-arm tactics in chapters 10–13 is precisely so that he does not have to exercise harsh discipline when he returns to Corinth: "This is why I write these things when I am absent, that when I come I may not have to be harsh in my use of authority" (13:10). His strategy and purpose in 2 Corinthians appears to be similar to his earlier letter, no longer extant, which the apostle tells us was written out of great distress and sorrow (2:1–4), but achieved its intended effect: "Even if I caused you sorrow by my letter, I do not regret it. Though I did regret it—I see that my letter hurt you, but only for a little while—yet now I am happy, not because you were made sorry, but because your sorrow led you to repentance. For you became sorrowful as God intended and so were not harmed in any way by us" (2 Cor. 7:8–9; cf. 1:23–2:11). It is clear that Paul is reluctant to exercise his authority in disciplining those under his care until every reparatory option has been exhausted. It is equally clear, however, that Paul is fully prepared to do so if necessary, in order that he might bring them to maturity and full restoration (13:11).

C. The Corinthians' Discipline of the Offender

The disciplinary action that Paul envisions he may have to implement when he returns to Corinth is closely paralleled by the disciplinary action the community has already undertaken, under Paul's guidance, against the unnamed brother (2:5–11; 7:11–13). The precise nature of the offence is not mentioned, nor is the form of the "punishment" (ἐπιτιμία, 2:6) executed by the larger body disclosed. In an earlier disciplinary situation Paul speaks cryptically of "handing the offender over to Satan" for the "destruction of his flesh" (1 Cor. 5:5),[26] without commenting on the meaning of this symbolic imagery. For the purpose of this study, the historical details of the form and means of the discipline are not significant. What is important is that these passages attest to the presence of disciplinary activity—both individual and corporate—among the Pauline communities, and Paul's stated goal in all this to bring them to maturity: "Everything we do is for your upbuilding" (12:19).

---

26 Paul probably does not mean physical death of the sinner, but rather that his "flesh" (= sinful disposition) would be purified. This is a very common meaning of "flesh" (σάρξ) in Paul's letters (Rom. 8:4–6; Gal. 5:13, 18).

"SEPARATE YOURSELVES . . . TOUCH NO UNCLEAN THING!" (6:17): DISCIPLESHIP THROUGH SEPARATION

Paul's abrupt call to separation in 6:14–7:1 represents the final discipleship theme to be considered in this survey of 2 Corinthians. Paul introduces the topic somewhat obliquely, warning against being "unequally yoked with unbelievers" (6:14). As he continues, however, the focus of his warning becomes clear, concerning frequenting pagan temples: "What agreement is there between the temple of God and idols? For we are the temple of the living God!" (6:16). And while this topic appears only here in 2 Corinthians, it is a subject Paul has already addressed extensively in 1 Corinthians 8:1–13 and 10:14–22. In 1 Corinthians 8, Paul's concern was that "the weak"—new believers whose worldview still regarded pagan deities as gods of some kind (8:7)—will be emboldened to participate in idolatrous activity when they see "the strong" believers whose worldview is monotheistic—and who thus know that there is only one God (8:4–6)—dining in pagan temples. In 1 Corinthians 10:14–22 Paul is concerned to reveal the spiritual reality behind the food and drink consumed in a temple precinct. In Paul's cosmology, the worshiper participates in the sacrifice of the food they consume, and the sacrifices at pagan altars are offered to demons (10:20–21).[27] In 2 Corinthians 6:14–7:2 Paul takes aim at the spiritually detrimental environment of pagan temples, which were often the scene of drunkenness and sexual frolicking.[28] Hence, he concludes with the admonition, "Let us purify ourselves from every defilement of flesh and spirit, perfecting holiness in the fear of God" (7:1).

From the Corinthian perspective, temples were not simply religious venues, but were integral to the social, civic, and political dynamics of a Roman city; even family traditions and rites of passage might involve a temple ritual.[29] Disentangling oneself from all connections with temple life would entail disengaging from the community, and it is no wonder that the Corinthians struggled with complying with this directive. Paul's initial expression of this issue in terms of being detrimentally affiliated with "unbelievers" (6:14) reveals the underlying problem of vital, but ultimately injurious, social connections between believers and unbelievers in Corinth.

---

27 Paul expands this concern in 10:23–33 to include eating meat sacrificed in pagan temples in the setting of a private dinner party.

28 For full details and primary sources see Ramsay MacMullen, *Paganism in the Roman Empire* (New Haven, CT: Yale University Press, 1981), 18–41.

29 On the importance of temples in daily life see Hubbard, *Christianity,* 124–27.

From Paul's perspective, the urgency of separation was predicated on the promise of: God's presence ("I will live with them and walk among them," 6:16); God's acceptance ("Come out from them and be separate, says the Lord. Touch no unclean thing, and I will receive you," 6:17); and the resulting fatherly intimacy ("I will be a Father to you, and you will be my sons and daughters," 7:18). Paul's rationale in these verses is drawn from the holiness code of Leviticus (6:18b=Lev. 26:12), and supported through a generous sampling of Old Testament soundbites and echoes, with particular reliance on the major prophets.[30] Paul's larger point is that separation from sin has always been a prerequisite for true fellowship with God, and the example of God's old covenant people should serve as a warning to his new covenant people. To the extent that discipleship aims at "perfecting holiness in the fear of the Lord" (7:1b)—and it certainly does—to that same extent disciples must make every effort to rid themselves of "every defilement of flesh and spirit" (7:1a).

This passage also brings to light the social implications of the call to discipleship, in that the journey toward Christlikeness sometimes entails separation from aspects of the larger society and culture when such interactions would involve moral compromise. Paul leaves the Corinthians with a stark choice: experience the presence and familial intimacy of God the father, or continue to be harmfully yoked with unbelievers in practices that effect estrangement.

CONCLUSION

Paul's goal in his life, teaching, and ministry was "to present every person fully mature in Christ" (Col. 1:28). The Corinthians, whom Paul judges to be immature (1 Cor. 3:1–4; 2 Cor. 10:7), carnal (1 Cor. 5:1–5; 2 Cor. 12:20–21), and in desperate need of restoration (2 Cor. 13:9, 11), require rigorous tutelage in the basics of Christian discipleship. To this end, Paul's strategy in 2 Corinthians is to hold up important examples for the Corinthians to follow (Jesus, himself, the Macedonians) and to emphasize the role of hardship in forming character and transforming perspectives. The apostle also reminds the Corinthians of the absolute necessity of separation from sin and warns of impending disciplinary action if his admonitions in this letter are not carried out. Paul's hope is that he will not have to deal harshly with his children

---

30 See Jer. 31:9; 32:38; Ezek. 20: 34, 41; 37:37; Isa. 52:11; Amos 3:13 [LXX]; 4:13 [LXX]; 2 Sam. 7:8, 14.

when he returns (13:10), but his more important goal is to fully disciple all believers under his care, which renders discipline a sometimes necessary component of discipleship. His assurance to the Corinthians is that "everything we do, beloved, is for your upbuilding" (12:19), which is emblematic of Paul the discipler.

CHAPTER 9

Living in Connection to the Resurrected Christ: Discipleship in Colossians and Ephesians

Clinton E. Arnold

Therefore, as you received Christ Jesus the Lord,
so walk in him, rooted and built up in him and established in the faith,
just as you were taught, abounding in thanksgiving.

Colossians 2:6–7

Therefore be imitators of God, as beloved children.
And walk in love, as Christ loved us and gave himself up for us,
a fragrant offering and sacrifice to God.

Ephesians 5:1–2

As in the other Pauline letters, the terms commonly translated "disciple" (μαθητής) and "make disciples" (μαθητεύω) are absent. So is the term for following Jesus (ἀκολουθέω). But the concept is richly present through a wide variety of terms, phrases, and images. In his important biblical theology of discipleship, Michael J. Wilkins addressed this question in a chapter titled, "The Epistles: Disciples in Other Words."[1] He rightly notes: "The writers of the Epistles draw upon the rich heritage of discipleship concepts from Jesus's ministry and communicate them in a powerful way for this age when the church is united with Christ as his

---

1 Michael J. Wilkins, *Following the Master: Discipleship in the Steps of Jesus* (Grand Rapids: Zondervan, 1992), 291–310. Mike's research on discipleship has been formative in my own thinking on discipleship. But, far more importantly to me, Mike has served as a friend and a mentor to me over the years after I joined the faculty of Talbot School of Theology (Biola University) in 1987. In the early years, Mike and I met regularly for lunch, team-taught a course together over a number of semesters, and became close friends. Mike was a deeply valued mentor to me, not only professionally in my teaching and research, but in family life and in growing in my life of following Jesus.

body."[2] The concept of discipleship has a prominent place in Colossians and Ephesians.[3]

THE MESSAGE OF COLOSSIANS AND EPHESIANS

Both Colossians and Ephesians are among the later Pauline letters and are traditionally grouped with Philippians and Philemon and called the Prison Epistles. Both letters make reference to Paul in Roman custody (Col. 4:18; Eph. 3:1, 4:1). Most commentators have understood this to be Paul's detention in Rome, which most likely took place A.D. 60–62 during the principate of Nero.[4] I take the two letters to be written in close proximity of time and directed to western Asia Minor—Colossians to a small city in the Lycus Valley approximately one hundred miles due east of Ephesus, and Ephesians to multiple house churches scattered throughout Ephesus and its environs.

Paul wrote Colossians to warn believers in that city of a dangerous teaching that was threatening the health of the church. Although the precise nature of that teaching and practice is widely disputed,[5] I have characterized it as a form of shamanism.[6] Someone within the church has surfaced as a leader who has a reputation for spiritual power and insight into the supernatural realm. This person is asserting himself as a community healer, exorcist, and spiritual guide The apostle Paul took strong

---

2 Wilkins, *Following the Master,* 309.

3 All Scripture translations are the author's own unless otherwise noted.

4 Other possible places of Paul's imprisonment include Caesarea (A.D. 58–60) and Ephesus (A.D. 52–55). Of course, any of these three options assumes the authenticity of the two letters. I have argued for the Pauline authorship of these two letters in other publications. See, especially, *Ephesians*, ZECNT (Grand Rapids, Zondervan, 2010), 46–50. There are a wide variety of views of time of composition, destination, and purpose among those who see Ephesians and Colossians as pseudepigraphical.

5 One of the more popular views in the past thirty years is that it is a form of Jewish mysticism by which the competing teacher was advocating a mystical ascent to heaven experience that would lead to worshipping God at his heavenly throne together with the angels. See, for example, Ian K. Smith, *Heavenly Perspective: A Study of the Apostle Paul's Response to a Jewish Mystical Movement at Colossae,* LNTS 346 (London: T&T Clark, 2006); Thomas J. Sappington, *Revelation and Redemption at Colossae,* JSNTSup 53 (Sheffield: JSOT Press, 1991); and James D. G. Dunn, "The Colossian Philosophy: A Confident Jewish Apologia" *Biblica* 76 (1995): 153–81.

6 See my "Initiation, Vision, and Spiritual Power: The Hellenistic Dimensions of the Problem at Colossae," in *The First Urban Churches: Volume 5: The Lycus Valley,* eds. J. R. Harrison and L. L. Welborn; Writings from the Greco-Roman World Supplement Series (Atlanta: SBL Press, 2017; "Sceva, Solomon, and Shamanism: The Jewish Roots of the Problem at Colossae," *JETS* 33 (2012): 7–26; and *The Colossian Syncretism: The Interface between Christianity and Folk Belief at Colossae,* WUNT 2/77 (Tübingen: Mohr Siebeck, 1995 [reprinted Eugene, OR: Wipf & Stock, 2015]).

exception to what this Sceva-like figure (see Acts 19:13–16) was doing, and wrote this letter to challenge the Colossians to resist his teaching. In making his case to this church, Paul's fundamental criticism of this rival teacher is that he is not a true disciple of Jesus Christ, viz. he is "not holding tight to the Head" (Col. 2:19). Paul also has a secondary purpose in writing the letter, and that is to provide teaching that would serve to facilitate their ongoing discipleship—that is, to instruct and encourage them in their spiritual growth as followers of Jesus Christ.

The purpose of Ephesians is different in that it was not written to address a crisis situation. Rather, Paul writes in large measure to encourage and instruct the readers in their discipleship with sensitivity to the challenges they face in their distinctive context. Many of the new believers in Ephesus converted to Christ from a background in folk Judaism, local religious practices (including adherence to the cult of the Ephesian Artemis[7]), as well as magic and astrological practices.[8] Paul endeavors to ground them in their new life in Christ by explaining Christ's relationship to the powers, and the difference this makes for them by virtue of their union with the resurrected and exalted Lord. He also addresses the unity of the church in a setting where there has been deep Jew-Gentile hostilities that undoubtedly were carried over into the Christian community to some degree. But more generally, and as he does in Colossians, Paul seeks to help and admonish these believers to cultivate a distinctively Christian lifestyle.

Thus, various forms of discipleship language and ideas pervade these two letters. Jesus is no longer physically present, but he is very much present in their lives, and the recipients of these letters are called to understand the nature of their relationship to him and to follow his leading as Head of the church.

THE CALL TO DISCIPLESHIP

Discipleship begins with the call of Jesus to follow him. The four fishermen—James, John, Peter, and Andrew—heard this "call" and immediately attached themselves to Jesus (Matt. 4:21; Mark 1:19–20). Jesus did not come to call the righteous but sinners (Matt. 9:13; Mark 2:17; Luke

---

7 See now the excellent volume by Michael Immendörfer, *Ephesians and Artemis: The Cult of the Great Goddess of Ephesus as the Epistle's Context*, WUNT 2/436 (Tübingen: Mohr Siebeck, 2017).

8 See my *Ephesians*, 41–46; *Ephesians: Power and Magic*, SNTSMS 63 (Cambridge: Cambridge University Press, 1989 [reprinted Eugene, OR: Wipf & Stock, 2001]).

5:32). His call to sinners anticipated the outcome of his passion and how he would give his life as a ransom for many (Mark 10:45). Written nearly a generation after the cross, Paul proclaims in Ephesians and Colossians that sinners can now experience redemption through the work of Jesus Christ (Col. 1:14; Eph. 1:7; 4:30). This is the heart of the gospel.

The Ephesians received this call when they "heard the word of truth, the gospel of your salvation" (Eph. 1:13). This new life of allegiance to Jesus Christ is "the calling to which you have been called" (Eph. 4:1; see also Eph. 4:4; Col. 3:15). It is the basis of hope for eternal life (Eph. 1:18; Col. 1:5).

The apostle Paul dedicated his life to the proclamation of this call. He tells the Ephesians that, "by God's grace and mighty power, I have been given the privilege of serving him by spreading this Good News" (Eph. 3:7 NLT). He is a διάκονος ("servant") of the gospel. He calls himself an ambassador of the gospel and earnestly desires to declare the gospel boldly, even in the intimidating circumstances of his Roman custody and his impending hearing before the Roman emperor (Eph. 6:19–20).

As in the parable of the wedding feast where the king sends out his servants to deliver invitations to all who would come (Matt. 22:1–14; Luke 14:16–24), Jesus bestows on his followers the commission to extend his call to people far and wide. The language of "filling" all things in Ephesians points to this commission (Eph. 1:23; 4:10). Thus, God gives to the church those whom he has gifted as "evangelists"—not only to share the good news and issue a call to enter a discipleship relationship with Christ, but these gifted individuals equip the members of the church to do this essential work (Eph. 4:12). By the early 60s, a generation after the death and resurrection of Christ, Paul can exult in the fact that the gospel "is bearing fruit and growing in the whole world" (Col. 1:5–6, NRSV).

FAITH AS THE RESPONSE TO JESUS'S CALL

The response of faith to the call of Jesus through the proclamation of the gospel is what constitutes becoming a disciple. As Wilkins notes, "the term *disciple* designated a believer in Jesus."[9] This is seen clearly in the book of Acts, where the whole group of "those who believed" (Acts 4:32) is subsequently referred to as "the full number of the disciples" (Acts 6:2). The term "disciple" is thus "simply the most common title

---

9 Wilkins, *Following the Master,* 111.

for a person who has made a commitment of faith to Jesus."[10] "Those who believe" becomes a common way that Paul speaks of disciples of Jesus Christ (Eph. 1:19).

Thus, the Ephesians entered this discipleship relationship with Christ by responding in faith to the gospel message. Paul says, "And you also were included in Christ when you heard the message of truth, the gospel of your salvation. When you believed, you were marked in him with a seal, the promised Holy Spirit" (Eph. 1:13, NIV; see also Col. 1:4; Eph. 1:15). This act of putting one's trust in Christ can also be termed "receiving" Christ. So Paul admonishes the Colossians, "as you received Christ Jesus as Lord, so walk in him" (Col. 2:6, NIV).

The sole basis for one's salvation is God's grace, but the means of receiving it is "through faith" (Eph. 2:8). The response of faith to the gospel results in a dynamic union with the risen Christ and an objective identification with him in his death and resurrection. Paul tells the Colossians that they "were also raised with him through faith in the powerful working of God, who raised him from the dead" (Col. 2:12). The living Christ now dwells in the hearts of believers through faith (Eph. 3:17).

THE CALL TO DISCIPLESHIP NOW EXTENDS TO GENTILES

One of the distinctive contributions of Ephesians is the teaching on how the gospel has extended beyond the Jews now to include the Gentiles. This is in fulfillment of Jesus's Great Commission that his initial band of Jewish disciples should now go "and make disciples of all the nations (πάντα τὰ ἔθνη)" (Matt. 28:19).

Ephesians paints a gloomy picture of the horrible plight of the Gentiles. They are "separated from Christ, alienated from the commonwealth of Israel and strangers to the covenants of promise, having no hope and without God in the world" (Eph. 2:12, ESV). In addition to that, they are "darkened in their understanding, alienated from the life of God because of the ignorance that is in them," their hearts are hard, their thinking is futile, they are callous, they have given themselves over to sensuality, they are greedy, and impure—in short, they are utterly separated from God (Eph. 4:17–19, ESV).

But the good news is that through the gospel, the Gentiles have now become fellow heirs of the grace of God together with their Jewish brothers and sisters. They are now "sharers together in the promise in Christ

10   Wilkins, *Following the Master,* 133.

Jesus" (Eph. 3:6, NIV). The Gentiles were once "far off" but now "have been brought near by the blood of Christ" (Eph. 2:13, ESV). Jesus is now also the source of peace between Jews and Gentiles. He has made this union possible by destroying "the dividing wall of hostility" (Eph. 2:14, ESV)—"the law of commandments expressed in ordinances" (Eph. 2:15, ESV). I take this to be a reference to the end of the Mosaic covenant (cf. Rom. 10:4), which is now no longer in force. This does not extend to the moral content of the Torah, which is still highly relevant as seen in the ethical teaching in these two letters, which reflects moral content from the Torah. But the Law no longer practically functions as a protective hedge to keep out the Gentiles as it did among many Jews in the first century. There is no longer a place for ethnocentrism and elitism because Christ "has made us both one" (Eph. 2:14). The hostility has effectively been destroyed since both groups have been reconciled to God in one body through the cross (Eph. 2:16; see also Col. 1:27).

IDENTIFICATION WITH JESUS'S DEATH, BURIAL, AND RESURRECTION AS THE BASIS OF DISCIPLESHIP

A discipleship relationship with Jesus could not happen apart from the cross. The blood of Christ is the means of atonement that makes union with a holy God possible. Thus Paul says, "But now in Christ Jesus you who once were far off have been brought near by the blood of Christ" (Eph. 2:13). The cross is the basis for forgiveness of sin, redemption, and reconciliation to God. The application of this work of Christ to believers is what enables them to receive their new identity as "saints" (ἅγιοι) (Eph. 1:1, 15, 18; 2:19; 3:8, 18; 4:2; 5:3; 6:18; Col. 1:2, 4, 12, 26). Believers are not just adherents to a master; they are adopted by God as sons and daughters (Eph. 1:5). They are both "saints" and "brothers" in Christ (Col. 1:2).

Believers are also uniquely identified with Jesus in his death, burial, resurrection, and ascension. This objective union with Christ in this complex of events is foundational to what it means to follow Christ in Ephesians and Colossians. Both of these letters use a series of verbs compounded with the preposition σύν ("together with") to give expression and emphasis to these crucial ideas. Paul declares in Colossians 2:12–13:

- "you were buried with him [συνταφέντες] in baptism";
- "you were raised with him [συνηγέρθητε] through faith in the power of God";

- "he made you alive with him [συνεζωοποίησεν]" (translations mine).

Similarly in Ephesians 2:6:

- "he made you alive with Christ [συνεζωοποίησεν]";
- "he raised you with him [συνήγειρεν]";
- "he seated you with him [συνεκάθισεν] in the heavenly places in Christ Jesus" (translations mine).

Participation with Christ in his death and resurrection results in a new life in union with him. This is the basis for defeating the pervasive power of sin and the flesh so that one can live in a manner that is pleasing to God. The call to a life of discipleship is now stated in different terms than it was before Jesus's passion. Paul says, "Since, then, you have been raised with Christ, keep seeking the things above, where Christ is, seated at the right hand of God" (Col. 3:1, NIV). Because of this and because "you have died, and your life is hidden with Christ in God" (Col. 3:3, ESV), believers can "put to death" vices and sinful behaviors (Col. 3:5–11; Eph. 4:25–32; 5:3–14) and appropriate virtues (Col. 3:12–17; Eph. 5:1–2).

Identification with Jesus in his resurrection also serves as the basis for standing against supernatural forces of evil. The concept of co-resurrection entails a participation with Jesus in his victory over the principalities and powers. Ephesians takes this a step further by asserting that believers also participate with Jesus in his enthronement at the right hand of God (Eph. 2:6). One needs to be cautious not to read into this any form of triumphalism over political powers; rather, it is an expression of the shared authority with Christ that believers now have over the demonic realm. Believers participate in God's great work of raising and exalting Jesus: "when he raised him [Jesus] from the dead and seated him at his right hand in the heavenly places, far above all rule and authority and power and dominion, and above every name that is named" (Eph. 1:20–21, ESV). Christians thereby have the shared authority with Christ to follow his example to "set the oppressed free" (Luke 4:18, NIV) and "to tread on serpents and scorpions, and over all the power of the enemy" (Luke 10:19, ESV).

THE PRESENCE OF JESUS WITH HIS DISCIPLES

After his resurrection from the dead and during one of his appearances to his disciples, Jesus promised his followers that he would be with them. He consoled them with the words, "And be sure of this: I am with you always, to the very end of the age" (Matt. 28:20). Colossians and Ephesians emphasize the ongoing presence of Jesus with his disciples—he in them and they in him.

Paul reveals that the content of the mystery that has been hidden for generations and that God has now revealed is "Christ in you, the hope of glory" (Col. 1:27). Jesus has not left his disciples as orphans, but has come to them in a profound way. There is a level of closeness and intimacy with Christ now available to his disciples that was not possible even when he was physically present on earth. In Ephesians, Paul speaks of Christ dwelling in the hearts of believers and mediating his incredibly vast love to them (Eph. 3:17–18). Paul's prayer for the Ephesians is that Christ would dwell in their hearts in increasing measure and that they would grow in their experience of Christ's love to the extent that they are filled up with all the fullness of God (Eph. 3:19). For Paul, the best illustration of the intimacy of connection that Christ shares with his people is the marriage relationship (Eph. 5:21–33). The ways the husband loves his wife, sacrifices himself for her, takes care of her and tends to her to the same degree that he does for himself, provides for her, and cherishes her point to the love and care that Jesus has for his people. Just as the husband and wife are "one flesh" (Eph. 5:31; Gen. 2:24), Jesus and his people are one body. At the end of this rich passage on marriage, Paul declares that "This is a profound mystery—but I am talking about Christ and the church" (Eph. 5:32, NIV).

Whereas Paul develops the metaphor of the church as the body of Christ in Romans 12 and 1 Corinthians 12, he expands that metaphor by making Christ the head of the body in Colossians and Ephesians. As head of the body, the risen Christ both leads his people and provides for their care and growth.[11] He is not aloof and waiting until the time of his return and eschatological consummation, but he is actively involved with his people by directing the ministry of the church. Every single member of the body is connected to Jesus as head and receives grace from him for doing their part in the ministry (Eph. 4:16; Col. 2:19). Each member is equipped to serve through the work of gifted leaders that God has given to the church (Eph. 4:12). In the outlook of Colossians and Ephesians, there is no distinction between clergy and laity; all receive God's grace to serve in accordance with their role in the body (Eph. 4:7).

---

11   See my "Jesus Christ: 'Head' of the Church," in *Jesus of Nazareth: Lord and Christ: Essays on the Historical Jesus and New Testament Christology*; Festschrift for I. Howard Marshall; eds. M. M. B. Turner and J. B. Green (Grand Rapids: Eerdmans, 1994), 346–66.

Closely related to the metaphor of head of the church is the fact that he is Lord of the church as well. When a person puts their faith in Christ, they receive Christ as Lord (Col. 2:6). Everything believers do should be done "in the name of the Lord Jesus" (Col. 3:17) and their aim in all that they do should be to "work heartily, as for the Lord" (Col. 3:23). He is their one Lord (Eph. 4:5) and to him they give their full allegiance.

Colossians and Ephesians also express the ongoing presence of Christ with his followers through the phrase "in Christ" and related expressions, which occur a total of thirty-eight times in the two letters ("in Christ" five times; "in Christ Jesus" eight times; "in the Lord" eleven times; and, "in him" fourteen times). Whenever anyone hears the gospel and responds in faith, they enter into a new sphere of existence in union with Jesus Christ. This phrase is central to the understanding of one's new identity in Christ. Believers are united to him in his past work on the cross, but they are also vitally linked to him in an ongoing dynamic relationship whereby he directs them, strengthens them, and helps them by his grace. All of life is now lived "in him."

The presence of Jesus with his disciples is mediated through the indwelling Holy Spirit. As Wilkins has noted, "Jesus emphasized that the Holy Spirit is key to discipleship."[12] Believers are "sealed" with the Holy Spirit when they put their trust in Christ upon hearing the gospel (Eph. 1:13). They can receive an ever deepening experience of the Holy Spirit through corporate worship and by yielding their lives to the Spirit's filling (Eph. 5:18–20). The Spirit guides believers in prayer (Eph. 6:18) and brings unity to the corporate community of believers (Eph. 4:3). It is the Spirit who works deep within the souls of believers to effect transformation and renewal (Eph. 4:23).[13]

Although there are thirteen references to the Spirit in Ephesians, the Spirit is explicitly referred to only once in Colossians (1:8). This could, in part, be explained by Paul's emphasis on Jesus as Lord and the presence of Jesus in the life of believers in that letter. Yet it cannot be missed that there is an indirect reference to the Holy Spirit in the "filling" and "fullness" language in Colossians (and Ephesians). The way Paul uses these terms (Col. 1:19; 2:9, 10) has its background in the temple of God in Jerusalem and the notion of God filling the temple with his presence

---

12 Wilkins, *Following the Master,* 120.
13 I take the term πνεῦμα ("spirit") in this verse to refer to the work of the Holy Spirit and not as a reference to the human spirit; thus, the verse should be translated, "you were taught in him . . . to be renewed by the Spirit in your mind" (4:21–23). See my *Ephesians,* 288–89.

and glory (e.g. "the glory of the Lord filled the temple"; Ezek. 43:5; 44:4). The language is evocative of the Holy Spirit as the presence of God in the new covenant temple. Thus, Paul says in Ephesians, that "in him you too are being built together to become a dwelling in which God lives by his Spirit" (Eph. 2:22).

JESUS EMPOWERS HIS DISCIPLES

Colossians and Ephesians emphasize the theme of divine supernatural enabling. This comes in fulfillment of Jesus's post-resurrection promise that, "you will receive power when the Holy Spirit has come upon you" (Acts 1:8, NASB). These two letters stress the availability of God's empowerment, most likely, because of the concurrent theme of conflict with hostile supernatural powers that Paul addressed as a major theme in both letters.

In Ephesians 6:10, Paul appeals to the believers at Ephesus to "be strong in the Lord and in the strength of his might." He then uses the metaphor of spiritual armor and weaponry to elaborate more extensively on this theme. Disciples of Jesus need to rely on God's power because they face overwhelming opposition from the realm of Satan and his principalities and powers (Eph. 6:12). But this opposition is not overwhelming if believers draw on their relationship to the risen Christ to stand up against supernatural attack. They do this, in part, by appropriating the means God has provided to acquire spiritual power, such as, knowing the truth of who they are in Christ (Eph. 6:14), trusting in Christ (6:16), standing on their salvation (viz. knowing the implications of what it means to be co-buried, co-resurrected, and co-enthroned with Christ) (Eph. 6:17; see also 2:6), and praying in the Spirit (Eph. 6:18).

It is crucial to keep in mind that this power is relational and does not depend on technique or ritual. It comes through a deep dependence upon the Lord Jesus Christ. Paul's teaching to the Colossian believers underlines this: "For in him the whole fullness of deity dwells bodily, and you have been filled in him, who is the head of all rule and authority" (Col. 2:9–10). This would have been a great encouragement to the Colossian believers given their fear of the demonic realm and their tendency to rely on ritual means for obtaining power. Their relationship with Christ is supremely sufficient for standing against every rule and authority. They share in Christ's authority over this realm.

The Holy Spirit is God's empowering presence in the life of his people. Consequently, Paul prays that "he may grant you to be strengthened with power through his Spirit in your inner being" (Eph. 3:16, ESV). This power at work within the lives of the disciples "is able to do far more abundantly beyond all that we ask or think" (Eph. 3:20, NASB). Similarly, Paul prays for the Colossians, that they will be "strengthened with all power according to his glorious might so you may have great endurance and patience" (Col. 1:11, NIV).

Jesus bestows his power on his people not for their personal gain or enjoyment. He empowers his people to engage in witness, growth, and resisting the work of the enemy. Jesus's goal is to sanctify his people that he might ultimately present them to himself holy and without blemish (Eph. 5:26; see also Col. 1:22).

GROWING TO BECOME LIKE JESUS

The goal of a disciple is to become like his master. Jesus said, "A disciple is not above his teacher, nor a servant above his master. It is enough for the disciple to be like his teacher, and the servant like his master" (Matt. 10:24–25, ESV). Paul reiterated this goal in Ephesians and Colossians. He told the Ephesians, "we are to grow up in every way into him who is the head, into Christ" (Eph. 4:15, ESV). He saw his own ministry as far more than evangelistic (entering a discipleship relationship), but extended to helping believers grow to become like their master. He declared, "He is the one we proclaim, admonishing and teaching everyone with all wisdom, so that we may present everyone fully mature in Christ" (Col. 1:28, NIV).

Wilkins rightly noted that, "Growth in discipleship should be understood as being synonymous with what we call Christian growth generally."[14] Although this is a process of becoming like Christ in his purity and holiness (ἁγιάζω; Eph. 5:26), throughout Colossians and Ephesians they have already achieved this status; they are ἅγιοι ("saints," see above). They have received this status through the gift of Christ in his bestowal of righteousness (Eph. 6:14), forgiveness of sins, reconciliation, adoption, and their identification with Jesus in his death, burial, and resurrection. But this provides the basis for realizing their call to become like their master.

Drawing on his Jewish background, Paul uses the term "walk" (περιπατέω; familiar to Hebrew speakers as haˉlak) to characterize the ethical conduct of believers. He calls on believers "to walk in a manner worthy of the Lord, fully pleasing to him" (Col. 1:10, ESV). This is the

---

14 Wilkins, *Following the Master*, 135.

obligation of everyone who enters a relationship with Jesus Christ. So, Paul admonishes the Colossians, "Therefore, as you received Christ Jesus the Lord, so walk in him" (Col. 2:6, ESV). He expresses this duty to the Ephesians as walking in a manner worthy of their calling (Eph. 4:1).

This new lifestyle will contrast sharply with the way they once walked (Col. 3:7). He tells the Ephesians, "at one time you were darkness, but now you are light in the Lord. Walk as children of light" (Eph. 5:8). Before becoming disciples of Christ, they walked in accordance with the world, the flesh, and the devil (Eph. 2:2–3), but now they are to live in accordance with their new nature being transformed by the power of the Spirit (Eph. 4:17–24).

Ephesians and Colossians describe this process in terms of "taking off the old self" and "putting on the new self" (Col. 3:9–11; Eph. 4:22–24). The "old self" (παλαιὸς ἄνθρωπος) is more than a set of habits, a mindset, or a lifestyle. It is a way of referring to believers in terms of their solidarity with Adam in his sin. He represents humanity in his fallenness and sinfulness. By contrast, Christ represents the new humanity. All who enter a discipleship relationship with Christ are united with him in his newness of life and have become a new creation in Christ. The relationship of every believer to the "old self" and "new self" needs to be seen in an eschatological perspective. This change of identity has already taken place, but it has not yet been realized in the daily lives of believers. Colossians stresses the already side of this tension by using the aorist participle to describe what has taken place: "having stripped off the old self with its practices and having put on the new self" (Col. 3:9–10). Ephesians, however, emphasizes the obligation of believers: "you were taught in him . . . to take off the old self that corresponds to your former manner of life . . . [and] to put on the new self that was created in the likeness of God in righteousness and holiness of truth" (Eph. 4:22–24). As in Romans 6:6, the old self has not totally been destroyed upon conversion.[15] It is still present and attempts to assert its control, just as the "flesh," in spite of the fact that Paul says it, too, has been crucified (Gal. 5:24). The difference is that, now, believers are no longer in slavery to the old self as an overwhelmingly compelling force. Its power has been broken and believers have the freedom to live in obedience to Christ. But more than that, their true identity is now determined by the new self, they are in a dynamic empowering relationship with the risen

---

15 See James D. G. Dunn, *The Theology of the Apostle Paul* (Grand Rapids: Eerdmans, 1998), 471.

Christ, and they possess the Spirit of God who is at work to transform them into the image of Christ.

After laying this foundation, Paul describes what transformation through the Spirit involves, focusing on three central aspects of the Christian life: vices and virtues, prayer, and community.

1. Vices and Virtues

First, Paul gives lists of vices that need to be eradicated from the lives of believers. In Colossians, he begins this list with the jarring command to "kill them" (νεκρώσατε; Col. 3:5). This image personifies the vices as alive, active, and powerful enemies. As John Owen explained in his classic work, *Of the Mortification of Sin in Believers*, "indwelling sin is compared to a person, a living person, called 'the old man,' with his faculties, and properties, his wisdom, craft, subtlety, strength; this says the apostle, must be killed, put to death, mortified—that is, have its power, life, vigour, and strength, to produce its effects, taken away by the Spirit."[16] Among the practices Paul specifically names in Colossians are sexual immorality, lust, greed, wrath, malice, slander, filthy talk, bitterness, and lying (Col. 3:5–9). He names a far more extensive list of evil practices in Ephesians that include these, but others such as, coveting, boasting, rage, yelling, malicious talk, dirty jokes, stealing, drunkenness, and others (Eph. 4:25–31; 5:3–20).

In place of these vices, Paul appeals to them to put on an array of virtues. These are pleasing to God and reflect the character and integrity of the Lord Jesus Christ. He exhorts the Colossians to "put on, then, as God's chosen ones, holy and beloved, compassionate hearts, kindness, humility, meekness, and patience" (Col. 3:12). He elaborates on a variety of other virtues and practices that would be consistent with their new identity as saints who belong to God. Similarly, in Ephesians, Paul commends numerous virtues that should characterize their lives as disciples of Christ. These include holiness, righteousness, blamelessness, wisdom, peace, patience, kindness, goodness, gentleness, faithfulness, tenderheartedness, truthfulness, humility, forgiveness, unity, and still others (Eph. 1:4; 4:1–3; 4:24; 4:25–5:2; 5:3–14).

The most important virtue of all is love. This is the epitome of what it means to be a follower of Jesus Christ. Paul tells the Colossians that love exceeds all the other virtues and that it "binds everything together

---

16 John Owen, *Of the Mortification of Sin in Believers* (Edinburgh: Banner of Truth Trust, 1967), 8. This volume was originally published in 1656.

in perfect harmony" (Col. 3:14). He exhorts the Ephesians, "Therefore be imitators of God, as beloved children. And walk in love, as Christ loved us and gave himself up for us, a fragrant offering and sacrifice to God" (Eph. 5:1–2). The language of "imitation" (μιμητής) is discipleship language meaning "to emulate" or "follow after." It is noteworthy that the only time this term appears in these two letters is to call believers to emulate the greatest example of love ever known—Jesus's self-sacrificial love that led him to a violent death on the cross for people who were undeserving. Jesus is the model for believers of self-sacrificial love (Eph. 5:25). The example that Jesus gives to his followers perfectly fulfills what he instructed his disciples to do in the Sermon on the Mount: "But I say to you, love your enemies" (Matt. 5:44; see also Luke 6:27, 35).

2. Prayer

Jesus taught his disciples to pray (Matt. 6:7–15; Luke 11:1–4) and Paul relied on this relational dependence to God and modeled its importance to his communities. He told the Colossians, "Devote yourselves to prayer, being watchful and thankful" (Col. 4:2, NIV). He saw prayer as the essence of how to stand against the attacks of spiritual powers, listing it as the final and most important weapon in the arsenal of believers. He says, "pray in the Spirit on all occasions with all kinds of prayers and requests. With this in mind, be alert and always keep on praying for all the saints" (Eph. 6:18). Paul begins both of these letters by reporting his regular prayers of thanksgiving to God for these believers (Col. 1:3–8; Eph. 1:16). He then lets each of these groups know that he is interceding regularly to God on their behalf and tells them, specifically, what kinds of things he is asking God to do for them (Col. 1:9–14; Eph. 1:15–23). For the Colossians, these requests include knowing God better, knowing his will, that they would live their lives in a manner worthy of the Lord, and for grace, wisdom, understanding, and strength. For the Ephesians, they include: knowing God better; for the Spirit's help and illumination; growing in understanding their hope, their value to God as his inheritance; and the vastness of God's power available to them. In Ephesians, he includes a second intercessory prayer report that picks up some of the same themes from the first and develops them (3:14–21). In particular, he prays that God would strengthen them, that Christ would dwell in their hearts in increasing measure (viz. that Christ would truly be Lord of their lives in every respect), and that they would know and experience Christ's love in all of its depths.

For Paul, prayer is also a time for worship, praise, and blessing God. He thus begins Ephesians with a moving and poetic expression of blessing God for all of his rich blessings to his people (Eph. 1:3–14). Both letters commend the singing of psalms, hymns, and spiritual songs as a mode of praise to God (Col. 3:16; Eph. 5:19–20). But prayer is also a time of laboring and even struggle. Paul commends to the Colossians the example of Epaphras who was "always struggling on your behalf in his prayers, that you may stand mature and fully assured in the will of God" (Col. 4:12). The advancement of the kingdom through the spread of the gospel is a major concern of Paul's in his prayers and in soliciting prayer from his communities, as he does from the Ephesians: "Pray also for me, that whenever I speak, words may be given me so that I will fearlessly make known the mystery of the gospel, for which I am an ambassador in chains. Pray that I may declare it fearlessly, as I should" (Eph. 6:19–20 NIV; see also Col. 4:3).

3. Community

Jesus taught that, "whoever does the will of my Father in heaven is my brother and sister and mother" (Matt. 12:50). Paul embraced this deeply and consistently referred to fellow believers as brothers and sisters (ἀδελφοί). The disciple of Jesus not only enters a relationship with Jesus, but is joined to other believers in a family relationship. Paul uses kinship terminology throughout Colossians and Ephesians (Col. 1:1–2; 4:7, 9, 15; Eph. 6:21, 23). His passion is to band these individual disciples together into bonded relationships in community where they serve one another, grow together, and reach out to the world filling it with the fragrance of the redemptive gospel of Christ.

Living in Christian community, however, means maintaining existing household relationships. Thus, Paul provides instructions to every member of the household on how to live as Christians within their household social structures (Col. 3:18–4:1; Eph. 5:22–6:9). He addresses three pairs of relationships: wives and husbands, children and fathers, and bondservants and earthly masters. The fact that he addresses wives, children, and bondservants first and as independent moral agents ascribes to them a social dignity that is unparalleled in the ancient world. There is much in these household codes that is counter to prevailing Greco-Roman culture and represents a distinctive vision for the Christian household that is deeply informed by Jesus Christ and his ethics.

The community of disciples lives in a world that can be dangerous and hostile to the message of Jesus. This is due to the ongoing influence of sin in the lives of people and because of the pervasive influence of hostile spiritual powers intent on thwarting and undoing the redemptive work of God in the world. Paul warns the Ephesians generally of the potential danger from the trickery and craftiness of certain people who engage in strategy of deception through their teaching (Eph. 4:14). This concern has already been realized at Colossae where a dangerous and deceitful teaching has emerged that is leading people away from Christ (Col. 2:4–5, 8–23). Paul's vision for maintaining the health and stability of the church is for all believers to maintain a close and vital connection to the exalted Christ who is the head of the church (Col. 2:19). This involves a dependence on fellow members of the body of Christ who become channels of God's grace to each of the members. In Ephesians, this includes relying on the gifted leaders of the church who teach and equip the members so they can stand firm and grow as a body (Eph. 4:7–16).

The vision that Paul casts for these disciples is not to remain inwardly focused, but to outwardly serve, each one according to the special grace that God has given (Eph. 4:7, 16). This involves a commitment to living a life of good works (Col. 1:10; Eph. 2:10). It involves taking the gospel of Christ to a lost world and "filling" the world with the extraordinary news of the redemption and salvation available in Christ Jesus (Eph. 1:23; 4:10; see also Col. 1:5). The spread of the gospel and building communities for teaching, learning, and growth is the heart of the Great Commission that Jesus gave to his original disciples (Matt. 28:18–20). Paul lives this pattern out and commends it in Colossians and Ephesians.

CONCLUSION

Although Jesus is no longer physically present for his disciples to hear, watch, and follow where he goes, he is present with his people—and profoundly so. He is with them and in them. And they are in him. There is a level of intimacy and closeness between Jesus and his people that can only be approximated by a comparison to marriage. This presence is not only a comfort and encouragement to Jesus's followers, it gives them direction and empowerment. Jesus is dynamically present with his disciples through the fact that they constitute his "body." And Jesus continues his ministry through this body that is present in far more locations than the incarnate Jesus could ever be. Through this expanding and growing body, Jesus continues to proclaim his good news of the possibility of redemption and reconciliation with God. Jesus functions as the head of this diverse yet unified body—providing it with direction and supplying it with strength; teaching; equipping; and the resources it needs to carry out its mission to fill the world.

The basis for the life of discipleship is not only the forgiveness of sin extended to believers through the blood of Christ shed on the cross, but also through identification with Jesus in his death, resurrection, exaltation, and new life. Because of this union with Jesus, believers are empowered to live a life of discipleship and to please God in every respect. They can stand against spiritual opposition, engage in the mission that God has given them, and reflect the moral character of Jesus in their lives.

Ephesians and Colossians thus expand upon, deepen, and enrich the concept of discipleship reflected in the Gospels. These letters reflect a post-resurrection perspective and endeavor to prepare believers for their life of discipleship in local Christian communities.

Looking to the Interests of Others: Discipleship in Philippians and Philemon

Joseph H. Hellerman

Jesus gave the definitive description of discipleship in Matthew 28:19–20a: "Go therefore and make disciples of all nations, baptizing them in the name of the Father and of the Son and of the Holy Spirit, teaching them to observe all that I have commanded you."[1] Discipleship involves an initial response to the call of Christ ("baptizing"), followed by a process of increasing alignment with the teachings of Jesus in both mindset and behavior ("teaching them to observe all that I have commanded you").

In what follows I will consider the latter aspect of discipleship as we see it reflected in two of Paul's letters: Philippians and Philemon.

JESUS'S CHALLENGE TO SERVANTHOOD

One of the most strikingly counter-cultural instructions Jesus gave to his followers—modeled in Jesus's life and his death—required a radical reconstruction of the social pecking order. To a pair of disciples jockeying for preeminent positions in the eschatological kingdom, Jesus replied:

> You know that those who are considered rulers of the Gentiles lord it over them, and their great ones exercise authority over them. But it shall not be so among you. But whoever would be great among you must be your servant, and whoever would be first among you must be slave of all. For even the Son of Man came not to be served but to serve, and to give his life as a ransom for many. (Mark 10:42–45, ESV)

The call to other-centered living is a timeless one that has forcefully confronted the social norms and personal propensities of Christians throughout history. The challenge proved particularly counter-cultural in the highly stratified honor culture of Roman antiquity. Yet for Jesus's

---

1 All Scripture translations are the author's own unless otherwise noted.

earliest followers the mindset and behavior reflected in Mark 10:42–45 essentially epitomized what it meant to be a disciple of Christ.

The inversion of social priorities surfaces, in various forms, throughout the gospel traditions (e.g., Matt. 20:24–28; Luke 22:24–27; John 13:1–17). The notion reappears as a key theme in Philippians and Philemon, where leveraging one's social position and resources in the service of others constitutes an indispensable aspect of Christian discipleship.

FOLLOWING AFTER JESUS IN PHILIPPIANS

Philippians can fairly be read as a commentary of sorts on Jesus's teaching in Mark 10, from a missionary in the trenches who modeled Christlike servanthood to others. Philippians exhibits three notable parallels to Jesus's teaching in Mark 10:

Theme	Jesus	Paul
A. Radical Reconstruction of Social Priorities	Mark 10:42–43	Philippians 2:3–4
B. Illustrated by Slave Imagery	Mark 10:44	Philippians 2:7
C. Exemplified in the Death of Jesus	Mark 10:45	Philippians 2:8

In Mark 10, Jesus (A) challenges his disciples to use any status or authority they might possess in the service of others (vv. 42–43), by drawing upon (B) slave imagery (v. 44) and (C) the example of his impending death (v. 45).

In similar fashion in Philippians, Paul (A) commends a radical reconstruction of Roman Philippi's honor culture to his readers (2:3–4); and uses the themes of (B) slavery as well (2:7) and (C) the death of Christ (2:8) to illustrate this crucial aspect of discipleship. I will examine each of these parallels and then consider several examples (D) of faithful discipleship in Paul's letter.

A. Radical Reconstruction of Social Priorities

Paul wrote Philippians to a community of Christians living in a Roman colony. Patristic evidence suggests that the Gospel of Mark was written in Rome. A brief overview of Roman cultural values and social codes will underscore the radical nature of Jesus's teaching in Mark 10, and it will helpfully illuminate the manner in which Paul contextualized Jesus's countercultural approach to honor and status in his letter to the Philippians.

Rome was arguably the most status-conscious culture in the ancient Mediterranean world—a people "obsessed with maintaining social distinctions and hierarchy," as a recent writer has noted.[2] Literary and archaeological data converge, moreover, to demonstrate that Philippi was the most characteristically Roman settlement in the East, when Paul arrived in Macedonia during his second missionary journey.

1. Roman Honor Culture

Two basic realities marked Rome's social values: (1) a profound degree of social stratification, and (2) intense competition among families for public honor within each social class.

Social Stratification. The Roman social hierarchy distinguished most basically between elites, who represented perhaps one to two percent of the empire's population, and non-elites. Further stratification, among both elites and non-elites, generated the following pecking order during the New Testament era:

The Elite Orders

Senators—@ 600
    Nobles
    New Men
Equestrians—@ 20,000
    Most Renowned
    Most Accomplished
    Excellent
Decurions—@ 150–200,000
    Two Council Leaders
    Other Decurions

The Non-Elite Orders

Citizens
Non-Citizens
    Free
    Freedman
    Slave

---

2 Helen Rhee, *Loving the Poor, Saving the Rich: Wealth, Poverty, and Early Christian Formation* (Grand Rapids: Baker Academic, 2012), 6.

Social status was generally an inherited trait in the Roman world, and social mobility, as we know it in society today, was rare. With some exceptions, wealth—a legal requirement for membership in the elite orders—was kept in the family and handed down from generation to generation.[3]

The social distinctions mapped above were inscribed in the legal system, and they were publicly communicated in a variety of ways. Clothing, for example, functioned as an important status symbol and was, in some instances, highly regulated. Persons in the empire also sat according to rank at public and private events. The hierarchy found expression in the courtroom, as well, where elite judges handed out different sentences for the same crime, depending on the status of the defendant.

Competition for Public Honor. Within each of the social classes listed above, competition for honor marked life at every turn.[4] Cicero aptly summarizes the centrality of honor in Rome's social economy:

> By nature we yearn and hunger for honor, and once we have glimpsed, as it were, some part of its radiance, there is nothing we are not prepared to bear and suffer in order to secure it. (*Tusc* 2.24.58)[5]

Since honor was "fundamentally the *public* recognition of one's social standing" by one's social peers, virtually every interaction with persons outside one's immediate family served as an arena in which to compete for personal and familial prestige.[6] Daily life among Rome's elites thus

---

3 My brief overview inevitably involves a degree of oversimplification. The traditional two-tiered view of wealth and poverty in the ancient world has been qualified in recent scholarship. See, for example, the works of Bruce W. Longenecker, *Remember the Poor: Paul, Poverty, and the Greco-Roman World* (Grand Rapids: Eerdmans, 2010), following Steve J. Friesen, "Poverty in Pauline Studies: Beyond the So-Called New Consensus," *JSNT* 26 (2004): 323–61. For a helpful introduction to class distinctions and legislation related to the social hierarchy during the Julio–Claudian era, see Susan Treggiari, "Social Status and Social Legislation," in *The Cambridge Ancient History, Vol. 10: The Augustan Empire, 44 BC–AD 69*, 2nd rev. ed., eds A. Bowman, et al. (Cambridge: Cambridge University Press, 1996), 873–904.

4 Honor may be defined as "the positive value of a person in his or her own eyes plus the positive appreciation of that person in the eyes of his or her social group" (Bruce J. Malina and Jerome H. Neyrey, "Honor and Shame in Luke-Acts," in *The Social World of Luke–Acts*, ed. J. H. Neyrey [Peabody, MA: Hendrickson, 1991], 25–26).

5 Trans. Carlin A. Barton, *Roman Honor: The Fire in the Bones* (Berkeley: University of California Press, 2001), 37.

6 Halvor Moxnes, "Honor and Shame," in *The Social Sciences and New Testament Interpretation*, ed., R. Rohrbaugh (Peabody, MA: Hendrickson, 1996), 19–40, at 20 (original italics).

became "a ceaseless, restless quest for distinction in the eyes of one's peers and of posterity."[7]

The quest for honor manifested itself in some culturally specific ways. Most prominent for the senatorial class was the hierarchy of public offices known as the *cursus honorum,* or race of honors. Successful senators who ascended the *cursus* amassed a corresponding set of increasingly prestigious titles, e.g., quaestor, aedile, praetor, prefect, consul, and proconsul.

The practice of urban benefaction, in turn, gave such individuals the opportunity to boast of these honors in public and thereby reinforce and enhance their status in the eyes of others. Thus Pliny—an esteemed senator who had won the titles of quaestor, tribune, praetor, prefect, and who, finally, ascended to the top of Rome's *cursus honorum* to become consul (and later became governor of Pontus and Bithynia)—instructs a client as follows:

> I have lately purchased with a legacy that was left to me a statue of Corinthian bronze [prized by Roman connoisseurs] . . . with a design of fixing it in some conspicuous place in my native province. . . . Pray, then, undertake this, as readily as you do all my commissions, and give immediate orders for a pedestal to be made. I leave the choice of marble to you, but *let my name be engraved upon it, and, if you think proper, my titles.* (*Ep.* 3.6, my italics)[8]

Honor, not wealth, was the most valuable commodity in the eyes of ancient Romans. Accordingly, Pliny invests money that he inherited in a statue which he situates in his homeland, in order publicly to associate his "name" with his "titles," and thereby remind passersby of the honors he won along Rome's *cursus honorum.*

2. Competition for Honor in Philippi

Cursus ideology and the related practice of urban benefaction were replicated among lower elite orders in local municipalities. Decurion families in Philippi, for example, competed for honor by funding publics works in the colony's forum. The following inscription, honors the Decimii family for their fountain project:

---

7   Jon E. Lendon, *Empire of Honour: The Art of Government in the Roman World* (Oxford, Clarendon Press, 1997), 35. Much of what follows summarizes Joseph H. Hellerman, *Reconstructing Honor in Roman Philippi: Carmen Christi as Cursus Pudorum,* SNTSMS 132 (Cambridge: Cambridge University Press, 2005), 3–108. See, too, Barton, *Roman Honor.*

8   Greco-Roman sources are cited from the Loeb Classical Library, unless otherwise noted.

> Lucius Decimius Bassus, the son of Lucius, from the tribe Voltinia, aedile of Philippi, has, on the basis of his will, ordered (this fountain) to be made for himself and for Lucius Decimius, the son of Lucius, from the tribe Voltinia, the quaestor and duumvir of Philippi, his father, and for Gaius Decimius Maxsimus, the son of Lucius, out of the tribe Voltinia, his brother, at a cost of 30,000 sesterces.[9]

The wealthy benefactor, Lucius Decimius Bassus, wants others to know that he spent the equivalent of more than thirty years of wages for the average Roman soldier, in order to build a fountain for Philippi's forum. "Voltinia" in the inscription identifies the family's Roman citizen tribe.

Not to be outdone, another elite family situated two inscriptions in Philippi's forum in close proximity to the Decemii project attested above. Both monuments were erected by Gaius Mucius Scaeva, who honors his father and his uncle, respectively:

> For Gaius Mucius Scaeva, son of Quintus, from the tribe Fabia, the first centurion of the Sixth legion, Ferrata, prefect of the cohort, on the basis of his own will, Gaius Mucius Scaeva, son of Gaius, has set up (this inscription).

> For Publius Mucius, son of Quintius of the tribe Voltinia, centurion of the Sixth Legion Ferrata, *duumvir iure dicundo* in Philippi, Gaius Mucius Scaeva, the son of Gaius, has set up (this inscription) on the basis of the will of Gaius Mucius Scaeva, son of Quintius, of the tribe Fabia.[10]

The close proximity in the Philippian forum of the Decimii inscriptions to those honoring members of the Mucii family speaks volumes about the way in which elite families competed for honor in a status-conscious Roman colony.

Note the concern to list titles acquired by the benefactors and their family members: "aedile," "quaestor," "duumvir," "centurion," "prefect." Local decurions replicated the senatorial *cursus* in miniature in towns like Philippi, even parroting titles such as "quaestor" and "aedile" from the *cursus* in Rome.

---

9 213/L347 (2nd c. CE). The inscriptions are numbered following Peter Pilhofer, *Philippi. Band 2: Katalog der Inschriften von Philippi* (Tübingen: J. C. B. Mohr, 2000 [rev. 2009]). The English translations are mine.

10 218/L352 (2nd half of 2nd c. CE); 219/L353 (2nd half of 2nd c. CE).

The following inscription outlines the *cursus* of yet another Philippian aristocrat:

> Publius Marius Valens, son of Publius, from the tribe Voltinia, honored with the decorations of a decurion, aedile, also decurion of Philippi, priest of the divine Antoninus Pius, duumvir, sponsor of games.[11]

A municipal career formally began with admission to the decurion council and the office of aedile (or, more likely, quaestor). An aristocrat would then set his sights on the primary honor of the decurion class, namely, the office of duumvir. The magistrates who beat and imprisoned Paul and Silas in Philippi held the office of duumvir in the colony (Acts 16:19–24).

The phenomenon of value replication, whereby local aristocrats like Philippi's decurions adopted the social values of senatorial elites in Rome, guaranteed that these values and associated practices would trickle down further, to the lower, non-elite, classes. As Horace colorfully expressed it, "Glory drags along the obscure no less than the nobly born bound to her shining chariot" (*Sat.* 1.6.23–4).[12]

Non-elite groups in Philippi included: a Bacchus cult; a group devoted to Cybele; a gathering that met to celebrate the Thracian god Suregethes; a Diana cult; an organization of persons dedicated to Dionysius; an association that venerated Isis and Serapis; and a cult that worshipped the god Silvanus.[13] Like the Jesus community in Philippi, these were small religious assemblies of less than fifty persons, made up of rural peasants, the urban poor, or other groups of commoners.

Nearly all of the inscriptions produced by these associations, moreover, include references to official titles held by their members. The most extensive epigraphic data comes from the Silvanus cult. Included is a detailed list of worshippers who financed a temple project. The inscription relates the names of those who contributed, the amount that each donated, and the contributor's honorific title, where applicable.

Non-elite groups consistently replicated in miniature the honor-seeking values and practices of their social betters among Philippi's elite

---

11   395/L780 (after 161 CE).
12   Trans. Lendon, *Empire of Honour,* 97.
13   340/L589 (Bacchus), 321/L377 (Cybele), 133/G441 (Suregethes), 451/L158, 519/L245 (Diana), 524/L103, 525/L104, 597/G221 (Dionysius), 252/L467, 307/G410 (Isis and Serapis).

decurion class. In the words of Ramsay MacMullen, they "ape(d) the high-sounding terminology of larger, municipal bodies, the nomenclature of officialdom . . . and constituted in every detail miniature cities."[14]

We can thus locate the characteristically Roman "restless quest for distinction" at every point along the social spectrum in ancient Philippi—competition for honor marked the lives of elites and non-elites alike.[15] It would have been quite natural for the church in the colony to adopt the same cultural values and social codes. Paul, however, had a very different vision for human relationships among those who sought to pattern their lives after Jesus.

3. Reconstructing Honor in Roman Philippi

To the small Jesus community that he had established in the very midst of this culture of competitive honor-seeking and self-promotion, Paul wrote the following:

> Do nothing from selfish ambition or conceit, but in humility count others more significant than yourselves. Let each of you look not only to his own interests, but also to the interests of others. (Phil. 2:3–4, ESV)

This, Paul proceeds to inform his readers, represents the "mind" (better, "mindset" NIV) "that was in Christ Jesus," and it is to be the mindset of Jesus's disciples, as well (2:5).[16] One can hardly imagine a more radical reconfiguration of relational priorities, given what we know about the values and practices of the dominant culture of the colony at Philippi.

The mindset to which Paul refers has to do with Christ's attitude toward his exalted position in the social pecking order of the universe and the way in which Christ chose to leverage the corresponding authority and power that were rightly his. In sharp contrast to local elites in Philippi—who used their resources to defend and augment their status in the public eye—the preincarnate Christ "did not consider

---

14 Ramsay MacMullen, *Roman Social Relations: 50 B.C. to A.D. 284* (New Haven, CT: Yale University Press, 1974), 76.

15 Lendon, *Empire of Honour*, 35.

16 This assumes that in verse 5 (a) τοῦτο picks up on the paranesis in the previous two verses, and (b) ὃ καὶ ἐν Χριστῷ Ἰησοῦ points ahead to the Christ narrative in verses 6–8. Christ thereby serves as Paul's example of the other-centered mindset reflected in 2:3–4, much as Jesus in Mark 10:45 offered himself as the example of the other-centered life he described in verses 43–44.

equality with God as something to be used for His own advantage" (v. 6, HCSB).[17]

Instead, Christ embarked upon what can only be viewed from the Roman perspective as a *cursus pudorum*, a race of ignomies, as he willingly descended a ladder of shame, from preincarnate glory ("the form of God" v. 6), to the slave-like status of the incarnation (v. 7), to the horror of public crucifixion (v. 8). The latter two stages of Christ's social pilgrimage conceptually parallel Jesus's teaching about discipleship in Mark 10.

B. Illustrated by Slave Imagery

In Mark 10:44, Jesus says to his disciples "whoever wishes to be first among you must be slave (δοῦλος) of all." In verse 45 Jesus portrays himself as the preeminent example of such a mindset. In Philippians 2:7, Paul informs us that Christ "emptied himself, taking the form of a slave, being born in human likeness." This is the only time that Paul associates the term δοῦλος with Jesus.

Slavery was a variegated phenomenon in antiquity. Many slaves worked on the large landholdings of their elite owners. Others suffered in the mines. Some served in extended households. Many were brutalized. Some became close friends of their masters and were later freed. Because of this diversity, scholars question the idea that all slaves belonged to a single social class in the Roman world.

What cut across all these expressions of the slavery, however, was the conviction that slave status was a shameful thing. Commenting on the inverse relationship that obtained between slavery and honor in the Roman world, Ramsay MacMullen summarizes, "That slavery even under a humane master negated pride and self-respect was its only essential evil, in the ancient mind." "Slavery," according to one Roman elite, was "the most shameful and wretched of states" (Dio Chrysostom, *Or.* 14.1).

When we consider the common legal status of slaves, inherited at birth—as opposed to the specific situations of individual slaves—the result is a rather uniform picture of slavery in the Roman world, and the referent "slave" takes on decidedly negative and socially shameful connotations in the symbolic universe of elite vocabulary. As a result, "Slave

---

17 The NIV's translation of ἁρπαγμόν is identical. The NRSV, "something to be exploited," is nearly synonymous. On this understanding of the crux, see N. T. Wright, "ἁρπαγμός and the Meaning of Philippians 2:5–11," *JTS* 37 (1986): 321–52. Further support for a sociological reading of the passage can be found in Hellerman, *Reconstructing Honor*, 129–56; see also idem, "μορφῇ θεοῦ as a Signifier of Social Status in Philippians 2:6," *JETS* 52 (2009): 779–97.

terminology almost always carries negative connotations in Greco-Roman literature."[18]

We now return to the slave terminology of Philippians 2:6, where it is important to note that δοῦλος does not refer here to the way that Jesus served others during his earthly ministry. Nor is δοῦλος used as a formal legal term to define his social class, since Jesus of Nazareth was not a slave but, rather, a free, non-citizen, peasant craftsman.

Rather, δοῦλος in Philippians 2:7 is used in a rhetorical sense to underscore the social stigma involved in the incarnation. The second participial clause explains the first: Christ took on "the form of a slave" by "being born in human likeness."[19] Peter Oakes elaborates, "Between being like God and being like a slave, there is the widest status gap imaginable by Paul's hearers. Paul is saying that for Christ to become human meant that deep a drop in status."[20]

The jarring imagery effectively targeted Paul's status conscious audience. For the preincarnate Son of God to become a human being was tantamount to assuming the shameful status of a Greco-Roman slave.

C. Exemplified in the Death of Jesus

The other-centered *ethos* of Christian discipleship—having the mindset of Christ—is exemplified, finally, in the manner in which Jesus chose to die. Christ reached the nadir of his pilgrimage down the ladder of shame when "he humbled himself and became obedient to the point of death—even death on a cross" (v. 8).

Treatments of the death of Christ in sermons and popular Christian literature typically highlight either the physical suffering involved in crucifixion, or the spiritual anguish Jesus experienced when he bore our sins on the cross. Paul focuses here on neither. Paul's concern in Philippians 2 is with the social stigma of crucifixion, the most publicly humiliating treatment a person could experience at the hands of others in the ancient world.

Paul does not elaborate on the other-centered purpose of Jesus's death, as Jesus himself does in Mark 10 ("to give his life a ransom for many"

---

18 Dale B. Martin, *Slavery as Salvation: The Metaphor of Slavery in Pauline Christianity* (New Haven, CT: Yale University Press, 1990), 46. See also Hellerman, *Reconstructing Honor,* 135–44.

19 Support for this reading can be found in Hellerman, "μορφῇ θεοῦ as a Signifier of Social Status," 790–92.

20 Peter Oakes, *Philippians: From People to Letter*, SNTSMS 110 (Cambridge: Cambridge University Press, 2001), 196.

[v. 45]). Paul focuses, instead, on the shame associated with Jesus's death—on what the crucifixion meant for Jesus, rather than what it meant for us.

However, Christ's other-centered mindset throughout his social descent in Philippians 2 cannot be far from Paul's mind. After all, this was a key aspect of Paul's gospel, and concern for other-centered living (vv. 3–5) is what initially launched Paul into his portrayal of the mindset of Christ (vv. 6–8). The notion will appear again, moreover, in the verses that follow (vv. 20–21). We may assume, with Peter Oakes, that "Jesus abandons his privileges *for the sake of others.*"[21]

D. Following After Jesus

Paul proceeds in the letter to offer three real-life examples of what it means to share the mindset of Christ—"not to be served but to serve" (Mark 10:45). The first is Timothy, whom Paul plans soon to send to Philippi.

1. *The Example of Timothy*

Echoes from language earlier in the chapter show that Paul views Timothy as an exemplary disciple of Jesus:

> For I have no one like him, who will be genuinely concerned
> for your welfare. For they all seek their own interests, not those
> of Jesus Christ. But you know Timothy's proven worth, how
> as a son with a father he has served with me in the gospel.
> (2:20–22, ESV)

Key phrases in verse 21 call to mind Paul's admonition in verse 4 of the chapter.

μὴ τὰ ἑαυτῶν ἕκαστος σκοποῦντες ἀλλὰ [καὶ] τὰ ἑτέρων ἕκαστοι (v. 4)

οἱ πάντες γὰρ τὰ ἑαυτῶν ζητοῦσιν, οὐ τὰ Ἰησοῦ Χριστοῦ (v. 21)

"The interests of others" (τὰ ἑτέρων [v. 4]) are now described as "those of Jesus Christ" (τὰ Ἰησοῦ Χριστοῦ [v. 21]), and understandably so, since Paul had previously offered Christ (vv. 6–8) as the preeminent example of other-centered living (vv. 3–4) earlier in the chapter.

We encounter another possible echo in verse 22, where Paul claims that Timothy "served" (ἐδούλευσεν) with him in the gospel. Paul employs δουλεύω seventeen times in his letters, so the occurrence here may offer

---

21 Oakes, *Philippians,* 116 (my italics).

little insight into Paul's understanding of discipleship. However, given the clear parallel between verse 4 and verse 21, outlined above, numbers of commentators assume that Paul has in view his description of Christ as δοῦλος (v. 7), when he uses ἐδούλευσεν of Timothy here in verse 22.[22]

Intentional concern (cf. σκοποῦντες [v. 4]; ζητοῦσιν [v. 21]) for "the interests of others" (v. 4; cf. "your welfare" [v. 21]) represents the heart of Christian discipleship precisely because "the interests of others" (τὰ ἑτέρων [v. 4]) are "those of Jesus Christ" (τὰ Ἰησοῦ Χριστοῦ [v. 21]). Timothy's "worth" (τὴν δὲ δοκιμὴν αὐτοῦ [v. 22]), in this regard, demonstrates that he is a model disciple.

2. The Example of Epaphroditus

Paul proceeds in the chapter to describe a second coworker who patterned his life after the example of Jesus:

> Still, I think it necessary to send to you Epaphroditus—my brother and co-worker and fellow soldier, your messenger and minister to my need; for he has been longing for all of you, and has been distressed because you heard that he was ill. He was indeed so ill that he nearly died. But God had mercy on him, and not only on him but on me also, so that I would not have one sorrow after another. I am the more eager to send him, therefore, in order that you may rejoice at seeing him again, and that I may be less anxious. Welcome him then in the Lord with all joy, and honor such people, because he came close to death for the work of Christ, risking his life to make up for those services that you could not give me. (2:25–30, NRSV)

Epaphroditus "nearly died" (v. 27) in his efforts to deliver a gift to Paul, while the apostle was in prison. Several verses later Paul describes his coworker's experience with words that intentionally call to mind the description of Jesus's other-centered pilgrimage earlier in the chapter:[23]

Jesus: γενόμενος ὑπήκοος μέχρι θανάτου (v. 8)

Epaphroditus: μέχρι θανάτου ἤγγισεν (v. 30)

---

22 Joseph H. Hellerman, *Philippians: Exegetical Guide to the Greek New Testament* (Nashville: B&H, 2015), 150; G. Walter Hansen, *The Letter to the Philippians* (Grand Rapids: Eerdmans, 2009), 197; Peter T. O'Brien, *The Epistle to the Philippians* (Grand Rapids: Eerdmans, 1991), 325.
23 Hansen views μέχρι θανάτου here as a "striking echo" of μέχρι θανάτου in verse 8 (*The Letter to the Philippians*, 205).

Near the end of his description of Epaphroditus, Paul instructs the Philippians to "honor such people" (v. 29).

Paul himself honored Epaphroditus a few verses earlier, when he granted him five titles: "brother . . . co-worker . . . fellow soldier . . . messenger . . . minister" (v. 26). Paul seldom uses even one title in apposition to another in his letters.[24] The use of five titles is truly exceptional. The proliferation of titles for Epaphroditus can be explained by the social setting of the colony at Philippi. Recall that each of the inscriptions from Philippi cited earlier included a list of honorific titles. Although one could cite similar evidence from elsewhere in the Roman Empire, Peter Pilhofer properly contends—from an extensive analysis of nearly eight hundred inscriptions from Philippi—that residents of the colony were "*especially proud* to display their ranks and offices."[25]

The biblical materials confirm the accuracy of Pilhofer's assertion. Only in the Philippian narrative in Acts 16, for example, does Luke use the proper technical terminology for magistrates and other officials in a Roman colony (στρατηγός = Lat. *duumvir* [16:20, 22, 35, 36, 38]; ραβδοῦχος [16:35, 38]; δεσμοφύλαξ [16:23, 27, 36]).[26] Only in his greeting in Philippians does Paul use titles for church leaders (ἐπίσκοπος καὶ διάκονος [1:1]). And now (2:25) Paul grants Epaphroditus five titles. Luke and Paul are both likely aware of the preoccupation with honorific titles that characterized social life in the colony.

Paul's radical reconstruction of the social values of the dominant culture is patently evident in his description of Epaphroditus.[27] Those who genuinely deserve the public titular recognition that the pagan residents of Philippi—elites and non-elites alike—so passionately pursued are persons like Epaphroditus who risk their lives ministering to others in the

---

24 He does so on occasion (e.g., Rom. 9:3; 1 Thess. 3:2; Philem. 1; two in Col. 4:7).

25 Peter Pilhofer, *Philippi. Band 1: Die erste christliche Gemeinde Europas* (Tübingen: J. C. B. Mohr, 1995) 142 [original italics. Pilhofer sees Philippi as exceptional in the degree to which honor and status were emphasized in the settlement, and he sees this reflected in Philippi's epigraphic database (*Philippi. Band 1*, 142–44).

26 Luke uses generic titles for local magistrates in other Roman colonies. Thus, Pisidian Antioch's *duumviri* are simply τοὺς πρώτους τῆς πόλεως, "the leading men of the city" (Hellerman, *Reconstructing Honor*, 112; following Pilhofer, *Philippi: Band 1*, 193). Note, as well, that Philippi is the only place among Paul's journeys that Luke calls "a Roman colony" (Acts 16:12), even though at least eight other settlements Paul visited in Acts were colonies (Pilhofer, *Philippi: Band 1*, 159–60). Only in Philippi, moreover, do local residents accuse the missionaries of "advocating customs that are not lawful for us as Romans to adopt or observe" (16:21). Clearly, for Luke, Philippi is distinctly Roman among the settlements Paul visited.

27 See, further, Hellerman, "Brothers and Friends in Philippi," *BTB* 39 (2009): 1–10; idem, *Philippians*, 156–57.

work of Christ (v. 30). When he instructs the members of the Jesus community in Philippi to "honor such people" (v. 29), Paul turns the relational values of the colony's honor culture on their head.

3. The Example of Paul

In Philippians 3, the apostle offers himself as a final illustration of what it meant to trade public recognition for the other-centered priorities of the gospel. The section begins with a catalogue of Paul's Jewish honors:

> If anyone else has reason to be confident in the flesh, I have more: circumcised on the eighth day, a member of the people of Israel, of the tribe of Benjamin, a Hebrew born of Hebrews; as to the law, a Pharisee; as to zeal, a persecutor of the church; as to righteousness under the law, blameless. Yet whatever gains I had, these I have come to regard as loss because of Christ. (3:4b–7, NRSV)

In verses 5–6, Paul departs from sentential grammar to list his honors in a staccato-like fashion that intentionally mirrors the chisel-and-stone economy of ancient epigraphy. Just like the honor inscriptions in Philippi, moreover, Paul lists his ascribed honors (natal status) first, followed by honors acquired later in life. Paul has essentially presented his Jewish honors in a Roman framework.[28]

Then, in a brazen affront to the cultural values of his audience, Paul labels these honors "rubbish" (σκύβαλα [v. 8]), willingly trading them (cf. ζημίαν [vv. 7–8]) for a new set of goals: "gain Christ . . . know Christ . . . attain to the resurrection from the dead" (vv. 8–11). The first two goals correspond roughly to Jesus's commandments in the Great Commission (Matt. 28:19–20): (1) "gain Christ" = justification = "baptize"; (2) "know Christ" = sanctification = "teaching them to observe all that I have commanded you."

Paul describes the process of discipleship (sanctification) in v. 10, where we learn that "to know Christ" is to know "the power of his resurrection in the sharing of his sufferings by becoming like him in his death."[29] The deep relational knowledge of which Paul speaks here in

---

28 Support for this reading can be found in Hellerman, *Reconstructing Honor,* 122–28.

29 NRSV, slightly modified. The first καί in verse 10 is epexegetical (cf. NIV: "I want to know Christ—yes, to know the power of his resurrection"). The two concepts δύναμιν τῆς ἀναστάσεως αὐτοῦ and κοινωνίαν τῶν παθημάτων αὐτοῦ (governed by a single article) are to be read together, as two aspects of the same experience (see Hellerman, *Philippians,* 189–90).

Philippians 3 is not something the apostle experienced as he prayed or meditated on Scripture in isolation from others. As the apostle writes these very words, he is suffering in prison, for the gospel, for the sake of others. Indeed, it was Paul's other-centered life of service that caused nearly all the suffering that we read about in his letters (cf. the catalogue in 2 Corinthians 11:25–28). Looking back on this life some years later, Paul would summarize: "I endure everything *for the sake of the elect,* so that they may also obtain the salvation that is in Christ Jesus, with eternal glory" (2 Tim. 2:10, emphasis added).

In a radical inversion of the honor values of ancient society, "the Son of Man came not to be served but to serve, and to give his life a ransom for many" (Mark 10:45). Paul patterns his life after Jesus, trading his Jewish honors to become like Christ "in his death" "for the sake of the elect."

E. Summary of Discipleship in Philippians

We can summarize Paul's understanding of discipleship in Philippians as becoming increasingly conformed to the other-centered mindset of Jesus, who (a) did not regard his divine status as "something to be exploited" to his own advantage (Phil. 2:6; cf. Mark 10:42–43), but instead, (b) traded the most exalted position in the universe for the abject status of a slave (Phil. 2:7; cf. Mark 10:44), finally (c) to become "obedient to the point of death" (Phil. 2:8) and thereby give his life "a ransom for many" (Mark 10:45).

FOLLOWING AFTER JESUS IN PHILEMON

Space limitations necessitate a briefer treatment of Philemon. The discussion assumes that Onesimus was Philemon's slave and that Philemon was one of Paul's converts who hosted a house church in Colossae.[30] Onesimus somehow wronged Philemon and ran away (v. 18). Paul encountered the fugitive slave while in prison in Rome and led Onesimus to Christ (v. 10).[31] Paul now sends Onesimus back to Philemon with a

---

30 The traditional reconstruction has been challenged in recent years but remains the scholarly consensus. See the discussions in Bernard Cho, "Subverting Slavery: Philemon, Onesimus, and Paul's Gospel of Reconciliation," *EvQ* 86 (2014): 99–115, at 100–102; and John G. Nordling, "Some Matters Favoring the Runaway Slave Hypothesis In Philemon," *Neotestimentica* 44 (2010): 85–121.

31 Circumstances surrounding the encounter remain unknown. Onesimus may have been imprisoned as a runaway slave (Cho, "Subverting Slavery," 107). Alternatively, Onesimus,

letter in which the apostle redefines the master-slave relationship according to the social realities of the gospel.

The challenge reaches its climax in verses 15–16:

> Perhaps this is the reason he was separated from you for a while, so that you might have him back forever, no longer as a slave but more than a slave, a beloved brother—especially to me but how much more to you, both in the flesh and in the Lord. (NRSV)

Philemon was the *paterfamilias* of his household. According to Roman law, he had absolute authority over all his extended family. To receive Onesimus back "as a slave" would have meant to treat him as a Roman master normally treated a runaway slave (*servus fugitivus*). Prospects for Onesimus were grim. Bernard Cho elaborates:

> [A]ssuming the cruel means by which masters disciplined common slaves, it is reasonable to conclude that no practical limits existed for slave-owners to express their anger on the *fugitivi*.[32]

Such were the expectations for a normal Roman household.

The conversion of Onesimus, however, meant that Philemon and his runaway slave now shared life together in a new household. And as a member of "the household of God" Philemon was to receive Onesimus back as "more than a slave, a beloved brother" (Eph. 2:19; 1 Tim. 3:15; Phlm 16).

It is difficult to tell whether or not Paul challenges Philemon to manumit Onesimus.[33] The issue, however, does not significantly inform the above discussion. For as Cho notes,

> Paul's thorough use of familial language with reference to Onesimus indicates that, even though Philemon could potentially

---

aware of the relationship between Paul and Philemon, may have sought out the apostle and asked him to intercede with his master on his behalf (S. Scott Bartchy, "Epistle to Philemon," *ABD*, vol. 5, eds. D. N. Freedman, et al. [New York: Doubleday, 1992], 305–10).

32 "Subverting Slavery," 106. For an informative overview of the treatment of slaves in Roman antiquity, see Cho, 102–07, and the works cited there.

33 Bartchy thinks so ("Philemon," 308), as does F. F. Bruce (*The Epistles to the Colossians, to Philemon, and to the Ephesians*, NICNT (Grand Rapids: Eerdmans, 1984], 217). Verse 21 may include an implicit request for manumission: "knowing that you will do even more than I say." Others challenge the manumission thesis given ancient social realities (Cho, "Subverting Slavery," 110, following John Barclay, "Paul, Philemon, and the Dilemma of Christian Slave-Ownership," *NTS* 37 [1991]: 161–86; Craig de Vos, "Once a Slave, Always a Slave? Slavery, Manumission, and Relational Patterns in Paul's Letter to Philemon," *JSNT* 82 [2001]: 89–105).

remain Onesimus's master, their relationship was now to be defined primarily on the basis of their being brothers and God's new humanity in Christ.[34]

For Philemon, at this crucial juncture in his pilgrimage as a follower of Jesus, a life of faithful discipleship means trading the status hierarchy and social norms of the Roman household for those of the family of God—a family in which "there is no longer slave nor free" (Gal. 3:28).[35]

And this is not a decision Paul intends for Philemon to make on his own, as would be natural for the *paterfamilias* of a Roman household. Paul addresses his challenging letter to Philemon, Apphia, Archippus, and the whole congregation, thereby proposing that "Onesimus's issue should be dealt with as a matter pertaining to the community of faith" (vv. 1–2).[36]

CONCLUSION: FOLLOWING JESUS AS A COMMUNAL DISCIPLINE

It remains only to remind ourselves of the social context of Christian discipleship that Paul envisioned when he penned Philippians and Philemon. For Paul, discipleship unfolds primarily in the community—not in the closet. That community, of course, is the Christian *ekklesia,* what we have come to call "the local church." And not only does discipleship unfold in community. The very integrity of the *ekklesia* itself, as a radically alternative social reality functioning under the lordship of Christ, is at stake in the choices we make as individual followers of Jesus.

The relational context of discipleship is perhaps most obvious in Philemon where, as we saw, a total revisioning of family—the most important social entity in the ancient world—constituted the very heart of Philemon's call to faithfully follow Jesus. Paul lovingly confronted Philemon

---

34 "Subverting Slavery," 112. Kirk D. Lyons, Jr. affirms, "Paul's intention was to promote an ideology affirming that within the church of Jesus Christ the primary relationship would be a pseudo-familial relationship among peers" ("Paul's Confrontation with Class: The Letter to Philemon as Counter-Hegemonic Discourse," *Cross Currents* 56 [2006]: 116–32, at 124). Sibling terminology surfaces four times in the letter (1, 7, 16, 20). See Hellerman, *The Ancient Church as Family* (Fortress: Minneapolis, 2001), for the solidarity involved in sibling relations in the ancient world, and the use of family language (e.g., ἀδελφός) as a rhetorical device to elicit family-like behavior.

35 On the letter's critique of the dominant culture's status hierarchy, see Lyons, "Paul's Confrontation with Class." It is not just Onesimus whose status is redefined in the letter. Lyons sees Paul "decasting" himself from his apostolic office by presenting himself in the greeting as a "prisoner of Christ Jesus," without the usual "apostle" or "servant of Christ" (325).

36 Cho, "Subverting Slavery," 108. As Calvin noted, "[Paul] seems to be thinking about the interests of the whole church rather than the private affairs of a single man" (cited in Lyons, "Paul's Confrontation with Class," 326).

with an important decision to make as an individual disciple of Christ. The consequences of that decision, however, would affect much more than Philemon's personal walk with God. Philemon's response would profoundly impact Onesimus and the house church as a whole. As Lyons rightly asserts, "[T]he transformation of Onesimus has fostered the collision of the two households."[37] Because Philemon was the *paterfamilias* of a large household that hosted the *ekklesia,* the integrity of the whole church was at stake in Philemon's response to Paul's request.

It is typical for westernized Christians to ask ourselves, "How can *I* become more like Jesus?" Paul's letter to Philemon encourages us to ask, as well, "How can *we* become more like Jesus?" Indeed, for Philemon the two questions could not be isolated from one another. And so it is for us, as well, since, almost without exception, the personal decisions we make at crucial crossroads in our spiritual lives affect the lives of others in the community—and the spiritual health of the church as a whole—for better or for worse.

A similarly radical revisioning of humans relations marks Paul's view of discipleship in Philippians, where the apostle wholly reconstructs the Roman honor system. Here, as well, genuine discipleship is a communal—not a private—enterprise, and the lives of individual disciples determine the integrity of the church as a whole.[38]

After all, one can adopt the mindset of Jesus, and learn to serve "the interests of others" (Phil. 2:4), only when one is in community with "others" in the context of church life and ministry (cf. "among you" Mark 10:43). This should be self-evident. But it needs to be emphasized, given our propensity as western evangelicals to value personal piety over the communal priorities of biblical Christianity.

Paul adopts a unique metaphor in Philippians, moreover, to drive this point home. More than half of the inscriptions unearthed in Philippi boast of the Roman citizenship of the person in view. The citizen franchise was a valued honor in a Roman colony like Philippi, possessed by perhaps one-third of the residents. It is no accident, in this regard, that only in Philippians does Paul use citizenship terminology as imagery for Christian community.

---

37 Lyons, "Paul's Confrontation with Class," 330.
38 Thus Paul addresses issues of community life in the passage (2:12–18) that directly follows his portrayal of the humiliation and exaltation of Christ in 2:6–11. We "work out [our] salvation" (v. 12) in our relationships with one another in the local church (v. 14), and the integrity of the church is at stake as we do (v. 15).

Followers of Jesus belong to a radically alternative socially reality (ἡμῶν γὰρ τὸ πολίτευμα ἐν οὐρανοῖς ὑπάρχει [3:20a]). They are to live in a manner worthy of their heavenly citizenship (Μόνον ἀξίως τοῦ εὐαγγελίου τοῦ Χριστοῦ πολιτεύεσθε [1:27a]). And they are to do so not as isolated individuals but in community with one another (στήκετε ἐν ἑνὶ πνεύματι, μιᾷ ψυχῇ συναθλοῦντες τῇ πίστει τοῦ εὐαγγελίου [1:27c]). Such is Paul's view of Christian discipleship in his letter to the Philippians.

CHAPTER 11

Discipled by God: Discipleship in 1–2 Thessalonians

David E. Briones

INTRODUCTION

Although the word "disciple" is completely absent from 1 and 2 Thessalonians,[1] the concept is certainly present. In fact, these letters project a rich theology of discipleship that has practical significance for the church today. But in order to discover it, one must examine the more explicit themes of holiness and imitation.[2]

Holiness (ἁγιωσύνη/ἁγιασμός) is widely considered the primary focus of the Thessalonian correspondence.[3] It comes especially to the fore when Paul combats sexual impurity (1 Thess. 4:3–8) and idleness (1 Thess. 4:9–12; 5:14; 2 Thess. 3:6–16). But holiness is also considered, according to Jeffrey Weima, "the key theme of discipleship."[4] Imitation is equally prominent in 1 and 2 Thessalonians. From the very start of this correspondence, Paul centers our attention on this important theme. He describes how the Thessalonians changed from idol worshippers to "imitators" (μιμηταί) of the apostles, of the Lord (1:6), and of other churches in Judea (2:14). He also presents himself as "a model to imitate [τύπον . . . μιμεῖσθαι]" when he refused remuneration for his gospel labors among them (2 Thess. 3:9; cf. 1 Thess. 2:1–12).[5] Thus, the attention given to imitation, and the pivotal role it plays in the Thessalonian correspondence, confirms the words of G. K. Beale: "The essence of discipleship is imitation."[6]

---

1 It is entirely absent from the Pauline corpus.

2 All Scripture translations are the author's own unless otherwise noted.

3 Jeffrey A. D. Weima calls it "the most important theme in 1 Thessalonians" ("How You Must Walk to Please God": Holiness and Discipleship in 1 Thessalonians," in *Patterns of Discipleship in the New Testament,* ed. R. N. Longenecker [Grand Rapids: Eerdmans, 1996], 98–119, at 98).

4 "How You Must Walk to Please God," 101; cf. also Andy Johnson, "The Sanctification of the Imagination in 1 Thessalonians," in *Holiness and Ecclesiology in the New Testament*, eds. K. E. Brower and A. Johnson (Grand Rapids: Eerdmans, 2007), 275–92.

5 All translations are my own, unless noted otherwise.

6 G. K. Beale, *1–2 Thessalonians*, IVPNTC (Downers Grove, IL: IVP Academic, 2003), 58. However, one must be careful not to conflate "imitation" and "discipleship." Victor A. Copan, "Μαθητής and Μιμητής: Exploring an Entangled Relationship," *BBR* 17 (2007): 313–23, argues that "the relationship between the terms is seen as the one concept (imitation) occurring within, though not limited to, the sphere of the other (discipleship)" (323).

Discipleship is therefore interconnected with the themes of holiness and imitation, and in these letters, Paul's approach to discipleship is on unique display through the relationship shared with the Thessalonians. Indeed, it is the warmth of this bond that sets the tone for Paul's discipleship strategy (see 1 Thess. 2:19–20; 3:5–13). Instead of stinging criticisms, like those levelled against the Corinthians, one mainly finds glowing commendation. He recalls their faith, love, and hope in the Lord Jesus Christ (1 Thess. 1:3–7; 2:14; 3:3–4), and he praises their increasing love for God, for one another, and for all (3:6–7, 11–13). Of course, they are far from perfect. In Paul's assessment, their faith is still "lacking" (3:10). They need to grow in their love "more and more" (4:1). Some are sexually promiscuous (4:3–8). Others grieve "as those who have no hope" (4:13). And still others are idle instead of hard-working (2 Thess. 3:6–15). Although this pales in comparison to the harsh judgments aimed at the Corinthians, the Thessalonians still had room for growth as disciples of Jesus Christ. Elucidating precisely how such growth is to be achieved is one of the most fascinating contributions to the topic of discipleship in 1 and 2 Thessalonians.

One of the key insights on discipleship gleaned from the Thessalonian correspondence is the leading role occupied throughout the process by God and his gospel—the powerful word about the crucified and risen Savior, Jesus Christ. Contrary to what many think, discipleship does not merely involve two human parties. Human actors play a real part, to be sure. Paul preaches and embodies the gospel to the Thessalonians. The Thessalonians accept the gospel, imitate Paul, and embody the gospel to others. This is discipleship at work. But from beginning to end, God superintends the entire process. He initiates, energizes, and completes all human effort in discipleship. As Paul says elsewhere, some water, others plant, but ultimately, the spiritual growth of disciples comes from God (cf. 1 Cor. 3:6). Indeed, God plays a fundamental role within discipleship, and this theological truth should significantly impact our practical understanding of the concept today.

In this essay, then, we will outline the triangular nature of discipleship "in Christ," examine the central role of God's gospel in the process, especially as it relates to becoming imitators, models, and mediators, and then conclude by considering the pursuit of holiness in the Christian life.

THE TRIANGULAR NATURE OF DISCIPLESHIP "IN CHRIST"

Every relationship "in Christ" necessarily has vertical and horizontal dimensions. As members of the body of Christ, believers are simultaneously joined to Christ as "head" (the vertical dimension) and to other "members" of the same body (the horizontal dimension; cf. Rom. 12; 1 Cor. 12; Eph. 4:15–16). All the while, God's grace empowers members of the body to serve one another (1 Cor. 12:4–7; Rom. 12:6). That being so, discipleship involves more than a human discipler and a human disciple. God plays a primary role in discipleship, triangulating the relationship and empowering those within it for the common good. In the context of Paul's letters to Thessalonica, discipleship involves Paul, the Thessalonians, and most importantly, God. After describing the specific identity of this God, we will show the ways in which God works through human agency. This will inform our understanding of the triangular nature of discipleship as well as lay the foundation for the following section on the progression of God's gospel in discipleship.

It is crucial to note that God is Triune—Father, Son, and Holy Spirit—a foundational doctrine affirmed at the beginning of 1 Thessalonians. "God the Father" (1:1, 3) is thanked by Paul (1:2) for the faith, love, and hope of the Thessalonians, because God, in his eternal decree, had elected them unto salvation (1:4). "The Lord Jesus Christ" (1:1) is the one in whom the Thessalonians hope (1:3), the one whom they imitate (1:6), and the one who will ultimately deliver them from the wrath to come (1:10). "The Holy Spirit" (1:5) is also powerfully at work in the lives of the Thessalonians, producing joy in the midst of affliction (1:6). This is the God Paul proclaims—Father, Son, and Holy Spirit.

In contradistinction to worthless idols (1:9; cf. Ps. 96:5), God initiates, energizes, and completes every human action on the horizontal level. Take, for example, God's activity in the Thessalonians' faith, love, and hope (1 Thess. 1:3; cf. 5:8). This triad of virtues sums up the Christian life, beginning with *faith*, persevering in *love* for God and neighbor, and anticipating with *hope* the new creation. But this triad is rooted in divine agency. The only reason they have faith, love, and hope is because of God's unconditional election (1:4)—in eternity past, he set his love on them and is calling them into his glorious kingdom (2:12; 2 Thess. 2:14, 16; cf. Eph. 1:4; Phil. 1:6).[7] When Paul speaks of this triad within time and space, he shows us how divine and human agency are not in

---

7 Peter O'Brien rightly notes "the immediate grounds for Paul's constant thanksgiving" is their faith, love, and hope of the Thessalonians, but "the ultimate basis" is "their election" (*Introductory Thanksgivings in the Letters of Paul*, NovTSup 49 [Leiden: Brill, 1977], 166).

competition with one another.[8] He boasts of *their* "faith" in suffering (2 Thess. 1:4), but still deems it fitting to "give thanks to God" that *their* "faith is growing abundantly" in the midst of affliction (2 Thess. 1:3). Paul calls *their* faith, "*your* faith" (1 Thess. 3:6), and yet he prays that God would "fulfill every . . . work of faith *by his power*" (2 Thess. 1:11; cf. also Eph. 2:8; Phil. 1:29). He calls *their* love, "*your* . . . love" (3:6), but that does not prevent the apostle from praying that "the Lord" would make them "increase and abound in love for one another and for all" (3:12), or from giving thanks to God as the one who "increases the love of every one of you for one another" (2 Thess. 1:3), or even from asking that "the Lord direct [their] hearts to the love of God" (2 Thess. 3:5). Paul also calls *their* hope, "*your* . . . hope" (1 Thess. 1:3), but he reminds the Thessalonians that "our Lord Jesus Christ" and "God our Father . . . loved us and gave us eternal comfort and good hope *through grace* [ἐν χάριτι]" (2 Thess. 2:16).

An important theological insight can be discerned from the above descriptions of faith, love, and hope: every human work is grounded in divine *grace*.[9] After all, it is "God who works in you, both to will and to work for his good pleasure" (Phil. 2:13). All is grace. Whether faith or love or hope, everything is a divine gift (1 Cor. 4:7; Rom. 11:36).[10] The gift of gifts, however, is the gospel of Jesus Christ. It brings faith, love, and hope into existence. It not only creates but also sustains Christians. The gospel is therefore not simply the means of conversion. It is the very life source of discipleship, and it is a gift from God. And yet, the gospel does not ring out directly from heaven. It is mediated. God uses frail jars of clay to showcase the treasure of the gospel to others (2 Cor. 4:7). This is the triangular relational pattern of discipleship. God works through Paul to disciple the church in Thessalonica. As Jan Lambrecht explains, "One can reconstruct the line coming from God and the Lord Jesus Christ and going through the apostles to the Thessalonians, and through them

---

8 John M. G. Barclay calls this "*non-contrastive transcendence*," insisting that God's sovereignty neither limits nor reduces human freedom, but grounds and enables it ("Introduction," in *Divine and Human Agency in Paul and His Cultural Environment*, eds. J. M.G. Barclay and S. J. Gathercole [London: T&T Clark, 2006], 1–8, at 7; author's italics).

9 This is further confirmed by the tripartite relational pattern in 1 Thessalonians 3:1–9, where, according to Andy Johnson, there is "a mutual mediation of God's grace, a reciprocity of grace that comes initially through Paul to the audience and then returns through the audience as sustaining grace to Paul" (*1 & 2 Thessalonians*, THNTC [Grand Rapids: Eerdmans, 2016], 91).

10 The word "grace" (χάρις) commonly means "gift" and often has the sense of something freely given. For an excellent analysis, see John M. G. Barclay, *Paul and the Gift* (Grand Rapids: Eerdmans, 2015).

further to others."[11] This "line" is nothing other than the progression of God's gospel, as it powerfully transforms many in its path into imitators, models, mediators, and therefore disciples of Christ. We now turn to consider how it progressed from God through Paul through the Thessalonians to others, and how all this relates to discipleship today.

THE PROGRESSION OF GOD'S GOSPEL IN DISCIPLESHIP

A. God as Source

The gospel is preached *by* Paul, but it is obviously not the gospel *of* Paul. It is, as the apostle so forthrightly puts it, "the gospel *of God*" (τὸ εὐαγγέλιον τοῦ θεοῦ, 1 Thess. 2:2, 8–9) and "the word *of God*" (λόγον θεοῦ, 2:13). Even when Paul calls it "our gospel" (τὸ εὐαγγέλιον ἡμῶν), he cannot help but to include a passive verb (ἐγενήθη) to indicate its heavenly origin (1:5) or a preposition to indicate his mediatorial role (ὃ ἐκάλεσεν ὑμᾶς <u>διὰ</u> τοῦ εὐαγγελίου ἡμῶν, 2 Thess. 2:14). God is the ultimate giver of this gift, whose subject matter is the person and work of the incarnate Son. It is "the gospel *of Christ*" (τὸ εὐαγγέλιον τοῦ Χριστοῦ, 1 Thess. 3:2) and "the gospel *of our Lord Jesus*" (τὸ εὐαγγέλιον τοῦ κυρίου ἡμῶν Ἰησοῦ, 2 Thess. 1:8). It is the good news about the crucified, risen, and reigning Savior who conquered sin and death through his incarnation, life, death, resurrection, and ascension. This is God's gift—indeed, the gift of gifts—that Paul proclaims as mediator, imitator, and model on behalf of the church.

B. Paul as Mediator, Imitator, and Model

The proclamation of God's gospel is described in clear terms by Paul. It came "in word, but also in power and in the Holy Spirit and with full conviction" (1 Thess. 1:5). Indeed, it proved to be economically, socially, politically, and even religiously disruptive in Thessalonica (cf. Acts 17:1–10).[12] It emerged out of "much conflict" (1 Thess. 2:2). It did not "spring from error or impurity or any attempt to deceive" or "words of flattery" or "a pretext for greed" (2:3, 5). Paul preached as one "approved by God to be entrusted with the gospel," always aiming to "please God" who tests his heart (2:4). His message was free of charge, because it was

---

[11] Jan Lambrecht, "Thanksgivings in 1 Thessalonians 1–3," in *The Thessalonian Correspondence*, ed. R. Collins (Louvain: Leuven University Press, 1990), 183–205, at 203.

[12] See C. Kavin Rowe, *World Upside Down: Reading Acts in the Graeco-Roman Age* (Oxford: Oxford University Press, 2009).

not a human word or message to be purchased but the very word of God to be received freely (2:6, 9). The church would have been exposed to the disreputable practices associated with human words, such as the Sophists and itinerant philosophers, who avariciously charged large sums of money for grandiloquent yet empty speeches and teachings. But when they heard God's heavenly word spoken through Paul, they knew this message was incomparable to anything they had heard before. They accepted the gospel "not as the word of men but as what it really is, the word of God [λόγον θεοῦ]" (2:13).

However, they did not simply hear God's gospel. They saw it. Paul, being united to Christ, proclaimed and embodied the gospel to the Thessalonians. He became what he proclaimed (cf. 2 Cor. 1:5; 4:10–12; Gal. 3:1). Or, as John Gillman puts it, "Paul not only gave what he had, but what he was."[13] What he *had* and what he *was* are summed up by the humiliation-exaltation pattern of the Christ event in 2 Cor. 8:9: "For you know the grace of our Lord Jesus Christ, that because he was rich, yet for your sake [δι' ὑμᾶς] he became poor, so that you by his poverty might become rich" (cf. Phil. 2:5–11). Christ, out of self-giving love, gave himself δι' ὑμᾶς ("for your sake"), so that others might be exalted. In similar fashion, Paul became an imitator of Christ and a model of the Christological pattern of humiliation-exaltation in Thessalonica.

After describing how the gospel came in word and power, he adds: "You know what kind of men we proved to be among you for your sake [δι' ὑμᾶς]" (1 Thess. 1:5). Encapsulated within that little prepositional phrase (δι' ὑμᾶς) is a Christoform model of discipleship,[14] one which played itself out in Paul's self-giving ministry: "So being affectionately desirous of you, we were ready to give [μεταδοῦναι] you not only the gospel of God but also our own selves [τὰς ἑαυτῶν ψυχάς], because you had become very dear to us" (2:8). Thus, Paul too, out of self-giving love, gave himself in order that others might be exalted. Here, Paul imitates Christ as a model for the church.

---

13 John Gillman, "Paul's Εἴσοδος: The Proclaimed and the Proclaimer," in *The Thessalonian Correspondence*, ed. R. Collins (Louvain: Leuven University Press, 1990), 62–70; cf. also Franz Laub, *1. und 2. Thesslonicherbrief* (Würzburg: Echter, 1985), 26–31. In the same vein, Gaventa asserts, "Apostles cannot give over the gospel without giving over something of themselves" (*First and Second Thessalonians,* Interpretation (Louisville: John Knox Press, 1998], 30).
14 By comparing δι' ὑμᾶς ("for your sake") in 1:5 to his use of the phrase in 2 Corinthians 4:15 and 8:9, it becomes readily apparent that his vocational labors are an embodiment of the gospel of Jesus Christ (cf. Stephen J. Kraftchick, "Death in Us, Life in You: The Apostolic Medium," in *Pauline Theology,* vol. 2, ed. D. M. Hay [Minneapolis: Fortress, 1993], 156–81, at 169–81; Michael J. Gorman, *Apostle of the Crucified Lord: A Theological Introduction to Paul & His Letters* [Grand Rapids: Eerdmans, 2004], 68–69, 155).

Two images, that of a mother and a father, further elucidate Paul's Christ-like model of discipleship. The image of "a nursing mother who cherishes her own children" is poignant (2:7).[15] A nursing mother, compelled by unrelenting love, gives herself for the physical sustenance and growth of her children. In the same way, Paul, overwhelmed by the self-giving love of Christ on his behalf (cf. Gal. 2:20), gives "his very self" (τὰς ἑαυτῶν ψυχάς) to his spiritual children. But he not only mothers them; he, as their father, also exhorts, encourages, and charges them "to live in a worthy man-ner [ἀξίως]" (1 Thess. 2:11–12). Only, for Paul, living in a worthy matter has little to do with cultivating an inherent spark of virtue within or ex-hibiting a philosophically refined inner disposition of the soul, as was the case among ancient philosophers. He desires the Thessalonians to live in a manner "worthy *of God* [ἀξίως τοῦ θεοῦ], the one who is calling [τοῦ καλοῦντος] you into his own kingdom and glory" (2:12). Calling language takes us right back to God's electing love in 1:4,[16] the primary cause of their Christian existence. But instead of using the aorist tense (as in 4:7; 2 Thess. 2:14; cf. Gal. 1:6; 1 Cor. 1:9), τοῦ καλοῦντος is in the present, indicating that God's past call is ongoing and effectual. It ensures their future in his "kingdom and glory," for "he who calls [ὁ καλῶν] you is faithful; he will surely do it" (5:24). Paul's discipleship tactic as a nursing mother and father is to cherish, exhort, encourage, and charge the church to love and live worthily in obedience to God, not *in order to* earn God's love but *because* God has set his electing love on them to guarantee their future.[17]

One particular—if not peculiar—way Paul embodied God's gospel be-fore the Thessalonians was by refusing financial support when he initially entered their city.[18] Since a father provides for his own children (cf. 2 Cor. 12:14), Paul gave himself by working "night and day, that [he] might not be a burden to any of [them], while [he] proclaimed to [them] the gospel of God" (1 Thess. 2:9). He lowered himself by plying a trade, so

---

15 For the precise meaning of and discussion surrounding the term τροφός, see Beverly Gaventa, *Our Mother Saint Paul* (Louisville: Westminster John Knox Press, 2007), 21–28.

16 Stephen Chester has made a compelling case for the close connection between election and calling. See *Conversion at Corinth: Perspectives on Conversion in Paul's Theology and the Corinthian Church*, SNTW (London: T&T Clark, 2003), 77–111.

17 Weima asserts that "though the Thessalonian Christians must live in a way that is worthy of God, such conduct in no way earns their salvation but rather is a response to the free and unmerited 'call' of God" (*1–2 Thessalonians*, BECNT [Grand Rapids: Baker Academic, 2014], 157).

18 Paul did, however, accept material assistance after leaving a church established by the gospel. See David E. Briones, *Paul's Financial Policy: A Socio-Theological Approach*, LNTS 494; (London: T&T Clark, 2013), 219–224.

that others might be lifted up. As he asks in 2 Cor. 11:7, "[D]id I commit a sin in humbling myself [ἐμαυτὸν ταπεινῶν] so that you might be exalted, because I preached God's gospel to you free of charge?" Just as Christ "humbled himself" (ἐταπείνωσεν ἑαυτόν) in Phil. 2:8, so, too, did Paul in 2 Cor. 11:7 (ἐμαυτὸν ταπεινῶν). He worked tirelessly in order to give the gospel free of charge, lest anyone think they had to pay for what he *had* and what he *was*. His refusal of financial support became a living embodiment of the grace of God in Christ.[19]

C. The Thessalonians as Imitators, Models, and Mediators

Paul certainly embodied Christ to the Thessalonians, but he also expected the Thessalonians to do the same. They, like their apostle, were to become imitators of Christ, models for the church, and mediators of God's gospel to others.

1. Becoming Imitators of Christ

Paul, in 2 Thessalonians 3:1, asks the Thessalonians to pray that the "word of the Lord may progress [τρέχῃ]," and then he inserts, "as happened among you." That progress is vividly depicted through the clever and repeated use of the verb "become" (γίνομαι) in 1 Thessalonians 1:5–2:14. Beginning in 1:5, the gospel "came" (ἐγενήθη) from God to Paul, and so Paul "became" (ἐγενήθημεν) a nonidentical embodiment of Christ to the Thessalonians (1:5b).[20] The Thessalonians then "became imitators" (μιμηταὶ . . . ἐγενήθητε) of Paul and the Lord (1:6), and "became imitators" (μιμηταὶ ἐγενήθητε) of the persecuted churches in Judea (2:14). All of this caused the Thessalonians to "become . . . beloved" (ἀγαπητοὶ . . . ἐγενήθητε) to Paul (2:8)—not because they were a stellar group of people but because their reception of the gospel and its effects confirmed their status as "elect" and "beloved by God" (ἠγαπημένοι ὑπὸ θεοῦ, 1:4; cf. 2 Thess. 3:13: ἠγαπημένοι ὑπὸ κυρίου).[21] Indeed, as Paul says, the transforming progression of the gospel "happened among [them]" (2 Thess. 3:1).

---

19 See the striking parallels between Philippians 2:5–11 and 1 Corinthians 9:12, 15, and 19 in Gorman, *Apostle of the Crucified Lord*, 260.

20 Three other instances of γίνομαι in 1 Thessalonians (2:1, 5, 7, 10) further depict the way the gospel shaped Paul and his ministry.

21 As Luther says, "It is not the imitation that makes sons, but the sonship [or, in this case, election] that makes imitators" (*Luther's Works* 27:263). Still, for a criticism of those who overly emphasize election in this regard, see John B. Webster, "Christology, Imitability, and Ethics," *SJT* 39 (1986): 309–26 at 312.

The Thessalonians were radically renovated by God's gospel. They went from idol worshippers to "imitators [μιμηταί] of us and of the Lord" (1 Thess. 1:6). The addition of the phrase "and of the Lord" is both unsurprising and unexpected.[22] It is unsurprising because, as we have seen, God in Christ is the ultimate giver of the gospel. It therefore makes sense that they would become, through their imitation of Paul, imitators of the divine giver (cf. Eph. 5:1: "be imitators of God").[23] But including the Lord in this imitation process is also unexpected. How did the Thessalonians imitate the Lord Jesus?[24] The γάρ clause gives us a clue: "*for* you received the word in much affliction, with the joy of the Holy Spirit" (1 Thess. 1:6). They received the divine gifts of grace and suffering, as the Philippians did. "For it has been granted [ἐχαρίσθη] to you that for the sake of Christ you should not only believe in him but also suffer for his sake" (Phil. 1:29). Still, even in the midst of suffering, they had the joy of the Holy Spirit (cf. 1 Thess. 4:8; Eph. 1:13–14). Therefore, as the Thessalonians beheld the crucified Christ in Paul's preaching (cf. 1 Cor. 1:23; 2:2; Gal. 3:1), they were united to him and subsequently imitated Paul and Christ by embodying the sufferings of Christ in the world (cf. 2 Cor. 1:5; Rom. 8:17).

Initially, they endured suffering with joy. But, over time, they became weary. Their Christian pilgrimage grew more and more challenging, even during Paul's stay with them. "For when we were with you, we kept telling you beforehand that we were to suffer affliction, just as it has come to pass, and just as you know" (1 Thess. 3:4). Disciples will grow weary in afflictions. That is inevitable. Therefore, reminding them of the Christological pattern of discipleship is important: humiliation precedes exaltation, and earthly suffering leads to eternal comfort. This was the pattern established by Christ, and so it will be for all those who participate in Christ by faith. Paul knew this pattern well. He reminded the Thessalonians that "God has not destined us for wrath, but to obtain salvation through our Lord Jesus Christ, who died for us so that whether we are awake or asleep we might live with him" (1 Thess. 5:9–10). One day, suffering will be overcome by life. One day, God will grant relief to the saints and deal justly with those who inflict suffering (1 Thess. 2:14–16; 2 Thess. 1:5–10). One day, Christians will fully experience the "eternal

---

22 References to "the Lord" refer to Christ (see 1:1, 3; 2:15, 19; 3:11; 4:1–2).

23 This passage is unique, insofar as Paul usually depicts himself as the object of imitation (see 1 Cor. 4:16; 11:1; Phil. 3:17; 2 Thess. 3:7, 9).

24 For different options, see Abraham J. Malherbe, *The Letters to the Thessalonians*, AB 32B (New Haven, CT: Yale University Press), 114.

comfort and good hope through grace" that is ours in Christ Jesus (2 Thess. 2:14). But until that day comes, afflicted disciples must treasure the words of Jesus: "In the world you will have tribulation. But take heart; I have overcome the world" (John 16:33).

2. Becoming Models and Mediators of God's Gospel

Despite persecution, the gospel of God transformed the Thessalonians from disciples to disciplers, from imitators to models. As Paul explains, they "became a model" (γενέσθαι . . . τύπον) to others—to believers and to non-believers—in Macedonia and Achaia (1:7–8). This occurred in three ways.

First, they became models by receiving "the word" (τὸν λόγον) in much affliction and joy of the Spirit (1:6). Second, they proclaimed the gospel verbally.[25] "For," Paul expounds, "the word of the Lord [ὁ λόγος τοῦ κυρίου] sounded forth from you" (1:8). Notice that they "received the word [ὁ λόγος]" in 1:7, but "the word [ὁ λόγος] . . . sounds forth" (ἐξήχηται; passive voice) from them to others in 1:8. They, like Paul, proclaimed God's gospel as mediators of divine grace. They freely gave what they freely received, but what they received and what they gave was not their own.[26] It was the word *of God* that "sounded forth" from them. *God's* gospel continued to progress.

The third way they became examples was nonverbally; that is, they embodied the gospel. "Your faith toward God has gone forth" (ἡ πίστις ὑμῶν ἡ πρὸς τὸν θεὸν ἐξελήλυθεν, 1:8). Some take this statement to imply verbal evangelistic activity,[27] but the parallel statement in the next verse ("how you turned to God [πρὸς τὸν θεὸν] from idols," 1:9) suggests that their "faith toward God" refers to their conversion. This also would have included the way they embodied the sufferings of Christ in 1:6 (see above). Through verbal and nonverbal communication, the Thessalonians proclaimed and embodied Christ to others. In so doing, they imitated and became models of their disciplers—of Paul and God in Christ.

3. Summary

That God in Christ disciples the Thessalonian church through Paul should be evident by now. If Paul's skillful arrangement of γίνομαι ("to

---

25 See James Ware, "The Thessalonians as a Missionary Congregation: 1 Thessalonians 1, 5–8," *ZNW* 83 (1992): 126–31, at 127.

26 Weima explains that "the Thessalonians were not the source from which the word sounded forth, but only the point from which it proceeded" (*1–2 Thessalonians*, 104).

27 See, e.g., Malherbe, *Thessalonians*, 117, 130–31.

become") and his depiction of the progress of God's gospel was not enough, we should recall 1 Thessalonians 2:13—it is, after all, the very word of God (λόγον θεοῦ) that powerfully works (ἐνεργεῖται) within believers. The church is ultimately discipled by her Lord. Or, perhaps more accurately, God disciples the church through the church, with his gospel at the center of this relationship. His gospel creates imitators to become models while also serving as a model itself to be imitated. But the question remains, what practical implications does this have for today?

The above presentation of the gospel's progression should change the way we view and practice Christian discipleship. First, since God is the source of grace and its transforming effects through the gospel, we are called to receive his grace and pass it on to others, not hoard or treasure it privately. God calls his people to give both what they *have* and what they *are* to one another, in word and deed.

Second, if God is the divine giver of grace and we mediate grace to one another, then our posture in discipleship should be one of divine dependency rather than self-sufficiency. In fact, our dependence runs in two directions: vertically (toward God), and horizontally (toward one another). Since God gives grace *to* believers *through* believers, we must depend on other believers to receive from God. This binds the discipler and disciple in a mutual bond where they equally depend on God through one another, indeed through an entire network of fellow believers in a given local church community. A leveling effect can be discerned in this relational pattern. God is the discipler, while believers are interdependent disciples (see 1 Thess. 3:1–9; Rom. 1:11–12; Phil. 4:10–20; 2 Cor. 1:3–11).[28]

Third, if the gospel of God is the means of discipleship, then the word of God—proclaimed and embodied—should primarily govern the shape and practice of Christian discipleship. We teach one another the gospel not only by declaring the promises of God in Christ to each other but also by exemplifying the gospel of God to one another, by serving another when sickness comes, by holding another when cancer appears, by forgiving another when sin hardens, by encouraging another when downtrodden. Christlike discipleship must be carried out in word and deed. If not, it does not contain the true mark of discipleship, as lived out by Christ himself (cf. John 5:24 and 13:1–17).

Having considered imitation in the context of discipleship, especially as it relates to the triangular pattern of relationships in Christ and the

---

28 For more on this relational dynamic, see David E. Briones, "Mutual Brokers of Grace: A Study in 2 Corinthians 1.3–11," *NTS* 56 (2010): 536–56.

progression of God's gospel, we now turn to examine holiness in the context of discipleship.

THE PURSUIT OF HOLINESS IN DISCIPLESHIP

"Holy, Holy, Holy is the Lord God Almighty" (Isa. 6:3). But can the same be said of his people? Yes, and no. We exist as those who are simultaneously justified and yet sinners. On the one hand, we are holy, sanctified, consecrated in Christ (e.g., 1 Cor. 1:30). On the other hand, we are called to pursue holiness in the Christian life (e.g., Rom. 6:19, 22). Holiness or sanctification should therefore be understood as a *status* and a *process*, a *sphere* in which we reside and a *goal* to which we strive. Put differently, it is a call to become who we are in Christ, with the imperative ("become") always flowing from and empowered by the indicative ("who we are in Christ"). In 1 Thessalonians 4:1–8, Paul not only affirms this twofold nature of sanctification (status and process) but also emphasizes God's role in the church's pursuit of holiness. More specifically, God in Christ is the ultimate source of the church's holiness or sanctification.

What is telling, theologically speaking, is that Paul articulates this truth in a prayer *before* calling on the Thessalonians to strive for holiness in 1 Thessalonians 4:1–8. After mentioning that something is "lacking in [the Thessalonians'] faith" (3:10), he immediately prays for Christ ("the Lord") to increase their "love" in order that their hearts might be established "blameless in holiness" (3:12–13). Interestingly, an increase in love is for the purpose of increasing one's holiness, and all this should be accomplished through dependence on Christ as the divine source. Only then does Paul turn in 4:1 to speak of their obligation to please God.

The apostle begins by reminding the Thessalonians of what they received from him: "how you ought [δεῖ] to live and please God" (4:1). Even though they fulfilled this obligation (δεῖ) in the past, Paul nevertheless encourages them to "do so more and more" (περισσεύητε μᾶλλον, 4:1; the same verb appears in the prayer of 3:12). They *must* obey "the will of God," and they *must* pursue sanctification or holiness (ἁγιασμός, 4:3). But how? One *must* "abstain from sexual immorality [τῆς πορνείας]," knowing "how to control [κτᾶσθαι] his own body [σκεῦος] in holiness [ἁγιασμῷ] and honor" (4:3–4). Apparently, some in the community were struggling to "control" or "master" their "body" or "vessel" (which may be a euphemism for genitalia).[29] Paul therefore gently yet firmly disciples them from sexual impurity to holiness in 1 Thessalonians 4:3–8. Just how he guides them toward that end is very informative for discipleship today.

Paul's discipleship strategy contains three movements. First, he communicates the seriousness of sexual sin and the need to resist it as God's covenant people. Since believers "ought" (δεῖ, 4:1) to obey the divine will to abstain from sexual immorality (4:3), Paul calls on them to separate themselves from the common, even culturally acceptable, practices of "sexual immorality" (πορνεία). This includes everything from cultic prostitution to fornication to homosexual activity.[30] Their conduct should be distinct from that of "the Gentiles who do not know God" (4:5; cf. Job 18:21; Ps. 79:6; Gal. 4:8–9). After all, "to know God" is to be in covenant relationship with God.[31] That is why Paul contrasts the *Gentile* Thessalonians who know God with other *Gentiles* who do not. He is reminding them of their new identity: They are a part of God's covenant people in Christ. And since he who called them is holy (1 Thess. 4:7; cf. Lev. 21:8), they also ought to be holy in all their conduct. They should be holy, for God is holy (Lev. 11:44; cf. 1 Peter 1:15). They must no longer conduct themselves like unbelieving Gentiles "in lustful passion" (ἐν πάθει ἐπιθυμίας, 4:4), a *self*-centered preoccupation with one's sexual desire. Rather, they must behave "with holiness and honor" (ἐν ἁγιασμῷ καὶ τιμῇ, 4:3), a *self*- and *other*-concern for purity, since sexual immorality dishonors oneself and others.[32] This explains why Paul commands the Thessalonians "not to transgress and wrong his brother in this matter" (4:6).[33] Sexual impurity dishonors our brothers and sisters in Christ, either by sharing in our sexually impure activity or by being implicated in such indecent behavior. Sexual sin poisons the body.

Second, Paul emphasizes the holiness of God and his inevitable judgment of sin. After issuing three exhortations to pursue holiness in 4:3–6a—(i) "abstain from sexual immorality" (4:3); (ii) "know how to control

---

29 Much debate surrounds the verb κτᾶσθαι and the noun σκεῦος. See Weima, *1–2 Thessalonians*, 268–73.

30 See Gary S. Shogren, *1 & 2 Thessalonians*, ZECNT (Grand Rapids: Zondervan, 2012), 159–60.

31 Weima, *1–2 Thessalonians*, 274.

32 Michael W. Holmes, *1 & 2 Thessalonians*, NIVAC (Grand Rapids: Zondervan, 1998), 126.

33 Some have thought that Paul here switches to a new topic: unethical business transactions (e.g., E. J. Richard, *First and Second Thessalonians*, SP [Collegeville, MN: Liturgical Press, 1995], 200–02). But it is much more likely to continue the discussion of sexual conduct. For convincing exegetical and contextual reasons, see Weima, *1-2 Thessalonians*, 275.

his own body in holiness and honor" (4:4); (iii) "no one transgress and wrong his brother in this matter" (4:6a)—Paul provides a reason for doing so: "because the Lord is an avenger in all these things, as we told you beforehand and solemnly warned you" (4:6b). The plural "all these things" (πάντων τούτων) includes all three exhortations above. Those who do not obey these commands will be held accountable by the Lord Jesus, an "avenger" (ἔκδικος) who will punish those who sin against God and others. This certainly would have come as a shock to the Thessalonians. Paul previously mentioned Jesus delivering them "from the wrath to come" (1:10), and he will later speak about God's people not being "destined for wrath" (5:9). Saying, therefore, that the Lord will punish the wicked *in the church* for their lack of obedience demonstrates the seriousness of sin, the holiness of God, and the inevitable outcome of *unrepentant* sexual sin: divine judgment.[34]

Third, Paul takes seriously God's role (i.e., agency) in the Christian's pursuit of holiness. The negative motivation of 4:6b—Jesus, as an avenger, will punish sin—is matched by the more positive motivation for holiness in 4:7: "for [γάρ] God has not called [ἐκάλεσεν] us for impurity but in holiness." With the aorist verb ἐκάλεσεν ("called"), Paul refers to God's eternal decree of election, as he did earlier. In 1:4, divine election (ἐκλογή) serves as the ultimate cause of his thanksgiving. In 2:12, he employs the present tense of καλέω to emphasize the continuing and effectual call of divine election. And now, in 4:7, divine election becomes a motivation for holiness. How so? The one who elected them for salvation is the one who faithfully commits himself to their growth in holiness, until the very end. As 1 Thessalonians 5:23–24 confirms: "Now may the God of peace himself sanctify you completely [ἁγιάσαι ὑμᾶς ὁλοτελεῖς], and may your whole spirit and soul and body be kept blameless *at the coming* of our Lord Jesus Christ. He who calls [ὁ καλῶν] you is faithful; he will surely do it" (cf. 1 Thess. 3:13; cf. 2 Thess. 3:3). Holiness therefore finds its beginning, middle, and end in God.

This is further amplified through the prepositional phrases of 4:7. The Thessalonians were not called for the purpose (ἐπί) of impurity but in holiness (ἐν ἁγιασμῷ). The unexpected preposition ἐν, in contrast with ἐπί, suggests that Paul intends to convey something other than purpose ("for the purpose of holiness"). If he wished to communicate purpose, he

---

34 *Repentant* believers in the church will not experience this type of judgment. To be sure, they will be judged *in accordance with* works that flow from faith in Christ (cf. Rom. 2:13; 14:10, 12; 2 Cor. 5:10), but this will not result in condemnation (cf. Rom. 8:1).

would likely have used the preposition ἐπί or εἰς. Instead, the preposi-tional phrase ἐν ἁγιασμῷ indicates a state or sphere in which the Thes-salonians currently reside, one very similar (if not identical) to being "in Christ." As 1 Corinthians 1:30 states, "Because of him you are in Christ Je-sus [ἐν Χριστῷ Ἰησοῦ], who became to us . . . sanctification [ἁγιασμὸς]." Consequently, the primary emphasis is "not on the readers' need to strive for sanctification but rather on the fact that Christian existence is to be lived in the sphere of God's holiness."[35] In other words, this text depicts holiness or sanctification as a *status* and a *process*, both of which are initi-ated, energized, and completed by divine agency through human agency. Both are necessary, but God's actions always precede human actions, much like the indicative always precedes the imperative. Mixing that order has detrimental effects. Only once people have been made holy (status) can they then become holy (process). As Dietrich Bonhoeffer puts it:

> As saints they are reminded and exhorted to be what they are. But this is not an impossible ideal, it is not sinners who are required to become holy, or that would mean a return to justi-fication by works and would be blasphemy against Christ. No, it is saints who are required to be holy, saints who have been sanctified in Christ Jesus through the Holy Spirit.[36]

Paul continues to underscore God's role in the pursuit of holiness in 4:8: "Therefore, whoever disregards this [call], disregards not man but God, who gives his Holy Spirit to you." The generic term "man" (ἄνθρωπος) refers to Paul. But if they were to persist in impurity, it is not Paul whom they would be "disregarding" or, more accurately in this context, "reject-ing" (ἀθετέω). They would be rejecting God. He is the one who, through the preaching and teaching of his gospel, calls and ultimately disciples the church. That is why Paul, in the very next verse, describes the Thessalo-nians as those who have been "taught by God" (θεοδίδακτοι, 4:9). It makes sense, then, that if they refuse to obey Paul, they actually refuse to obey God. No wonder Paul places them "under oath before the Lord to have this letter read to all the brothers and sisters" (5:27). It is the very word of God, and Paul anticipates it will have a dynamic effect on believers.

What is even more striking is how Paul goes on to describe God in 4:8, as the one "who gives his Holy Spirit to you." If they choose to reject

---

35 Charles A. Wanamaker, *The Epistles to the Thessalonians,* NIGTC (Grand Rapids: Eerd-mans, 1990), 157.
36 Dietrich Bonhoeffer, *The Cost of Discipleship* (New York: Simon & Schuster, 1995), 281.

God, they would not be merely rejecting the one who *commands* their obedience, but the very one who *enables* their obedience. As a fulfillment of Old Testament promises concerning God's Spirit indwelling his people in the messianic age (Ezek. 37:6, 14; cf. 11:19), the Holy Spirit breathes life into dry bones, not only at the beginning of salvation (1 Thess. 1:5–6; cf. Rom. 5:5; Gal. 4:6; 2 Cor. 1:22) but also as a continuing presence: God is "the one who is giving" (τὸν διδόντα) his Holy Spirit (1 Thess. 4:8). He is not "*an option* against sin," Gordon Fee insists, but the very "dynamic that makes Paul's argument against sexual impurity possible."[37] This renders reliance on divine grace an essential component in the believer's pursuit of holiness. As Andy Johnson insightfully notes, "The priority of divine grace is therefore in, with, and under every line of these letters [i.e., 1 and 2 Thessalonians], making any holiness that characterizes this church a holiness that is derived from God the Father in the sphere of Christ the Son, through the activity of the Holy Spirit."[38] And yet, disciples *must* obey the will of God. They *must* abstain from sexual immorality. God works, and the believer works. But it is the indwelling Spirit where divine and human agency come together. As Augustine famously prayed, "Lord, command what you will, but give what you command."[39] We have no recourse to holiness apart from our Triune God.

In sum, Paul's discipleship strategy strikes a perfect balance. He brings the Thessalonians under the word of *promise* (i.e., what God has done, is doing, and will do for believers) and the word of *command* (i.e., what duty God requires of believers). *Grace* and *truth* come through the apostle's teaching, but the apostle is not ultimately the one teaching them. They are "taught by God" (4:9). May we, as twenty-first-century saints, strike the same balance as we disciple God's people, jointly coming under the *promise* and *command* of the gospel, mediating grace to one another by imitating and modeling Christ, and pursuing holiness with gratitude in our hearts. But we must remember, first and foremost, that those who come under the gospel of God are ultimately discipled by the God of the gospel. If we forget this, we neglect a foundational truth of discipleship: God initiates, energizes, and completes all of our discipling efforts. May God grant us this vision of triangular discipleship, and the practical benefits that come as a result.

---

37 Gordon D. Fee, *God's Empowering Presence: The Holy Spirit in the Letters of Paul* (Peabody, MA: Hendrickson, 1994), 53 (original italics).

38 *1 & 2 Thessalonians*, 228.

39 *Confessions*, 10.29.

CHAPTER 12

Faithful Stewardship in God's Household: Discipleship in the Letters to Timothy and Titus

Andreas J. Köstenberger

The Letters to Timothy and Titus (LTT) make an important contribution to the New Testament's teaching on discipleship, yet they do so in terms rather different than the Gospels, the book of Acts, or even Paul's earlier writings.[1] For this reason it is important to be open to terminological and conceptual diversity in the New Testament if one is to capture the LTT's teaching on discipleship and to mine these letters for relevant passages, themes, and subthemes. In the following essay, we will take as our point of departure the grounding of these letters in Paul's apostolic mission, involving his apostolic delegates, and explore how these themes relate to discipleship, both with regard to the kind of modeling that occurs between the apostle and his delegates and the way in which discipleship to Christ is directed through disciple-on-disciple relationships. This will be followed by an exploration of the importance of safeguarding sound apostolic teaching and of being God's stewards over his household, the church. It is in the matrix of these themes and conceptualities that we find a rich and fruitful deposit of apostolic teaching on discipleship.[2]

THE APOSTOLIC MISSION

The theme of discipleship in the LTT is inextricably tied to the apostolic mission. One of the most important questions regarding the LTT is the way in which these writings are grounded in the mission of the early church in general and in the mission of Paul in particular and thus convey his apostolic authority. Most likely, these letters were written after the other ten Pauline letters included in the New Testament canon, as they are concerned with cementing Paul's legacy and establishing the church

---

1 This essay adapts relevant portions from the biblical-theological exposition in the present author's *Commentary on 1–2 Timothy and Titus*, BTCP (Nashville: B&H Academic, 2017). Used by permission.
2 All Scripture translations are from CSB unless otherwise noted.

at the onset of the subapostolic period. In this regard, it is of some importance whether or not these instructions are grounded directly in the mission of the apostle. If so, Paul himself prior to his martyrdom would have conveyed his instructions regarding the ordering of the church to his apostolic delegates, who in turn were to pass these on to others. In this way, discipleship would have formed an integral part of the way in which the early church's mission was carried out in practical terms, in the form of close disciple-to-disciple relationships and life-on-life mentoring. Thus, the contents of these letters would constitute an integral part of the apostolic foundation of the church, which was to remain authoritative throughout subsequent history.

The New Testament documents are properly viewed as "documents of a mission," recording the inauguration of the work of Jesus and its extension through his followers.[3] Whether or not one holds to Pauline authorship, it is evident that the LTT represent an extension of Paul's mission to the Gentiles as he interacts with his delegates in Ephesus and Crete. After an initial visit to Ephesus, Paul established a mission work there (Acts 18:19–21). In Ephesus, Paul left Timothy with an established church to confront false teaching that is detrimental to Paul's larger mission (1 Tim. 1:3–4), teaching contrary to the sound doctrine that "conforms to the gospel concerning the glory of the blessed God, which was entrusted to me" (1 Tim. 1:11). In Crete, Titus is to complete the setting up of churches throughout the island by appointing qualified local church leadership (Titus 1:5).[4]

On a Pauline reading of these letters, in particular, it is clear that the LTT are "mission documents" by which Paul guides and encourages his delegates in their ministries with regard to an established and a more recent work.[5] The centrality of mission in the LTT is captured well by C. E. Ho, who speaks of the "missionary outlook" of these letters, which

---

3 I. Howard Marshall, New Testament Theology: Many Witnesses, One Gospel (Downers Grove, IL: InterVarsity, 2004), 34–35 (even though Marshall places those letters at a later point of composition subsequent to the earthly departure of Paul).

4 Wieland argues on the basis of parallels between the letter and the distinctive culture of Crete that Titus is "understood most satisfactorily as a product of early Christian mission and an intriguing example of creative missionary engagement with a specific environment." George M. Wieland, "Roman Crete and the Letter to Titus," NTS 55 (2009): 338–54, at 354.

5 Barram notes that "inasmuch as Paul's letters aim to nurture the faith of established Christian communities, they are themselves *mission in action*—tools used by Paul to fulfill the terms of his apostolic commission. Everything in Paul's letters—autobiographical details and travel itineraries, theological assertions and benedictions, even the epistolary and rhetorical framing of the letters—serves a missional function for the apostle." Michael D. Barram, *Mission and Moral Reflection in Paul*, StBibLit 75; New York: Peter Lang, 2006), 136.

convey an "overarching framework of thought that has missions at its center."[6] Indeed, the LTT, and 1 Timothy and Titus in particular, portray the apostle as engaged in the mission to which God called him, relying on delegates to handle matters in particular locales as he is engaged in travel or occupied elsewhere.[7] Specifically, in conjunction with the larger idea of his mission, we find Paul speaking of his appointment as a preacher, apostle, and teacher of the Gentiles (1 Tim. 2:7; cf. 2 Tim. 1:11). Paul's apostolic mission, in turn, entails mentoring his close followers, in particular his apostolic delegates, who joined him in his mission and as the next generation of disciples would continue his mission work and apostolic legacy.

In 2 Timothy, Paul seeks to prepare Timothy for assuming the mantle of Paul's mission. The letter closes with the intriguing statement that at Paul's first defense "the Lord stood with me and strengthened me, so that I might fully preach the word and all the Gentiles might hear it" (2 Tim. 4:17). The connection between "all the Gentiles" and the "fullness" or "completeness" of Paul's proclamation of the apostolic message indicates that more is in view than Paul being able to complete his presentation without interruption on this occasion. Paul's words in 2 Timothy 4:6–7 indicate that he believes he has reached the end of his life and ministry, which supports an understanding of "fully proclaim" that has the Gentile world in view. In any case, Paul has his larger mission in mind, and specifically passing on his apostolic legacy to the disciples he had been mentoring in many cases for several decades, as he closes his final canonical letter.[8]

Not only does Paul expect his apostolic delegates to participate in his Gentile mission, he expects individual congregations to do so as well: "The theme of *witness* that underlies much of the ethical teaching reveals one important way in which the Christian communities are to participate in the

---

6   Chiao Ek Ho, "Mission in the Pastoral Epistles," in *Entrusted with the Gospel: Paul's Theology in the Pastoral Epistles*, eds. A. J. Köstenberger and T. L. Wilder (Nashville: B&H Academic, 2010), 241–67, at 242. Ho's work in this essay is grounded in his dissertation, "Do the Work of an Evangelist: The Missionary Outlook of the Pastoral Epistles" (PhD thesis, University of Aberdeen, 2000).

7   Note also the future plans Paul has for his own travels (1 Tim. 3:14–15) and those of his associates (Titus 3:12–13).

8   Towner argues that what Paul says in his figurative statement of 2 Timothy 4:7 "on the historical (and missiological) plane translates into 'I have fully accomplished my mission to the Gentiles.'" Philip H. Towner, "1–2 Timothy and Titus," in *Commentary on the New Testament Use of the Old Testament*, eds. G. K. Beale and D. A. Carson (Grand Rapids: Baker, 2007), 891–918, at 911.

mission to the Gentiles."[9] To use the language of Titus 2:10, it is in this way that believers whose character and conduct reflect their Christianity "adorn the teaching of God our Savior."[10] Another way in which believers are to participate in Paul's mission is through *prayer*. In 1 Timothy 2:1–6, the apostle urges that prayers be uttered for all people, including kings and those in authority. While these latter prayers may also have the salvation of the rulers themselves in view, "Christians who pray for the authorities of state and city implore God 'to let them create the necessary free space in which the expansion of the gospel is possible.'"[11]

Paul's apostolic identity is explicitly affirmed at the outset of each of the LTT[12] and is evident throughout.[13] Although the letters are addressed to his delegates—who doubtless need little reminder of Paul's status as an apostle—they are apparently not meant to be received solely and privately by Timothy and Titus but also to be heeded by their respective congregations.[14] Paul's apostolic authority finds forceful expression in the authoritative language used,[15] whether in the form of direct commands or third-person imperatives addressed to the congregations.[16] Paul considers himself able to speak authoritatively not only to the congregations at large but also to their local leadership[17] and to Timothy and Titus in

---

9   Philip H. Towner, "The Pastoral Epistles," in *New Dictionary of Biblical Theology*, eds. T. D. Alexander, et al. (Downers Grove, IL: InterVarsity Press, 2000), 333 (emphasis added). See on this point more thoroughly idem, *The Goal of Our Instruction: The Structure of Theology and Ethics in the Pastoral Epistles*, JSNTSup 34 (Sheffield: Sheffield Academic Press, 1989), 169–99.

10   Ho rightly argues that "the ethical posture of the Pastorals is not defensive and merely inward-looking as some commentators have suggested but is also outward-looking and missionary in orientation" ("Mission in the Pastoral Epistles," 242; note his treatment of the "good witness" motif on 245–46).

11   Eckhard J. Schnabel, *Early Christian Mission*, vol. 2: *Paul & the Early Church* (Downers Grove, IL: InterVarsity, 2004), 1470, citing Peter Lampe and Ulrich Luz, "Nachpaulinisches Christentum und pagane Gesellschaft," in *Die Anfänge des Christentums: Alte Welt und neue Hoffnung*, eds. Jürgen Becker, et al. (Stuttgart: Kohlhammer, 1987), 185–216, at 213. See also I. Howard Marshall, "Biblical Patterns for Public Theology," *EuroJTh* 14 (2005): 73–86, at 79–83.

12   1 Tim. 1:1; 2:7; 2 Tim. 1:1, 11; Titus 1:1.

13   The word ἀπόστολος appears only four times in the LTT (1 Tim. 1:1; 2:7; 2 Tim. 1:1, 11) but words and concepts reflecting apostolic authority are common.

14   This is suggested by the closing plurals in 1 Timothy 6:21, 2 Timothy 4:22, and Titus 3:15, as well as the third-person imperatives in the letters.

15   E.g., βούλομαι (1 Tim. 2:8), διαμαρτύρομαι (2 Tim. 4:1), οὐκ ἐπιτρέπω (1 Tim. 2:12), παραγγέλλω (1 Tim. 6:13), παραγγελία (1 Tim. 1:5, 18), and παρακαλέω (1 Tim. 1:3; 2:1).

16   E.g., 1 Tim. 2:11; 3:10, 12; 4:12; 5:4, 9, 16, 17; 6:1, 2; Titus 2:15; 3:14. Such imperatives are conspicuously absent from 2 Timothy, and nearly so from Titus.

17   E.g., 1 Tim. 5:17.

particular who as apostolic delegates are portrayed as outranking local church leaders.[18]

More than once, Paul speaks of his apostolic office, which may be part of his strategy to legitimate the authority of his teaching and directives (and thus that of his delegates) over against the false teachers. For example, after Paul opens 1 Timothy by addressing the issue of false teaching at Ephesus (1:3–11), he uses his own contrasting example to highlight the nature of his gospel as one of mercy, grace, and transformation rather than genealogies, myths, and law (1:12–17). In this connection, Paul goes on to refer to the juncture at which Jesus appointed him to his service, that is, Paul's ministry as an apostle (1:12), and draws particular attention to the gracious nature of his apostolic calling. Correspondingly, just as Jesus appointed the twelve apostles and Paul, so Paul is charged with training a new generation of disciples who in turn will train yet others (2 Tim. 2:2). Later in the letter (and similarly in 2 Timothy), Paul reiterates certain aspects of his gospel and observes that it was for the proclamation of this very gospel that he was called to be a preacher, apostle, and teacher of the Gentiles (1 Tim. 2:7; 2 Tim. 1:11).

In 2 Timothy, a particular emphasis emerges on the apostle's suffering that runs through the entire letter.[19] As Paul the prisoner (1:8, 16; 2:9) opens the letter, the topic of his suffering at once comes to the fore (1:8–12). In verse 8, the veteran apostle challenges Timothy not to shrink back from the proclamation of the gospel or from associating with Paul as the Lord's prisoner. Instead, Timothy must join with Paul in suffering for the gospel; thus, discipleship is shown to involve identification with Christ even when such proves costly and results in suffering for his name's sake. After stepping back for a big-picture look at the gospel in verses 9–10 and highlighting his own appointment as a preacher, apostle, and teacher of that gospel, Paul acknowledges that it is because of this very appointment that he is currently suffering. In what follows, he engages the language of his challenge to Timothy as he points to himself as a model for Timothy. Just as Timothy must not be ashamed of Paul and his gospel proclamation but should join him in suffering for the gospel (1:8), so Paul is suffering for the gospel and is not ashamed (1:10–12). Given this correspondence in language, the grounds for Paul's lack of shame are

---

18 E.g., 1 Tim. 1:3–5, 18; 4:11, 12; 5:7, 21; 6:2, 13, 17; 2 Tim. 2:14; 4:1–2; Titus 1:3; 2:15.
19 The vocabulary of suffering in the LTT as a whole is largely confined to 2 Timothy and includes κακοπαθέω (2x: 2 Tim. 2:9; 4:5), συγκακοπαθέω (2x: 2 Tim. 1:8; 2:3), πάθημα (1x: 2 Tim. 3:11), and πάσχω (1x: 2 Tim. 1:12), as well as the use of διώκω in 2 Tim. 3:12.

implied to be Timothy's as well: Paul knows the God in whom he trusts, and he is convinced that God will guard his deposit.

This discipleship progression—from Paul to Timothy to faithful men to others—is significant in its connection with the suffering that accompanies the apostolic ministry as well. In fact, 2 Timothy reflects a passing of the torch from Paul to Timothy, and 1:8–12 suggests that Timothy may have been fearful with regard to the suffering his own ministry would continue to entail. After an aside regarding those who have deserted him (1:15) and one who has remained loyal to him (1:16–18), Paul returns to encouraging Timothy, continuing to tie suffering to the ministry of the gospel as he calls his foremost disciple to be strong in Jesus's grace (2:1). Paul also urges Timothy to perpetuate Paul's gospel ministry in the lives of other trustworthy men and to share in his suffering. In particular, Timothy is called to share in suffering as a good soldier of Christ Jesus, which may imply continuity with Jesus's suffering as well. The need to be prepared to suffer rejection in this world for Christ's sake is an inexorable entailment of following the Crucified One yet constitutes an often-overlooked element of Christian discipleship.

At the same time, it is of note that in spite of the connection between Paul's and Jesus's suffering (cf. 2 Cor. 1:5–7; 4:8–14; Col. 1:23–26), and in spite of 2 Timothy's oblique references to Jesus's suffering (1:8; 2:8–10), the suffering of Jesus is nowhere directly mentioned in the letter. Instead, Jesus is overtly portrayed—doubtless for Timothy's encouragement—on the other side of the grave, having abolished death and having brought life and immortality to light through the gospel (1:10), having risen from the dead (2:8), and serving as the righteous judge of the living and the dead (4:1, 8). To be sure, Paul's suffering for the gospel is tied to the death of Christ in 2:11, but only as part of what is probably a preformed tradition, and as a passing protasis ("If we died with him") on the way to a hopeful apodosis ("we will also live with him"). In 2:9, Paul reiterates that it is the gospel for which he, bound as a criminal, is suffering. Because God's gospel message is not bound, however, Paul is willing to endure all things for the sake of God's elect (2:10). Paul's suffering thus leads to a desirable end, similar to the way in which dying with Christ leads to being alive with him (2:11).

After reminding Timothy to avoid the false teachers who are described at some length in 3:1–9, Paul points out that in contrast to these individuals, Timothy has known and followed Paul's example.[20] One aspect of Paul's model that Timothy should continue to emulate as part of his discipleship is that of accepting persecution and suffering. Timothy is familiar with the persecutions and sufferings Paul underwent on his first missionary journey in Pisidian Antioch, Iconium, and Lystra (3:11; cf. Acts 13:49–52; 14:4–6, 19–22), which came to a head when Jews from the first two cities caught up with him at Lystra, stoned him, and left him for dead outside the city. Even this last instance of persecution, however, is included in Paul's affirmation that "the Lord rescued me from them *all*" (2 Tim. 3:11).

Remarkably, then, Paul ties together the virtue of godliness, so characteristic of the letters to Timothy, with suffering for the gospel: "In fact, *all who want to live a godly life* in Christ Jesus will be persecuted" (2 Tim. 3:12). A striking contrast is thus established with the preceding verses 1–9 and the following verse 13. On the one side are those who display only an outward veneer of godliness (3:5), in particular the false teachers whom Timothy must confront. On the other side are Paul (model of right teaching, moral living, and proper affections), Timothy, and all those who desire to live in a godly way. The theme of godliness receives particular emphasis in the LTT where it typically designates "a particular way of living that reflects knowing God and being in a close, reverent relationship with him."[21] It also provides a distinguishing mark between true disciples of Christ such as Paul's apostolic delegates and the false teachers.[22]

As 2 Timothy draws to a close, Paul challenges Timothy one final time to "endure suffering" (4:5). His own suffering is reflected shortly thereafter in his reference to Psalm 22 in the latter half of chapter 4. These kinds of connections place the suffering of Paul and his apostolic delegates, as well as other faithful believers, against the backdrop of an entire biblical trajectory of righteous suffering that encompasses David, the prototypical righteous sufferer (especially at the hands of Saul), and the latter-day son of David, Jesus Christ, who was the suffering Servant and endured a violent cross-death to atone for the sins of humanity (e.g., 1 Peter 2:21–25;

---

20 On the nuance of παρηκολούθησάς ("followed") here, see Ceslas Spicq, *Les épîtres pastorales*, 4th ed., Études bibliques 39 (Paris: Gabalda, 1969), 781. To be sure, Timothy has farther to go in imitating Paul—hence Paul's exhortations throughout the letter—but the term here does not *merely* mean that Timothy carefully observed Paul, as shown by the contrast with those characterized in the previous verses.

21 See Köstenberger, *Commentary on 1–2 Timothy and Titus*, with references to additional scholarly works. See the entire discussion of godliness in the LTT on 498–503.

22 Köstenberger, *Commentary on 1-2 Timothy and Titus*, 502–3.

cf. Isa. 52:13–53:12). In this way, Paul's apostolic mission, reaching to the ends of the earth and including the Gentile nations, is shown to involve (vicarious) suffering that finds validating biblical-theological precedent in previous servants of the Lord such as David and, climatically, Jesus himself (cf. Col. 1:24). This also shows that suffering is part of Christian discipleship: just as Jesus suffered, and Paul is suffering, so their followers are likewise called to suffer.

THE ROLE OF APOSTOLIC DELEGATES

The apostolic mission, rooted in the Great Commission and carried forward in Paul's mission to the Gentiles, significantly involves the use of apostolic delegates who carry out the apostle's orders.[23] Both in terms of close one-on-one committed discipleship relationships, and in terms of cultivating Christlike character and conduct and mentoring others to do the same, the apostolic mission and the role of apostolic delegates contribute significantly to the biblical teaching on Christian discipleship. Notably, while nomenclature used for Timothy and Titus in the LTT is diverse,[24] neither is said to be an apostle. There is a sense in which they might be considered such in a nontechnical sense—Paul's *apostoloi*, sent by the apostle with his authority backing them as they act as his representatives.[25] Time and again, Timothy and Titus are instructed to authoritatively communicate Paul's instruction; on Paul's behalf, they are

---

23 Cf. Frances Young, *The Theology of the Pastoral Letters* (Cambridge: Cambridge University Press, 1994), 67, who views the apostolic mission as taking place between two epiphanies or imperial visits of Christ, at which time authority is vested in the apostle and his delegates, who in turn are over God's household, the church.

24 In 1 and 2 Timothy, Timothy is spoken of as Paul's true or beloved child in the faith (1 Tim. 1:2, 18; 2 Tim. 1:2; 2:1), as a good servant of Christ Jesus (1 Tim. 4:6), as a man of God (1 Tim. 6:11; 2 Tim. 3:17), as a good soldier of Jesus Christ (2 Tim. 2:3), as a workman (2 Tim. 2:15), and as the Lord's servant (2 Tim. 2:24; "servant of the Lord" is probably meant to refer to church leaders in addition to Timothy but likely includes Timothy as well). Elsewhere in the New Testament, Timothy is said to be a disciple (Acts 16:1), Christ's servant (Phil. 1:1), and God's coworker (1 Thess. 3:2), as well as Paul's helper (Acts 19:22), coworker (Rom. 16:21), child in the Lord (1 Cor. 4:17), and brother (2 Cor. 1:1; Col. 1:1; 1 Thess. 3:2). Titus, not nearly as prominent in the New Testament, is spoken of as Paul's brother (2 Cor. 2:13), partner (2 Cor. 8:23), coworker (2 Cor. 8:23), and true child in their common faith (Titus 1:4).

25 In connection with "apostolic delegates," consider the significance of the laying on of hands by Paul in 2 Timothy 1:6, cf. 1 Tim. 4:14. Cf. John Fleter Tipei, *The Laying on of Hands in the New Testament: Its Significance, Techniques, and Effects* (Lanham, MD: University Press of America, 2009), 268: "In the manner of a Jewish Rabbi who ordains his own student to become a teacher of the Law, so Paul ordains Timothy as his delegate in order to preserve the established apostolic teaching."

to command,[26] teach,[27] urge,[28] remind,[29] and insist on[30] the things Paul has set forth, tasks that continue to be vital as entailments of Christian discipleship.

Regarding Timothy, his marching orders in 1 Timothy pertain to his correction of those who teach false doctrine in the church (1:3–4). Throughout the letter, Paul issues instructions on this and other matters, not only to Timothy directly but also to the congregation. As Paul's delegate, Timothy is responsible to convey Paul's instructions to the congregation and to hold people accountable to follow these instructions. This is regularly made explicit as Paul pauses to instruct Timothy to "command and teach these things" or the like.[31] As to the specific church-related responsibilities given to Timothy, he is to (1) stop the false teachers from teaching false doctrine (1:3–4); (2) authoritatively communicate what Paul is commanding and teaching in the letter (4:6, 11; 5:7; 6:2, 17); (3) provide a godly example for the congregation (4:12, 15–16); (4) devote himself to the public reading of Scripture and to the exhortation and teaching that follow from such reading (4:13); (5) exhort various members of the congregation in the context of the church family, giving consideration to their age and gender, possibly in relation to guiding them away from false teaching they may have embraced to proper belief and behavior (5:1–2);[32] (6) honor true widows by regulating the church's support program (5:3–16); (7) handle accusations against elders by accepting only substantiated charges and rebuking persistently sinning elders in the presence of the congregation (5:19–21); and (8) avoid haste in appointing men to the office of elder (5:22). While there is a sense in which Timothy's role as Paul's apostolic delegate is unique, there is also a sense in which the aforementioned characteristics are part and parcel of faithful discipleship—and particularly church leadership—in any age.

In 2 Timothy, Paul seems less concerned with church matters and more intent on encouraging Timothy to remain loyal to Paul and his gospel in spite of the suffering that is the lot of a servant of the gospel. That said,

---

26 1 Tim. 1:3; 4:11; 5:7; 6:17.
27 1 Tim. 4:11; 6:2.
28 1 Tim. 5:1; 6:2; 2 Tim. 4:2.
29 2 Tim. 2:14; Titus 3:1.
30 Titus 3:8.
31 1 Tim. 4:11; 5:7; 6:2.
32 It is likely that these verses are not wholly generic, merely giving general instruction to Timothy as to the way in which he should relate to various groups in the congregation. That this is the case is suggested by the immediately preceding admonition of 4:16: Timothy is to keep a close watch on his own life and doctrine and should follow Paul's teaching carefully, because in doing so he will help preserve both himself and those who listen to him.

church matters are by no means out of view: as Paul's delegate, Timothy, is to (1) entrust Paul's teaching to other faithful men for its perpetuation (2:2); (2) remind the congregation of Paul's teaching (2:14); (3) charge the congregation not to engage in the fruitless debates that apparently characterized the false teachers (2:14, 16); (4) kindly and adeptly correct his opponents, with gentleness and without quarreling (2:24–25); (5) engage in "the faithful presentation of the Christian message to the church with the accompanying discipline that is needed for people who are tempted not to listen or to heed it"[33] (4:2); and (6) do the work of an evangelist, that is, proclaim the gospel (4:5). Again, the essential tasks of faithful mentoring, cultivation of Christlike character, and diligent preservation of the apostolic teaching continue to be of paramount importance for every disciple of Christ, in particular church leaders.

The letter to Titus, similar to 1 Timothy, provides a straightforward statement of Paul's purpose for his delegate (1:5). In general terms, Titus is to complete aspects of Paul's mission to Crete that have remained unfinished; more specifically, he is to appoint elders in the cities of Crete where Christian congregations have been established. In addition he is, (1) along with the elders he appoints, to silence the false teachers present in the churches (1:9–14); (2) to teach what is consistent with healthy doctrine, urging proper conduct to various age groups within the church (2:1–6); (3) to model good works and blameless teaching (2:7–8); (4) to authoritatively declare and remind the Cretan believers of Paul's teaching and to exhort and rebuke his hearers as necessary (2:15–3:1; 3:8); (5) to avoid participating in worthless disputes with the false teachers (3:9); and (6) after warning factious people twice, to reject them, which probably involves their formal exclusion from the congregation. Like Timothy, Titus thus serves as a model disciple who provides a vital paradigm for Christian discipleship and its various entailments in the context of the local church.

A. Responsibilities of Apostolic Delegates

This survey of responsibilities given to Timothy and Titus provides insight into the role of an apostolic delegate. In an important sense, as mentioned, the role of an apostolic delegate is salvation-historically unique in that it is tied to a unique period in salvation history, namely that of

---

33 I. Howard Marshall (in collaboration with Philip H. Towner), *A Critical and Exegetical Commentary on the Pastoral Epistles*, ICC (Edinburgh: T&T Clark, 1999), 799. This includes preaching the word, and doing so in an urgent way, reproving, rebuking, and exhorting the hearers.

the apostolic era. In a broader, generic sense, however, the principles discussed above also translate to faithful discipleship in the church of any age and provide a template for how disciples of Christ are to live and act in concert with other committed disciples as they carry out the mission of preaching the gospel and of validating it by the lives they live.

1. The role of apostolic delegate entails a considerable measure of *authority*. This is evident in the strong language of command Paul uses when speaking of their interaction with their respective congregations, their significant role in appointing elders and excluding false teachers from the congregation, their role of teaching apostolic doctrine, and Paul's insistence that their congregations are not to reject or despise them (1 Tim. 4:12; Titus 2:15).

2. Their authority is not *intrinsic* but *delegated*. Time and again, Paul insists that they teach and urge their congregations to heed the instructions and commands he is issuing.[34] Similarly, Paul insists that they bring the Scriptures to bear upon their congregations: It is the God-breathed Scriptures that equip the man of God (2 Tim. 3:16–17), and it is to the public reading and exhortation and teaching of this Scripture that Timothy must devote himself (1 Tim. 4:13). Similarly, disciples of Christ today should be mindful that their authority ultimately derives from Christ and the gospel rather than being vested in and of themselves.

3. The *preservation and perpetuation of the apostolic teaching* is paramount in their work: They must be sure to teach what is consistent with sound doctrine (1 Tim. 4:16; Titus 1:9), fight against false teaching (1 Tim. 1:3–4), and entrust Paul's teaching to faithful men (2 Tim. 2:2). The importance of identifying faithful believers who then can be mentored thoroughly by mature Christian leaders cannot be overstated. While preaching Christian sermons is essential, it is not sufficient merely to engage in verbal proclamation to a larger audience. In addition, there is a need for close one-on-one relationships in which the Christian life is modeled in a variety of settings and which provide much-needed accountability, encouragement, guidance, and support.

---

34 As Margaret M. Mitchell shows ("New Testament Envoys in the Context of Greco-Roman Diplomatic and Epistolary Conventions: The Example of Timothy and Titus," *JBL* 111 [1992]: 641–62, at 649–51), this was commensurate with the standard role of an envoy in Greco-Roman culture, although Paul's own conception of his delegates may well have been shaped more significantly by the role of the Jewish *shaliah* or his own role as an apostle of Christ.

4. The role of Timothy and Titus as apostolic delegates was *temporary*: Timothy is envisioned as leaving Ephesus to come to Paul (2 Tim. 4:9, 11–13, 21), and a similar situation obtains with Titus (Titus 3:12; cf. 2 Tim. 4:10). Similarly, Paul indicates that Timothy's ministry of bringing Scripture to bear on the Ephesian congregation is to be done "until I come" (1 Tim. 4:13), which implies that Paul will take the reins back at that time. Regarding the temporary nature of the assignments extended to Paul's apostolic delegates, their role in some respects resembles that of an interim pastor who may be called in during times of crisis or transition to provide stability and if needed healing or even correction in a local church. In this way, their role differs from that of a permanent, resident staff of pastors or elders and provides additional help and support along a spectrum of possible tasks depending on the particular needs of a given congregation at a particular point in time.

5. Paul's apostolic delegates were *competent*. As Mounce notes, "The often-painted picture of Timothy as a weak, timid person is not supported by the evidence. He was Paul's 'first lieutenant,' someone Paul felt comfortable sending into difficult situations, as he did repeatedly throughout Acts."[35] This assessment is underscored by Phil. 2:19–22, where Paul speaks of Timothy's "proven worth."

Why did Paul send delegates to churches, as opposed to going himself? Doubtless at least part of the reason lies in the multiplicity of needs Paul encountered in the many churches under his care. Many congregations required special attention beyond what their nascent leadership could provide, but Paul could physically be in only one place at a time. Through his delegates, however, his apostolic presence could extend to numerous churches (see, e.g., 1 Tim. 3:14–15). The same principle of delegation may prove useful in a missions or church-planting context today as a pastor's or church planter's ministry is multiplied and extended to faithful delegates who serve under the overall jurisdiction of the lead pastor or senior church planter.

B. God's Household

By conceiving of the local church in terms of a household or family, the LTT make a vital contribution to our understanding of the biblical teaching on discipleship. The LTT in their entirety contain *paraenesis*, that is,

---

35 William D. Mounce, *Pastoral Epistles,* WBC 46 (Nashville: Thomas Nelson, 2000), lviii.

ethical instruction and exhortation.[36] This body of teaching is to be understood in the context of first-century Greco-Roman education[37] and the depiction of the church as God's household. Within the household, moral conduct is imperative, as are properly aligned relationships and adherence to tradition. This pertains to God's household, the church, just as it did to the natural household in the first-century Greco-Roman world: "The predominant concern is about correct relationships, duties and obligations in a community which regards itself as a teaching environment with a pattern of virtuous behavior and a set of authoritative writings."[38] Thus the household was the primary place where ancient education took place.[39] This, in turn, explains why Paul was perturbed when certain false teachers invaded households (e.g., 2 Tim. 3:6) and sought to infiltrate them with their teaching which was contrary to apostolic doctrine.

Throughout the LTT, reference is made to some in the church who were perpetrating teachings contrary to Paul's gospel. In response, Paul's delegates were to preserve and perpetuate what Paul taught, and Paul uses a number of terms to describe this apostolic teaching,[40] usually in contexts where it is contrasted with false teaching. If false teaching is rightly understood as the main problem faced across the three letters, it would make sense to say that "the fundamental interest of the Pastorals would appear to be 'healthy' or 'sound teaching.'"[41] Vocabulary covering the content of Paul's apostolic mission is diverse and includes references to "healthy teaching," "the truth," "the faith," "the word of God," and "the deposit."[42]

---

36 See Young, *Theology*, 78, who cites terminology such as παραγγέλλω, παραγγελία, παρακαλέω, παράκλησις, μανθάνω, παιδεία, and παιδεύω. See also Claire S. Smith, *Pauline Communities as "Scholastic Communities": A Study of the Vocabulary of 'Teaching' in 1 Corinthians, 1 and 2 Timothy and Titus,* WUNT 2/335 (übingen: Mohr-Siebeck, 2012), who after thorough examination concludes that E. A. Judge's characterization of believing communities as "scholastic" (or, better, "learning communities") is appropriate in the cases of Corinth, Ephesus, and Crete.

37 As Young (*Theology*, 79) notes, "The education of mind and body through *paideia* was the classical Greek ideal" (citing relevant literature in n. 2).

38 Young, *Theology*, 83.

39 Cf. Young (*Theology*, 82), who states, "Indeed, it was in the household that much education and training must have taken place. The head of the household was responsible for the appropriate nurture of family and servants."

40 Key terms in the LTT include διδασκαλία (1 Tim. 1:10; 4:6, 13, 16; 5:17; 6:1, 3; 2 Tim. 3:10, 16; 4:3; Titus 1:9; 2:1, 7, 10) and ὑγιαίνω (1 Tim. 1:10; 6:3; 2 Tim. 1:13; 4:3; Titus 1:9, 13; 2:1, 2).

41 Young, *Theology*, 74.

42 See in this conjunction also the remembrance theme in the LTT, on which see esp. 2 Tim. 2:8–10.

Whereas the LTT feature Paul's instructions to his apostolic delegates assigned to care for congregations in his place, explicit terminology related to the church appears only intermittently.[43] This should not be surprising, however, as the church is presupposed throughout these letters. Paul uses the common New Testament term for the church, ἐκκλησία, only three times in the LTT, all in 1 Timothy (3:5, 15; 5:16). More common is the depiction of the church as "God's household," whether explicitly (οἶκος θεοῦ; 1 Tim. 3:15; cf. 3:4, 5) or implicitly (see, e.g., 1 Tim. 5:1–2; Titus 2:1–10).

The concept of God's people as a family is not unique to Paul but finds its roots in the Old Testament, where God's people Israel are physically descended from Jacob (later renamed Israel). As early as Genesis 46:27, the nascent nation is referred to as "the house of Jacob," a phrase which, along with "the house of Israel," occurs approximately 170 times in the Old Testament.[44] The familial nature of the people of God is carried into the New Testament where, in the teachings of Jesus and Paul, the spiritual relationship among believers is highlighted over against their ethnic characteristics (see, e.g., Matt. 12:46–50; Rom. 8:14–16).

While the phrase οἶκος θεοῦ can be rendered as either "house of God" (e.g., Matt. 12:4) or "household of God" (e.g., Eph. 2:19), the latter is commonly in view in the LTT.[45] Based on the premise that believers are members of one and the same spiritual family, Paul depicts them as members of a joint household, a concept with a rich background in the Jewish and particularly the Greco-Roman world.[46] While the concept of God's household thus builds on the reality of the church as the family of God, the LTT use this household metaphor to convey how Paul's apostolic

---

43 See also Young's interesting discussion of Paul as teacher (e.g., 1 Tim. 2:7) and of Timothy and Titus as "philosopher-chaplains" in keeping with contemporary educational mores in first-century Greco-Roman culture (*Theology*, 89–90).

44 The phrase normally refers to the people of Israel as a whole (e.g., Exod. 19:3; Lev. 17:10), though on a few occasions it refers specifically to the northern kingdom of Israel (e.g., 1 Kings 12:21; 20:31).

45 F. Alan Tomlinson, "The Purpose and Stewardship Theme within the Pastoral Epistles," in *Entrusted with the Gospel: Paul's Theology in the Pastoral Epistles*, eds. A. J. Köstenberger and T. L. Wilder (Nashville: B&H Academic, 2010), 52–83, at 69–70 and 75–82, demonstrates that the controlling metaphor in the LTT is household stewardship, pointing to the use of stewardship language at important junctures in the letters: e.g., οἰκονομίαν θεοῦ (1 Tim. 1:4), παραγγελία (1 Tim. 1:5, 18), ἐκκλησία θεοῦ, παραθήκη (1 Tim. 6:20; 2 Tim. 1:12, 14), παρατίθημι (2 Tim. 2:2), ἐπιστεύθη (Titus 1:3), θεοῦ οἰκονόμον (Titus 1:7). In addition, there is not only a focus on the household of God but on the literal household as well (1 Tim. 3:4–5, 12; 5:4, 8, 13–14).

46 The designation of the church as the "household of God" occurs first in Ephesians 2:19. It is not surprising that Paul draws on this imagery again when writing to Timothy in Ephesus.

delegates should carry out their roles and how believers should conduct themselves in the church.[47]

The household metaphor used for the church in the LTT would have resonated deeply with Paul's audience.[48] In the Greco-Roman world, the household was the foundational unit of society. Rather than viewed as a matter of expediency or social construction, it was held to be divinely instituted and a foundational part of the natural order,[49] consisting not only of the nuclear family but also of slaves and the extended family. The male head of the household, the *paterfamilias*, served as the final authority responsible for overseeing the affairs of the entire household, all of whom were expected to follow his guidance in every respect.[50] For example, they were to worship his gods, though in addition they might also have been devoted to other gods privately. At times, this authority was delegated to a steward (οἰκονόμος) whose role was to manage some aspect of the household. Because the household was viewed as the integral societal unit, its proper ordering was considered to be essential to the health of society. Consequently, a large volume of philosophical works was dedicated to the right ordering of the household and the proper conduct of its members.[51]

---

47 This is not a unique theme in the LTT but is more developed there than in Paul's other letters (see 1 Cor. 4:1–2; 9:17; Col. 1:25; Gal. 6:10; Eph. 2:19; 3:14–15). McCartney, "House, Spiritual House," 509–11; Towner, *Letters to Timothy and Titus*, 57, 273; idem, "Pauline Theology or Pauline Tradition in the Pastoral Epistles: The Question of Methodology," *TynBul* 46 (1995): 287–314, at 308.

48 For relevant literature, see John K. Goodrich, "Overseers as Stewards and the Qualifications for Leadership in the Pastoral Epistles," *ZNW* 104 (2013): 77–97; Malcolm B. Yarnell, "*Oikos Theou*: A Theologically Neglected but Important Ecclesiological Metaphor," *Midwestern Journal of Theology* 2 (2003): 53–65; Korinna Zamfir, "Is the ἐκκλησία a Household (of God)? Reassessing the Notion of οἶκος θεοῦ in 1 Tim. 3.15," *NTS* 60 (2014): 511–28, esp. 526–28. See also D. G. Horrell, "From ἀδελφοί to οἶκος θεοῦ: Social Transformation in Pauline Christianity," *JBL* 120 (2001): 293–311; Abraham J. Malherbe, "Overseers as Household Managers in the Pastoral Epistles," in *Text, Image, and Christians in the Graeco-Roman World: A Festschrift in Honor of David Lee Balch*, eds. A. C. Niang and C. Osiek (Eugene, OR: Pickwick, 2012), 72–88.

49 Luke Timothy Johnson, *The First and Second Letters to Timothy*, AB 35A (Garden City, NY: Doubleday, 2001), 149. Young's summary is apt: "the theology of the Pastorals unquestionably assumes that God is the apex of a hierarchically ordered society in which obedience is a prime value. The church is God's household, and he is King of the Universe. By God's grace and favour, Christians are members of his household" (*Theology*, 94).

50 On the power and responsibilities of the *paterfamilias*, see L. Michael White, "Paul and Pater Familias," in *Paul in the Greco-Roman World: A Handbook,* vol. 2, ed. J. P. Sampley (New York: Bloomsbury T&T Clark, 2016).

51 Mark Harding, *What Are they Saying about the Pastoral Epistles?* (New York: Paulist, 2001), 47–48; Karen Jobes, *1 Peter*, BECNT (Grand Rapids: Baker, 2005), 181–83; Craig S. Keener, "Family and Household," in *Dictionary of New Testament Background*, eds. C. A. Evans and S. E. Porter (Downers Grove, IL: InterVarsity Press, 2000), at 353–68; H. Kuhli,

The household imagery, while appropriating language and conceptualities from Greco-Roman culture, nonetheless finds its theological foundation in the Old Testament and Jesus. Therefore, rather than reflecting a capitulation to the standards of the culture in order to survive, household imagery is an apt metaphor for describing the unique relationships believers have with one another as committed followers and disciples of Christ, which reflects biblical theology and would have resonated with people living in a culture where the household was considered to be the foundational unit of society.[52]

Not only is the household metaphor the predominant way in which Paul conceives of the church in the LTT, this designation occupies a central place in his purpose for writing. The reference to the church as God's household in 1 Timothy 3:15, for instance, is part of Paul's purpose statement, suggesting that "1 Timothy is not merely *ad hoc* instruction but rather has application to the 'household' more broadly."[53] While the immediate occasion is given in 1 Timothy 1:3–4 (dealing with false teachers), the instructions that follow are not so narrowly construed as to be limited to the original context. Thus the entire letter, not merely small portions of it, is predicated upon the conception of the church as God's household, which provides a fertile ground for close one-on-one mentoring relationships in the context of Christian discipleship.

Consequently, Paul's concern for rightly ordering the household of God is connected to his mission to the Gentiles as he promotes "God's plan" (1 Tim. 1:4), that is, his redemptive arrangement.[54] His desire is to see that believers carry out their responsibilities as members of God's household, living appropriately in light of the coming return of Christ. As Towner observes:

"οἰκονόμος," in *Exegetical Dictionary of the New Testament*, eds. H. R. Balz and G. Schneider (Grand Rapids: Eerdmans, 1991), 2:499; D. G. McCartney, "Household, Family," in *Dictionary of the Later New Testament & Its Developments*, eds. R. P. Martin and P. H. Davids (Downers Grove, IL: InterVarsity Press, 1997), 511–13; Philip H. Towner, "Households and Household Codes," *Dictionary of Paul and His Letters*, eds. G. F. Hawthorne, et al. (Downers Grove, IL: InterVarsity Press, 1993), 417–19; Carolyn Osiek and David L. Balch, *Families in the New Testament World: Households and House Churches* (Louisville: Westminster John Knox, 1997), 82–83; David C. Verner, *The Household of God: The Social World of the Pastoral Epistles*, SBLDS 71 (Chico, CA: Scholars, 1983), 28–29.

52 See Tomlinson, "Purpose and Stewardship," 68; Benjamin L. Merkle, "Ecclesiology in the Pastoral Epistles," in *Entrusted with the Gospel: Paul's Theology in the Pastoral Epistles*, eds. A. J. Köstenberger and T. L. Wilder (Nashville: B&H Academic, 2010), 173–98, at 176.

53 Tomlinson, "Purpose and Stewardship," 53, with reference to Andreas J. Köstenberger, L. Scott Kellum, and Charles L. Quarles, *The Cradle, the Cross, and the Crown: An Introduction to the New Testament* (Nashville: B&H Academic, 2009), 646.

54 Tomlinson, "Purpose and Stewardship," 68–69; Towner, *Letters to Timothy and Titus*, 238.

As Paul applies [the idea of God's οἰκονομία] to Christian existence, the term is expansive, encompassing the whole social, political, and religious world of life in much the same way as the Emperor would take to himself the role of the father or householder and regard the Empire and its inhabitants as his household. Understood this way, the whole of life is subject to the divine will (or is meant to be). The implications for a Christian understanding of the church in the world and mission are enormous.[55]

The household imagery becomes particularly salient in the discussion of *order* in the church. Paul's first directive in 1 Timothy is to deal with the opponents, whose teaching promotes empty speculation. This is set in contrast with the apostolic pattern of instruction, which promotes "God's plan" (1 Tim. 1:4). Paul's use of the word "plan" calls to mind the stewardship of a household. This term relates specifically to God's way of ordering his redemptive plan while preparing the way for Paul's explicit discussion of God's household.[56] As mentioned, this is one of Paul's central purposes in writing the LTT.[57] God has a distinct way of ordering the world at large and his church in particular,[58] and the teaching Timothy is to correct produces a way of life that is opposed to this order.[59] Timothy and Titus, as Paul's apostolic delegates, are charged with helping to bring order to the church so that the members of God's household conduct themselves properly (e.g., 1 Tim. 1:5; 3:14–15; 2 Tim. 2:4–15; Titus 1:13–14), and members of God's household today should endeavor to do the same as they live out their Christian lives in community as committed followers of Christ.

The reference to Timothy being given instruction also uses stewardship language (παρατίθεμαί), seeking to ensure that the household is run properly (1 Tim. 1:18).[60] This same idea is present in Paul's statement to Titus that the elder is "God's administrator" (θεοῦ οἰκονόμον; Titus 1:7). First Timothy also contains an interesting variation on the common household codes in the New Testament (1 Tim. 2:1–6:2). In this

---

55 Towner, *Letters to Timothy and Titus*, 69; idem, *Goal of Our Instruction*, 172.
56 Towner, *Letters to Timothy and Titus*, 112–14.
57 Johnson, *1 Timothy, 2 Timothy, Titus*, 149.
58 In 1 Timothy 1:4, the οἰκονομία of God is further designated as being in reference to the faith, οἰκονομίαν θεοῦ τὴν ἐν πίστει.
59 Towner, *Letters to Timothy and Titus*, 113.
60 Tomlinson, "Purpose and Stewardship," 78–79.

extended section, Paul addresses the proper ordering of God's household, discussing the church at large (2:1–7), men and women (2:8–15), elders/overseers (3:1–7), deacons (3:8–13), Timothy himself as the servant of Christ Jesus (chap. 4), different age groups (5:1–2), widows (5:3–16), elders (5:17–25), and slaves (6:1–2), with occasional general instructions interspersed. These exhortations have been influenced by the language of traditional Greco-Roman household codes, a form Paul likely chose because of his overriding conception of the church as God's household.[61] The emphasis on teaching throughout the letters, therefore, does not merely reflect a concern with proper doctrine for its own sake but with being a faithful steward in the household of God, rightly ordering the people of God to carry out the mission of God.[62]

The idea of order, in turn, dovetails with the notion of *authority*. This is seen most clearly in Paul's designation of elders as God's administrators (Titus 1:7) and the injunction that an elder/overseer who is unable to manage his own household cannot be expected to be able to oversee the church (1 Tim. 3:4–5). In addition, the concept of authority may be present where household imagery is absent, such as in the authority Paul has granted to Timothy and Titus as his apostolic delegates and in the instructions to appoint elders/overseers who will lead the churches. The language does not, however, suggest that there should be a rigid structure of authority imposed upon the church where it actually functions as a household.[63]

The implicit assumption is that the ultimate *authority*, and thus the source of *order*, is God; elders are simply *stewards*. Titus and Timothy, while functioning in unique roles as apostolic delegates, are nonetheless not heads of households. Even Paul is not the *paterfamilias*; that role belongs to God alone: The church is *his* household (1 Tim. 3:15). Those with authority in the household serve with delegated responsibility and are accountable to God, each other, and the members of the household. This set of assumptions should cause us to take Paul's instructions that much more seriously. God's household is not ours to order as we see fit. Inasmuch as God has given us instructions, it is incumbent upon us to follow them. This is not to suggest that the LTT answer every question we may have regarding church order, structure, and authority, but it does

---

61 Towner, *Goal of Our Instruction*, 170–71.
62 Towner, "Pauline Theology or Pauline Tradition in the Pastoral Epistles," 310–11.
63 Mounce, *Pastoral Epistles*, 221; Tomlinson, "Purpose and Stewardship," 68; Towner, *Letters to Timothy and Titus*, 238.

serve as a reminder that the church is not ultimately ours to structure or lead as we desire.

While household imagery does not demand that each person in the local body fill a particular role corresponding to a role in the household, it nonetheless helps convey the idea that there is proper behavior in the church, just as there is in the home. Specifically, the members of God's household, as in the natural family, are said to be related to one another as spiritual fathers and mothers, sons and daughters, and brothers and sisters (1 Tim. 5:1–2; Titus 2:1–6). Christian discipleship thus has an important family dimension. In this way, the LTT demonstrate a certain degree of fluidity in moving from a discussion of the church as household to issuing commands to people in their natural households. As Verner rightly notes, Paul "never addresses the subject of the household life of church members as a topic in its own right. Rather, whenever he introduces the topic of household life, he does so in the course of discussing one aspect or another of life in the household of God."[64] The LTT thus contain both instructions directly pertaining to life in the household of God—such as how Timothy and Titus are to relate to members of the household—as well as instructions on how members of God's household should conduct themselves in their own households. As Towner observes, "Just as there are rules of accepted behavior, relationships to observe, and responsibilities to fulfill within the household, so there are analogous patterns to be observed in God's church."[65]

CONCLUSION

The theme of discipleship in the LTT is grounded in Paul's apostolic mission. As an extension of his apostolic authority, Paul tasks apostolic delegates such as Timothy and Titus with appointing church leadership in newer works and with confronting false teachers and removing errant elders in the case of more established churches. While their role is unique in some respects, Paul's apostolic delegates also provide an important template of how Christian discipleship is to be exhibited in committed one-on-one discipleship and mentoring relationships in a local church context.

One important aspect of Paul's mission in which his apostolic delegates are enjoined to share is that of suffering for the gospel. Similarly,

---

64 Verner, *Household of God*, 128.
65 Towner, *Letters to Timothy and Titus*, 273–74.

believers today must be prepared to suffer rejection in the world as followers of the crucified Christ. Their mission is set within the context of the church conceived as God's household in keeping with Jewish and Greco-Roman households. This entails the authority of the *paterfamilias* and also involves caring for the needs of the various members of the household, including older and younger men and women, slaves, and widows. Caring for the family of God thus involves the same kind of loving provision and protection as that exercised by the father in a natural household. In all these ways, in particular with regard to conceiving of church leadership in terms of household management, the LTT provide a significant contribution to the New Testament's teaching on discipleship.

CHAPTER 13

The Lost Concept Recovered: Discipleship in Hebrews

Victor S. Rhee

Anyone who reads through the Bible will find that the word "disciple," which is the translation of the Greek term μαθητής, appears frequently in the Gospels and Acts.[1] Because of the frequency of the word, numerous books and articles have been written on the topic of disciple and discipleship in recent decades. However, a survey of literature indicates that very little work has been done on the topic of discipleship in Hebrews. According to my research, only one such essay has been written, by William L. Lane.[2] Although Lane's essay is helpful for the understanding of the concept of discipleship in Hebrews, a more comprehensive work needs to be done on this topic in this important letter. Perhaps the reason for the lack of interest in this topic is due to the absence of the term μαθητής in Hebrews. But does this necessarily mean that teaching on discipleship is missing in Hebrews? One of the purposes of this essay is to demonstrate that models of discipleship are clearly presented by the author of Hebrews, even if the term μαθητής and its cognate words are not used.

In addition, even though terms such as "disciple," "discipleship," and "disciple-making" are commonly used by many Christians, the understanding of these terms is different from one person to another.[3] Some argue that the word "disciple" (μαθητής) means merely a learner, regardless of whether or not a person is a believer.[4] Others suggest that a disciple is a Christian who is dedicated in his walk with the Lord, who is at a higher

---

1 All Scripture translations are the author's own unless otherwise noted.
2 See William L. Lane, "Standing Before the Moral Claim of God: Discipleship in Hebrews," in *Patterns of Discipleship in New Testament,* ed. R. N. Longenecker (Grand Rapids: Eerdmans, 1996), 203–24; The volume edited by Fernando F. Segovia (*Discipleship in the New Testament* [Philadelphia: Fortress, 1985]), does not include an essay on discipleship in Hebrews.
3 The following different views are an adaptation from Sung Yul (Victor) Rhee, "The Concept of Disciple in Luke-Acts" (ThM thesis, Talbot School of Theology, 1989), 2–3; See also Michael J. Wilkins, *Following the Master: A Biblical Theology of Discipleship* (Grand Rapids: Zondervan, 1992), 25–34.
4 See Charles Caldwell Ryrie, *Balancing the Christian Life* (Chicago: Moody Press, 1969), 178. Kenneth S. Wuest, *Wuest's Word Studies from the Greek New Testament* (Grand Rapids: Eerdmans, 1973), 1:54.

level of spiritual life.[5] The problem is complicated by those who maintain
that a disciple is simply someone who is a believer in Jesus.[6] It is beyond
the scope of this essay to discuss these different views in detail. For the
purpose of this essay, I will adopt the view that a disciple is someone who
has come to trust Jesus as the Lord and Savior for eternal life, and has entered a life of following Jesus.[7] All genuine believers in Jesus are disciples
of Jesus. What, then, is the meaning of the word "discipleship"? It is a way
of life for believers as God intends us to live as recorded in the Bible.[8] In
other words, discipleship is not just for believers who are at a higher level
of Christian life, but it is for all the believers in Christ, regardless of one's
level of spiritual maturity. With this definition in mind, I will examine the
concept of discipleship in Hebrews. To accomplish this purpose, I will
first discuss the phenomenon of the absence of the term μαθητής ("disciple") in the epistles and the book of Revelation. Then I will examine the
terms and concepts related to discipleship in the book of Hebrews.

THE ABSENCE OF THE TERM "DISCIPLE" IN HEBREWS

The term μαθητής ("disciple") is used 261 times in the Gospels and
Acts (233 times in Gospels; twenty-eight times in Acts). Since both Jesus and the writers of the Gospels considered the concept of disciple to
be important, one would expect that the word μαθητής would appear in
the Epistles and Revelation. It is surprising, however, that the term is not
used outside the Gospels and Acts. Does the absence of a term mean that
there can be no concept of disciple or discipleship in the epistles and Revelation? Karl H. Rengstorf, for example, argues that there is no concept
of master-disciple relation in the Old Testament because the term itself is
absent.[9] In response to this assertion, Michael J. Wilkins maintains that
"the comparative lack of terminology should not be the primary reason

---

5 See Gary W. Kuhne, *The Dynamics of Discipleship Training : Being and Producing Spiritual
Leaders* (Grand Rapids: Zondervan, 1977), 13; J. Dwight Pentecost, *Design for Discipleship*
(Grand Rapids: Zondervan, 1971), 11.
6 See Dietrich Bonhoeffer, *The Cost of Discipleship*, rev. ed. (New York: Macmillan, 1963),
63–64.
7 Wilkins, *Following the Master,* 40.
8 In my ThM thesis, I have demonstrated from Luke-Acts that the word "disciples" is synonymous to "believers" or "Christians." I have also examined the lifestyle of the disciples of
Jesus. See Rhee, "The Concept of Disciple in Luke-Acts," 51–91, 92–111.
9 Karl H. Rengstorf, "μαθητής," *TDNT*, eds. G. Kittel and G. Friedrich; trans. G. Bromley
(Grand Rapids; Eerdmans, 1967), 4:427. For a similar view, see also Joseph A. Fitzmyer, *Luke
the Theologian: Aspects of His Teaching* (New York: Paulist Press, 1989), 119.

for suggesting a corresponding lack of the concept being found."[10] Wilkins has convincingly demonstrated that other terms and expressions found in the Old Testament clearly point to the idea of discipleship (e.g., covenant relationship of Israel with God; relationships of certain individuals with God; relationship between God and the nation of Israel).[11] Wilkins's methodology of searching for the concept of discipleship even when the specific term is not present is instructive. I am also of the opinion that the terms and concept of discipleship can be found in Hebrews, even though the word "disciple" (μαθητής) itself was not used by the author.

What terms, then, were used in place of "disciple" outside the Gospels and Acts?

William Sanday provides a helpful insight that after the departure of Jesus, the term was substituted by "brethren" (ἀδελφοί) and "saints" (ἅγιοι) in the epistles and Revelation to indicate their relation to each other and to non-Christian society.[12] But an examination of the terms in Acts reveals that ἅγιοι ("saints") began to emerge in Acts already from the early years of the beginning of the church (9:13, 32; 9:41; 26:10). It is interesting to observe that this word was used along with "disciple" in the immediate context. In 9:10, Ananias was referred to as a "disciple." Then in 9:13 Ananias says to the Lord that Paul did much harm to the "saints" at Jerusalem. In the context of 9:32–44, Luke employs "saints" in verse 32, then he switches back to the word "disciple" in verses 36 and 38. In 9:41, he reverts back to "saints." In 26:10, Paul testifies that, before his conversion, he locked up many "saints" in prison. Luke indicates in 9:1 that these saints are none other than the disciples. Luke also employs the verbal form ἁγιάζω to refer to believers in Christ (Acts 20:32; 26:18, "those who have been sanctified [ἡγιασμένοις]"). With the interchangeable use of these terms, Luke implies that the transition is already taking place away from the term μαθητής ("disciples").

Another word that Luke uses along with μαθητής in Acts is ἀδελφός ("brother"). The word is used in a singular form three times with reference to Paul after his conversion (9:17; 22:13; 21:20). Luke also uses the plural form of the word (ἀδελφοί ["brothers"]) thirty-two times to refer to the believers in Christ (e.g., 1:15; 6:3; 9:30; 11:1; 12:17; 14:2; 15:1, 36; 16:2;

---

10 Michael J. Wilkins, *The Concept of Disciple in Matthew's Gospel: As Reflected in the Use of the Term Μαθητής*, NovTSup 59 (Leiden: Brill, 1988), 52.

11 Wilkins, *Following the Master*, 56–57.

12 William Sanday, *Inspiration: Eight Lectures on the Early History and Origin of the Doctrine of Biblical Inspiration* (London: Longmans, 1914), 289.

17:10; 18:27; 28:14). Combining the singular and plural forms, the word is used thirty-five times in Acts. But the word μαθητής is used only twenty-eight times. A comparison of the occurrences reveals that a transition of expression was taking place in Acts, even from the earliest period of the church. In some instances, Luke uses both terms (μαθητής and ἀδελφός) to it indicate that these two terms are interchangeable (cf. 6:1–3).

What is the significance of this analysis? The word study suggests that the terms used to refer to followers of Jesus were going through a transition even from the beginning stages of the Jesus movement. Just as the use of some terms was becoming more common, so the use of others, such "disciple" (μαθητής), was becoming less common. Thus, the early appearance of words such as "saints" (ἄγιοι) and "brethren" (ἀδελφοί) in Acts helps to explain the absence of the word "disciple" (μαθητής) in Hebrews, and in other epistles and Revelation.[13]

TERMS AND CONCEPTS FOR DISCIPLES AND DISCIPLESHIP IN HEBREWS

In the Gospels and Acts, discipleship is portrayed as the relationship between Jesus and his followers. Does Hebrews present the same kind of relationship between the Savior and believers? Answering this question requires an examination of the titles of Jesus as described by the author of Hebrews and the terms used for the followers of Jesus Christ. These findings will be compared with titles used in the Gospels and Acts to see if there is continuity or discontinuity between the writers of the Gospels and Acts and the author of Hebrews.

A. Descriptions of Jesus in Hebrews

In the Gospels the two most common titles for Jesus used by his followers are "Lord (κύριος)" (Matt. 7:21; 8:2; Mark 7:28; Luke 5:8; 7:6; 9:59; John 6:34; 11:3; 13:6) and "Master (ἐπιστάτης) " (Luke 5:5; 8:24, 45). People also called him "Savior" (Luke 2:11; John 4:42), "Immanuel" (Matt. 1:23), and "Christ" (Matt. 16:16; 26:68; 27:22). Jesus is also described as the light of the world (John 8:12), the good shepherd (John 10:11), the door (John 10:7, 9), the bread of life (John 6:35, 41), and so on. Can one find any of these descriptions about Jesus in Hebrews? What other terms were used to describe Jesus? With these questions in mind, I

---

13 For a detailed discussion on the reasons for the absence of the term μαθητής, see Wilkins, *Following the Master*, 281–90.

will proceed to discuss the terms, titles, and metaphors that the author of Hebrews uses to describe Jesus.

1. Jesus Is the Final Spokesperson of God's Revelation for the Salvation of Humanity

Hebrews 1:1–2a reads, "In the past God spoke to our ancestors through the prophets at many times and in various ways, but in these last days he has spoken to us by his Son." The term πολυμερῶς ("at many times") suggests that God's speaking in the Old Testament was fragmented, coming in multiple segments or portions at different times. The term πολυτρόπως ("in various ways") speaks of the diverse ways that God spoke through the prophets.[14] Both words speak of the progressive nature of God's revelation which is completed in his Son.

2. Jesus Is Heir of All Things

The expression "whom he appointed heir [κληρονόμον] of all things" (1:2b) is probably an allusion to Ps. 2:8—"Ask me, and I will make the nations your inheritance, the ends of the earth your possession." What is the inheritance that Jesus has come to possess? The word for "all things" (πάντων) in Greek can be either masculine or neuter, which means it may refer to either the whole universe or humanity. In the immediate context the collocation of the words "world" (1: 2c) and "all things" (1:3) suggest that "all things" may be considered neuter, referring to the universe. However, the author's use of the neuter form of πᾶς in other parts of Hebrews to refer to people suggests that "all things" may also include humanity (2:10; 3:4, 6). For this reason, the inheritance the Son has come to possess includes both the universe and humanity.[15]

3. Jesus Is the Creator of the World

Hebrews 1:2c reads, "through whom also he made the worlds [τοὺς αἰῶνας]." This verse indicates that the Son is the agent through whom the whole universe came into existence. This thought is further developed in 1:10–12; the Son is the one who laid the foundation of the earth, and the heavens are the works of his hands. Moreover, 1:3b indicates that the Son

---

14   Harold W. Attridge, *The Epistle to the Hebrews: A Commentary on the Epistle to the Hebrews,* Hermeneia (Philadelphia: Fortress, 1989).

15   For a more detailed discussion, see Victor (Sung Yul) Rhee, "The Role of Chiasm for Understanding Christology in Hebrews 1:1–14," *JBL* 131 (2012): 341–62, at 347.

upholds (φέρων) all things by the word of his power. Jesus is not only
the direct agent of creation, but also the one who is holding the world
together by the word of his power. The author's use of the present participle φέρων suggests that upholding has to do with an ongoing activity
of the Son, which involves not only the support of the universe, but the
carrying forward all things toward the fulfillment of God's purpose.[16]

4. Jesus Possesses the Nature of God

Hebrews 1:3a reads, "being the radiance [ἀπαύγασμα] of his glory and
the exact representation [χαρακτήρ] of his nature." The term ἀπαύγασμα
may be translated as either "reflection" in a passive sense or "radiance"
in an active sense.[17] Those who understand the meaning of the word
as a "reflection" tend to interpret the phrase in 1:3a as the glory of God
manifested in the perfection of the Son in his earthly life.[18] I consider that
the author of Hebrews has the active meaning in mind with the use of
ἀπαύγασμα in Hebrews 1:3a.[19] The author employs the word to express
the relationship between God and the Son; the Son is the radiance of
God's glory in his preexistent state. Another term that describes the Son
is χαρακτήρ, which has the idea of "the seal" or "impression" on a coin in
a figurative sense.[20] The significance of the word is that the Son bears the
very mark of God's nature, as the image and inscription on a coin exactly
matches the original form in the device.[21] Along with ἀπαύγασμα, it also
speaks of the essential nature of Christ in his preexistent state.

5. Jesus Is the Purifier of Our Sins

In 1:3c, the author shifts his description of the Son from preexistent to incarnate using the participial phrase, "after making purification

16 Philip Edgcumbe Hughes, A Commentary on the Epistle to the Hebrews (Grand Rapids:
Eerdmans, 1977), 45.
17 BDAG, 99.
18 John A. T. Robinson, The Human Face of God (Philadelphia: Westminster, 1973), 155; L. D.
Hurst, "The Christology of Hebrews 1 and 2," in The Glory of Christ in the New Testament: Stud-
ies in Christology in Memory of George Bradford Caird, eds. L. D. Hurst and N. T. Wright (Oxford:
Clarendon, 1987), 151–64, at 155–56.
19 For scholars who understand ἀπαύγασμα in a positive sense, see William L. Lane,
Hebrews 1–8, WBC 47a (Dallas: Word Books, 1991), 13; Craig R. Koester, Hebrews: A New
Translation with Introduction and Commentary, AB (New York: Doubleday, 2001), 176; Hughes,
A Commentary on the Epistle to the Hebrews, 42.
20 Ulrich Wilckens, "χαρακτήρ," TDNT, eds. G. Kittel and G. Friedrich; trans. G. Bromley
(Grand Rapids: Eerdmans, 1973), 9:420.
21 F. F. Bruce, The Epistle to the Hebrews, rev. ed., NICNT (Grand Rapids: Eerdmans, 1990), 48.

[καθαρισμόν] of sins." This is a summary statement of what Jesus has accomplished in his earthly life; Jesus Christ had provided purification of sins through his sacrificial death on the cross. The word καθαρισμός is used only once in Hebrews, in 1:3c. But the author employs the verb καθαρίζω and its cognates in other parts of Hebrews to develop the idea of purification (καθαρίζω [9:14, 22, 23; 10:2]; καθαρότης [9:13]; καθαρός [10:22]). The context of these passages shows that these words are used with reference to the sacrificial death of Christ for the forgiveness of sins.[22] With the announcement of the subject of "purification" in 1:3c, the author also anticipates the theme of Christ's high priesthood, which he further develops in other parts of the letter.

6. Jesus Is the Exalted Son

Hebrews 1:3d reads, "he sat down at the right hand of the Majesty on high." This verse is an allusion to Psalm 110:1, which the author quotes in 1:13, and alludes to further in other parts of the epistle (8:1; 10:12; 12:2).[23] What is the significance of "sitting at the right hand?" It stands for the symbol of Christ's power and honor as the ruler of the universe after his ascension into heaven. In this verse the author does not use the word "resurrection" (ἀνάστασις) in describing Jesus having been raised up from the dead. In Hebrews the word ἀνάστασις occurs only twice (6:2; 11:35), and with both occurrences speaking of the resurrection of believers. Christ's resurrection is referred to only once, in 13:20, with the expression of "bringing again from the dead." It is apparent that the author considers both resurrection and exaltation as one event.[24]

7. Jesus Is the Lord

The primary referent of the word "Lord" (κύριος) in Hebrews is God the Father (7:21; 8:8, 9, 10, 11; 10:16, 30; 12:5, 6, 14). But the author also uses the term to refer to Jesus ("so great a salvation . . . which was spoken through the Lord" [2:3]; "our Lord was descended from Judah" [7:14]; "the true tabernacle, which the Lord pitched" [8:2–3]; "Jesus our Lord" [13:20]). In addition, the title is used by God the Father himself to

22 Paul Ellingworth, *The Epistle to the Hebrews: A Commentary on the Greek Text*, NIGTC (Grand Rapids: Eerdmans, 1993), 102.
23 See Hans-Friedrich Weiss, *Der Brief an die Hebräer: Übersetzt und Erklärt*, Kritisch-exegetischer Kommentar über das Neue Testament 13 (Göttingen: Vandenhoeck & Ruprecht, 1991), 150–51.
24 Attridge, *The Epistle to the Hebrews*, 46.

refer to his Son Jesus. Hebrews 1:10 reads, "You, Lord [κύριε], in the beginning, laid the foundation of the earth, and the heavens are the works
of your hands." The immediate context (1:8–12) reveals that the Son who
is addressed as "God" (ὁ θεός) in verse 9 is also called "Lord" (κύριε) in
verse 10. Here, the author considers Jesus to be the preexistent Son and
the creator of the universe.[25]

8. Jesus Is a High Priest

Jesus being the high priest of the new covenant is one of the epistle's
major themes. The author implies this theme in 1:3 ("after having made purification of sins"), and officially announces it in 2:17 ("a merciful and faithful high priest"). Afterwards, he further develops this profile in 3:1–5:10,
though in reverse order: a *faithful* high priest (3:1–6) and a *merciful* high
priest (4:14–5:10). Then, in 6:20, he introduces Jesus as a high priest after
the order of Melchizedek. In 7:1–10:18 the author delineates this theme in
great detail. The aim of this section is to make a contrast between Christ's
high priesthood after the order of Melchizedek and the Levitical high priesthood.[26] Finally, in 10:19, the author describes Jesus as "a great priest" to
encourage the believers not to forsake their faith in Christ (10:19–39).

9. Jesus Is the Great Shepherd

The author of Hebrews brings the sermon to closure by invoking the
benediction in 13:20–21. In verse 20, Jesus is referred to as "the great
Shepherd of the sheep." What might have been the reason for the insertion of the adjective "great" (μέγας)? Lane suggests that the formulation
of the benediction is the author's reflection on Isaiah 63:11–14 (LXX),
which refers to God's appointment of Moses as a leader for the deliverance of Israel from Egypt.[27] If Lane's observation is correct, the implication
seems clear: The author's intention is to make a contrast between the old
covenant and the new covenant. Whereas Moses is the shepherd of the
sheep whom God led out in the old covenant, Jesus is the great shepherd
of the sheep whom God brought up from the dead in the new covenant.[28]
This contrast, marked by the use of "great" (μέγας), is also implied in the

---

25 For a detailed discussion of the relationship between "Lord" (κύριε) and "God" (ὁ θεός)
see, Victor (Sung Yul) Rhee, "Christology in Hebrews 1:5–14: The Three Stages of Christ's
Existence," *JETS* 59 (2016): 717–29, at 726–27.

26 Lane, *Hebrews 1–8*, 111.

27 William L. Lane, *Hebrews 9–13*, WBC 47b (Dallas: Word, 1991), 561.

28 Lane, *Hebrews 9–13*, 562.

expressions "great high priest" (4:14) and "great priest" (10:21). In both verses the author seeks to contrast the Levitical priesthood in the old covenant with Christ's high priesthood in the new covenant.

10. Summary

The analysis of the portrait of Jesus in Hebrews reveals that the author of Hebrews is in line with the tradition of the Gospels as they describe Jesus. Jesus is the creator and sustainer of the universe. He possesses the divine nature. He is a person within the triune God. As a preexistent Son, he became an incarnate Son and made known to us the finality of God's revelation with regard to the salvation of humanity. He made purification for sins by offering up his own body (i.e., once-for-all sacrifice) for the people. As the exalted Lord, Jesus intercedes for us as a high priest of the new covenant. He is the Lord and the great shepherd of believers. The titles of Jesus in Hebrews basically outline who Jesus is and what he has accomplished for humanity, just as one finds in the Gospels.

B. Terms and Concepts for Disciples in Hebrews

It is evident from our analysis of Acts above that Luke used "saints" (ἅγιοι) and "brethren" (ἀδελφοί) along with "disciple" (μαθητής) to indicate that changes were taking place with respect to these terms after the ascension of Jesus. In Hebrews also the plural form ἅγιοι is used three times as an expression for believers in Christ—once with ἀδελφοί ("holy brethren" [3:1]), twice without it ("saints" [6:10; 13:24]). In addition, the author employs the phrase "those who are sanctified" as a way of referring to believers (οἱ ἁγιαζόμενοι [2:11]; τοὺς ἁγιαζομένους [10:14]). The author also makes use of "brethren" (2:11, 12, 17; 3:12; 10:19; 13:22) as a favorite term for believers in Christ. He also uses a singular form ἀδελφός (13:23) to describe Timothy (i.e., "our brother Timothy"). From this study we may safely infer that Hebrews was following the traditional meaning of these expressions as commonly used by believers from the beginning of Christianity. But the combination of ἀδελφοί and ἅγιοι (i.e., "holy brethren") in 3:1 is a unique expression, occurring within the New Testament only in Hebrews. The author also describes believers with the term μέτοχοι ("partakers of the heavenly calling" [3:1]; "partakers of Christ" [3:14]; "partakers of the Holy Spirit" [6:4]; "partakers [12:8]), which is used only in Hebrews.

An examination of the Gospels also reveals that Jesus depicts discipleship as a familial relationship. He taught that the one who does the will of the Father who is in heaven is one's brother, sister, and mother (Matt. 12:46–50; Mark 3:31–35; Luke 8:19–21). In his earthly ministry as the incarnate Son, Jesus referred to God as his Father (e.g., Matt. 10:32, 33; 18:35; John 6:32; 10:15) and even called God his Father (e.g., Matt. 26:39; Luke 22:42; John 17:1, 5). Moreover, Jesus taught that God is the heavenly Father of all believers (Matt. 5:16, 45; 6:9), and called his followers "my brethren" (Matt. 28:10; John 20:17). Careful study of Hebrews similarly describes the relationship between Jesus and believers is described in familial terms.

First, the family relationship can be observed from the language of sonship. The author of Hebrews presupposes that God is the Father of Jesus ("God . . . has spoken to us in his Son" [1:2]; "You are my Son" [1:5]; and Jesus is the Son [3:6]). The author also portrays believers as sons ("in bringing many sons to glory" [2:10]; "God deals you as with sons" [12:6]). Next, Jesus is also described as πρωτότοκος ("the firstborn" [1:6]), and believers as πρωτοτόκων ("the firstborn ones" [12:23]. The use of singular and plural forms implies that a family concept is in view. The plural form "firstborn" refers to the people of God who share the inheritance of the Son, who is the firstborn in God's family.[29]

Second, the idea of Son having been appointed as "heir" of all things (1:2) shows the family relationship between Jesus and believers (1:2). The word "heir" and its related words in Hebrews indicate that the inheritance relates to the future salvation of believers. For example, angels are the ministering spirits sent out to render service for the sake of those who inherit (κληρονομέω) salvation (1:14). In the context of 6:9–12, the promise of inheritance is the future salvation of believers (6:9). Jesus is the heir of the eternal salvation that God has promised to believers, and believers have the privilege of sharing in his inheritance. In this sense, we are fellow heirs with Christ (cf. Rom. 8:17).

Third, the concept of family may be detected from the idea of solidarity between the Son and believers. In Hebrews 2:10–18, the author explains how God the Father and the Son accomplish the salvation of humanity by way of a family relationship. God the Father is the one who brings to perfection the author of salvation (i.e., Jesus) through suffering, namely death on the cross. Jesus is the one who leads many sons (i.e., believers) to glory (2:10).[30] "The one who sanctifies" is the Son. "The ones

---

29   Gareth Lee Cockerill, *The Epistle to the Hebrews,* NICNT (Grand Rapids: Eerdmans, 2012), 655.

30   The agreement of the case, number, gender (accusative, singular, masculine) between πολλοὺς υἱοὺς εἰς δόξαν ἀγαγόντα ("for the purpose of bringing many sons to glory") and

who are sanctified" are the sons (2:11). In what ways does Jesus identify himself with those who believe in him? He does this by (1) calling believers "brethren" and "children whom God has given me" (2:11–13); (2) sharing with humanity in flesh and blood ("he himself partook of the same" [2:14–15]); (3) becoming a merciful and faithful high priest; and (4) offering help to those who are tempted (2:17–18; cf. 4:14–16).

To sum up, the author of Hebrews continues with expressions which were developed in the early period of the church after the ascension of the Lord Jesus. As for the concept of family, Hebrews follows the teaching of Jesus in that God is the Father, Jesus is the big brother as our Lord and Savior, and we are brothers and sisters in the Lord. The terms and concepts used in Hebrews clearly suggest that the idea of discipleship is not lost, but merely described with different words.

WHAT DISCIPLESHIP IN HEBREWS INVOLVES

In many parts of the Gospels (especially in Luke) Jesus speaks of the cost of being his disciple (e.g., Luke 9:23–27; 9:57–62 [cf. Matt. 8:19–22]; 14:25–35; 18:24–30). Luke also records in Acts what discipleship involves, such as proclaiming the gospel in the midst of persecution (Acts 4:1–22; 5:27–33; 8:1–4), perseverance in faith (Acts 14:21–22), being devoted to the teaching of the apostles and prayer (Acts 2:42; 5:42), and sharing material goods among the believers (Acts 2:45; 4:32–37). Can we find any of these discipleship qualities in Hebrews? A careful analysis of Hebrews shows that the author indeed displays many qualities of discipleship.[31]

A. Christ-Centered Teaching

Hebrews 13:17–19 suggests that the author of Hebrews was one of the prominent leaders in the church. He must have been the chief spokesperson among the leaders because he was the one who was writing this word of exhortation (13:22).[32] Being absent from the church, he gives a sermon in written form in a critical situation by reminding the congregation who

---

τὸν ἀρχηγὸν τῆς σωτηρίας αὐτῶν ("the author of their salvation") points to Jesus as the one who brings many sons to glory. Attridge understands that "the one who leads many sons to glory" is God (*The Epistle to the Hebrews*, 82).

31 Lane rightly asserts, "Evidence of extended and thoughtful reflection on the subject of Christian discipleship can be found throughout Hebrews. Hebrews is, in fact, a sermon on the cost of discipleship" ("Standing Before the Moral Claim of God," 204).

32 Barnabas Lindars, "The Rhetorical Structure of Hebrews," *NTS* 35 (1989): 382–406, at 386.

Jesus is, and what he has done for them. He accomplishes this purpose
by carefully structuring his message with the literary device known as
"alternating genre." The author uses the alternating sections of doctrine
and exhortation five times to encourage his readers to remain faithful to
Christ. This may be illustrated as follows:[33]

Doctrine (D)	Exhortation (E)
1:1–14: Divinity of the Son (God's revelation through his Son)	*2:1–4:* Do not drift away
2:5–18: Humanity of the Son (solidarity with humanity)	*3:1–4:16:* Do not fail to enter God's rest
5:1–10: Jesus the merciful high priest	*5:11–6:20:* Do not fall away
7:1–10:18: Jesus the superior high priest	*10:19–39:* Do not willfully live in sin
11:1–40: Loyalty to God through enduring faith	*12:1–29:* Endure and do not reject God's word

In the first alternating structure the author encourages the readers
not to drift away from faith in Jesus (2:1–4) in light of the finality of the
revelation given through the Son (1:1–14). In the second alternating
structure the readers are exhorted to enter God's rest (3:1–4:16) with
the teaching on the humanity of Jesus (2:5–18). In the third alternating
section the author again warns the readers against falling into apostasy (5:11–6:20) by reminding them that believers have a merciful high
priest who is appointed by God according to the order of Melchizedek
(5:1–10). In the fourth alternating structure the author urges the readers
not to go on living in sin (10:19–39) based on the superior high priesthood of Christ (7:1–10:18). Lastly, in the fifth alternating section, the
author reminds his readers to focus on Jesus (12:1–29) by urging them
to be loyal to God through enduring faith (11:1–40), followed by the
conclusion of his sermon (13:1–25). The significance of the discussion
of the alternating sections of doctrine and exhortation is that the author
is quite intentional about driving home the centrality of Christ in his
exhortation to his congregation.

33 Victor (Sung-Yul) Rhee, *Faith in Hebrews: Analysis within the Context of Christology, Eschatology, and Ethics,* StBibLit 19 (New York: Peter Lang, 2001), 64–242. What follows is a brief
summary of the detailed analysis of the alternating sections of doctrine and exhortation in
Hebrews.

More specifically, the expressions "we must pay much closer attention (2:1), "consider Jesus, the apostle and high priest of our confession" (3:1), "if we hold fast our confidence and the boast of our hope (3:6), "let us press on to maturity" (6:1), "let us hold fast the confession" (10:23), and "fixing our eyes on Jesus" (12:2) are the author's ways of reminding believers to redirect their attention to Jesus, the author and perfecter of faith. Just as the author of Hebrews is very much Christ-centered in his exhortation as a spiritual leader of the congregation, those who are in leadership positions need to be intentional about helping their congregations to turn their focus to the Lord Jesus in the discipling process.

B. Paying Attention to the Word of God

Hebrews 2:1 reads, "For this reason we must pay much closer attention to what we have heard, so that we do not drift away from it" (NASB). What is the content of the message that the readers have heard? The conjunction "therefore" (διὰ τοῦτο) suggests that "what we have heard" refers back to the words that God has spoken through the Son in 1:1–2. Since God has spoken to us by his Son in these last days, and the Son is superior to the angels, we ought to pay all the more closer attention to what we have heard.[34] In addition, 2:3 indicates that "what we have heard" (2:1) refers to the message of salvation that was first spoken through the Lord (i.e., Jesus), and proclaimed by the followers of the Lord Jesus. Lane observes that the Greek word for "to pay attention" (προσέχειν) in 2:1 has a similar meaning to "hold fast" (κατέχω) in 3:6, 3:14, and 10:23, where readers are urged to hold fast to their confession of faith.[35] The implication of the verb is that "the community had grown lax in their commitment to Christ and were neglecting the Christian message."[36] The author's exhortation to pay closer attention involves not only listening to the words, but the action of holding fast to what they had believed in the beginning.

Negligence of God's word by believers is also described by the analogy of the disobedience of the wilderness generation in 3:7–4:13. The word of God is described in terms of the voice of God (e.g., "Today, if you hear his voice, do not harden your hearts" [3:7–8, 3:15; 4:7]). The author implies that some members of the faith community may be in danger of disobeying God's word, just as the wilderness generation failed to

---

34 Attridge, *The Epistle to the Hebrews*, 64.
35 Lane, *Hebrews 1–8*, 37.
36 Lane, *Hebrews 1–8*, 37.

appropriate the word of God by faith (4:1–2). For this reason, he exhorts readers to be diligent to enter that rest (4:11) by reminding them that the word of God is living and active and sharper than any two-edged sword (4:12). The implication is that God's word will bring about judgment on them for their disobedience.

C. Imitating Jesus

The author employs the noun μιμητής ("imitator") in 6:12, and the verb μιμέομαι ("to imitate") in 13:7 to describe the idea of imitation. In addition, he also brings out the importance of imitating Jesus through the context in different parts of the epistle. To begin with, the context of 3:1–19 indicates that believers need to imitate the faithfulness of Jesus. The author exhorts readers to consider Jesus, the apostle and high priest of our confession (3:1). What aspect of the life of Jesus does the author encourage believers to consider? The overall emphasis of 3:1–6 is on Christ's fidelity to the service of God. In this context the admonition to consider Jesus is tantamount to imitating the faithfulness of Jesus. The author elaborates on the faithfulness of Jesus by comparing it with that of Moses; while Moses was faithful as a servant, Jesus was faithful as a Son (3:2, 5–6). The point of comparison between Moses and Jesus is on their faithfulness in *serving* within God's house. For this reason the exhortation to consider Jesus should be understood as a call to imitate the faithfulness of Christ.[37] Moreover, the exhortation to consider the faithfulness (or, trustworthiness) of Jesus is reinforced by the negative example of the unfaithfulness of the wilderness generation (3:7–19). In 3:7a the author exhorts the readers not to harden their hearts when they hear his voice. Then, he quotes Psalm 95 (94 LXX) to emphasize that the Israelites were not able to enter God's rest because they had failed to obey the word of God (3:7b–11, 15–19). The author's point is this: "Do not be like those people who have perished in the wilderness because of their unfaithfulness [ἀπιστία] to God. Instead, consider the faithfulness of Jesus. Be like Jesus."

Next, Hebrews 12:1–3 highlights the importance of perseverance by reminding believers that they need to imitate Jesus, who has endured sufferings and even death on the cross. In this passage, the author employs the image of athletes who run a race in a stadium, and exhorts the readers to run their race with endurance. Westcott observes from this passage

---

37   Rhee, *Faith in Hebrews*, 96.

that Jesus is the perfect example of faith which one ought to imitate.[38] How does the author develop his exhortation to endure the sufferings as Jesus did? Verse 3 reads, "For consider Him who has endured such hostility by sinners against Himself" (NASB). This verse is a reiteration of the previous verse (12:2), which is a summary of the sufferings and death of Jesus on the cross. The term "cross" (σταυρός) used in 12:2 is the only use of this word in Hebrews.[39] But other terms, such as "shame" (αἰσχύνης [12:2]), "suffer" (πάσχω [2:18; 5:8; 9:26; 13:12]), and "suffering" (πάθημα [2:9, 10; 10:32]), were also used to convey the significance of the cross of Jesus. Pointing to the supreme example of Jesus who endured the sufferings on the cross, the author exhorts readers to run with endurance the race that is set before them by fixing their eyes on Jesus, the author and perfecter of faith (12:2). The titles "author" and "perfecter" circumscribe the dual aspects of the saving work of Jesus Christ: he is the author (or, the founder) in a sense that he started eternal salvation for his people, and he is the perfecter in that he will see them through to finish the course.[40]

D. Emulating Other Exemplars of Faith

The author presents a negative example of those who have fallen away from faith in 6:4–8 by describing that it is impossible to restore them again to repentance. Then he exhorts the readers to be imitators of those who through faith and patience inherit the promise (6:9–12). The point of the contrast between 6:4–8 and 6:9–12 is clear: Do not be like those who have fallen away, but imitate the faith of those who have persevered throughout their lives. The phrase "faith and patience" (πίστεως καὶ μακροθυμίας) may be translated "faith, that is, patience."[41] Or, it could be understood as "persevering faith."[42] In Hebrews, faith involves endurance or steadfastness. To illustrate the enduring aspect of faith, the author of Hebrews brings in Abraham's example of steadfastness in 6:13–15 to show that Abraham obtained the promise of God by waiting for it

38 B. F. Westcott, *The Epistle to the Hebrews: A Historical and Theological Reconsideration* (London: Macmillan, 1889), 395.

39 Lane, *Hebrews 9–13*, 414.

40 William Manson, *The Epistle to the Hebrews: A Historical and Theological Reconsideration* (London: Hodder and Stoughton, 1951), 83.

41 James H. Moulton, *A Grammar of New Testament Greek—Vol. 3: Syntax* (Edinburgh: T&T Clark, 1963), 335.

42 Erich Grässer, *Der Glaube im Hebräerbrief* (Marburg: N. G. Elwert Verlag, 1965), 28; Ellingworth, *The Epistle to the Hebrews*, 333.

patiently. The purpose of including the example of Abraham's faith in
these verses is for readers to imitate the steadfastness of Abraham. This
idea is supported by the argument in 6:16–18, which speak of the irrevo-
cable nature of God's oath as mentioned in Gen. 22:16–17. The purpose
of God intervening with an oath is indicated by the conjunction ἵνα ("in
order that") in Heb. 6:18: the purpose is for believers to receive strong
encouragement to hold fast the hope that lies ahead of them. It is evident
that the author relates 6:13–15 to 6:16–18 with the theme of an oath to
show that the readers need to emulate Abraham's enduring faith. God's
unchanging purpose provides a strong motivation for believers to imitate
the trust and steadfastness of Abraham.[43]

The author also indicates that emulating Abraham's faith is related to
the believers' imitation of Christ (6:19–20). The author describes that
we have taken refuge to lay hold of the hope set before us. The idea of
hope goes back to the faith of Abraham, who waited for God's promise
patiently (6:13–15). The implication is that as Abraham hoped for what
God had promised him, believers in the new covenant should also hope
for that which is set before them. What then is the object of the believer's hope? An examination of the Greek construction reveals that it is
the hope that enters within the curtain in the heavenly sanctuary where
Jesus has already entered as forerunner by becoming a high priest according to the order of Melchizedek.[44] The Greek word for "forerunner"
is πρόδρομος, which occurs only here in the New Testament. In classical
Greek the term denotes "running ahead" in a figurative sense.[45] Likewise,
Jesus being the forerunner for us in verse 20 means that Jesus is the model of faith that his followers should emulate. As Jesus entered within the
veil as a forerunner, believers ought to imitate the act of Jesus in entering
inside of the curtain (i.e., the heavenly sanctuary). In summary, the author's exhortation to imitate those who inherit the promises (6:12) and
Abraham's enduring faith is tantamount to imitating Christ.

The theme of imitating the exemplars of faith, which the author ex-
pounded in Hebrews 6:9–20, is elaborated more fully in Hebrews 11,
which is commonly known as a "faith chapter." In the immediate context
(10:32–39) the author exhorts the believers to endure in the midst of the
trials they are facing in their Christian walk. He does this by calling the

---

43 Lane, *Hebrews 1–8*, 152.
44 Lane, *Hebrews 1–8*, 153. For the analysis of Hebrews 6:18–19, see Rhee, *Faith in Hebrews*, 127.
45 BDAG, 867.

readers to remember their former days when they endured great suffering, partly by being made public spectacles through reproaches and tribulations, and partly by becoming partakers of those believers who were
persecuted for the sake of Christ (10:32–34). Based on this reminder, the
author exhorts the readers not to abandon their confidence (i.e., faith in
Jesus), which has a great reward (10:35). The reason for it is indicated by
the conjunction γάρ ("for") in 10:36: "for you have need of endurance, in
order that you may receive the promise of God after you have done the will
of God." Here, reference to "you have need of endurance" in 10:36 implies
that the believing community should expect more severe persecution in the
near future.

It may be noted that Hebrews 10:36–39 is an announcement of the
theme that will be discussed in 11:1–12:13.[46] The author of Hebrews
sets the tone for what follows by citing Habakkuk 2:4 (LXX) in Hebrews
10:38. The exemplars of faith in 11:1–40 and the supreme example of
the faith of Jesus in 12:1–3 are a further elaboration on the quotation
from Habbakuk, "but my righteous one shall live by faith" (10:38a). The
exhortation to endure discipline in 12:4–13 corresponds to the theme
introduced in 10:38b, "and if he draws back, my soul will take no pleasure in him." This is supported by the author's repeated use of the verb
"to discipline" (παιδεύω [12:6, 7, 10]) and the noun "discipline" (παιδεία
[12:5, 7, 8, 9, 11]).[47] Thompson rightly observes that both 10:32–39 and
12:1–11 have a common theme of "endurance" in the midst of sufferings,
and that chapter 11 is in the middle of these two sections.[48]

It is in this context that the author's exposition of the exemplars of faith
in Hebrews 11:1–40 is to be understood. Hebrews 11 may be compared
to a diamond under light. Just as one sees the beautiful reflections of rays
shining through it, so are the aspects of faith exemplified by the men and
women of faith in this chapter. There are many qualities of faith that these
Old Testament saints display.[49] Some of the examples are: suffering and
dying for the sake of righteousness (11:4 [Abel]; obedience to God's word
(11:7 [Noah]), believing in God's promises (11:8–10, 17–19 [Abraham];

---

46 Albert Vanhoye, *La Structure littéraire de l'Épître aux Hébreux*, 2nd ed. (Paris: Desclée de
Brouwer, 1976), 182.

47 For a detailed discussion of 10:32–39 and 12:4–13, see Rhee, *Faith in Hebrews*, 171–79,
232–35.

48 James W. Thompson, *The Beginnings of Christian Philosophy: The Epistle to the Hebrews*,
CBQMS 13 (Washington, DC: Catholic Biblical Society of America, 1982), 69.

49 For a detailed analysis of the aspects of faith in Hebrews 11, see Victor (Sung Yul) Rhee,
"Chiasm and the Concept of Faith in Hebrews 11," *BibSac* 155 (1998): 327–45.

11:11–12 [Sarah]), and so on. But the overall emphasis of faith is for the readers to be steadfast in their walk with God. In other words, the author of Hebrews exhorts them to persevere through trials, temptations, sufferings, and persecution, by emulating the life of the heroes and heroines of faith in Hebrews 11:1–40, and ultimately by imitating Jesus, the author and perfecter of faith, who endured the cross (Heb. 12:1–3).

E. The Importance of Community

In the life of discipleship these days there is a tendency for believers to think in terms of an individual relationship with Jesus, and personal spiritual growth (e.g., *my* daily reading and meditation of God's Word, *my* prayer life, *my* spiritual maturity, *my* desire to imitate Jesus). We tend to neglect the spiritual development of the faith community as a whole. It is true that Hebrews does have a role for individual discipleship. This is evident from the singular use of the indefinite pronoun τις ("anyone"). For example, Hebrews 3:12–13 reads, "Take care, brethren, that there not be in any one [τινι] of you an evil, unbelieving heart that falls away from the living God. But encourage one another . . . so that none [μὴ . . . τις] of you will be hardened by the deceitfulness of sin" (NASB). In Hebrews 4:11 the author also exhorts the readers to enter that rest in order that anyone (τις) may not fall by the same example of disobedience.[50]

But a close look at Hebrews reveals that the emphasis is more on the discipleship of the faith community as a whole, rather than that of an individual person in the church. One can find even from a casual reading of Hebrews that the author makes use of the plural personal pronouns "we," "us," and "you" throughout the epistle.[51] The intention seems to be clear; he wants to let the audience realize the importance of the faith community in the Christian life.

What are some specific ways that the author brings out the communal aspects of discipleship? First, he does this with the idea of believers being "the house of God." While speaking of the faithfulness of Christ by way of comparison with that of Moses, the author points out that

---

50 For other examples, see Hebrews 10:28–29 and 12:15–16.
51 The author employs the various forms of ἡμεῖς and ὑμεῖς in his letter (e.g., ἡμεῖς: 1:2, 5; 2:1, 3; 3:1, 6; 4:13; 10:26; 12:5, 25; 13:20; ὑμεῖς: 3:8, 9; 3:12, 13; 4:1, 7; 5:12; 6:9–11; 10:34–35; 13:7). The author also expresses the communal idea through the use of the hortatory subjunctive mood of verbs (e.g., προσερχώμεθα ["let us draw near," 4:16]; φερώμεθα ["let us press on," 6:1]; κατέχωμεν ["let us hold fast," 10:23]; κατανοῶμεν ["let us consider," 10:24]; τρέχωμεν ["let us run," 12:2]; ἀναφέρωμεν ["let us offer up," 13:15]).

those who have come to believe in Jesus are God's house (οἶκος), which speaks of the community of believers (3:1–6). Hebrews 10:21 also mentions that Jesus is a great priest over the house of God (i.e., believers as a whole).

Second, the idea of the community is expressed with the term "partakers" (μέτοχοι). For example, believers in Christ are called "partakers of a heavenly calling" (3:1), "partakers of Christ" (3:14), and "partakers of discipline" (12:8). This term, along with "brethren" (ἀδελφοί [3:1]), connotes the family relationship of believers. This family relationship was brought about by Jesus (i.e., "he is not ashamed to call them brethren"; "I will proclaim your name to my brethren" [2:11–12]). With these expressions, the author has in mind the community of those who are called into the presence of God, who enjoy privileged access to him.[52]

Third, the communal aspect of discipleship can be observed from the believers' ministry to one another. Hebrews 6:10 indicates that the believers in the community have lived out their Christian life, and are still doing so because of their faith in God and love for him. Their love for God was expressed through ministry to his people.[53] The plural term ἅγιοι ("saints") does not refer to a particular or special class of believers, but to all believers in the faith-community.[54] The author's addressing of the audience as "holy brethren" (3:1) and the exhortation to greet all the saints (13:24) indicates that ἅγιοι is general enough to encompass all the believers in the community.

What, then, are some ways that believers in Christ can minister to other saints in the faith-community? In 6:10 the author does not present specific ways of serving others. But he does this in other parts of his epistle. Some examples will be adequate enough to illustrate this point. Firstly, believers need to encourage one another daily, so that none of the members will fall away from the living God, and be hardened by the deceitfulness of sin (3:12–13). Secondly, believers are to stimulate one another to love and good deeds, and not to forsake the assembling together (10:24–25). Thirdly, believers need to have the courage to identify with those who are persecuted for the sake of Christ (10:32–36; 13:2–3). Fourthly, believers in Christ need to support the leaders and pray for them, so that they may be able to exercise the leadership with joy, and not with grief (13:7, 17, 18). Lastly, believers in the Lord should help others

---

52 Lane, *Hebrews 1–8*, 74.

53 George H. Guthrie, *Hebrews*, NIVAC (Grand Rapids: Zondervan, 1998), 222.

54 Attridge, *The Epistle to the Hebrews*, 175.

to take Jesus seriously in their Christian lives, and encourage them to fix their eyes on Jesus, the author and perfecter of faith (3:1; 12:1–2).

CONCLUSION

Who, according to Hebrews, is a disciple of Jesus Christ? A disciple is a true believer who has decided to follow Jesus with his or her life. In other words, *all* genuine believers in Jesus are disciples of Jesus. What, according to Hebrews, does discipleship refer to? It denotes a way of life for believers in Jesus as prescribed in the Word of God. The present study has revealed that the author of Hebrews carries on the tradition of the Gospels and Acts concerning the concept of discipleship, even though the term "disciple" (μαθητής) is not used in the epistle. The word "disciple" (μαθητής) is replaced by other terms such as "saints" (ἅγιοι), "brethren," "holy brethren," "those who are sanctified," "partakers of heavenly calling, of Christ, and of the Holy Spirit." As for the titles of Jesus, although the word "Master" is not used, the author continues to employ "Lord" and "Christ." He also employs other expressions (e.g., "great shepherd," "high priest," "author and perfecter of faith") to summarize the life and work of Jesus which are recorded in the Gospels.

This study also reveals that the qualities of discipleship are abundant in Hebrews, even though the term "disciple" is absent. What does discipleship involve, according to the author? (1) Discipleship in Hebrews is Christ-centered. (2) It involves paying attention to the word of God. (3) It necessitates being faithful to God as Jesus was as a Son. (4) It entails imitating Jesus by enduring sufferings and hardship. (5) It involves emulating other exemplars of faith who have followed in the footsteps of Jesus. (6) And lastly, discipleship in Hebrews is not merely an individual relationship with Christ, but more importantly, it involves the spiritual growth of the faith community as a whole.

There are many other principles of discipleship which may be elaborated (e.g., brotherly love [13:1–7]; moving toward maturity [5:11–6:3]; lifestyle of living sacrifice [13:15–16]). But it is hoped that the results of this study have sufficiently demonstrated that the concept of discipleship is not lost in Hebrews amid the disappearance of the term, but is faithfully preserved through a host of other terms that offer instruction for followers of Jesus Christ.

CHAPTER 14

Single-Mindedness vs. Duplicity: Discipleship in James

Craig L. Blomberg and Ben R. Crenshaw

More so than any of the other New Testament epistles, James presents the reader with an uninterrupted sequence of ethical instruction.[1] Whereas other letters at times have extended theological reflection, so that a study of the theme of discipleship has to sift through the writer's discussions looking for the most relevant texts, James deals with the topic from start to finish. We might be tempted, therefore, to summarize discipleship in James by saying simply, "Read the book and do everything it says and avoid everything it warns against."[2] Imperatives abound at every turn.

Such an approach, however, would beg the question of whether there are one or more unifying themes in James's letter. The days of Martin Dibelius's influential form-critical study of the letter, in which he found only discrete units of thought loosely linked together by catchwords,[3] have long since given way to detailed proposals about a very careful and complicated structure of this epistle.[4] Such redaction—and even literary-critical studies of the letter—exhibit considerable disagreement about the precise nature of that structure, but there is a reasonable groundswell of support for the notion of three key themes. Ever since Peter Davids designed his entire, excellent commentary around the programmatic article of Fred Francis, more and more scholars have accepted that something along the lines of "trials and temptations," "wisdom

---

1 All Scripture translations are NIV unless otherwise noted.

2 This is why Darian R. Lockett groups the ethical injunctions into the way of God and life vs. the way of the world and death ("Structure or Communicative Strategy? The 'Two Ways' Motif in James' Theological Instruction," *Neotestimentica* 42 [2008]: 269–87).

3 Martin Dibelius (*James*, Hermeneia [Philadelphia: Fortress, 1975], 3) spoke of "a text which strings together admonitions of general ethical content." Catchwords helped to move from one theme to the next, pithily punching out memorable ethical aphorisms without creating any continuity in thought or development in theology (2).

4 See the thorough survey of proposals in Mark E. Taylor, *A Text-Linguistic Investigation into the Discourse Structure of James* (London: T&T Clark, 2006). Cf. also Mark E. Taylor, "Recent Scholarship on the Structure of James," *CBR* 3 (2004): 86–115.

and speech" and "riches and poverty" form three pervasive concerns in this little letter.[5]

The greatest amount of agreement comes with the conviction that James 1 forms an introduction to these themes, possibly cycling through them twice in verses 2–11 and 12–27 or thereabouts. It is also widely acknowledged that these themes continue to recur in chapters 2–5, but here is where any even slight consensus breaks down, despite our support for Davids's notion (though not his exact pericope divisions) that the three topics account for most of the rest of the epistle in precisely the reverse sequence from the order in which they are introduced in chapter 1.[6] Nevertheless, we still have not arrived at a "big idea," to use Haddon Robinson's widely applauded homiletical concept,[7] for the ethical injunctions of the entire epistle, though no principle of the rhetoric of the ancient Mediterranean world absolutely requires that there be one. Still, the concept was common enough that it is worth asking if there is a "golden thread" that runs through even the three main themes, tying the teaching on discipleship in James together.

One way of envisioning this is to select one of the three themes as subsuming the other two. Too often, as Elsa Tamez highlights, North American (or European) commentators have "intercepted" the letter of James and muted its force by treating it as a document of abstract proverbs rather than a missive tied very close to specific, agonizing circumstances of its audience.[8] If one allows even a little bit of mirror reading, however, it seems clear that many in James's churches are poor day-laborers in agricultural settings, who are being exploited and oppressed by not always receiving their daily wages (5:4). In worst-case scenarios, when this persists among the poorest of the workers, they are required to take out loans which they may not be able to repay,

5 Peter H. Davids, *The Epistle of James,* NIGTC (Exeter: Paternoster; Grand Rapids: Eerdmans, 1982); Fred O. Francis, "The Form and Function of the Opening and Closing Paragraphs of James and 1 John," *ZNW* 61 (1970): 110–26. Particularly appreciative of Davids's outline is John Painter, "James," in *James and Jude,* Paideia, eds. John Painter and David A. deSilva (Grand Rapids: Baker, 2012), 56–59.
6 Cf. Craig L. Blomberg and Mariam J. Kamell, *James,* ZECNT (Grand Rapids: Zondervan, 2008).
7 Haddon W. Robinson, *Biblical Preaching: The Development and Delivery of Expository Messages,* 3rd ed. (Grand Rapids: Baker, 2014), 15–26.
8 Elsa Tamez, *The Scandalous Message of James: Faith without Works Is Dead,* rev. ed. (New York: Crossroad, 2002), 1. For the view that James is responding to temptations to react to oppression by joining pre-Zealot groups promoting violent rebellion, see Jim Reiher, "Violent Language: A Clue to the Historical Occasion of James," *EvQ* 85 (2013): 228–45.

eventually landing themselves in debtors' prison where they may eventually die (v. 6). For those not yet in such dire straits, there is still the strong temptation to take out their frustrations against one another in church (4:1–2), since the absentee landlords who are the true objects of their anger are not immediately accessible. When more well-to-do individuals do come to their churches, believers kowtow to them, discriminating themselves against the poorest in their midst, in hopes of receiving their economic favor (2:1–4).[9]

It is possible, therefore, to envision the problem of poverty vs. riches as creating the trials and temptations that James addresses in more generalizable terms and as necessitating godly wisdom and proper speech. Alternately, if one is less convinced of this very specific *Sitz im Leben*, one may start where James begins, with trials and temptations (1:2–4) and see the socioeconomic problems as just one kind of external circumstance that can either be a test to refine us (v. 12) or a temptation to seduce us (vv. 13–15). The need for wisdom from above (3:17) displayed in more listening than speaking (1:19) then follows in all of these many contexts.[10] The third option is to see careful speech as the overarching topic. Robert Wall, for example, finds 1:19 with its triad of injunctions to be "quick to listen, slow to speak and slow to become angry" as previewing the three main topics of the rest of the body of the letter.[11] The way in which each of these three key themes can be seen to lead to the other two, of course, does make us wonder if all we are demonstrating is their interconnectedness. If there actually is a uniting principle, we may have to look elsewhere.

---

9 Cf. also Elsa Tamez, "James: A Circular Letter for Immigrants," *RevExp* 108 (2011): 369–80. In light of such specific circumstances, it is hard to go along with the notion of a plurality of recent commentators that James is merely an abstract, "apostolic letter to the diaspora" designed to dispense general wisdom, especially when no independent example of this literary genre is known other than short letters embedded in larger works. For other options, see Craig L. Blomberg, "Genre in Recent New Testament Commentaries," in *On the Writing of New Testament Commentaries: Festschrift for Grant R. Osborne on the Occasion of his 70th Birthday*, eds. S. E. Porter and E. J. Schnabel (Leiden: Brill, 2013), 73–90, at 87, and the literature there cited.

10 So, e.g., D. Edmond Hiebert, *The Epistle of James: Tests of a Living Faith* (Chicago: Moody, 1979). More recently and with more rhetorical sophistication, see Matt. Jackson-McCabe, "Enduring Temptation: The Structure and Coherence of the Letter of James," *JSNT* 37 (2014): 161–84. On wisdom as the primary solution and antidote to persecution, see John C. Poirier, "Symbols of Wisdom in James 1:17," *JTS* 57 (2005): 57–75, esp. 60–62.

11 Robert W. Wall, *Community of the Wise: The Letter of James*, New Testament in Context (Valley Forge, PA: Trinity Press International, 1997).

Sophie Laws offered the intriguing proposal that we should focus on the theme of single-mindedness in James.[12] Mariam Kamell (now Kovalyshin), in her commentary coauthored with Craig Blomberg, made a similar suggestion that we find persuasive. The length of the introductions in the commentary series in which that volume appeared, however, prevented this suggestion from being developed in any detail.[13] The scope of this essay permits only slight expansion, but we may at least attempt a fresh exposition in light of a decade of scholarship that has appeared since the Blomberg-Kamell volume was published. The thesis we are proposing is that *the heart of James's thinking about discipleship consists of the need for the believer to grow in the likeness of God (cf. 3:9) as ever more single-minded in their focus on the things of God, minimizing the duplicity that too often besets them with the discrepancy between thoughts and even words, on the one hand, and actions on the other.*

EXEGESIS

After James's greetings in 1:1, he immediately commands his listeners to "consider it pure joy" whenever they confront trials (v. 2). The Greek term behind "pure" is merely πᾶς, often translated "all," but "consider it all joy" in English too easily misleads people into thinking that "all" is the direct object of the verb rather than an adjective modifying "joy." James is not calling us to treat all things as joyful but rather to think about trials in a purely joyous fashion.[14] We certainly may not feel happy; emotions cannot be commanded anyway. But our outlook may reflect a deeply seated conviction that God can use these experiences to grow our character (vv. 3–4a) so that we become "mature and complete, not lacking anything" (v. 4). The two adjectives in this phrase could also be translated "perfect" and "whole,"[15] so that it is clear that the theme of unidirectional focus continues.

As James moves from trials (vv. 2–4) to wisdom (vv. 5–8), he enjoins believers to ask God for what they need because he gives ἁπλῶς (v. 5), which is usually rendered "generously." The more common meaning of the word, though, is "simply," in the sense of "straightforward" or "singly focused."[16]

---

12 Sophie Laws, *The Epistle of James,* BNTC (London: A & C Black, 1980), 29–32. Cf. also Tamez, *Scandalous Message of James,* 46–56; Richard Bauckham, *James,* New Testament Readings (London: Routledge, 1999), 177–85.

13 Blomberg and Kamell, *James,* 261–63.

14 Cf. Chris A. Vlachos, *James* (Nashville: B&H, 2013), 15–16.

15 BDAG, 995–96 and 703–4, respectively.

16 Cf. BDAG, 104. Horst Balz and Gerhard Schneider (*Exegetical Dictionary of the New Testament,* 2 vols. [Grand Rapids: Eerdmans, 1990], 1:124) give "sincerely, uprightly" for

No doubt that leads to generosity, which is primarily in view here, but the root meaning of the term is not entirely left behind, because by verse 8, James will be likening the fickle believer to a δίψυχος or "double-minded" individual. James may well have coined this word, making its etymology ("two-souled") more significant than it otherwise might be.[17] God dispenses wisdom unswervingly, so believers should not doubt that he will give it to them (vv. 6–7). Verses 9–11 do not as obviously contain our theme, as they introduce the issue of wealth and poverty. In fact, what is clearest is the reversal of contexts that they promise poor and rich Christians. In each case, however, James's point is to pay consistent attention to the life to come, so that circumstances in this life are not weighted more than they deserve.

With the second cycle of the three themes in 1:12–27, single-mindedness becomes more explicit again. With respect to trials, believers must "persevere" (from ὑπομένω). Various English translations also use "stand firm," "endure" or "remain steadfast."[18] A single-minded focus is certainly in view. They must also not blame God, as if he were trying to tempt them to sin, because God is unequivocally devoted to providing only good things for his people (vv. 13b, 18) and he does not change in this respect (v. 17). As Mariam Kamell nicely phrases it, "with the bold statement of 1:17 James again affirms God's unchanging nature as the generous giver of all that is good, and also demonstrates the singleness, the purity of God's nature especially as it is revealed in his desire to give the good things his people need."[19]

If 1:19 does not preview the rest of the body of James's letter, it at least appears to account for the structure of verses 20–26.[20] Here begins his

---

their main definitions but suggest "without ulterior motives" for the use in James 1:5, and note Dibelius's (*James*, 79) "without hesitation." Dan G. McCartney (*James,* BECNT [Grand Rapids: Baker, 2009], 89) explicitly contrasts it with the "doubleness" of the doubter in 1:18 and defines it here as "not devious" and "without complications or double-dealing." Douglas J. Moo (*The Letter of James*, PNTC [Grand Rapids: Eerdmans, 2000], 59) explains it as God's "single, undivided intent."

17   Stanley E. Porter, "Is *dipsuchos* (James 1,8; 4,8) a 'Christian' Word?" *Biblica* 71 (1990): 469–98. The word occurs in 1:8 in conjunction with ἀκατάστατος, which can mean "restless" or "rebellious" (cf. 3:8 where it appears again. In the contexts of 1:8 and 4:8, δίψυχος concerns "instability of thinking, commitment, and direction, which is expressed in indecision"; Painter, "James," 67.

18   Cf. also Moisés Silva, *New International Dictionary of New Testament Theology and Exegesis* (Grand Rapids: Zondervan, 2014), 4:566; Dan G. McCartney, *James,* BECNT (Grand Rapids: Baker, 2009), 87.

19   Mariam J. Kamell, "The Implications of Grace for the Ethics of James," *Biblica* 92 (2011): 274–87, at 278.

20   William R. Baker and Thomas D. Ellsworth, *Preaching James* (St. Louis: Chalice, 2004), 32.

emphasis on the tongue, and the contrast between "simplicity" and duplicity sums up most of what James has to say. Unless we are slow to speak, we wind up being quick to anger, which works contrary to the righteousness God desires (vv. 19–20). We must not merely hear the word, but do it—obeying it or putting it into practice (v. 22). An illustration drives the point home. How ridiculous it is to see a problem with one's grooming or appearance in a mirror but then take no corrective action (vv. 23–24).[21] One's treatment of a problem should be consistent with its diagnosis. Hence the call to look into the "perfect law that gives freedom"—the Torah as fulfilled in Christ and subsumed under the new covenant[22]—and *continue* in it (v. 25). An unyielding determination to follow God's will emerge as a result.

Verses 26–27 belong together grammatically, but topically verse 26 concludes James's reflections in this context on the tongue, while verse 27 returns to God's concern for the poor. It also rounds out James's introduction and provides the transition to the body of his letter. Verse 26 pursues the need for consistency between one's claims and one's behavior, while verse 27 returns to what is "pure and faultless," this time using the language of ritual purity ("clean and undefiled") but applying it to moral matters instead—helping the most destitute in society, even while remaining morally unblemished by the fallen world. The goal is to avoid the duplicity so common among those who commendably are involved in trying to do good in the muck and grime of society but end up being corrupted instead. But believers must equally avoid the duplicity of talking a good game, so to speak, about the priority of helping the physically and socially needy while in reality doing nothing or very little to alleviate their suffering (whether or not James has that specifically in mind when he spoke of bridling the tongue in v. 26).[23]

Chapter 2 joins two subsections—one against discrimination in favor of the rich (vv. 1–13) and one on the need for faith to produce good deeds (vv.

---

21 Commentators have caused unnecessary confusion by trying to take the behavior here as something that could be imagined. The whole point is how absurd it would be to behave this way. See William R. Baker, "James," in *James—Jude: Unlocking the Scriptures for You*, eds. William R. Baker and Paul Carrier (Cincinnati: Standard, 1990), 137. Cf. also James L. Boyce, "A Mirror of Identity: Implanted Word and Pure Religion in James 1:17–27," *Word & World* 35 (2015): 213–21.

22 Mariam J. Kamell, "Incarnating Jeremiah's Promised New Covenant in the Law of James," *EvQ* 83 (2011): 19–28. McCartney (*James*, 123) agrees and adds that it refers also to "Torah that has reached its ultimate redemptive purpose."

23 Verse 27 can be seen to form the thesis statement for the entire letter. See Blomberg and Kamell, *James,* 80. On this verse, cf. also Mariam Kamell, "James 1:27 and the Church's Call to Mission and Morals," *Crux* 46 (2010): 15–22.

14–26). The latter begins with an illustration of the horrible hypocrisy of wishing the neediest people well without lifting a finger to help them when one is clearly in a position to do so (vv. 14–17). In that sense, the topic that so many since Luther have touted as the centerpiece of James's letter, for good or for ill, is really just an outgrowth of the theme of riches and poverty.[24] The entire chapter may thus be seen as unpacking that theme in more detail than its introduction in 1:9–11 and 26–27 permitted.

Single-mindedness vs. duplicity, however, characterizes all parts of 2:1–26 as well. The favoritism and discrimination in favor of the rich and to the detriment of the poor illustrated in verses 1–4 represent the duplicity that Christians must eschew. Interestingly, the verb in verse 4 that means to "discriminate" in this context (διακρίνω) is the same one James used in 1:6 for "doubting." Both meanings derive from the root concept of making a distinction or differentiation between two or more things.[25] This can be a positive activity, as when the term means to "discern." But when it turns into unfair, unequal treatment or the inability consistently to head in the same direction, then it becomes a negative quality to be avoided. That inconsistency is exacerbated when one shows favoritism to the rich, as verses 5–7 go on to explain, because they are precisely the people hauling the poor believers into court, probably to get them to pay the debts they owe precisely because the rich have not paid them their due![26]

The solution is to be singly focused in obedience to the royal (or "kingdom") law, most likely identical to the "law that gives freedom" (vv. 8–13; see esp. vv. 8, 12).[27] Even one transgression makes a person a sinner (vv. 9–11) and the law of tit-for-tat retribution applies to the judgment of the unmerciful (v. 13). Fortunately, one major arena in which God is gloriously inconsistent is in his provision of salvation due to his mercy and *not* based on what we deserve (v. 12)! But, as other parts of Scripture detail, the atonement Jesus provided is consistent with a deeper logic of satisfaction and justice, but James does not go into that issue here.

The rest of chapter 2 simply repeats, illustrates and demonstrates the refrain that "faith" without works is dead, useless or unable to save (vv.

---

24 For excellent overviews of the history of reception, see Dale C. Allison, Jr., *A Critical and Exegetical Commentary on the Epistle of James*, ICC (London: Bloomsbury T&T Clark, 426–41; and David B. Gowler, *James through the Centuries*, Wiley Blackwell Bible Commentaries (Oxford: Wiley Blackwell, 2014), 173–203.

25 BDAG, 231.

26 See esp. William J. Brosend II, *James & Jude*, NCBC (Cambridge: Cambridge University Press, 2004), 62–66. Cf. also Moo, *Letter of James*, 108–9.

27 Davids, *Epistle of James*, 114; Moo, *Letter of James*, 111–12.

14, 17, 20, 26). Tucked into the middle of this discussion is James's allusion to the *Shema* of Deuteronomy 6:4, the cardinal Jewish confession of the oneness of God. It is easy simply to turn the expression, "God is one" (εἷς ἐστιν ὁ θεός) into an affirmation of monotheism—there is only one God—and there is no doubt that this belief was absolutely foundational in ancient Jewish thought. But the wording of the statement, both in the Hebrew of Deuteronomy and the Greek of James 2:19, suggests that it first of all means that God is "simple" or undivided, a unified being.[28] That is why he is uniformly faithful to his covenant promises and why being remade in his image should lead his people to increasingly single-minded attention to his will, so that professions of faith unfailingly lead to deeds of mercy. In fact, Daniel Block argues that even more than an affirmation of God's integrity, the *Shema* was "a cry of allegiance, an affirmation of covenant commitment in response to the question, 'Who is the God of Israel?'"[29] In other words, the integrity and single-mindedness of God should be reflected in his people.

Chapter 3 returns to the theme of the tongue and the speech it produces (vv. 1–12). James then juxtaposes more on wisdom (vv. 13–17), suggesting that he sees wisdom and speech as a unified concept. Chapter 4 brings up the misuse of speech again (vv. 1–12), suggesting that all of 3:1–4:12 unpack the second of the three main themes introduced in chapter 1. But where do the sins of the tongue come from? After explaining why the issue is so important and such a barometer of Christian maturity (3:1–2)—because one's words can have powerful and irreversible effects for both good and bad (vv. 3–6)—James puts his finger on the nub of the matter. Unlike the animal kingdom, the tongue is untamable (vv. 7–8). The natural word of plants and springs demonstrates a consistency that human beings often do not (vv. 9–12). In other words, there is a unique duplicity in praising God and cursing those made in his image that the rest of creation does not and cannot replicate (vv. 7–12). In a

---

28 This is an application of Colwell's rule. In his treatment of it, Daniel B. Wallace (*Greek Grammar beyond the Basics* [Grand Rapids: Zondervan, 1996], 256–70) moves beyond predicate nouns to include all predicate nominatives, including an example with the numerical pronoun (p. 265). Vlachos (*James*, 95) rightly concludes from both the most likely original textual reading and the grammar that the translation should be "God is one" but then erroneously adds that this translation and "There is one God" both "amount to the same confession of monotheism." Cf. also Patrick J. Hartin, "The Letter of James: Faith Leads to Action (The Indicative Leads to the Imperative)," *Word & World* 35 (2015): 222–30, at 223.
29 Daniel L. Block, "How Many Is God? An Investigation into the Meaning of Deuteronomy 6:4–5," *JETS* 47 (2004): 193–212, at 211. Cf. also Barbara E. Bowe, "Friendship with God: Discipleship in the Letter of James," *The Bible Today* 44 (2006): 286–90, at 289.

wonderful understatement, James declares, "my brothers and sisters, this should not be" (v. 10).[30]

Wisdom from above (i.e., heaven) as opposed to that which comes from the world, the flesh and the devil is similarly demonstrated by good deeds (v. 13). It is first of all "pure" (ἁγνός), the third different Greek word the NIV has rendered this way, and another term that could refer to ritual cleanliness now applied to moral holiness (v. 17).[31] By beginning the list of virtues that define godly wisdom with the modifier "first," James suggests that this is the foundational character trait, without which the others have little significance.[32] "Then" (ἔπειτα), a term that sometimes denotes a specific chronological sequence,[33] all the others come into play. Included as the last two are ἀδιάκριτος and ἀνυπόκριτος. If we preserve the morphology in English translation, these yield "not discriminating [against someone]" and "not hypocritical." As previously in James, the goal is to avoid double-mindedness, inconsistency or duplicity as much as possible.

Chapter 4 continues the pattern of vices as emerging from contradictory or warring impulses in people (v. 1). We try to acquire things by the wrong means (v. 2) or we use the right means but with the wrong motives (v. 3). In what Luke Johnson thinks is the thesis of the entire epistle, verse 4 declares that such people are metaphorically adulterous, unfaithful to their God to whom they should be exclusively wedded.[34] They think they can be friends with God while also being friends with the fallen world, which James insists is not possible. Friendship in the ancient Mediterranean world was often conceived of in terms of sharing one's soul with someone else, in joining one's life in a single purpose and cause with them, which explains how James can make such an absolute dichotomy in this verse.[35] For the second time in his letter, James uses

---

30 McCartney (James, 192) suggests that "this might be more idiomatically rendered 'This cannot be!'—not that cursing and blessing coming from the same mouth is impossible, but that it is radically inconsistent."

31 For a detailed study, see Darian Lockett, Purity and Worldview in the Epistle of James (London: T&T Clark, 2008).

32 Ralph P. Martin (James, WBC [Waco, TX: Word, 1988], 133) notes that purity means that one is "free of the moral and spiritual defects that are the marks of the double-minded."

33 BDAG, 361. Allison (James, 581) takes the "first . . . then" construction to refer to "relative importance rather than time."

34 Luke T. Johnson, "Friendship with the World/Friendship with God: A Study of Discipleship in James," in Discipleship in the New Testament, ed. F. F. Segovia (Philadelphia: Fortress, 1985), 176–83.

35 Cf. Bowe, "Friendship with God," 287.

the neologism "double-minded" (v. 8b) to characterize these competing allegiances. As Barbara Bowe observes, this state of double-mindedness "leaves one constantly in doubt; in fact, it paralyzes and renders one incapable of any good action."[36] Instead, Christians should submit themselves in all things to God, metaphorically washing their hands and purifying their hearts (vv. 7–8a), and not just individually but in their entire communities, which is where much of their duplicity was being acted out.[37]

Slander likewise exemplifies one kind of duplicitous speech (vv. 11–12). Speaking (falsely) about or against another person causes a person to sit in judgment over the Law (v. 11), because the Law proscribes slander, and this particular moral principle remains every bit in force in the age of the new covenant, too. As in 2:19, James appeals to the Shema to support his commands: "there is only one Lawgiver and Judge, the one who is able to save and destroy (4:12).[38] Again the word order supports the more woodenly literal sense of "the Lawgiver and Judge is one" (εἷς ἐστιν ὁ νομοθέτης καὶ κριτής).[39] God always speaks truly about people and so should we. He alone can fairly mete out judgment, so we should trust him to do so and not try to take vengeance into our own hands. In fact, for James, the role of judge was the only activity of God which believers were *not* to imitate.[40] Instead of judging others, we should be more concerned to be doers of the law God has given us (4:11; cf. 1:22).

At 4:13, James shifts back to the theme of wealth and poverty.[41] The greatest disagreement on the outline of James, even at the level of the individual pericopes, comes as one moves into chapter 5. The first paragraph clearly sticks to this topic (5:1–6). But a number of commentators end the body of the epistle precisely at 5:6.[42] Yet verses 7–11 appear to

---

36 Bowe, "Friendship with God," 288.
37 Here James echoes Paul's implicit expectation that Christian discipleship and sanctification would primarily be a communal effort, not an individual one (for a thorough treatment of the Pauline corpus, see James M. Howard, *Paul, the Community, and Progressive Sanctification: An Exploration into Community-Based Transformation within Pauline Theology* [New York: Peter Lang, 2007]).
38 Kim Huat Tan, "The Shema and Early Christianity," *TynBul* 59 (2008): 181–206, at 198.
39 Cf. Martin, *James*, 164; Allison, *James*, 637 (with reference to the *Shema*).
40 Kamell, "Implications of Grace for the Ethics of James," 279.
41 Verses 13–17 also continue with the theme of presumption that is covered in verses 11–12. Given the fact that in verese 10 James commands us to humble ourselves, verses 11–17 could be two examples of the opposite of humility: being presumptuous in judging others and in our economic productivity. In both cases we act as if we can sit in God's place or that we don't need him—both traits evidenced by those who are friends with the world (v. 4).
42 Davids, *Epistle of James*, 29; Ben Witherington III, *Letters and Homilies for Jewish Christians: A Socio-Rhetorical Commentary on Hebrews, James and Jude* (Downers Grove, IL: IVP, 2007), 405; Painter, "James," 47.

be the antidote to precisely the socioeconomic hardships and exploitation depicted in verse 6. Verse 12 has puzzled many readers and Bible translators. Should it stand alone as a self-contained paragraph? Probably not. As William Baker has argued, this verse is probably tied to the problem sketched in verses 1–6. Debtors made solemn vows to repay loans even when it was unlikely they could make good on their promises.[43] The allusion to Jesus's teaching in the Sermon on the Mount on not taking oaths (Matt. 5:34–37) suggests that they may have been involved in some of the same casuistry—swearing by various things related to God that were not the same as God and therefore that they felt might not be as binding— though admittedly this is only speculation. Again, James stresses the need for single-mindedness in both intention and spoken confirmation—even under duress and oppression—avoiding at all costs the personal duplicity that verbal oath-taking often masked.

Whatever one makes of the ceremony of anointing the sick person with oil in 5:14, the last main pericope in James (5:12–18) clearly presents prayer as the main antidote to whatever illnesses are in view. Verbs or nouns for prayer appear seven times in as many verses, and eight times if we include the injunction to "sing songs of praise" in verse 12b. The kind of prayer enjoined is "the prayer offered in faith" (v. 15). Out of context, this verse seems like a blank check: Just have enough faith and you will be made whole! Of course, most of the time it doesn't work, which then leads people to heap on themselves or others enormous guilt trips for not having enough faith. Instead of coming to this conclusion, James expects his listeners to remember what he said only one chapter earlier. People in their planning should always leave room for God's will to override theirs (4:15).[44] Like so many of James's teachings, this passage too seems to allude to a teaching of Jesus, again from his Great Sermon.[45] In what has come to be called the "Lord's Prayer," he teaches his disciples to pray, "your will be done" (Matt. 6:10). By definition, then, a prayer offered in faith will always leave the door open for God's will to be different from the will of the

---

[43] William R. Baker, "'Above All Else': Contexts of the Call for Verbal Integrity in James 5.12," *JSNT* 54 (1994): 57–71.

[44] Cf. Douglas J. Moo, *James*, TNTC, rev. ed. (Downers Grove, IL: IVP, 2015), 235–36. Cf. McCartney, *James*, 227. *Contra* attempts to take sickness and healing as more spiritual than physical to alleviate the tension caused by 5:15, see Gary S. Shogren, "Will God Heal Us—A Re-Examination of James 5:14–16a," *EvQ* 61 (1989): 99–108.

[45] Most recently, see Alicia J. Batten, "The Jesus Tradition and the Letter of James," *RevExp* 108 (2011): 381–90.

person praying (with Jesus's prayer in Gethsemane as the classic example—Mark 14:35–36 pars.).[46]

James next illustrates the prayer of faith with an Old Testament example from the ministry of Elijah (1 Kings 17:1, 18:42–45). Not only were
the objects of the prayer unlikely to occur without direct divine interven-
tion (an unusually long period of time without rain, followed by a deluge
to end the drought), but James stresses that Elijah prayed "earnestly."
Some translations prefer "fervently." The Greek employs a cognate da-
tive (προσευχῇ προσηύξατο), an emphatic way of stressing the action of
the verb.[47] "Single-mindedly" could just as easily be the concept in view,
cementing James's overarching point that prayers for healing should be
made with earnestness and unwavering devotion, knowing that God can
heal but trusting him if he doesn't.

In what seems like an abrupt and is certainly a non-epistolary closing,
verses 19–20 commend the restoration of a wandering sinner. The very
concept of "wandering" (from πλανάω) is the opposite of traveling in a
straight line, which is how a single-minded focus would guide a person.
Right to the very end of the letter, then, the emphasis on linear rectitude
vs. faithless duplicity permeates every main section of this epistle. We
must be single-mindedly devoted to God in our discipleship of the mind
and single-mindedly committed to putting his will into practice in our
discipleship in the world.[48]

CONTEMPORARY REFLECTION

Today's Western world needs many more models of single-minded
service to God. Because God is one (and because there is only one God),
our commitment to him must be unswerving. The orthodox doctrines
that we readily confess must be consistently backed up by deeds of mercy that genuine, saving faith produces. Crucial applications address the
areas of trials and temptation, wisdom and speech, wealth and poverty.
The problem of evil is one of the perennially greatest challenges to belief

---

46 Keith Warrington, "James 5:14–18: Healing Then and Now," *International Review of
Mission* 93 (2004): 346–76, at 358–59. Cf. Scot McKnight, *The Letter of James*, NICNT (Grand
Rapids: Eerdmans, 2011), 441.

47 A. K. M. Adam, *James: A Handbook on the Greek Text*, BHGNT (Waco, TX: Baylor University Press, 2013), 104.

48 For excellent general treatments on discipleship of the mind, see James W. Sire, *Disciple-
ship of the Mind* (Downers Grove, IL: InterVarsity Press, 1990); and J. P. Moreland, *Love Your
God with All Your Mind: The Role of Reason in the Life of the Soul*, rev. ed. (Colorado Springs:
NavPress, 2012).

in a God who is active in the affairs of humanity. It is also one of the biggest reasons some people apostatize.[49] Scripture suggests there is no such thing as gratuitous evil (esp. Rom. 8:28).[50] All human suffering can be explained as part of God's larger, beneficent purposes for creation, even if, like the back side of a tapestry,[51] we cannot see the beautiful picture being woven and even if, in some instances, we will not understand until the life to come. Thus an unswerving allegiance to God in Christ means that we will draw closer to him in times of hardship and difficulty rather than moving away and becoming cynical. But this allegiance is predicated upon God's character as demonstrated in Scripture and experienced in our own lives (e.g., Jas. 1:17), not upon our ability to determine how God is working even in the midst of evil circumstances, because we sometimes cannot. We will, however, look for the ways he wants us to persevere and grow in our likeness of him through even the worst of trials. We will not use external evil as a provocation for us to sin personally but as the impetus to run into Jesus's arms, as it were, and cling ever more tightly to him.

James 3:2b highlights the power of words. "Anyone who is never at fault in what they say is perfect, able to keep their whole body in check." Words reveal the thoughts and attitudes of the heart; if one can control that which can so easily slip out and do irreparable damage, they have the ability (δυνατός) themselves in other moral arenas as well.[52] Of course, being able to do something doesn't mean that a person *will* do it, but at least they have only themselves to blame if they succumb (recall 1:14–15). The truly wise person will nevertheless seek as direct and straightforward a trajectory with their speech as possible, saying what they mean, telling the truth, not requiring oaths, encouraging rather than condemning others. They will avoid duplicity and hypocrisy at every turn.

---

49 On which, see esp. Scot McKnight and Hauna Ondrey, *Finding Faith, Losing Faith: Stories of Conversion and Apostasy* (Waco, TX: Baylor University Press, 2008).

50 But this verse must be translated with its adverbial accusative as "in all things, God works . . . ," as in the NIV. See esp. Carroll D. Osburn, "The Interpretation of Romans 8:28," *WTJ* 44 (1982): 99–109. For a good exchange on the definition and nature of gratuitous evil, see Kirk R. MacGregor, "The Existence and Irrelevance of Gratuitous Evil," *Philosophia Christi* 14 (2012): 165–80; and Ross Inman, "Gratuitous Evil Unmotivated: A Reply to Kirk R. MacGregor," *Philosophia Christi* 15 (2013): 435–45.

51 To use the wonderful analogy Edith Schaeffer made famous in her ministry of teaching and writing.

52 Cf. Painter, "James," 115; Alec Motyer, *The Message of James: The Tests of Faith* (Leicester: IVP, 1985), 120–21.

The issue of the disparity between wealth and poverty in the modern world is doubtless the hardest for most Western Christians to address. We who live in middle-class comfort or better are like the proverbial fish in the water that don't even know there is life on dry land. Or we make brief forays into the most impoverished parts of the world for short-term ministry of some kind and "inoculate" ourselves against the realities of the Majority World without having any single-minded devotion through-out our lives to make a difference. Instead, we need to take regular stock of our income and spending patterns, how we can free up more to help others who are much worse off, both when sudden disasters create acute but temporary needs as well as for those perennially challenged, both via nontoxic charity and via systemic or structural changes that can be made.[53] We need to recognize the areas in which governments can and can't help, in which the private sector does and doesn't make a difference, and in which churches and individual Christians should and shouldn't address.[54] The issues are complex and there are no quick fixes, but we have made significant progress over the past twenty-five years,[55] which should encourage us that we can continue to make considerable more improvement in others' lives, though never at the expense of sharing with them Jesus and the salvation he uniquely offers.[56]

Discipleship in James, of course, goes beyond a single-minded de-votion to the three major themes of his letter. His recurring teaching on prayer suggests that this needs to be an important concern for us as well. James 4:2 contains some of the more neglected biblical teaching that helpfully addresses the oft-heard question, "why pray if God will accomplish his will anyway?" The short answer is that he has two kinds of will—unconditional and conditional. He will implement his uncondi-tional will whether anyone prays for it or not. But there are some good

---

53   For an excellent study of what is and is not harmful, see Robert D. Lupton, *Toxic Charity: How Churches and Charities Hurt Those They Help, and How to Reverse It* (New York: Harper-Collins, 2011); and for specific guidance on how to help the poor without unintentionally hurting them, see Steve Corbett and Brian Fikkert, *When Helping Hurts: How to Alleviate Pover-ty Without Hurting the Poor . . . and Yourself* (Chicago: Moody Publishers, 2012).

54   Cf. further Craig L. Blomberg, *Christians in an Age of Wealth: A Biblical Theology of Steward-ship* (Grand Rapids: Zondervan, 2013), 194–242.

55   See esp. Scott C. Todd, *Fast Living: How the Church Will End Extreme Poverty* (Colorado Springs: Compassion International, 2011).

56   Of course, the ways we are duplicitous, often unwittingly, in the use of our wealth go far beyond what we have space to include here. See esp. John de Graaf, David Waan and Thomas H. Naylor, *Affluenza: How Overconsumption Is Killing Us—And How to Fight Back*, 3rd ed. (San Francisco: Berrett-Koehler, 2014).

things that he would like for people to have that he has decided to give them if and only if they pray: "you do not have because you do not ask God" (4:2). The verbal aspect of the present tense verbs here and elsewhere in both James (recall 1:5) and its antecedent texts in the Sermon on the Mount (Matt. 7:7–8 par.) suggest that sometimes we have to ask repeatedly.[57] James 4:3, of course, then reminds us that our motives come into play as well.[58] But these caveats should not blind us from the basic point. Sometimes we "have not" because we "ask not" (v. 2, KJV). There can be little greater incentive to prayer!

Despite those who have relegated James to some "early Catholic" stage of the developing church, in the late first or even early second centuries, when all lively hope of a quickly arriving parousia had vanished,[59] such a hope in fact does appear in this letter. Chapter 5 has even been criticized for being too quietist or insufficiently activist, with its trio of references to Christ's return. Verse 7 insists that believers should be patient "until the Lord's coming," which is made possible because that coming "is near" (v. 8). The little paragraph then closes with the strongest statement of the three: "The Lord is standing at the door!" (v. 9). To be sure, this does not exclude the possibility of what from a human vantage point appears to be a long interval of time. Jews had been wrestling for at least eight centuries with the tension between the repeated declarations of their prophets that the Day of the Lord was at hand and the lack of the arrival of the messianic era. They had already appropriated Psalm 90:4 that a thousand years are like a day in God's sight to help address this tension.[60] Second Peter 3:8 would later take the same tack. But whatever the timing, the point for Christian living remains the same. God will one day right all wrongs. We do not have to abandon all hope of justice.

At the same time, James's eschatology does not override social activism. In 1:27 James exhorts his hearers to tangibly care for orphans and widows, and in 5:10–11 he circles back to the proper use of speech when

---

57 Vlachos, *James*, 25, 132. David L. Mathewson and Elodie Ballantine Emig (*Intermediate Greek Grammar: Syntax for Students of the New Testament* [Grand Rapids: Baker, 2016], 113) prefer to speak of aspect of the present tense as the perception of "action as in progress, as developing or unfolding" rather than as simply repeating or continuous.

58 As when "the gift-giving God is here manipulated as a kind of vending machine precisely for the purpose of self-gratification" (Johnson, *Letter of James*, 278).

59 For the most recent, detailed set of arguments for a very late date for James well into the second century, based on early and later Catholic features and several other elements as well, see David R. Nienhuis, *Not by Paul Alone: The Formation of the Catholic Epistle Collection and the Christian Canon* (Waco, TX: Baylor University Press, 2007), 99–161.

60 Richard J. Bauckham, "The Delay of the Parousia," *TynBul* 31 (1980): 3–36.

the prophets and Job are used as models of the right response to injustice. The "prophets who spoke in the name of the Lord" are hardly an example of either passivism or pacifism—they may not have countenanced violent revolt but their denunciatory rhetoric against personal and social sin gives us the permission and the responsibility to follow in their steps.[61] Job likewise persevered—he never cursed God and died—but his just outrage and complaints at the expense of his friends' orthodox but misapplied theology is what earned him God's praise (see esp. Job 42:7).[62] Mature disciples, then, according to James, will speak out persistently and boldly on behalf of the downtrodden and exploited, even when others, even within the Christian community, might try to silence them.

Some have alleged that there is little or nothing distinctively Christian in James.[63] A letter about ethical living, fulfilling the Law, commending Job, Elijah and the prophets and focusing on the right response to difficult external circumstances, especially socioeconomic discrimination and disparity, with proper speech and prayer could easily have been written in Second Temple Judaism prior to the life and times of Jesus. Whether or not this is the case, the letter is Christian as we have it, with its references to the Lord Jesus Christ in 1:1 and 2:1 and with no textual evidence to suggest they were added after the rest of the letter was complete. What is more, at least some of the other uses of "the Lord" in the letter probably refer to Jesus and not just to God (esp. in 4:15; 5:7, 8, 14).[64] So, while discipleship for James's Jewish-Christian congregations may from one perspective look a lot like discipleship could have looked in certain non-Christian Jewish assemblies of the same day, we must recognize the "faith" that inevitably produces works is *Christian* faith and not merely Jewish monotheism. Rightly understood, there is no "works-righteousness" in James, just as texts like Galatians 5:6 and Ephesians 2:10 remind us that Paul assumed that good works would flow from saving faith. But it may be better to say for James that genuine Christian faith includes within it Christian works.[65]

---

61 Painter, "James," 164; Christopher Church, "James," in *Hebrews—James*, eds. Edgar. V. McKnight and Christopher Church, SHBC (Macon, GA: Smyth & Helwys, 2004), 407.

62 Tamez, *Scandalous Message of James*, 44; McKnight, *Letter of James*, 420–21.

63 Allison (*James*, 32–51) does not go quite so far but sees James's milieu as Ebionite Christianity in which boundaries between Judaism and Jewish Christianity were not necessarily drawn and included individuals of both persuasions.

64 William R. Baker, "Christology in the Epistle of James," *EvQ* 44 (2002): 47–57

65 The classic little article of Joachim Jeremias ("Paul and James," *ExpTim* 66 [1955]: 568–71) is still very helpful at this juncture. Cf. esp. Hartin, "The Letter of James: Faith Leads to Action," *Word & World* 35 (2015): 231–40; and Mariam Kamell Kovalishyn, "Endurance unto

If those who date James early, to the mid to late 40s, are correct,[66] then here we are very close to our Christian roots. James may be the oldest known Christian document. It may not be much of an exaggeration, therefore, to say that in the Letter of James are the very foundations of New Testament discipleship. People must become followers of Jesus and then live out a life of single-minded deeds of mercy, responding properly to trials and temptations, growing in godly wisdom as particularly exemplified by the correct use of the tongue in their speech, and using their wealth to help the poor in whatever ways they can.[67] To whatever extent contemporary concepts of discipleship match up with this agenda, they may be said to capture the essence of the earliest form of Christianity.

Salvation: The Witness of First Peter and James," *Word & World* 35 (2015): 231–40. Four studies that all nuance the classic solution in various helpful but not always complementary ways are: Timo Laato, "Justification According to James: A Comparison with Paul," *TJ* 18 (1997): 43–84; C. Ryan Jenkins, "Faith and Works in Paul and James," *BibSac* 159 (2002): 62–78; David R. Maxwell, "Justified by Works and Not by Faith Alone: Reconciling Paul and James," *ConcJ* (2007): 375–78; and Alexander Stewart, "James, Soteriology, and Synergism," *TynBul* 61 (2010): 293–310.

66   Davids, *Epistle of James*, 2–22; Moo, *Letter of James*, 25–27; Donald Guthrie, *New Testament Introduction*, 4th ed. (Leicester: IVP, 1990), 749–53.

67   Arriving at similar conclusions following a different methodology is Christopher Church, "A 'Complete' Ethics: James' Practical Theology," *RevExp* 108 (2011): 407–15. Particularly important is his conclusion, "God is, for James, the very model of the kind of integrity expected of community members" (415).

CHAPTER 15 ▬▬▬▬▬▬▬▬▬▬▬▬▬▬▬▬▬▬▬▬▬

Suffer, Strive, and Stand for Holiness: Discipleship in 1–2 Peter and Jude

Robert L. Cavin

Although 1–2 Peter and Jude share the label "catholic epistles," typically they are not discussed together.[1] Scholars often examine 2 Peter and Jude as a pair because they parallel one another in language and thought in numerous places.[2] First Peter, on the other hand, stands apart having been written to meet decidedly different needs. Yet, a common theme runs through all three epistles, namely how God's people should respond to internal and external pressures to jettison Christian thinking and living. Each author sounds the alarm by calling on disciples to grow in their faith by knowing God's Word, reflecting Jesus, and rejecting tempters who seek the capitulation of gospel-centered beliefs and behaviors. Thus, all three epistles offer much guidance for the embattled disciple of Jesus who faces temptation from desires, suffering from persecution, and duplicity from false teachers.[3]

DISCIPLESHIP IN 1 PETER

A. Holy War

In 1 Peter, disciples live in a war zone that has the potential to refine genuine faith. But dark forces, though defeated (3:22), continue to battle against disciples to thwart God's call to holiness. This view surfaces through examination of Peter's descriptions of human existence and sins as wounds, the gospel as freedom or release, the devil and evil desires as warring enemies, and God's call for disciples to arm themselves in the battle for holiness.[4]

---

1 "Catholic" means "general, universal" for the epistles are addressed, not to individual persons or churches, but to the church at large.
2 Gene L. Green, *Jude and 2 Peter,* BECNT (Grand Rapids: Baker Academic, 2008), 159.
3 All Scripture translations are NIV unless otherwise noted.
4 See chapter three in Robert L. Cavin, *New Existence and Righteous Living: Colossians and 1 Peter in Conversation with 4QInstruction and the Hodayot,* BZNW 197 (Berlin: de Gruyter, 2013), 31–85, for a detailed exploration of the connection between redemption in Christ and moral enablement in 1 Peter.

1. Human Existence and the Wounds of War

Peter views humanity as deeply flawed. In contrast to the eternal word of God, the "flesh" (σάρξ, 1:24) is temporary and fleeting like withering grass and fading flowers.[5] It lives for human desires, not God's will (4:2), because it suffers from "evil desires" (ἐπιθυμίαι, 1:14; cf. 2:11; 4:2, 3) and commits sins which are offenses against God's holiness and cause deadly wounds (2:24).[6]

2. Freedom and Healing

Outside of faith in Christ, judgment looms (4:5, 17–18), the wounds of sin remain, and captivity continues. Thankfully, through faith in the preached gospel (1:12, 25; 4:6), disciples are redeemed (1:18) by the ransom payment of Christ's death (1:19) on the cross (2:24).[7] Redemption brings new birth (1:3, 23) and a coming salvation (1:5, 9, 10; 2:2).[8] Redemption also secures freedom (2:16) from the wounds of sin (2:24), the coming judgment (4:17), and a sinful pattern of life (1:18; 4:3). Freed, and now "God's slaves" (2:16), disciples are to live all of life to God's glory (4:11).[9] Thus, Peter exhorts living rightly as a response to God's merciful redemption.

Christ's ransom payment proves effective for several reasons. Not only was Jesus chosen before creation (1:20), but he was perfect in life and death, like a sacrificial lamb without spot or blemish (1:19). He was also raised to life (1:21; 3:18, 21), glorified (1:21), and will return (1:13; cf. 2:12; 4:13; 5:1, 4).

3. The Enemies

Although redeemed, disciples continue to wage war against enemies that once held them captive (2:11). These insidious foes seek to derail disciples from trusting God and living rightly. Five verses provide significant "intel" (1:14; 2:11; 4:2, 3; 5:8), highlighting Peter's view that

---

5   Cf. LXX Isa. 40:6, 8.

6   Cf. Isa. 53:5–6.

7   Andrew Mutua Mbuvi, *Temple, Exile, and Identity in 1 Peter,* LNTS 345 (London: T&T Clark, 2007), 86–89. See also, George Eldon Ladd, *A Theology of the New Testament* (Grand Rapids: Eerdmans, 1974), 433.

8   John Hall Elliott, *1 Peter: A New Translation with Introduction and Commentary,* AB 37B (New York: Doubleday, 2000), 534.

9   Fritz Neugebauer, "Zur Deutung und Bedeutung des I. Petrusbriefes," *NTS* 26 (1979): 61–86, at 84–85.

humanity battles two adversaries, evil desires (ἐπιθυμίαι) within the human person and the devil who prowls around the world.[10]

Evil desires play a significant role in Peter's theology.[11] They describe nonbelievers' lives (4:3), and prior to faith in Christ, evil desires controlled disciples' behavior (1:14). Even after redemption, the flesh of Christians still contains evil desires (2:11). This poses a risk to disciples because evil desires have the potential to be as dangerous as they were prior to redemption.[12] This is because evil desires crave and desire in a manner contrary to God's holiness.[13] Therefore, pitted against God's will (4:2) and left unchecked, evil desires may thwart disciples from living good lives (2:11–12).

If evil desires remain unchanged, is the flesh of Christians unaffected by redemption? Peter uses the term "flesh" (σάρξ, or its derivation) to refer to bodily, human existence, not the power of sin.[14] In 1 Peter, the death and resurrection of Jesus does not change the flesh of Christians. Thus, to be human is to be "in the flesh" (ἐν σαρκί, 4:2), with flesh that contains evil desires being an enemy that wars (2:11) within the disciple.

While evil desires are an internal threat, the devil is an external enemy that "prowls around like a roaring lion looking for someone to devour" (5:8). Thus, Christians face both an external enemy, the devil who seeks to devour them, and an enemy within, evil desires that plague their flesh. To succeed in following Jesus, disciples must fight these enemies by abstaining from evil desires (2:11) and resisting the devil (5:9).[15] In this light, Peter's exhortation to arm yourselves (4:1) sounds a battle call to disciples fighting an ongoing "holy war."

---

10   "Lust, desire, passion." In BDAG s.v. ἐπιθυμία.

11   Occurring 4x (1:14; 2:11; 4:2; 3, always plural).

12   That 1 Peter depicts an internal battle within the disciple between good and evil, see Cavin, *New Existence and Righteous Living*, 59. On psychological dualism, see John G. Gammie, "Spatial and Ethical Dualism in Jewish Wisdom and Apocalyptic Literature," *JBL* 93 (1974): 356–85, at 358. That pre-redemption ἐπιθυμίαι "of humans" (4:2) are the same as disciple's "evil desires" (2:11), see Leonhard Goppelt, *A Commentary on I Peter*, ed. F. Hahn; trans. J. E. Alsup (Grand Rapids: Eerdmans, 1993), 156.

13   Goppelt, *A Commentary on I Peter*, 157.

14   Cavin, *New Existence and Righteous Living*, 59–60. In various contexts, σάρξ refers to finite existence on earth (1:24); bodily existence of Christ (3:18); bodily existence which contain ἐπιθυμίαι that wage war against the "soul" (2:11); physical body in baptism (3:21); bodily suffering of Christ and of believers (4:1 [2x]); existence lived pursuing *either* ἐπιθυμίαι or "God's will" (4:2); or physical earthly lives (4:6).

15   Cavin, *New Existence and Righteous Living*, 63.

4. Living as God's House

Peter utilizes a rich collection of Old Testament metaphors to describe redemption's impact on the identity of a disciple. Disciples are living stones, a spiritual house, and a holy priesthood (2:5).[16] Collectively, the stones become the house of God (4:17). Founded "on" Christ the cornerstone (2:6) and formed by the Spirit, God lives in this new temple.[17] Additional temple imagery is seen in the description of disciples as a holy priesthood (2:5) and priestly kingdom (2:9). By reinterpreting these Old Testament metaphors, describing them as spiritual (2:5), and saying that the Spirit of God rests upon (4:14) the community, Peter signals that the eschatological outpouring of the Spirit has occurred.[18]

The new identity (people/temple/priests of God, 2:9–10) signals the calling, responsibilities, and life of disciples. First, as holy priests, disciples are to offer spiritual sacrifices (2:5). By this, "Peter sees the church in terms of Israel's priestly function," meaning that disciples are consecrated to serve God.[19] Second, "these offerings are spiritual in that they are inspired by and offered through the Spirit" and result in material sharing with other disciples.[20] Third, the priestly function calls disciples to declare the praises of God for his redemption. In this light, disciples are set apart "as God's chosen race, royal priesthood, holy nation," to display God's "power, grace, and mercy."[21]

5. The Ongoing Battle for Holiness

Peter is deeply concerned that disciples live holy lives to reflect the character of the One who redeemed them.[22] Quoting Leviticus 11:44, Peter appropriates God's holiness command to Israel and applies it to Christians: "But just as he who called you is holy, so be holy in all you do; for it is written: 'Be holy, because I am holy'" (1 Peter 1:15–16). Peter fleshes out this overarching command through other, specific exhortations, such as a call to live good lives among unbelievers (2:12). In all areas of life, the

---

16 See Bertil E. Gärtner, *The Temple and the Community in Qumran and the New Testament* (New York: Cambridge University Press, 1965), 75, that the metaphor of "living stones" is unique among New Testament authors.

17 Peter H. Davids, *The First Epistle of Peter,* NICNT (Grand Rapids: Eerdmans, 1990), 87.

18 Gärtner, *Temple,* 73.

19 Cf. Exod. 19:6. See Davids, *The First Epistle of Peter,* 87.

20 Davids, *The First Epistle of Peter,* 89.

21 Karen H. Jobes, *1 Peter,* BECNT (Grand Rapids: Baker Academic, 2005), 163.

22 See William L. Schutter, *Hermeneutic and Composition in 1 Peter,* WUNT 2/30 (Tübingen: Mohr Siebeck, 1989), 93, that God's holiness command pertains to the new identity.

people of God are called to manifest God's very presence among unbelievers who, though they may revile Christians' "good behavior in Christ"
(3:16), will ultimately be ashamed and come to praise the One who seeks
to redeem them (2:9, 12; cf. 3:1). Thus, Christians' holy lives serve as
witnesses to God's presence and activity in the world.

The imperative to be holy, a process of growth arising from salvation
(2:2), rests upon the indicative.[23] God's merciful election (1:3) resulted in
faith in Christ, removal of sins, redemption, new birth (1:3, 23), and new
existence as the people of God (2:10). Because of the change wrought by
faith in Christ's resurrection and in obedience to God's command, disciples must rid themselves of sinful behaviors (2:1, 11). However, because
of the real and present danger of evil desires waging war within them
(2:11), and the devil who seeks to devour them (5:8), disciples must
prepare for war.

Thus, "prepare your minds for action" (1:13 [NRSV]) serves as a call to
arms. English translations of 1:13 obscure the poignant image conveyed
in Greek of a tunic being tucked in one's belt in preparation for "work
or war."[24] The battle plan includes not conforming (1:14) to evil desires,
which had led to a licentious pattern of life (4:3) prior to redemption
and were contradictory to a redeemed life (1:15).[25] The main strategy
hinges on following Christ's model (2:21) during the pitched struggle.
Thus, Peter exhorts believers to arm themselves (4:1) with the attitude of
Christ, that is an all-encompassing trust in God that provides weapons
of immeasurable power to defeat the desires of the flesh and the devil, in
order to win the battle against sinning.

B. Entrusting Oneself to God to Respond Like Jesus

Innocent suffering poses many challenges to faith as the crucible of
suffering leads to questions regarding God's nature, presence, and care.
Why would God allow innocent suffering? How could any good come
from it? And, how should Christians respond to it? While 1 Peter does
not provide exhaustive answers to such pressing questions, it does shed
valuable light on the purposes of God, the path for disciples to choose,

---

23 Philip L. Tite, "Nurslings, Milk and Moral Development in the Greco-Roman Context: A
Reappraisal of the Paraenetic Utilization of Metaphor 1 Peter 2.1–3," *JSNT* 31 (2009): 371–
400, at 391–95.

24 See Davids, *The First Epistle of Peter*, 66, that ἀναζωσάμενοι τὰς ὀσφύας τῆς διανοίας
ὑμῶν (1 Peter 1:13) commands one to "gird the hips of your minds."

25 Cavin, *New Existence and Righteous Living*, 63.

and some functions of innocent suffering in both the world and the lives of Christians who rightly respond to it.

1. Innocent Suffering according to God's Will

In 1 Peter, suffering is "according to God's will" (4:19; cf. 3:17),[26] originates in the calling of God,[27] and is certain (4:14).[28] Suffering stems from persecution, not from discipline for sin.[29] Experienced by disciples around the world (5:9), suffering proves and refines genuine faith (1:6–7). Therefore, disciples should not be surprised by their innocent suffering (4:12).

Obedience to God's command to "be holy" (1:15) results in innocent suffering. Why? Practically, holiness means that speech and behavior reflect the holy God who mercifully bought redemption. Holiness entails rejection of worldly mores; therefore, disciples must rid themselves of "all malice and all deceit, hypocrisy, envy, and slander of every kind" (2:1). They must cease from "evil things that godless people enjoy—their immorality and lust, their feasting and drunkenness and wild parties, and their terrible worship of idols" (4:3 [NLT]). However, holiness surprises unbelievers who slander disciples (4:4) and speak maliciously against their "good behavior in Christ" (3:16).

2. Innocent Suffering and Doing Good

In the midst of slander and persecution, Christians are called to do good (2:15; 3:17; 4:19), being mindful of God who finds such behavior commendable (2:19) and will bestow upon them "praise, glory and honor when Jesus Christ is revealed" (1:7).[30] "Doing good" (2:12, 14, 20; 3:6, 17; 4:19) in the name of Christ (4:14) defines suffering rightly.[31] While evil desires within the disciple yearn for retaliation and retribution, Peter exhorts disciples not to repay evil in kind, but instead bless persecutors (3:9). This is the pattern modeled by Jesus (2:21),

---

26 Floyd V. Filson, "Partakers with Christ: Suffering in First Peter," *Interpretation* 9 (1955): 400–12, at 405.

27 Cf. "called" 1:15; 2:9, 21; 3:6, 9; 5:10. See David Hill, "On Suffering and Baptism in I Peter," *NovT* 18 (1976): 181–89, at 185.

28 See Paul J. Achtemeier, *1 Peter: A Commentary on First Peter,* Hermeneia (Minneapolis: Fortress, 1996), 307, that "εἰ . . . combined with a verb in the indicative mood (ὀνειδίζεσθε), . . . has the force not so much of 'if' as of 'when'."

29 Cavin, *New Existence and Righteous Living,* 32–33.

30 On "commendable" (χάρις) in 2:19, see Goppelt, *1 Peter,* 200–01.

31 Cavin, *New Existence and Righteous Living,* 33.

who, instead of retaliating, entrusted himself to God (2:23), refrained from deceitful speech, turned from evil, sought and pursued peace (3:10–11), exemplifying God's commands in the Hebrew Scriptures (Ps. 34:12–14).[32] Just as Christ demonstrated restraint when reviled, so should disciples, for this is their calling (3:9; cf. 2:21, 23). Like Christ, their speech is to be pure, without deceit (3:10; cf. 2:22), and their behavior good (3:17; cf. 2:15), so that charges by unbelievers might be proven baseless (3:16; cf. 2:12).

Good behavior in Christ acts as a witness and may result in some unbelievers believing in Christ.[33] For example, the lifestyle of a Christian wife may lead an unbelieving husband to faith in Jesus (3:1).[34] Good behavior in Christ leads unbelievers to ask disciples about their source of hope, providing an opportunity to explain the gospel (3:15).[35]

Despite hardships, disciples are to take comfort in the knowledge that suffering is for a "little while" (5:10) until Christ's glorious return (1:7, 13; 2:12; 4:13; 5:1, 4). Moreover, disciples may rest knowing that God intimately cares (5:7) and will restore his people by his mighty hand (5:6). Such knowledge serves to encourage disciples to endure (5:12) and do good until Christ returns.

3. Adopting the Attitude of Jesus to Stop Sinning

Disciples are called to suffer like Jesus.[36] Leaving an example, Christ provided *the* model for innocent suffering, and disciples are to "follow in his steps" (2:21). Peter combines the extremely rare word ὑπολιμπάνω ("leaving behind," 2:21) with the equally rare term ὑπογραμμός ("a model of behavior, example," 2:21) to depict an instructor leaving behind letters for pupils to trace in order to learn the alphabet.[37] The phrase denotes

---

32 Cavin, *New Existence and Righteous Living*, 78.
33 Eduard Lohse, "Parenesis and Kerygma in 1 Peter," in *Perspectives on First Peter*, ed. C. H. Talbert (Macon, GA: Mercer University Press, 1986), 58–59, notes that by "their love and good deeds they are to bear witness to the truth of their faith" (2:12, 15, 20: 3:1, 6, 17; 4:7–11, 15, *et passim*). Also, Torrey Seland, "Resident Aliens in Mission: Missional Practices in the Emerging Church of 1 Peter," *BBR* 19 (2009): 565–611.
34 See Aída Besançon Spencer, "Peter's Pedagogical Method in 1 Peter 3:6," *BBR* 10 (2000): 109–19. Also John Hall Elliott, *A Home for the Homeless: A Sociological Exegesis of 1 Peter, Its Situation and Strategy* (Philadelphia: Fortress, 1981), 108, 111.
35 Lauri Thurén, *Argument and Theology in 1 Peter: The Origins of Christian Paraenesis*, JSNTSup 114 (Sheffield: Sheffield Academic Press, 1995), 218, notes that Christians' good behavior may lead unbelievers to praise God.
36 J. Ramsey Michaels, *1 Peter*, WBC 49 (Dallas: Word, 1989), 144.
37 See, BDAG s.v. ὑπογραμμός, "lit. 'model, pattern' to be copied in writing or drawing."

mirroring a pattern to develop the ability to reproduce that pattern as habit. This model, or pattern, by Jesus "places one under obligation,"[38] an obligation enabled through Christ's "enlivening power of salvation."[39]

Christ's salvation carries the expectation that disciples "might die to sins and live for righteousness" (2:24). But evil desires in the flesh war against this outcome. However, by trusting God in the face of unjust persecution, that is following Jesus's model, disciples gain the ability not to sin (4:1). That is the meaning behind 4:1–2.

> Therefore, since Christ suffered in his body, arm yourselves also with the same attitude [ἔννοια], because he who has suffered in his body is done with sin. As a result, he does not live the rest of his earthly life for evil human desires, but rather for the will of God.

In other words, rightly handling innocent suffering by imitating Christ's example (2:19–25) enables disciples to be holy.

A key to grasping Peter's theology lies in rightly interpreting 2:23, 4:1–2, and 4:19. Christ's paradigmatic example centers on his "attitude" (ἔννοια) in the midst of unjust suffering.[40] Peter describes Christ's attitude in 2:23—"When they hurled their insults at him, he did not retaliate; when he suffered, he made no threats. Instead, he entrusted himself to him who judges justly." Herein lies Christ's decision to place himself within the hands of God the Father. This mind-set included "Christ's subordination to the divine will during his innocent suffering (1:2c; 2:21–23 [as God's servant]; 3:17–18), his resistance to wrongdoing and retaliation (2:22–23b), and his trusting commitment of his cause to God (2:23c)."[41]

As I have explained elsewhere, in 4:1, Peter calls disciples to follow in Christ's steps by adopting Christ's mind-set ("attitude").[42] Found

See also J. N. D. Kelly, *A Commentary on the Epistles of Peter and of Jude*, HNTC (New York: Harper and Row, 1969), 120. That ὑπογραμμός is not found in the LXX nor elsewhere in the New Testament, see Edward Gordon Selwyn, *The First Epistle of St. Peter: The Greek Text, with Introduction, Notes and Essays* (London: Macmillan, 1947 [reprinted, 1961]), 179.

38 Goppelt, *1 Peter*, 204.

39 John Hall Elliott, "Backward and Forward 'In His Steps': Following Jesus from Rome to Raymond and Beyond. The Tradition, Redaction, and Reception of 1 Peter 2:18–25," in *Discipleship in the New Testament*, ed. F. F. Sergovia (Philadelphia: Fortress, 1985), 184–209, at 202.

40 *Contra* Ivan T. Blazen, "Suffering and Cessation from Sin according to 1 Peter 4:1," *AUSS* 21 (1983): 27–50, at 44, who concludes that ἔννοια refers to the "*thought* of Christ's suffering for righteousness' sake and his consequent victorious lordship (3:18–4:1)," including his defeat of the hostile powers. I argue instead that ἔννοια refers to Jesus's attitude during innocent suffering of total reliance upon God, the one who judges justly (2:23).

41 See Elliott, *1 Peter*, 713.

42 Cavin, *New Existence and Righteous Living*, 76–84.

only in 1 Peter 4:1 and in Hebrews 4:12, "attitude" (ἔννοια) means "the content of mental processing, thought, knowledge, insight."[43] In 2:23, Peter defines the content of Christ's "attitude" as entrusting himself to God. Peter rephrases his exhortation of 4:1 in 4:19—"So then, those who suffer according to God's will should commit themselves to their faithful Creator and continue to do good." After explaining that suffering is God's will, Peter explicitly calls disciples to entrust themselves to God.

Why does Peter call disciples to adopt Christ's attitude when experiencing unjust persecution? By giving up the desire to retaliate, and instead placing retribution in the hands of "the one who judges rightly" (2:23; cf. 4:19), disciples submit to God's will and, thereby, no longer live for the desires of humankind (4:2). Entrusting oneself to God, which is the very attitude of Christ, proves decisive in the battle against the desires of flesh (2:11–12), enabling disciples to live in a manner that confounds and amazes unbelievers (4:4).[44]

During innocent suffering from persecution, disciples must choose to trust in God as creator (4:19), redeemer (1:18), and righteous judge (1:17; 2:23; 4:5; 16–19), by adopting Christ's attitude and letting "go of their desire for recompense, retaliation, and vengeance."[45] Failure to do so arouses evil desires, self-will, and sinning. But, by adopting the attitude of Christ, disciples experience two outcomes. First, God's will (4:2) and mighty hand (5:6) guides their lives. Second, and as a result, suffering rightly, somehow, battles against the evil desires in the flesh, enabling the disciple not to sin. So, instead of embittering disciples, suffering has the potential to lead to holiness if the disciple entrusts herself to God. Correctly understood, then, innocent suffering in the manner of Jesus provides the opportunity to exercise faith that is refined by testing (1:6–7), conquer the flesh, and win the battle to be holy.

DISCIPLESHIP IN 2 PETER AND JUDE

A. Strive to Grow in Your Faith

Second Peter and Jude share many themes. "There is clearly a relationship" between the two epistles, evidenced by the fact "that the same topics are covered in largely the same order, often using the same or almost

---

43 BDAG s.v. ἔννοια explained in Cavin, *New Existence and Righteous Living*, 81.
44 Cavin, *New Existence and Righteous Living*, 83.
45 Cavin, *New Existence and Righteous Living*, 84.

the same words."[46] For our understanding of discipleship, shared themes will be discussed together, while unique contributions by each author will be handled separately.[47]

1. The Source and Function of Faith

In 2 Peter, the first few verses drive home the centrality of receiving faith in "our God and Savior Jesus Christ" (1:1), who bought salvation (2:1).[48] Faith arrives by accepting the promises and call of Christ, a call made attractive by his glory and goodness.[49] Faith provides divine power for separating oneself from evil desires (1:4) and for living a holy life, an assumed goal made explicit in 3:11. Divine power flows from an all-encompassing knowledge of Christ (1:3), knowledge that is relational as well as intellectual, resulting in an ethical lifestyle.[50] Through faith, a disciple "may participate in the divine nature" (1:4), which foregrounds a dynamic relationship with God and highlights the disciple's responsibility to acquire, and thereby participate in, the moral character of Christ.[51] With faith and effort through God's enabling power, the disciple has everything needed for "life and godliness" (1:5–15).[52]

2. The Command to Grow in the Faith

Exhortations arise from the recently laid theological foundation. Repeated three times, the command to "make every effort" or "apply all diligence" to grow in the faith and live rightly serves as a structural beam

---

46 Peter H. Davids, *The Letters of 2 Peter and Jude*, PNTC (Grand Rapids: Eerdmans, 2006), 136, 141.

47 That shared themes and reuse of material by another "does not mean that they share the same background and context" or "theological outlook," see Richard Bauckham, *Jude, 2 Peter*, WBC 50 (Nashville: Thomas Nelson, 1983), 143. Rightly, Gene L. Green, "Second Peter's Use of Jude: Imitatio and the Sociology of Early Christianity," in *Reading Second Peter with New Eyes: Methodological Reassessments of the Letter of Second Peter*, eds. R. L. Webb and D. F. Watson, LNTS 382 (New York: T&T Clark, 2010), 12, notes that "we should not assume that the letters counter identical heresies."

48 That "use of the title 'God' for Jesus is rare in the New Testament" and reflects Peter's view that "Jesus is God yet distinct from God and does not think that there is more than one God," see Terrance Callan, "The Christology of the Second Letter of Peter," *Biblica* 82 (2001): 253–63, at 259, 263. That ἀγοράζω means "purchase" from slavery, see Callan, "The Christology of the Second Letter of Peter," 550.

49 Michael Green, *2 Peter and Jude*, TNTC (Leicester: InterVarsity Press; Grand Rapids: Eerdmans, 1987), 71–72.

50 ἐπίγνωσις occurs in 1:2, 3, 8; 2:20. See Davids, *2 Peter and Jude*, 165.

51 Gene L. Green, *Jude and 2 Peter*, BECNT (Grand Rapids: Baker Academic, 2008), 185–87.

52 Cf. 1 Thess. 4:7–8. See Green, *2 Peter and Jude*, 71.

for 2 Peter.[53] Motivation to obey flows out of gratitude for receiving faith (1:1), which should lead believers to godliness (1:3) by allowing them to escape corruption caused from evil desires (1:4).[54] As they follow Christ in all areas of life, disciples are called to grow in the faith by developing virtues that reflect the character of Christ.[55]

Peter lists seven virtues in which to grow (1:5–7). While not exhaustive, the series highlights the moral character of a Christlike disciple. For example, "goodness" (ἀρετή) foregrounds virtuous deeds toward others.[56] "Knowledge" (γνῶσις) carries the Hebraic notion of practical wisdom in Proverbs.[57] "Perseverance" (ὑπομονή) refers to "steadfast endurance in the face of suffering evil" while placing one's trust in God.[58] And "godliness" (εὐσέβεια) restates the call of 1:3. Significantly, the virtues do not reflect the life of a desert father but instead convey a communal dynamic—"brotherly love" (φιλαδελφία) requires fellow humans with whom to practice warmth and caring, and "love" (ἀγάπη) envisions godly self-sacrifice for others. In sum, Peter paints with broad strokes the long road of discipleship, one he will reiterate in closing—"what kind of people ought you to be? You ought to live holy and godly lives" (3:11).[59]

The command to grow contains both a promise and a warning. In obedience, the disciple should expect fruitfulness (1:8). However, disobedience and lack of growth results in a grim diagnosis. Such a person is blind and nearsighted (1:9). The colorful description of "spiritual blindness" arises from the recipients' needs, as Peter writes to warn disciples about false teachers who live contrary to the gospel and deny the return of Jesus. Nearsighted likely describes the licentious false teachers who lack the ability to see his second coming in the distance. Verse 10 contains

---

53 E.g., 1:5, 10; 3:14.
54 That receiving faith creates an obligation of reciprocity to the Chief Benefactor Jesus Christ, see Frederick W. Danker, "2 Peter 1: A Solemn Decree," *CBQ* 40 (1978): 64–82, at 80.
55 Michael J. Wilkins, *Following the Master: A Biblical Theology of Discipleship* (Grand Rapids: Zondervan, 1992), 123, states eloquently, "Discipleship is becoming like Jesus as we walk with him in the real world."
56 Green, *Jude and 2 Peter*, 192.
57 In agreement with Charles Bigg, *A Critical and Exegetical Commentary on the Epistles of St Peter and St Jude*, ICC (Edinburgh: T&T Clark, 1901), 253, of an intended difference between γνῶσις ("practical wisdom," 1:5) and ἐπίγνωσις (1:2, 3, 8; 2:20) conveying a more comprehensive sense of intellectual and personal knowledge leading to an ethical lifestyle.
58 Bauckham, *Jude, 2 Peter*, 186.
59 On discipleship as a "long road of obedience," see Eugene H. Peterson, *A Long Obedience in the Same Direction: Discipleship in an Instant Society* (Downers Grove, IL: InterVarsity Press, 2000).

the promise. If the disciple strives to make her calling and election sure, then she will never stumble but will receive a rich welcome into the eternal kingdom (1:11), a vivid picture of a heavenly celebration at Christ's return.

Peter concludes this section with a reminder to disciples to guard against complacency (1:12–15). Although the recipients *currently* possess a firm grasp of the truth, being firmly established requires *ongoing* diligence. Stasis is not possible in discipleship. Present knowledge offers no guarantee of future fruit. Disciples must press forward in knowing Christ and living rightly or risk regressing, and then failing, to receive "a rich welcome into the eternal kingdom" (1:11).

3. The Reliable Basis of Faith

Peter gives two reasons for writing. First, the Lord has revealed to him that his death approaches (1:13–15), and second, he seeks to build every disciple's faith on the bedrock of historical accounts. On the second reason, verse 16 bears stating: "We did not follow cleverly invented stories [σεσοφισμένοις μύθοις] when we told you about the power and coming of our Lord Jesus Christ, but we were eyewitnesses of his majesty." Bigg notes that μύθοι ("stories")

> by itself might mean merely "fables," such as the legendary history of the heathen gods, "false tales," "fictions"; . . . [But] the addition of σεσοφισμένοι ["cleverly invented"] shows that it must, bear the . . . sense of "a fiction which embodies a truth," "an allegorism." The False Teachers, or some of them, must have maintained that the Gospel miracles were to be understood in a spiritual sense, and not regarded as facts. . . . [They had] allegorical explanations of the gospel; they denied the literal sense, but professed to hold fast the spiritual. It is obvious how this mode of exegesis might be applied to the Second Advent.[60]

Peter's point is that history matters.[61] God acted in time and space to reveal the divine nature of Jesus who will return visibly (1:16–19).

Peter gives two reasons that disciples may rely on their accounts about Jesus: First, they were eyewitnesses to Jesus's transfiguration on the

---

60 Bigg, *St Peter*, 265–66.
61 Cf. 1 Cor. 15:13.

mountain (1:16–18)⁶²; second, they are prophets who received the words of God from the Holy Spirit (1:20–21). Disciples of every age need to hear Peter's call to sound scriptural exegesis and its bearing on discipleship. When Scripture makes a historical claim, the disciple must take that claim with all seriousness.⁶³ This is why Peter exhorts disciples to pay attention to the prophetic words of Scripture; its light illuminates a "dark place" (1:19). While certainly God's word illuminates spiritual darkness through faith in God's historical resurrection of Jesus, it also defeats the darkness in culture through disciples who shine the light of the gospel in word and deed.⁶⁴

B. Strive against False Teachers

Disciples follow Jesus within a particular cultural milieu that shapes ideas and beliefs about acceptable behavior. However, according to Scripture, the Christian looks to God, not to culture, to know not only the boundary lines God has given but the Giver of those lines. Knowledge of God and of Jesus empowers the disciple, through faith, to respond in obedience to the gracious gift of salvation found in Christ (1:1–3). Faith, then, is the basis for a new relationship with God, the source of a new way of life, and the power to live accordingly. However, in every age, disciples face those who propose beliefs and practices counter to God's revealed way. Thus, disciples must guard against those who would lead them to accept the norms and mores of culture instead of faithfully following Jesus.

1. Characteristics of the False Teachers

The threat of heretical leaders serves as the backdrop to both 2 Peter and Jude.⁶⁵ Both authors labor to protect the "beloved" (ἀγαπητοί, 2 Peter 3:8, 15, 17; Jude 3, 17, 20) from leaders who deny Jesus as Lord by their behavior and reject authority. Their lack of genuine faith, as well as

---

62 Cf. Matt. 17; Mark 9; Luke 9. See Richard Bauckham, *Jesus and the Eyewitnesses: The Gospels as Eyewitness Testimony* (Grand Rapids: Eerdmans, 2006).
63 On the historical reliability of the gospels, see J. P. Moreland and Michael J. Wilkins, eds., *Jesus under Fire: Modern Scholarship Reinvents the Historical Jesus* (Grand Rapids: Zondervan, 1995). See also Craig L. Blomberg, *The Historical Reliability of the Gospels* (Downers Grove, IL: IVP Academic, 2007).
64 Green, *2 Peter and Jude*, 228.
65 For simplicity, I will refer to the heretics in both epistles as "false teachers" recognizing that the heretics in Jude appear to be pseudo-prophets from outside the congregation (Jude 4) while the heretics in 2 Peter appear to be false teachers arising from within the churches (2:1, 13).

the fruit such faith should produce, leads them to slander angelic beings (Jude 8), boast, and seduce the weak.

The false teachers claim knowledge, wisdom, and maturity to deliver God's word to God's people. But both authors denounce these "teachers" as ungodly charlatans because their teaching encourages, and their lives reflect, immorality, licentiousness, debauchery, and "sensual indulgence, especially sexual immorality" (ἀσέλγεια, 2 Peter 2:2, 18; Jude 4).[66] Rightly, Bigg comments, "grandiose sophistry is the hook, filthy lust is the bait, with which these men catch those whom the Lord had delivered or was delivering."[67]

Each author provides additional details about their opponents. Peter combats those who allegorize Scripture and deny Jesus's return. Jude fights against faultfinding, antinomian charismatics who divide the church.[68] Promulgating their unique "visions," they twist God's word to teach "grace without repentance or even grace that grants license to sin."[69] In sum, and in line with apostolic warnings, both authors aim to persuade the recipients to reject false teachers, wolves among them, who represent a real and present danger to the church. Despite the passage of almost two millennia, twenty-first-century disciples face pressures not unlike those faced in the first century. Therefore, disciples must labor to recognize false teachers, reject their unbiblical views, and follow scriptural commands to separate themselves from false teachers.[70]

2. Old Testament Examples of God's Judgment

Peter and Jude share similar methods of persuasion, providing a model on how to confront heresy and to follow Jesus. Both authors rely on scriptural stories to do the heavy lifting. That is to say, the authors allow God's word to vilify and judge the false teachers.[71] Both authors point to rebellious angels (2 Peter 2:4; Jude 6), sexual perversion in Sodom and Gomorrah (Gen. 18–19), and the prophet Balaam's greedy attempt to use the gifts and word of God to prosper himself (Num. 22–24, cf. Deut. 23:4–5). And, each author addresses the needs of their recipients by highlighting unique and salient reference points:

---

66   E.g. ἀσέλγεια in 2 Peter 2:2, 7, 18 and Jude 4. See Bauckham, *Jude, 2 Peter*, 38.

67   Bigg, *St Peter*, 285.

68   Stephan Joubert, "Persuasion in the Letter of Jude," *JSNT* 58 (1995): 75–87, at 79.

69   Davids, *2 Peter and Jude*, 44–45.

70   Cf. Matt. 7:15–20; Acts 20:29.

71   Richard Bauckham, "James, 1 and 2 Peter, Jude," in *It Is Written: Scripture Citing Scripture: Essays in Honour of Barnabas Lindars,* eds. D. A. Carson and H. G. M. Williamson (Cambridge: Cambridge University Press, 1988), 303–17, at 314.

Jude	2 Peter
The Exodus generation who died in the wilderness because of their grumbling and fingerpointing against God and his appointed leader (Jude 5)	God's judgment of wickedness resulting in the flood (Gen. 6–9; 2 Peter 2:5)
The "way of Cain" that highlights the impact of a jealous heart (Gen. 4; Jude 11)	God's saving of Lot who rejected the immorality of Sodom and Gomorrah (Gen. 19; 2 Peter 2:7)
The story of Korah that illustrates God's judgment of those who divide God's people in an attempt to gain power (Num. 16; Jude 11)	

Scriptural stories serve at least four functions. First, they clarify God's condemnation of sin. Second, they reveal the false teachers' fate. Third, hopefully, they dissuade the recipients from following suit. And, fourth, they demonstrate the role that God's word should play in shaping disciples' thinking, decisions, and behavior.

3. Effects of the False Teachers

Both authors highlight the devastation caused by false teachers. Peter points to disciples led into "shameful ways" (2:2) and enticed back into sin (2:18), thus bringing harm (2:3, 13), "disrepute" (2:2), and "blemishes" (2:13) on the gospel and the church. Jude echoes these sentiments adding that the congregation will be divided because of the false teachers (Jude 19). In sum, the false teachers exploit and abuse people for their own ends, divide congregations, and damage the church's witness by bringing the gospel into disgrace.

4. Destiny of the False Teachers

In this light, Peter and Jude declare God's coming judgment with dark and visceral language.[72] Peter exclaims that condemnation hangs over the false teachers, and "their destruction has not been sleeping" (2:3). As

---

72 Wilkins, *Following the Master*, 139, notes that "Jesus taught that judgment was an inescapable factor in human existence. It is the factor that will condemn the unbeliever but will also separate out those who have professed discipleship but whose profession is unreal" (cf. Matt. 7:21–23).

"brute beasts" meant to "be caught and destroyed" (2:12), the false teachers await "the day of judgment" (2:9) and the "blackest darkness" (2:17) "for the harm they have done" (2:13). Jude strikes similar macabre notes proclaiming that at Jesus's return, their long-ago-written condemnation for ungodly ways (Jude 4) will culminate in judgment, woe, and places in the "blackest darkness" (Jude 10, 13–14).

The pronouncements flow from the authors' strategic use of Old Testament stories that emphasize punishment.[73] That is to say, "the past is prophetically linked to the present. . . . [The Lord comes, warlike and with volcanic force."[74] God will destroy those who teach falsely and abuse his church.

5. Guarding against False Teaching

Identifying false teachers in order to reject not only their teaching, but the teachers themselves, forms the core of both epistles. The false teachers have "secretly" slipped into the congregation (Jude 4) and have "secretly" introduced "destructive heresies" (Jude 4; 2 Peter 2:1). Distortions of the truth are their stock-in-trade, and herein lies a challenge in recognizing false teaching. It is rarely all false. Like a poison pill embedded in a filet mignon, distortions may appear "fine-sounding" and "persuasive."[75] Thus, Peter exhorts "wholesome thinking" on the words of the prophets and Jesus (3:1), and Jude urges disciples to reflect on and contend for the faith that was "entrusted to God's holy people" (Jude 3).

To expose the false teachers, Peter and Jude encourage disciples to be "fruit inspectors." A true teacher will display the fruit of moral character grown through the Spirit in obedience to God's commands, while a false teacher will lack both the Spirit and fruit (Jude 12, 19; 2 Peter 2:17) because of ongoing sin (Jude 4, 16; 2 Peter 2:2, 10, 14). Neither author expects perfection, but instead they call out the false teachers for whom the gospel has become a cover for sin. Having turned their backs on the "sacred commands" received in God's word (2 Peter 2:21), the false teachers expose the heresy in their teaching by their very lives.

Disciples, therefore, must identify and remove such leaders to prevent themselves from traveling the path to destruction. Rightly, Webb

---

73 Robert L. Webb, "The Eschatology of the Epistle of Jude and Its Rhetorical and Social Functions," *BBR* 6 (1996): 139–51, at 144.

74 On the use of Old Testament typologies to depict God's judgment against the false teachers, see J. Daryl Charles, "'Those' and 'These': The Use of the Old Testament in the Epistle of Jude," *JSNT* 38 (1990): 109–24, at 112.

75 Cf. Col. 2:4 for deception by "fine-sounding arguments."

concludes, "the crux of the matter is, what will the *readers'* judgment be?"[76] Will they pronounce judgment, guard themselves, and act, or receive the fate destined for the false teachers?

C. Strive to Live Rightly, Sure of Christ's Return

Since Jesus's ascension, people have been trying to "read the tea leaves" as to the time and date of the *parousia*. Within a few decades, some Christians were already questioning if Jesus would return, while others wondered if they had missed it (1 Thess. 4:13–5:3)! After two millenia, the march of time has the potential to dim enthusiasm for Jesus's imminent return. And, the cacophony of voices that scoff at the mere idea of the *parousia* can drown out the call of Christ. Therefore, disciples must increase the volume of Scripture to drown out background interference, hear God's promises of Jesus's imminent return, and live accordingly.

1. Thinking Rightly about Christ's Return

Peter and Jude write with urgency because "scoffers" signal "the last days" (Jude 1:18; 2 Peter 3:3).[77] Peter confronts false teachers who scoff at the *parousia* and teach that the passage of time without Christ's return proves that the end is not imminent and Christ will not return (2 Peter 3:4). He senses the exigency of the task because "the day of the Lord" could be at any time (3:8–10). Thus, Peter desires to "stimulate" (3:1) disciples to think rightly in order to live rightly as "the day" approaches (1:19; 2:9; 3:7, 10, 12). While Jude does not write to counter a denial of the *parousia*, he also writes with urgency to counter false teachers who pervert God's grace into a license for immorality (Jude 4). Thus, disciples must grow in the apostolic teaching (Jude 3, 17, 20) to live in such a manner that they will stand in his glorious presence without fault (Jude 24).[78]

Peter counters the false teachers by arguing that the Scriptures reveal a known, and imminent, future. Alluding to creation and the flood, Peter notes that God has created and destroyed before (3:5–6), and he will do so again. Peter's argument connects the origins and destiny of creation to ethics. The One who created *ex nihilo* judged his creation. The past foreshadows a rapidly approaching future when God will purify and cleanse

---

76 Webb, "The Eschatology of the Epistle of Jude," 149.

77 Hans C. C. Cavallin, "The False Teachers of 2 Peter as Pseudo-Prophets," *NovT* 21 (1979): 263–70, at 270.

78 Joubert, "Persuasion in the Letter of Jude," 79.

his creation through fire (3:7, 10, 12), creating "a new heavens and new earth" (3:13). Therefore, thinking rightly on the *telos* of creation should bear heavily on life today.

Furthermore, Peter urges disciples not to forget that God experiences time differently than humankind (3:8).[79] His "delay" will end with prophecy being fulfilled and "the day of the Lord" arriving unexpectedly (3:10).[80] In this light, disciples must realize that God's "slowness" points to God's desire that all come to repentance (3:9).[81] But, when God's patience ends and Christ returns, the entire *cosmos* (earth and heavens, visible and invisible) will be purified by fire (3:7, 10–12).[82] Peter draws from a deep reservoir of evocative Old Testament prophecies about the coming "day of the Lord" so that disciples think rightly about Christ's return.[83]

2. Living Rightly because of Christ's Return

Since God will execute fiery judgment when Christ returns, Peter asks the rhetorical question, "What kind of people ought you to be?" (3:11). His answer, "you ought to live holy and godly lives," (3:11) rests upon the goal of being "found spotless, blameless" at Christ's return (3:14; cf. Jude 24). A known future should shape present behavior because disciples are "looking forward" (3:14) to "a new heavens and new earth" (3:13).[84]

In sum, both Peter and Jude exhort disciples to grow and be built up in knowledge of the faith that leads to godliness. Exhortations such as "be on your guard" (Jude 17) recognize the formidable forces at work to derail these efforts. Nevertheless, disciples are responsible to the Lord for digging into the deep things of God, building themselves "up in the most holy faith" (Jude 20), growing in the grace and knowledge of Christ (2 Peter 3:18), and not being led astray. Such knowledge includes application of God's Word to all areas of life as the disciple waits expectantly for Christ's return (2 Peter 3:12; Jude 21).

---

79 "With the Lord a day is like a thousand years, and a thousand years are like a day."
80 Cf. Ezek. 12:26–27; Hab. 2:2–3; Matt. 24:44.
81 Cf. Ezek. 18:23, 32.
82 Note that Hebrew prophets warn that the "day of the Lord" represents the dramatic culmination of human history and the arrival of God's judgment (e.g., Isa. 13:6, 9; 24:21–22; Jer. 46:10; Ezek. 30:3–4; Joel 1:15; 2:11, 31; Amos 5:18–20, Obad. 1:15, Zeph. 1:14; 3:8, Zech. 14:1–3; Mal. 4:1–2).
83 The Hebrew Scriptures describe "the day of the Lord" as a cataclysmic event (e.g., Isa. 66:15, 16, 22), dark and terrible for those who have rejected God, "a cruel day, with wrath and fierce anger" (Isa. 13:9) and "a time of doom for the nations" (Ezek. 30:3).
84 Cf. Isa. 65:17–18a, 25.

CONCLUSION

Belief and practice prove inseparable for the Christian who absorbs the exhortations in 1–2 Peter and Jude. In other words, *orthodoxy* and *orthopraxy* are two sides of the same coin minted when faith in Jesus creates a new person destined for eternity with God. First and Second Peter and Jude concur—a disciple's life must align with God's call to be holy while awaiting the glory to be revealed at Jesus's return. This call to live rightly applies during periods of persecution because the furnace of innocent suffering, when married with trust in God, refines the disciple for coming glory. Furthermore, Christians must grow in their faith, recognizing and rejecting those whose teaching and behavior stray from God's commands. Entrusted with the gospel, disciples who think and live rightly will bear fruit in word and deed, providing witness to the beauty and power of the gospel that changes people by God's merciful grace.

CHAPTER 16

Walking in the Light:
Discipleship in John's Letters

Karen H. Jobes

A s the work of Michael Wilkins has demonstrated, Christian discipleship is a major theme throughout the New Testament.[1] It is also the
essence of a vital, flourishing relationship with God in our lives today. So
both in terms of understanding ancient Christianity and for its spiritual
value in transforming lives today, no other topic exceeds that of Christian
discipleship in importance for the big picture of life.[2]

The topic of discipleship is at the heart of John's letters but, unlike the
Gospels and Acts, the Greek nouns conventionally translated as *disciple*
(μαθητής, μαθήτρια) and the verb to *be* or to *make disciples* (μαθητεύω)
do not occur at all in 1, 2, and 3 John. Oddly in fact, these words don't
occur in *any* of the New Testament epistles even though there are about
250 occurrences in the Gospels and Acts. This, of course, does not mean
that discipleship isn't a topic in the epistles, just that other terms are used
there. Wilkins discusses this interesting observation at length, suggesting
that the terms used to refer to Christian disciples in the epistles (believers,
brothers/sisters, servants, church, and Christians) reflect "the relationships of these disciples to their risen Lord [as opposed to the historical
man Jesus], to the community, and to society."[3]

THE METAPHOR OF WALKING

The major image of Christian discipleship in John's letters is *walking in
the light* (1 John 1:7; 2:6) and *walking in the truth* (2 John 4; 3 John 3, 4).
But how do these images relate to discipleship when that term isn't used?
Two aspects must be considered: 1) the metaphor of walking and 2) the
symbolism of light.

---

[1] Michael J. Wilkins, *Following the Master: A Biblical Theology of Discipleship* (Grand Rapids:
Zondervan, 1992). This essay is written in honor of his lifetime of work in service to Jesus
Christ.
[2] All Scripture translations are NIV unless otherwise noted.
[3] Wilkins, *Following the Master*, 288, 291–310.

During Jesus's earthly ministry he explicitly called to himself a small number of men with the imperative, "follow me!" (Matt. 4:19; 9:9; Mark 1:17; 2:14; Luke 5:27; John 1:43; 21:19, 22). They came to be known as the twelve disciples, and later the twelve apostles. As Jesus taught the crowds, he extended that command to follow him to all who would be his disciples (Matt. 8:22; 10:38; 16:24; 19:21; Mark 8:34; 10:21; Luke 9:23, 59; 14:27; 18:22; John 10:27; 12:26). Jesus came not simply to appear on earth, as significant as that appearance was, but to reconcile those who would *follow him* with God the Father. Just as first-century rabbis had students (disciples) who followed them (cf. John 1:38), many of Jesus's disciples physically took leave from their occupations and homes to *walk* with Jesus throughout Galilee, Judea, and the Decapolis, listening to his teaching, witnessing his miracles and his interactions with people, agonizing over the horror of his crucifixion, and being awestruck by his resurrection.

Though our place in history means we cannot literally follow Jesus as the Twelve and others once did, we can still hear his teaching, witness his miracles and interactions with people, agonize over the horror of his crucifixion, and be awestruck by his resurrection because all of that has been recorded and preserved in the extant New Testament Gospels. "Following" Jesus and "walking with" Jesus are nearly synonymous, and when applied to living, it entails that his disciples will do as he would do. It was natural that Jesus's apostles should use the metaphor of walking to refer to a way of life in their later writings that form the New Testament.

"Walking" as a metaphor for how one lives life wasn't invented by the apostles but was already a familiar metaphor from the Old Testament. Fellowship with God, which is the essence of discipleship (cf. 1 John 1:5–7), was first expressed as God *walking* with Adam and Eve in Eden (Gen. 3:8). Both Noah and Enoch were said to have *walked* with God (Gen. 5:22, 24; 6:9) and God commanded Abraham to *walk* blamelessly before him (Gen. 17:1). Psalm 1:1 blesses "the one who does not *walk* in the counsel of the wicked" (italics added). "Walking" refers metaphorically to how one conducts oneself in life.

In the ancient world walking was the most common way of going somewhere, even rather long distances by today's standards. Walking is deliberate, directional movement that takes intention and effort. It implies continuing progression over time, starting at one point and moving toward another. And so the metaphor of walking implies life is a journey toward a final destination that takes intent and effort.

It is the apostle John who distinctively brings together the concepts of following Jesus and walking to refer to Christian discipleship in the Fourth Gospel. If written as traditionally believed to be by John, the son of Zebedee, he had left his fishing nets as a very young man to literally follow Jesus (Mark 1:19, 20 and parallels). John walked with Jesus for those three years before his crucifixion, but also witnessed the dawn of new creation in the resurrection of Jesus. Tradition teaches that John lived for several decades after Jesus's resurrection, preaching and teaching before writing the Gospel and letters that bear his name. He had both followed by walking with the earthly Jesus and walked with the risen Christ. Therefore, when John describes discipleship as "walking in the light," what does the metaphor entail?

Whether or not 1, 2, and 3 John were written by the same author as the Fourth Gospel, the message, themes, motifs, images, and vocabulary are so similar that the letters cannot be best understood apart from reading them within the context of the Gospel. There, in John 8:12, Jesus himself is reported to have brought together his command that his disciples *follow* him and the metaphor of *walking*: ἐγώ εἰμι τὸ φῶς τοῦ κόσμου· ὁ ἀκολουθῶν ἐμοὶ οὐ μὴ περιπατήσῃ ἐν τῇ σκοτίᾳ, ἀλλ' ἕξει τὸ φῶς τῆς ζωῆς ("I am the light of the world. Whoever *follows* me will never *walk* in darkness, but will have the light of life," emphasis added). John's Gospel shows the world stumbling in the darkness of ignorance and sin until the genuine Light comes into the world (John 1:9). With the incarnation of Jesus, authentic light floods into the dark world, inviting people to step into it. Sadly, many prefer the darkness. As many interpreters have recognized, light in John's Gospel (and his letters) symbolizes true revelation from God. One need not agree with Bultmann's redactional theory of John's Gospel to agree that here, "Jesus describes himself as the Revealer."[4] While the symbol of light is both ubiquitous in ancient religions and polyvalent in John's writings, all that light symbolizes in this context can be subsumed under what Jesus came to reveal of the true and full nature of God. For when John's Gospel introduces Jesus as "the one and only Son, who is himself God," he also tells of the purpose of Jesus's coming into the world: to reveal the unseen God (John 1:18).

Jesus makes this statement during or soon after the Feast of Tabernacles in Jerusalem within the context of the mounting disbelief and rejection by Jewish leaders as he pursued his God-sent ministry. He is in the temple,

---

4   Rudolf Bultmann, *The Gospel of John: A Commentary,* eds. R. W. N. Hoare and J. K. Riches; trans. G. R. Beasley-Murray (Oxford: Basil Blackwell, 1971), 342.

presenting to them, and to all who hear, the choice of either believing he is who he claims to be or of dying in the darkness of sin (8:24). The acceptance or rejection of Christ is not a neutral decision of religious choice. Rejection of the revelation of God that Christ brings is in itself a sin. Acceptance of the revelation offered, expressed as faith in the person of Jesus the Christ, is described metaphorically as *following* Jesus. Believing in Jesus and following him are synonymous in John's writings.[5] Jesus describes his followers as his sheep who know and listen to his voice, that is, who recognize and receive the revelation he brings (John 10:15–16). He said, "I am the light of the world. Whoever follows me will never walk in darkness, but will have the light of life." Believing Jesus is who he says he is brings one out of the darkness to have, and henceforth to walk in, the light of life (τὸ φῶς τῆς ζωῆς). The phrase is to be understood either as an epexegetical genitive (the light that *is* life) or a genitive of source (the light that produces life). Either way, to have the light of Jesus, who reveals the Father, is to have life eternal (John 17:3). As Bultmann pointed out, the revelation is not something taught apart from who Jesus is, as if it were some sort of *gnosis*. "The light which the believer has is always the light that Jesus *is*."[6]

The symbol of light, ubiquitous in various religions, alludes here to rich ideas in the Old Testament, such as the light of God's presence during the Exodus (Exod. 13:21) and the psalm declaring, "The LORD is my light" (Ps. 27:1). Judaism also considered light to be a symbol of Torah (cf. Ps. 119:105; Prov. 6:23), which was God's previous revelation of himself.[7] Given these previous associations, Jesus's astounding claim that he was in some way God's presence and Torah would not have been lost on the Jewish leaders in the Temple courts. Jesus's subsequent claim in John 8:58 to an existence that was pre-Mosaic and even pre-Abrahamic was so scandalous it provoked an attempt to kill him ("before Abraham was born, I am!").

The call to *follow* Jesus, by believing he is who he said he was and to *walk* in that revelation, is re-expressed in similar words in John's letters. There, rather than calling his readers to an initial belief in Jesus Christ (cf. John 20:31), John is calling them at a confusing time to *continue* to walk in Christ's revelation, which in the Gospel is expressed as *remaining* (μένω) in Christ (John 15), that is, *continuing* to live in the revelation that Jesus has brought.

---

5   Andreas J. Köstenberger, *John*, BECNT (Grand Rapids: Baker Academic, 2004), 254.

6   Bultmann, *Gospel of John*, 344 (original italics).

7   C. H. Dodd, *The Interpretation of the Fourth Gospel* (Cambridge: Cambridge University Press, 1988), 84.

WALKING IN THE LIGHT IN JOHN'S LETTERS

All of John's discourse in the letters flows from the theological state-ment that opens the body of 1 John: "God is light; in him there is no dark-ness at all" (1:5).[8] In John's Gospel Jesus is the light who reveals God's pure light; in 1 John that revelation is presumed (1 John 1:1–4) and the symbol of light shifts somewhat to the nature of the God who has been revealed by Jesus as the basis for distinctively Christian living, living that is described as walking in the light (1 John 1:7).

In both the Old Testament and New Testament, walking as a metaphor for living can be positive, moving one toward God, or negative, moving away from God. John distinctively speaks of the proper Christian life as walking in the light as opposed to walking in the darkness (1 John 1:6; 2:11). In other words, every human being is walking through this life toward some future destination. According to John, the difference be-tween life and death is how one walks and where one walks. Each way has its consequences. Because darkness is the absence of light, to walk in darkness is to be blind to the revelation of God and, therefore, not to see where one is heading (1 John 2:11). In other words, walking in the darkness is living without the revelation of eternal life brought by Jesus Christ. Without that revelation, one has no moral compass calibrated to God's will and cannot walk with certainty toward a destination with him.

The metaphor of walking implies deliberate, directional movement that takes intention and effort. In his letters John unpacks the metaphor as it applies to Christian life and ethics. Christian discipleship is *deliber-ate*, starting with one's initial belief that Jesus is who he says he is. It is directional, moving consistently in a direction toward God as revealed by Christ. Discipleship is not a random meandering through the various spiritualities and religions the world offers. Jesus Christ is the one whom the Christian disciple is to follow. In John's Gospel, the Son came into this world to reveal the Father and, in God's greatest act of love, to secure redemption on the cross. When that mission was complete he "returned" to the Father, promising that he was going to a place where his disciples would one day follow (John 13:36; 14:4). Jesus made exclusive claims, declaring himself to be the *only* way to God the Father in a world that was

---

8 The author of the letters will be referred to as John for simplicity, without overlooking the various theories about actual authorship, which lie outside the scope of this essay. See my analysis of this topic elsewhere: Karen H. Jobes, *Letters to the Church: A Survey of Hebrews and the General Epistles* (Grand Rapids: Zondervan, 2011), 399–412; idem, *1, 2 & 3 John*, ZECNT (Grand Rapids: Zondervan, 2014), 22–29.

already filled with religions and philosophies: "I am the way and the truth and the life. No one comes to the Father except through me" (John 14:6). Therefore, walking in the light has a specifically christocentric focus.

John writes his first letter to remind his readers, both then and now, that walking in the revelation of Jesus takes sustained intention and effort. John's letters are pastoral notes originally written to people who had come to faith in Christ but who had been shaken deeply by some sort of schism in the church. John writes to reassure them of their eternal life based on faith in Christ and implores them to make the intention and effort of continuing to believe in spite of the confusing and difficult times they were in (1 John 5:13). There were people in the Johannine churches, just as there are now, who, though perhaps well-intentioned, were leading believers astray (1 John 2:26), leading them out of the light of the revelation that Jesus brought and back into the shadows of darkness. The content of the three letters reflects the issues involved, though we can't reconstruct the details as specifically as we'd like. However, this lack of specificity also allows a broader application of the letters for today's situations.

As Wilkins explains John's distinctive view of Christian discipleship, he points out that "the central characteristic of the disciple is belief or acceptance of Jesus's claims vis-á-vis the Father."[9] The Fourth Gospel presents people in various stages of belief in response to Jesus, and shows those who would be called disciples in a process of increasing understanding and perception of who Jesus is. It was not enough to consider Jesus a wonder-worker or a great religious teacher or a hopeful national leader, and many turned back from following him in response to his teaching about himself and his mission (e.g., John 6:51–58). Even one of the Twelve, Judas Iscariot, followed Jesus physically but never came to a place of truly realizing who Jesus was in relation to the Father, mistaking him for some sort of political Messiah. The central mark of true discipleship then, as now, was to perceive the truth about Jesus's identity and mission, and it was precisely on that point that John's letters had to focus.

Whatever the schism in the Johannine churches, it went to the heart of Christology (1 John 1:3; 2:18–24; 4:1–3, 14; 5:9–12, 20). And as Wilkins points out, abiding in Jesus's words is the first mark of the true disciple.[10] John writes 1 John with a passion to see his readers continue to believe rightly about Jesus and to prove themselves true disciples, unlike "those who went out from us" whom John labels as antichrists (1 John 2:18–19).

---

9 Wilkins, *Following the Master,* 226.
10 Wilkins, *Following the Master,* 230.

Despite the association of antichrist with the book of Revelation and end-time prophecy, 1 John is the only book of the New Testament that mentions antichrists, and always in the plural. Contrary to popular depictions of a singular embodiment of evil in antichrist in the final days of the world, John here identifies as antichrists those who by their teaching and practices deny the authentic gospel and mislead Christians, whether in the first century or the twenty-first. (This is not to deny that there may someday be a powerful leader who is the final instantiation of antichrist views, but that is an interpretation of Revelation's beast imagery and not a direct teaching of John's letters.) Whatever the false teachers in the Johannine churches were spreading, it was a heresy that threatened to destroy the essence of Christian faith, even perhaps while claiming to be compatible with it. It was, therefore, anti-, or opposed to, the revelation that Jesus brought.

But apparently John first has to establish the grounds of his authority to exposit the revelation that Jesus brought. This he does in 1 John 1:1–4, emphasizing that he stands in the apostolic tradition as one who has heard and seen and perceived and touched the life that was with the Father and appeared in history during his lifetime. Two references to visual sense occur: one, the physical sense of seeing with the eyes, but the second, a perception of the significance of what was seen physically.[11] In the Fourth Gospel disciples were those people who not only saw the signs that Jesus did but understood and believed the significance of the signs as indicators of Jesus's identity (e.g., John 2:11). The emphasis on the physicality of Jesus is not so much here an antidocetic polemic—though these statements certainly challenge docetic ideas—as it is a reminder that the apostles were men who originally followed Jesus during his earthly ministry and were designated by him to be the authentic interpreters of his message after his resurrection. They are the ones who saw and heard and touched Jesus, but also who perceived the true significance of what they saw and heard and touched. While this group includes the original eyewitness disciples, it also includes those who have not seen Jesus and yet believe the authentic apostolic witness (John 20:29). John asserts his apostolic authority in the face of those teachers in the church who apparently did not stand in that tradition and who were teaching wrongly about who Jesus was and where spiritual authority was to be found. False teachers, perhaps even well-intentioned, may have claimed to receive revelation from the Spirit (cf. the promise of John 16:13, 14) but in their

---

11 Jobes, 1, 2, & 3 John, 47.

error did *not* bring glory to Jesus Christ. We, too, live in a world of many voices claiming spiritual authority representing many different religions as well as various Christian beliefs. Therefore, 1 John is as relevant to our Christian discipleship as it was for its original readers.

If walking in the light means to believe Jesus is who he said he was, Christology—knowing and believing the truth about Jesus—is the central issue in Christian discipleship according to 1 John, as it is in the Fourth Gospel. Thinking rightly about Jesus is the central issue in John's letters that unpacks what it means to walk in the light of God's revelation in Christ. He wants his readers to be purposeful and thoughtful in their living, always moving in the right direction toward a destination with Christ (cf. John 14:3). John speaks authoritatively of who Jesus is, and what he came to do, specifically in John's letters teaching us to deal rightly with sin and to love one another as an expression of love for God. These three topics—correct belief about Jesus, dealing rightly with sin, and loving one another—are intertwined in John's letters and mutually informing. They cannot be completely separated in a discussion of each.

In John's letters Christian discipleship is described both as walking in the light of Christ's revelation—implying intention, effort, and direction in life—and yet also as remaining, abiding, or continuing (μένω) in it, implying a constancy of belief throughout life. These two concepts may seem at first glance to be contrary, with walking being an image of movement and abiding an image of staying put. But both images contribute to our understanding of Christian discipleship. The inevitable sweep of time moves us through our lives as we walk through each season of life. We are to live through each season in the light of Christ's revelation. And rather than wander into other religions or ideals, we are to abide, or remain, in that light of Christ's revelation through every season of life.

ABIDING IN RIGHT BELIEF

John relates abiding in God to keeping God's commands (1 John 3:24), but he defines God's command not as, for instance, the Ten Commandments, but as believing in Jesus. "And this is his command: to believe in the name of his Son, Jesus Christ, and to love one another as he commanded us" (1 John 3:23). As the Fourth Gospel shows, not every sort of belief about Jesus is authentic faith that brings us into right relationship with God. First John was written to people who had an authentic Christian faith in Jesus Christ (1 John 5:13), but who had been exposed to heretical teaching about Christ that could mislead them back into darkness. John writes to reassure them that the faith they already hold is the true faith, and exhorts them to let that belief remain in their hearts so that they may remain (abide) in the Son and the Father (1 John 2:24). Apparently the false teachers who had left the Johannine churches had *not* continued in the teaching of Christ and had effectively left the faith (2 John 9). And so the message about discipleship in 1 John is the same as in John's Gospel: Abide in the teachings from and about Jesus concerning who he is, the Son of God.

Although we don't know the details of the false teaching that disrupted the Johannine churches, three passages in 1 John indicate it was a Christological error and give us some hints. First, 1 John 2:18–29 raises the issue of those who had left the church(es), people who self-identified as Christian but who did not remain in the apostolic teaching about Christ and therefore, appropriately, did not remain in the congregations. They apparently denied that Jesus was the Christ (2:22), denying his identity as the eternal Son of God (2:23). This point was at the very heart of John's gospel—that people believe Jesus is the Son of God and have eternal life in his name (John 20:30–31). Therefore, to deny Jesus's identity as the Son of God by believing he was merely a religious teacher or wonder-worker or anti-Roman zealot was to destroy the life-giving gospel.

The second point of false teaching is raised in 1 John 4:1–6, where false teachers apparently denied that Jesus Christ has come in the flesh. This was likely a teaching that denied the necessity of the Incarnation of the Son in Jesus and overemphasized the spiritual existence of the Christ. One entailment of denying the Incarnation is that the human life of Jesus becomes largely irrelevant, whereas in the apostolic Gospels it is the human life, death, and resurrection of Jesus that earns redemption for all. Without the incarnation of the eternal Son of God there is no atonement, no forgiveness of sin, and no eternal life for us.

Thirdly, in 1 John 5:6–12 there is the mysterious statement that Jesus Christ came not by water only, but by water and blood. Here John appears to remind his readers of the blood of Jesus shed on the cross as a necessary part of God's testimony about his Son (1 John 2:2). In other words, the water of Jesus's baptism when God announced, "This is my Son" (Matt. 3:13–17; Mark 1:9–11; Luke 3:21–22), is a necessary but insufficient event as far as the gospel is concerned. Without the crucifixion and resurrection, belief in the identity of Jesus as a "Son of God" in the sense of a true and anointed teacher of religion is insufficient.

Attempts to integrate Greek philosophies or ancient worldviews into Christian teaching—such as what later was labeled Docetism, Gnosticism, and the Montanist movement—may have caused the antichrist Christology that disrupted the Johannine churches. We don't know the details. But John does say that belief in the crucifixion and resurrection of the incarnate, eternal Son of God is at the heart of the apostolic gospel, and that eliminates many false ideas about who Jesus is that are still with us today.

THE ETHICS OF JOHANNINE DISCIPLESHIP

Jesus Christ brought revelation from God not only about his own identity as the incarnate, eternal Son, but in his life and teaching provided the moral foundation of how God has created us to live. Whoever claims to abide in Christ must live as Jesus did (1 John 2:6). This, of course, does not mean adopting the cultural lifestyle of first-century Palestine, and it does not mean we should expect to replicate Jesus's miraculous powers at will. Within John's letters we find teaching on two topics about what it does mean to abide in Christ: to deal rightly with sin and, closely related, to love one another.

A. Dealing Rightly with Sin

Jesus came to break the cycle of sin by "taking sin away" (1 John 3:5). And so to abide in Christ, to continue to walk in the light of Christ's revelation, means that Christian disciples must deal rightly with sin. John states that no one who abides in Christ continues to sin (1 John 3:6). To sin is to walk in darkness toward spiritual death. But does John teach that to walk in the light and to abide in Christ is to somehow become sinless like Jesus?

The dualism that John presents in both his Gospel and letters between light and darkness, life and death, righteousness and sin might suggest that John believed Christians should be and could be sinless. In his discussion of discipleship expectations, Wilkins observes that the ideal of perfectionism will almost certainly frustrate a person into either complacently denying sin or just walking away from the faith.[12] He highlights the importance of correctly understanding the life of discipleship to which Jesus calls us. And so as much as John wished it

---

12 Wilkins, *Following the Master,* 340–41.

true that his Christian readers not sin (1 John 2:1), he also recognized that people with authentic Christian faith *do* sin. To walk in the light of Christ does not mean that a person is sinless, but Christian discipleship as John defines it calls us to the intent and effort to avoid sin, and then to deal rightly with sin when it does occur.

Sin that is dealt with rightly is sin that is confessed in the name of Jesus, our advocate with the Father (1 John 1:9; 2:1). But apparently there were at least three ideas about sin in the Johannine church(es) that John needed to correct (1 John 1:5–2:2): to lie about our sin, to claim to be sinless, to claim to have never sinned. God is light in whom there is no darkness (1 John 2:5), which in the context of morality and ethics means that God alone defines righteous moral standards. God claims that we have sinned, and sent his Son to provide the remedy for our sin. Therefore, to deny our sin in any way is to call God a liar (1 John 1:10)!

There are many ways we can fail to deal rightly with sin. We can ignore it; we can rationalize and excuse it; we can redefine what we do as not sin. But the one who walks in the light of Christ will agree with God about what is sin, will confess it, and will avoid doing it again. Confession of sin in Christ's name, not pretending we are without sin, is the way to deal rightly with it.

B. Johannine Love

A major characteristic of Christian discipleship in John's Gospel and letters is love for one another.[13] "God is love. Whoever lives in love lives in God" (1 John 4:16). "Anyone who loves their brother and sister lives in the light" (1 John 2:10). "Anyone who does not love remains in death" (1 John 3:14). The challenge for Christians today is to correctly define this love that characterizes a true disciple of the Lord. If you ask people on the street what love is, you might expect answers such as: "Love is a feeling"; "love is a commitment"; or even, "love is sexual union." As theologian Jonathan Wilson has observed, "Love is a terribly debased term today, almost beyond rescue as a description of the good news of the kingdom come in Jesus Christ."[14] Sadly, Christians who uphold God's definition of sin as revealed in Scripture are often accused of being *unloving* people, as if love by any definition trumps the truth

---

13 Wilkins, *Following the Master,* 232–33, 237.

14 Jonathan R. Wilson, *For God So Loved the World: A Christology for Disciples* (Grand Rapids: Baker Academic: 2001), 131.

of God's Word. Is it loving to allow others to walk in darkness? But in fact, the opposite of love is not hate but sin. In his second letter, John defines love as walking in obedience to the Father's commands (2 John 6). Scripture throughout teaches that sin involves not only rebellion against God but at the same time wronging another person. John writes that by living in the light we avoid making others stumble (1 John 2:10). And so John's emphasis on sin and love in the letters are, to a large extent, two sides of the same coin of Christian discipleship. We love others by not sinning against them. Instead, when we walk in the light, we have fellowship with one another (1 John 1:7).

John's letters provide some help in defining the love that characterizes the Christian disciple not as a feeling but as the action of meeting the needs of others (1 John 3:17). John learned this from both the teaching of Jesus and the example of his life.[15] On the final night of his earthly life, after kneeling before his disciples to wash their feet, Jesus gave them a new command, "Love one another. As I have loved you, so you must love one another. By this everyone will know that you are my disciples, if you love one another" (John 13:34–35). The love that Jesus prescribes is an action of humility and service that benefits others.

The love that John learned from Jesus flows first from God's revealed love for us (John 3:16; 1 John 4:19). The eternal Son of God became a human being so that he might meet our greatest need for an atoning sacrifice for our sin (1 John 4:10). When a person believes that Jesus is the Son of God who sacrificed himself for our sin that we may have eternal life, the Holy Spirit enables them to love both God and others rightly (1 John 4:13–16). And John defines that love enabled by the Spirit to follow the same pattern as Christ's love in meeting the needs of others. "If anyone has material possessions and sees a brother or sister in need but has no pity on them, how can the love of God be in that person? Dear children, let us not love with words or speech but with actions and in truth" (1 John 3:17–18; cf. the Parable of the Good Samaritan in Luke 10:25–37). Elsewhere I write,

> This definition of love doesn't exclude warm feelings or commitments, but it means that Christians should live in a way that considerately responds to the needs of those around them. It means making life-sustaining resources available to meet the needs of those in dire circumstances—providing clean water,

---

15 Wilkins, *Following the Master,* 232–33, 237–39.

food, clothing, shelter, and of greatest importance, the true
gospel of Jesus Christ. [16]

First John closely links love for God to love for other human
beings: "Whoever claims to love God yet hates a brother or sister is a liar. For whoever does not love their brother and sister,
whom they have seen, cannot love God, whom they have not
seen. And he has given us this command: Anyone who loves
God must also love their brother and sister" (1 John 4:20, 21).

John's presentation of the love Christian disciples are to have for others
confirms Wilkin's observation that the terms used for Christian discipleship
in the New Testament epistles "describe the *relationships* of these disciples
to their risen Lord, to the community, and to society."[17] To walk in the light
as John defines it is a very relational endeavor. In the Fourth Gospel the
disciple's intimate relationship to the Lord is pictured as sheep following
the shepherd (John 10) and branches of a vine (John 15:1–8). In John's
letters, following a situation that had strained and divided the church, a
relationship of love for others becomes prominent. Christian discipleship
is formed, strengthened, developed, and honed as we live in relationships
with those who come into our lives in every sphere and season.

For Christian disciples today John's call to love means choosing a lifestyle that does not hog so much of the world's goods that others are forced
to go without. It means being mindful of how others in our church congregations may be struggling. It means paying attention to what is hap-
pening to people in other neighborhoods, other regions, and around the
world so that our resources can be directed to relieve their need. And it
means that to truly love others we must continue to invite them into the
light of Christ's revelation, even when the world misjudges that as hateful.

AUTHENTIC DISCIPLESHIP

Wilkins summarizes his definition of a disciple of Jesus Christ as
"one who has come to Jesus for eternal life, has claimed him as Savior
and God, and has embarked upon the life of following him."[18] Christian
discipleship is the process of living our lives in this world in the light of
the revelation of God in Christ that Jesus brought into it, empowered

---

16 Jobes, *1, 2 & 3 John*, 160–61.
17 Wilkins, *Following the Master*, 288 (italics added).
18 Wilkins, *Following the Master*, 342.

by the Holy Spirit not to sin and to love others, all the while becoming more fully like Jesus. It requires us to be molded from start to finish by the apostolic teaching found in Scripture, such as John presents with authority in his letters and to live in community with others following Jesus, walking in the light.

CHAPTER 17

Witnesses for the Lamb: Discipleship in Revelation

Buist M. Fanning

In his inimitable way, George Caird suggests that Revelation tends to provoke an initial frustrated query, "What on earth is *this* all about?" that moves to a more reflective but still perplexed question, "What *on earth* is it all about?"[1] A brief overview of what the book actually *is* all about will show how very relevant it is for life on earth, especially for our lives as Christ's disciples in the here and now.

INTRODUCTION

Revelation is, above all, a book centered on God.[2] It confronts us with who God is and what is he doing in this world, with a special focus on what is to come and how we should live now in anticipation of that future. It is filled with powerful images of God's glory, power, holiness, and sovereignty. But in his majesty and dominion, God remains present and engaged with his world across all the ages. We see him on his heavenly throne (15x), extolled as Creator (3:14; 4:11; 10:6; 14:7; 21:5) and Redeemer (5:9; 7:10; 12:10; 19:1), and feared as the Judge to whom all will give an account (6:16–17; 11:18; 14:10, 19; 19:15; 20:11). Among the most distinctive terms in Revelation are the divine titles "Almighty" (9x in Revelation; only once elsewhere in New Testament), "Alpha and Omega" (used of God the Father in 1:8 and 21:6, and of Christ in 1:17 and 22:13), and "who was and is and is to come" (1:4, 8; 4:8; cf. 11:17; 16:5). These titles portray God as the all-powerful ruler and sovereign over all things, who created and now sustains his universe while bringing all things to their divinely intended fulfillment.[3] The worship that John

---

1 G. B. Caird, *A Commentary on the Revelation of St John the Divine,* HNTC (New York: Harper & Row, 1966), 1.

2 See Richard Bauckham, *The Theology of the Book of Revelation* (Cambridge: Cambridge University Press, 1993), 23–53; and G. K. Beale, "Revelation (Book)," in *New Dictionary of Biblical Theology,* eds. T. D. Alexander, et al. (Downers Grove, IL: InterVarsity Press, 2000), 356–57.

3 Bauckham, *Theology,* 27, says about the title "Alpha and Omega": "God precedes all things, as their Creator, and he will bring all things to eschatological fulfillment. He is the origin and goal of all history. He has the first word, in creation, and the last word, in new creation."

shows being offered to God in heaven serves as a model of the fitting and proper worship to be offered to him on earth by all its inhabitants. It shows us that devotion to and communion with such a God are the most important things to which we could give ourselves.[4]

More particularly, Revelation is a book about God's work of judgment and redemption through Christ leading to the renewal of all things. From beginning to end John's topic is "things that must soon take place" (1:1; 22:6; cf. 1:19; 4:1), for "the time is near" (1:3; 22:10) and Christ is "coming quickly" (3:11; 22:7, 12, 20). As in the rest of the New Testament, Jesus Christ is seen as the focal point of history, for God's people Israel and the rest of humanity as well as for all of creation. His incarnation, death, resurrection, and exaltation ensure God's victory over evil for all time (1:5–6, 17–18; 3:7; 5:5, 9–10; 11:15). But we must wait for his return as the Lion of Judah, the King of kings and Lord of lords to bring this victory to earth in its fullness (1:6; 5:5; 10:6–7; 11:15–18; 14:1; 19:11–21; 21:1–5; 22:16).

In many ways, then, Revelation recaps the story of the Bible as a whole from creation to new creation. It is firmly anchored in the Old Testament story of Israel's kings and prophets and in the gospel of God's saving grace through Christ. To these it adds the glorious climax of biblical revelation, visions of deliverance and renewal that will bring humans into direct worship of and communion with God and the Lamb forever in a restored creation (21:1–22:5). In the process it shows the privileged status and responsibility that Christ's disciples possess now while the ongoing story of God's redemption works its way out in the real world in which we live.

WHAT DISCIPLESHIP LOOKS LIKE IN REVELATION

In order to trace how Revelation contributes to the portrayal of discipleship in the New Testament, it will be convenient to treat the themes and characteristics of discipleship in the book under two main headings. First, the themes that are essentially continuous with the picture of discipleship found in the rest of the New Testament, ones that confirm or reinforce the larger picture but do not add to it because they are not developed in any detailed way in Revelation. These will be treated rather briefly. And second, themes in the book that are distinctive in their portrayal of Christian discipleship. These may have parallels with features found in other New Testament books, but Revelation's contribution to the larger picture is unique.

---

4 All Scripture translations are the author's own unless otherwise noted.

A. Discipleship in Revelation: Continuities

Among the features of Christian discipleship in Revelation that are similar to what is found in the rest of the New Testament are certain *traits* that are understood to characterize disciples and *terms* used to describe disciples. None of these is developed extensively or in distinctive ways, but some of them do occur frequently in the book. The concept of discipleship is found in Revelation, but outside of the Gospels and Acts the term "disciple" itself does not occur in the New Testament.[5]

Several of the significant but undeveloped *traits* that Revelation associates with disciples are found in Christ's messages to the seven churches (chs 2–3), but other passages supplement them. These are characteristic behaviors that the churches are commended for or called to display.[6] Here are some of the most important. First, love for God and people is cited as the indispensable mark of a Christian (2:4–5, 19; cf. Mark 12:28–31; John 13:34–35), and it is implied in the image of the bride or wife of the Lamb, made ready and devoted to her bridegroom (19:7–9; 21:9). The churches are also commended for faith (2:19; 13:10; 14:12), unflagging endurance in the face of difficulties (1:9; 2:2–3, 19; 3:10; 13:10; 14:12), and loyalty to Christ (2:13; 3:8). Also important are hearing and obeying God's word or commands (1:3; 3:3, 8, 10; 14:12; 22:7, 9), usefulness and zeal to serve Christ in this world (3:15–17), discernment about false doctrine and evil conduct (2:2, 6, 20, 24), and repentance when they sin (2:5, 16; 3:3, 19). Christians are also commended for tireless acts of obedience (2:2–3; 14:13), holiness (3:4, 18; 7:14; 19:8),[7] growth in obedience or service (2:19), and maintaining that obedience over the long term (2:25–26).

When we move from *traits* to specific *terms* that are used to refer to disciples, the following are most important. First, references to "slaves/servants/service" occur in significant places (e.g., 1:1; 7:3; 19:2; 22:6). Occasionally the term "servant/slave" (δοῦλος) refers to God's prophets (10:7; 11:18) or even to Moses (15:3) or John (1:1), but generally it

---

5 Michael J. Wilkins, *Following the Master: A Biblical Theology of Discipleship* (Grand Rapids: Zondervan, 1992), 281–90.
6 What Jesus says to the *corporate* body of believers also extends as a commendation or challenge to the *individual* Christians who make up the congregation (see the individual focus in the call to listen and the promise to the "overcomer" at the end of each message).
7 Revelation makes clear that Christians' "white garments" as a symbol of their purity and holiness is not something they have merited or accomplished on their own, but they obtain them from Christ (3:18) in view of his sacrificial death for them (7:14), a righteousness given by God (19:8) but lived out in their day-by-day faithfulness and obedience to him (3:4).

describes Christians. Its use with possessives referring to God (my, his, of
God) alludes to divine ownership and the disciple's surrender of personal
rights and loyalty to God alone.[8] It also implies deeds of humility and
sacrifice that give evidence of a life lived not for self but for Christ and the
gospel (2:19; 6:11; 19:2; cf. Mark 8:34–35; 10:42–45).

Another common term for disciples in Revelation as in the Epistles is
"saints, holy ones." This is used to refer to Christians in connection with
their prayers (5:8; 8:3–4), their persecutions (13:7; 16:6; 17:6; 18:24),
their endurance and faith (13:10; 14:12), their righteous deeds (19:8),
and their reward for faithfulness (11:18).

A clear term for discipleship, the verb "follow," is used in the description "who follow the Lamb wherever he goes" (14:4), but it occurs in a
highly debated passage in Revelation, the text about a group of 144,000
who stand with the Lamb on Mount Zion (14:1–5). Aune treats this as the
most important passage on discipleship in the book and explains its details
accordingly.[9] It certainly seems like a natural point of focus, but there is
little consensus about the identification of this group or about the other
images used to describe them in these verses. Out of an impulse to see
them as comparable to Christian disciples portrayed in the rest of the New
Testament, the understanding of who they are and how they are described
in 14:3–5 is sometimes forced into a mold that does not fit the context, in
my opinion. They are taken to be Christians of all ethnic backgrounds celebrating in heaven Christ's spiritual victory over evil (singing a new song on
Mount Zion). They have resisted spiritual idolatry (they are chaste virgins
in a figurative sense). They had been martyred for their faith (they follow
the Lamb wherever he goes) as a sacrificial offering (like firstfruits of the
redeemed who are offered to God in worship). Their innocence and commitment to truth led them to be slaughtered at the hands of God's enemies
(no lie was found; they are blameless).[10] From a certain point of view these
are plausible interpretations, but they misconstrue a number of contextual
indicators that should point us in a different direction.

---

8 One reference implies God's jealousy that a false-teacher would be allowed to lead "his
servants" astray (2:20).

9 David E. Aune, "Following the Lamb: Discipleship in the Apocalypse," in *Patterns of
Discipleship in the New Testament,* ed. R. N. Longenecker (Grand Rapids: Eerdmans, 1996),
270–77.

10 For most of these conclusions about the passage, see Aune, "Following the Lamb,"
271–77; Robert H. Mounce, *The Book of Revelation,* rev. ed. (Grand Rapids: Eerdmans, 1998),
263–69; and Stephen S. Smalley, *The Revelation to John: A Commentary on the Greek Text of the
Apocalypse* (Downers Grove, IL: InterVarsity Press, 2005), 353–60.

This group is almost certainly to be identified with the 144,000 mentioned in 7:1–8 since key details are the same (the distinctive number, their marking "on their foreheads," their association with Israel, their status as God's "servants" or his "redeemed"). The descriptions in 14:3–5 add further details, but it is clear that the same group from 7:1–8 is in view. Unfortunately, the interpretation of both of these passages suffers from a neglect of ethnic Israel and a tendency to collapse Old Testament prophetic expectations about the future into a form of Christian eschatology that is either supersessionist (the church replaces Israel) or that effaces all ethnic differences among the redeemed (ethnic distinctions are no longer relevant). As a result, important clues for interpretation of what the text actually says in the context of its ancient background are missed or misread.

I argue along with others that these "followers" represent one specific group of faithful ethnic Israel, regathered from among the nations where they had been scattered.[11] They have turned to Christ in faith at some point during the future time of severe tribulation described in Revelation 6–16 and are physically and spiritually protected by God so that they will be able to stand with their Messiah (among other Christians) in Jerusalem when he begins his earthly reign there (14:1–5; 20:1–10). The visions of 7:1–8 and 14:1–5 thus affirm the widespread ancient Jewish expectation of the regathering in the end times of all the tribes of ethnic Israel, of "Israel as a whole," not just a remnant. This expectation appears elsewhere in the New Testament (Matt. 19:28; Luke 22:30; Rom. 11:25–29) and is a common motif in the Old Testament (e.g., Deut. 30:1–5; Isa. 11:10–16; Jer. 23:5–8; Ezek. 37:15–28) and in other ancient Jewish literature.[12] Thus they are distinct from the innumerable multiethnic group described in 7:9–14. Many commentators see that multitude as identical with the 144,000 (i.e., the Jewish-Gentile church that takes on the role of the "true" or renewed Israel), who will be protected spiritually but not physically in the final woes, but the role of this 144,000 among the larger body of Jewish and Gentile followers of Christ is much more specific. As

---

11 Buist M. Fanning, *Revelation,* ZECNT (Grand Rapids: Zondervan, forthcoming). For variations on this view, see Albert Geyser, "The Twelve Tribes in Revelation: Judean and Judeo-Christian Apocalypticism," *NTS* 28 (1982): 388–99; Rebecca Skaggs and Thomas Doyle, "Revelation 7: Three Critical Questions," in *Imagery in the Book of Revelation,* eds. M. Labahn and O. Lehtipun (Leuven: Peeters, 2001), 161–81; and Joel R. White, "The 144,000 in Revelation 7 and 14: Old Testament and Intratextual Clues to Their Identity," in *From Creation to New Creation: Biblical Theology and Exegesis,* eds. D. M. Gurtner and B. L. Gladd (Peabody, MA: Hendrickson, 2013), 179–97.

12 Tobit 13:3–5; Sir 48:10; *Apoc. Ab.* 29:14–17; *2 Bar.* 29:1–3; 32:1–2; 40:2; 78:1–7; *T. Benj.* 9:2; *4 Ezra* 13:40, 48–49; *Pss. Sol.* 15:4–9; 11QTemple 57.5–6.

a result, the descriptions of them in 14:3–5 display some indirect indi-cations of what general Christian discipleship should be like, but they cannot be taken as directly applicable to the topic. This would be like arguing that Old Testament believers were all Nazirites (Num. 6:1–21).

A more contextually consistent reading of 14:1–5 should see the 144,000 as the specific group of ethnic Jewish converts to Christ whom God seals for protection from physical destruction (following the pro-phetic parallel in Ezekiel 9:1–11) as a sign that he will chasten Israel but not destroy her in the coming judgment and restoration. Along with their special privilege this group takes on a special representative role (taken from all the tribes, numbered in a way that symbolizes the completeness of God's mercy on Israel as well as Israel's role as the firstfruits or van-guard of God's redemption that starts with Israel and expands to all the nations of the world) and displays a special consecration (sexually pure and undistracted, devoted to whatever Christ asks of them, and com-pletely irreproachable in speech and conduct). Some of their characteris-tics apply to Christian disciples more broadly (following Christ no matter what, committed to the truth, and above reproach), but some do not (Jewish virgins, the vanguard of the redeemed, protected from physical harm in the midst of the tribulation).

B. Discipleship in Revelation: Distinctives

Other discipleship themes in Revelation are distinctive in comparison with the rest of the New Testament. Most of these have parallels with features found in the other books, but Revelation's contribution to the topic is unique. The five closely related themes that follow trace its distinctive contribution.

1. The Environment for Discipleship

A major counterpoint to the picture that Revelation gives of God in his majesty and sovereignty (see Introduction) is the implacable but ultimate-ly futile enmity against God by the powers of evil that have spoiled his creation. All that is said in the book about following Jesus must be seen against the backdrop of aggressive, satanic evil directed against God, his Messiah, and his people. The fallen world's hostility to God's redemptive work is not a new theme (cf. John 15:18–25; 17:13–19), but Revelation clearly shows the truth of Jesus's words to his disciples: "If you belonged to the world, it would love you as its own. As it is, you do not belong to the world, but I have chosen you out of the world. That is why the world hates you" (John 15:19, NIV). Revelation portrays with vivid intensity the opposition that Christians will face as they seek to follow Christ in this world. God's good creation itself is not evil, but it has been coopted for evil purposes in resistance to its Creator.

An important dimension of this hostile background for discipleship is its cosmic and age-long character. Satan's implacable struggle against God began long ago and continues through the present age in spite of the decisive defeat he suffered in Christ's death and resurrection (Rev. 2:10–13; 12:3–9). And he will wage war against God and his people with heightened intensity in the days immediately preceding Christ's second coming (12:10–13, 17; 13:7). Sometimes such attacks come in the form of overt persecution, including social ostracism, personal slander, economic discrimination, physical assault or imprisonment, and even death (1:9; 2:9–10, 13; 13:15–17). But Satan's opposition can also manifest itself in times of peace and prosperity in the form of false teachings (2:2, 20, 24) or temptations that lull us into complacency (3:17–19) and easy conformity to the sinful practices of the world (2:20; 18:3–4).[13]

Revelation's answer to this ominous conflict is its vision of God's sovereign control of events on earth even now and his coming reversal of what appears to be the irresistible victory of evil in the world (5:9–10; 11:15–18; 19:6). He is still on his heavenly throne, engaged with his people and his world and anticipating their ultimate security and presence with him forever in his restored creation (7:13–17; 21:1–5; 22:1–6). Evil powers hold sway only because in the mystery of his redemptive purpose he allows it for a time, but "the power structures of the world [are] illusory and temporal."[14] The victory of the Lamb and his Father has already been accomplished and soon will be realized completely in judgment and renewal on earth, so Christians can stand confident even now because of that victory (5:5; 12:11; 13:7; 21:7). But in the midst of pervasive hostility and temptation to assimilate to the world's values, disciples must have a clear vision of who is Lord of this world after all and where its history is headed. John's apocalyptic visions provide a vivid glimpse of the true

---

13 Aune, "Following the Lamb," 269–70; Loren T. Stuckenbruck, "Revelation: Historical Setting and John's Call to Discipleship," *Leaven* 8 (2000): 27–31; and John Sweet, "Maintaining the Testimony of Jesus: The Suffering of Christians in the Revelation of John," in *Suffering and Martyrdom in the New Testament: Studies Presented to G. M. Styler by the Cambridge New Testament Seminar,* eds. W. Horbury and B. McNeil (Cambridge: Cambridge University Press, 1981), 101–03

14 Mitchell G. Reddish, "Martyr Christology in the Apocalypse," *JSNT* 33 (1988): 85–95, at 92.

King of kings and Lord of lords (17:14; 19:16) and summon us to give
him our full allegiance in all things.

2. The Testimony of Jesus

The debated phrase "the testimony/witness of Jesus" (ἡ μαρτυρία
Ἰησοῦ) is a central part of Revelation's teaching about Christ and Christian discipleship.[15] Early in the book it has a clearly subjective sense:
Jesus's *own* testimony about God and his ways that was his mission in his
earthly life and death (1:2, 5, 9). He bore witness faithfully by clear word
and costly action, so that all humanity could see the truth about God and
his saving purposes (John 3:31–36; 18:37). But as the book moves along
it shifts to an objective sense and refers to believers' testimony *about* Jesus that they communicate by their conduct and verbal witness (12:17;
19:10; 20:4; cf. 6:9; 12:11).[16] John speaks about this in patently mimetic
terms: Jesus faithfully bore witness despite opposition even to the point
of suffering and death, and his followers are called to do likewise.[17] John
mentions Jesus as "the faithful witness" (1:5; also 3:14) and describes his
own confinement on Patmos as "because of . . . the witness of Jesus" (1:9).
Then he records Jesus's commendation of the Christians at Pergamum for
their fidelity to his name in their hostile surroundings "even in the days of
Antipas, my faithful witness, who was killed among you" (2:13). A later
vision presents followers of Christ under attack from Satan, who defeated
him "because of the blood of the Lamb and because of the word of their
testimony, and they did not love their life even when faced with death"
(12:11, NASB).[18] The parallel with Jesus's fidelity to God is unmistakable

---

15 Aune, "Following the Lamb," 281–83; Bauckham, *Theology*, 72–73. See also Sarah Under-
wood Dixon, *The Testimony of the Exalted Jesus: The "Testimony of Jesus" in the Book of Revelation*
(London: T&T Clark, 2017), who argues that "the testimony of Jesus" refers to his witness in
Revelation itself (cf. 1:2; 22:18, 20).
16 Some argue (e.g., J. Beutler, "μαρτυρία," *EDNT* 2:392–93; Sweet, "Maintaining the Testimony of Jesus," 103–5) that "testimony/witness of Jesus" (6x in Revelation) always carries
the subjective sense, since they understand verses that describe Christians as "holding" to this
witness (12:17; 19:10) to mean being faithful to what Jesus taught. But it makes more sense
in these later contexts to understand that John subtly shifts the phrase "testimony/witness
of Jesus" to mean Christians' proclamation, in turn, of what they know about Jesus and the
God he came to reveal (e.g., John 15:26–27; 1 John 1:2; 4:14). So, as verses like Revelation
6:9 and 12:11 show, what Christians hold fast to or maintain in the face of opposition is the
task of bearing witness about Jesus. But much of what is said above about Christian "witness"
would hold true whether we take "testimony/witness of Jesus" as subjective or objective.
17 Christians' imitation of Christ in bearing witness is, of course, a limited one that falls far
short of the uniqueness, authority, and power of his witness as God's Son.
18 See also 17:6, portraying Babylon as drunk "with the blood of the witnesses of Jesus."

and it reflects the nuances of the call to discipleship in Mark 8:31–38 (i.e., the Son of man will give his life; his followers must also take up a cross and lose their lives for his sake and the gospel's, not being ashamed of his words).[19]

The theme of "witness" in Revelation holds two important lessons for what it means to be Christ's disciple in the world in which we live today.[20] First, and quite astounding, is its call for us to reach out to an unwelcoming world with our gospel witness. We must testify to the truth about God's gracious salvation in Jesus Christ, offered even to those who are antagonistic to him. By speaking and living out the truth of God in Christ, we truly exemplify his instructions to love our enemies and to pray for and do good to those who hate us (Luke 6:27–28). Instead of withdrawing from the hostile world and leaving it to its deserved judgment, we are called to bear winsome witness by our conduct and our verbal testimony to the Lamb who "redeemed for God with [his] blood people from every tribe and language and people and nation" (5:9).[21] An active, witnessing presence of Christians truly *in* the world rather than separate from it (John 17:11–19) mirrors the seeking, self-giving love of God (John 3:16) and of Christ (Mark 10:45; Luke 19:10).

The second lesson also reflects Jesus's rubric in John 17: Though *in* the world, we cannot be *of* the world but must be set apart from it by God's truth (John 17:15–19). Revelation communicates this by its constant warnings against complacency and assimilation to the godless ideology and conduct of the surrounding culture (2:2, 20, 24; 3:17–19; 14:9–10; 18:3–4). If we fail in love for God and people or care little for holiness and faithfulness or adopt the "truth" that appeals most to the world around us, then we will have nothing to offer to our contemporaries and will not be witnesses for the Messiah we claim to follow.

---

19 This pattern does not mean, however, that "witness" and related words in Revelation had already come to denote "martyr" (i.e., one who bears witness by giving his life). That comes only at a later stage in the linguistic development of the Greek words. See J. Beutler, "μάρτυς," *EDNT* 2:395; and Reddish, "Martyr Christology," 86.

20 On both of these points, see Bauckham, *Theology*, 159–64.

21 This is the first of seven occurrences in Rev. of this or similar phrasing referring to the multicultural impact of the gospel (cf. 7:9; 10:11; 11:9; 13:7; 14:6; 17:15). God's redemption is not just for "people like us," but for all the nations. Some of these verses refer to the peoples still under Satan's control, who need to be set free by the gospel. See Richard Bauckham, *The Climax of Prophecy: Studies in the Book of Revelation* (Edinburgh: T&T Clark, 1993), 326–37.

3. Jesus's Victory and Ours

Just as "witness" is a characteristic action of Jesus that disciples imitate, so Christians are called to participate in his "victory" (i.e., νικάω, to conquer, prevail, overcome) in the cosmic struggle against godless evil. This expectation is repeated seven times in the promises to the overcomer in Jesus's messages to the churches, but especially the final one, "To the one who overcomes I will give the right to sit with me on my throne, as I myself overcame and sat down with my Father on his throne" (3:21).[22] But as with the theme of witness, the call to imitate Jesus in "victory over evil" is a limited and relative one that needs to be unpacked a bit further to understand its significance for discipleship.

Again here, the theme of "victory" for Christ and for Christians in Revelation must be seen in light of the environment of evil already discussed above. In fact, the key verb νικάω is sometimes used to refer to the "victory" of Satan and his minions over God's people during the final period of severe affliction for the world (11:7; 13:7). In spite of these setbacks, divine triumph is assured because of Christ's death and resurrection. The slain Lamb now standing in the center of God's heavenly throne room "has overcome" so that he can open the scroll and set God's judgment and redemption in motion (Rev. 5:5; cf. 3:21). His full victory that has already been won will be established completely on earth through the events portrayed in the rest of Revelation. One entailment of his resurrection (implied but not directly stated) is the victory over death that Christians will themselves experience as a result.[23] This focus on the cross and resurrection is one stage of victory for Christ and Christians portrayed in the book.[24]

A second stage is the victory that Christ's followers are urged to achieve by the faithful way they live their lives throughout the inter-advent age and especially in the time of intense suffering in the final days. "Overcoming" in this sense is likewise set against the backdrop of the universal

---

22 One issue that sometimes arises regarding these promises is the question—also raised elsewhere about the demands of discipleship—whether "overcomers" are understood to be those who suffer martyrdom for their faith or a group of more committed or obedient Christians as over against other believers who are less spiritual. The first two promises (2:7, 11) make it clear that these are references to Christians in general, those who genuinely believe in Christ, who by virtue of God's new birth find the ability to endure in faith against idolatry and persecution (cf. 1 John 4:4; 5:4–5; Rev. 13:10; 14:12; 21:5–7).

23 For example, the Christian as "overcomer" is promised access to the tree of life and God's paradise (2:7), no harm from the second death (2:11), and secure inclusion in the book of life (3:5), all based on redemption in Christ (1:5–6; 5:9–10; 7:14–17).

24 See Bauckham, *Theology*, 70, for mention of these stages.

and age-long struggle of all that is evil, including the Devil and the world system he controls (1 John 2:13–17; 4:2–4), against God and his saving purpose. Christians are caught in the middle of this conflict and are called to faithful endurance even if it means suffering and martyrdom (Rev. 1:9; 13:10; 14:12). For us to be victorious or prevail in this struggle means resisting evil and falsehood in our lives and in our churches, staying faithful to God by not conforming to the world's values or worshipping false gods (see the exhortations in chs 2–3; also 18:4). This is the sense in which Christ's followers are said to "overcome" Satan (12:11) and the Beast (15:2). But such a victory will be gained by virtue of what Christ has already accomplished, not by human efforts but by enduring faith in him (1 John 4:4; 5:4–5; Rev. 21:5–7).

The third stage of victory in Revelation is the conquest Christ achieves against the satanic and earthly forces of evil arrayed against him at his second coming (17:14; cf. 19:15–21). These are the armies assembled by the Antichrist to resist the establishment of the Messiah's rule (Ps. 2:1–12; Rev. 11:15–18; 12:10), whom he will summarily defeat and consign to judgment (Rev. 19:14–16, 20–21). Even though these portrayals are highly symbolic with metaphors that are clearly not to be read with wooden literalism (a sword coming from his mouth, forces mounted on horses), they do not refer to a purely transcendent, spiritual battle. They point to Jesus's actual return to this earth and his victory over a coalition of military forces (demonic and human) gathered to resist the coming of his kingdom in this world (cf. Dan. 7:13–14, 27; Acts 1:11; 1 Cor. 1:7–8; 2 Thess. 1:7–10; 2:6–12).[25] The important point is that victory in this battle is achieved by Christ alone. Though angelic and human armies accompany him (cf. 17:14; 19:14), their role is minimal or nonexistent since Christ's power and authority is what secures complete and immediate victory (19:14–16, 19–20).[26] This means there is no support in Revelation for violent attacks against religious foes, no "jihad" to defeat

25 George Eldon Ladd, *A Commentary on the Revelation of John* (Grand Rapids: Eerdmans, 1972), 252–53; and Allan J. McNicol, *The Conversion of the Nations in Revelation*, LNTS 438 (London: T&T Clark, 2011), 59–61. For a defense of this view, see Fanning, *Revelation* (forthcoming).
26 These verses show that John's correlation of Lion and Lamb in Revelation 5:5–6 is not intended to "reinterpret" prophetic expectations of a powerful Davidic Messiah who conquers and judges God's foes and replace them with a martyred victim who persuades by "the invincible power of self-negating, self-sacrificing love" (Caird, *Revelation*, 73–75). See this view also in Bauckham, *Climax*, 213–15; Reddish, "Martyr Christology," 88–90; and Sweet, "Maintaining the Testimony of Jesus," 113–17. Both images (Lion of Judah and slaughtered Lamb) are true, and we should not collapse one into the other just because it has greater appeal to modern sensibilities.

the enemies of the gospel. The book's teaching on Christian victory co-heres exactly with Paul's words about "not be[ing] overcome by evil but overcom[ing] evil with good" and leaving all vengeance with God (Rom. 12:17–21).

4. Intimacy with Our Savior Now and Forever

Partly in consolation for the rigors of discipleship portrayed in the preceding sections, Revelation also provides a wonderfully attractive pic-ture of the intimacy with Christ that comes for his disciples. To follow him opens up a personal *relationship* with him, not just a religious affil-iation or doctrinal persuasion. He knows us through and through, and we come to know him more and more (cf. John 10:14–15, 27–28). This comes out in Revelation in regard to our communion with him in both the present and the future.

The messages to the churches (chs 2–3) are replete with indications that the risen Jesus knows his people intimately and wants them to draw near to him in turn. In 2:1 he cites his presence among the lampstands (i.e., churches) from 1:12–13 but adds the detail "who walks among" them. He repeatedly says, "I know . . ." in regard to their character and circumstances (e.g., 2:2, 9, 13, 19). A particularly poignant example is 2:13, "I know where you live . . .", as he consoles those in Pergamum about their dangerous situation. The old spiritual that laments, "Nobody knows the trouble I've seen, nobody knows my sorrow," is not true for the Christian. Actually, in the version that Louis Armstrong recorded, the next stanza says, "Nobody knows but Jesus." He knows us profoundly even if no one else does or cares to. We can be confident that he sees our struggles and our successes, and he will act authoritatively in discipline or reward (2:12, 16–17). Whether his all-seeing knowledge of us is a source of comfort or distress depends on our response to him. Even when he must rebuke (e.g., 3:19–20), he appeals to his follower out of great love to turn back and find the warmth of restored communion with him-self ("I will come in to him and share a meal with him and he with me").

The invitation to table fellowship, as in 3:20, holds true of our pres-ent relationship with Christ, but it also anticipates the coming messianic banquet or marriage supper of the Lamb (Isa. 25:6–8; Matt. 8:11; 26:29; Luke 14:15; 22:30; Rev. 19:9) that the redeemed will enjoy when Christ returns. The image of the bride or wife of the Lamb, made ready and de-voted to her bridegroom and soon to be joined to him forever (19:7–9;

21:9), is another image of the disciple's intimate personal relationship with Christ that begins now but comes to its full form in the future. One of the benefits of focusing on eschatology, as Revelation does, is the power of such teaching to encourage us through the difficulties and sorrows of life in this present broken world. As we glimpse the future God has in store for us, especially the hope of enjoying his presence forever in intimate communion with him, our perspective is renewed and our spirits are lifted. It gives us hope to endure in our individual situations in the present but also eagerness to experience what God can do for all of his creation in spite of its present longings and "groanings" (Rom. 8:18–25).

Revelation speaks of that future dimension of our intimacy with Christ also in verses like 2:7 and 3:12 (which allude to 21:1–7 and 22:1–5). Whatever difficulties may come to faithful Christians in this life, they pale in comparison to the glorious blessings promised to them at the consummation. "To eat from the tree of life that is in God's paradise" (2:7) echoes the entire biblical story of divine redemption from beginning to end. It points to a divine renewal of all of creation, not just to the spiritual salvation of individual humans, and to God's provision for humanity's needs in a life lived in obedience to and intimate fellowship with him.[27] "Paradise" represents the original, Edenic context for such face-to-face communion with God—a life that humans lost in the fall but that God intends to restore in his renewal of all things in the future. The promise in 3:12 of being identified by God's name and by the name of the new Jerusalem captures the covenantal theme of God dwelling among his people as *their* God and the redeemed serving and worshipping him directly as *his* people (20:3; 22:3–4).[28] God's intent is that such a life of personal communion would begin even now and grow throughout our lives as disciples, so that the consummation to come in the future will be the natural fulfillment of a process begun already in the here and now in our walk with Christ.

5. Personal Transformation according to God's Design

Closely related to the glorious future that is coming for Christians is a further dimension of discipleship that also begins in our present experience

---

27 N. T. Wright, *Surprised by Hope: Rethinking Heaven, the Resurrection, and the Mission of the Church* (New York: HarperOne, 2008), 104–06.

28 Jonathan Lunde, *Following Jesus, the Servant King: A Biblical Theology of Covenantal Discipleship,* BTL (Grand Rapids: Zondervan, 2010), 43–44, 65, 69, mentions the covenantal dimensions of this Edenic renewal, but he does not develop them at length.

and culminates in the new creation. It concerns the promise of *individual* transformation in the midst of God's wider *cosmic* re-creation. One of the central tenets of the New Testament's theology of discipleship is the transformation of the believer that is often called "progressive" sanctification and then "final" sanctification, that is, being conformed to Christ's likeness more and more until the process is made complete in his glorious presence (Rom. 8:29; 2 Cor. 3:18; 1 John 3:2).[29] Revelation's unique contribution to this doctrine is to focus on the individual Christian's transformation to be like Christ but tailored to God's design for each specific believer.

This point, however, is expressed in a single verse in the book using highly symbolic language that is subject to various interpretations, although it gains a bit more support from another verse using similar imagery to make a different point. The reader can judge how convincing the following interpretation is. The key verse is 2:17, the third of the promises to the overcomer, and one that like other such promises refers ultimately to blessings the Christian will enjoy in the new heaven and new earth (Rev. 21–22). It pledges several things: first, "hidden manna" (symbolic of full provision from God for all that is needed for human life at its best; "hidden" now in heaven but ready to be revealed in the eschaton; cf. 7:16–17; 21:6–7; 22:1–3). The further things promised are "a white stone, and inscribed on the stone a new name that no one knows except the one who receives it." These items are simply and clearly worded but the range of options for what they signify is daunting. At least seven different possibilities are proposed for the significance of the "white stone," but it probably represents an entry pass or a favorable verdict, that is, some kind of approval of the individual for the status that has been reached.[30] The "new name" inscribed on the stone is also debatable. A parallel promise in 3:12 pledges that the "new name" of Christ will be written on the overcomer, but that appears to be a different blessing (related to divine ownership), since here in 2:17 the "new name" on the stone will be unknown except to "the one who receives it." The name of Christ would of course be known already, so the "new name" in 2:17 is most likely a divinely given name specific to that individual Christian.

Another parallel in Revelation helps, I think, to fill out the picture. In 19:12 we find "a name written" on Jesus Christ at his glorious return "that no one knows except he himself." These texts (2:17; 19:12) reflect

---

29 Wilkins, *Following the Master*, 342–47.
30 See Grant R. Osborne, *Revelation*, BECNT; Grand Rapids: Baker, 2002), 148–49, for details.

the biblical idea that the "name" of a person is indicative of his or her true identity or role, and so a "new name" can symbolize a change of character or status or perhaps an intent that a change would occur (e.g., Abram/ Abraham, Simon/Peter).[31] Likewise a new circumstance can reveal that an existing name, one already known, has a depth of meaning and relevance not previously appreciated.[32] That seems to be the point in 19:12, since Christ's private name is likely to be either the name given in 19:13 ("the Word of God") or more likely the one in 19:16 ("King of kings and Lord of lords"), a name whose profound meaning is now understood by others, not just by Jesus himself.

Similarly, in 2:17 Jesus promises to give the overcomer a "new name," an identity and character hardly imagined now but which represents the full transformation of his or her person and gifts according to God's good design for that person in Christ. The significance of this for discipleship is that as individual Christians we are called to live toward the future God has for us. As part of the new creation I will receive a new name from Jesus. How I live in the present is largely determined by how I see myself now and in the future, and God's revelation in Scripture should inform that image. The God who loves me infinitely and the Savior who knows me and shepherds me through all of life wants to mold me into the "best version of me" possible,[33] a unique human conformed to Christ. I need to discover and inhabit Christ's intent for my life, not my own self-chosen identity or one molded by the overpowering culture around me (i.e., autonomous, self-absorbed, independent of God).[34] My identity and conduct in the present is formed from my history and heritage as well as my destiny and hope for the future, and God is at work in me to bring about such transformation through the process of discipleship.

SUMMARY

Those who live in anticipation of the fulfillment of God's prophecies of future redemption are often caricatured as "too other-worldly to be of

---

31 L. Hartman, "ὄνομα," EDNT 2:519–20.
32 G. K. Beale, The Book of Revelation. NIGTC (Grand Rapids: Eerdmans, 1999), 953–56; and Smalley, Revelation, 490–91.
33 This phrase is adapted from John Ortberg, The Me I Want to Be: Becoming God's Best Version of You (Grand Rapids: Zondervan, 2010).
34 See this point explored especially in regard to sexual identity and ethics (both hetero- and same-sex conduct) in Stanton L. Jones and Mark A. Yarhouse, "Anthropology, Sexuality, and Sexual Ethics: The Challenge of Psychology," in Personal Identity in Theological Perspective, eds. R. Lints, et al. (Grand Rapids: Eerdmans, 2006), 118–36.

any earthly good." They are seen as pessimistic escapists, happy to see the culture decay with no investment in what is just or good in today's society. But the teaching of Revelation on discipleship, in the framework of its view of God and his intent for humans and their world, shows that this should not be the case either corporately or individually. Because of its vision of God and of the future, the book calls Christians to stand firm in the present age against the dominant ideology of religious and moral apostasy and bear consistent witness in life and word to the true God. We are called to Christlike living in the real world, to fidelity and gracious outreach, not assimilation or withdrawal or isolation, even in the face of insidious and deadly opposition.[35] We do this in part because the church corporately is "an inaugurated form of the future kingdom of God"[36] on earth. It displays ahead of time what God's redeemed and reconciled human society can look like in pursuing righteousness, joy, and peace among people of diverse backgrounds. And we do this individually because the Savior who knows each of us as his own is transforming us in preparation for a glorious future of communion with him. He calls us to live like him and for him now and engage with others as winsome witnesses for the true and living God, the Almighty, who controls all of history.

---

35 Bauckham, *Theology*, 16–61.
36 Craig A. Blaising and Darrell L. Bock, *Progressive Dispensationalism* (Wheaton, IL: Bridge-Point, 1993), 286; cf. 285–91.

PART 2

Discipleship Today

CHAPTER 18

Knowing What Jesus Knew: Discipleship and the Development of the Christian Mind

J. P. Moreland

It was 10:00 a.m. on a Saturday in early December, and I had just returned home from a late breakfast with friends. As I walked in the front door, I saw my twenty-year-old daughter, Allison, sitting on the living room floor next to the fireplace. It was her junior year at Biola University (where I teach), a mere eighteen miles from our home, and she had come home for the weekend. As I focused on her, she was reading a fairly large book, and tears were streaming down her cheeks.

I asked her what was wrong. "Dad," she said, "I am reading a book on the historical background to the Gospels for Dr. Wilkins's class, and it is by far the best class I have ever had at Biola." I asked her why and she replied, "Dr. Wilkins's lectures, his person, the readings he has assigned have made me feel closer to and understand Jesus more than ever before in my life. I am falling in love with Jesus, thanks to Dr. Wilkins, and I can't stop crying as I draw near to Him by reading about the world He lived in. It makes Him more real."

That was eighteen years ago, and Allison still refers to that class as a turning point in her life. That is the impact Mike Wilkins routinely has on people. He is a brother, friend, colleague, first-rate scholar, a natural born leader, a man full of integrity, and a Jesus lover/follower. And I am in his debt for the impact he had on my daughter. That is why I jumped at the chance to contribute to a book honoring him.

Mike has a big heart, but he also has spent his Christian life loving God with his mind, and my assignment is to honor Mike by further elaborating on this aspect of walking with Jesus. Accordingly, in what follows, I will, first, explain how the current intellectual crisis in the church has harmed us terribly, and I will make clear exactly what is at stake in this crisis. Second, I will briefly sketch out a picture of Jesus as "the smartest man who ever lived," as Dallas Willard used to say repeatedly, as one who knew and used logic quite effectively, and who knew what he was talking about. Finally, I shall close with a list of reasons why we should love God with our minds, and briefly offer some practical advice for improving in this area of the Christian life. Let us begin in earnest, then, and look at the crisis of knowledge that is spewing chaos in Western culture.

THE CURRENT CRISIS OF KNOWLEDGE IN THE WEST

In 1941, Harvard sociologist Pitirim A. Sorokin wrote a book entitled *The Crisis of Our Age*. Sorokin divided cultures into two major types: sensate and ideational. A sensate culture is one in which people only believe in the reality of the physical universe capable of being experienced with the five senses. A sensate culture is secular, *this* worldly, and empirical. By contrast, an ideational culture embraces the sensory world, but goes on to accept the notion that an extra-empirical immaterial reality can be known as well, a reality consisting of God, the soul, immaterial beings, values, purposes, and various abstract objects like numbers and propositions. Sorokin noted that a sensate culture eventually disintegrates because it lacks the intellectual resources necessary to sustain a public and private life conducive of corporate and individual human flourishing. After all, if we can't know anything about values, life after death, God, and so forth, how can we receive solid guidance to lead a life of wisdom and character?

As we move through the early portion of the twenty-first century, it is obvious that the West, including the United States, is sensate. To see this, consider the following. In 1989, the state of California issued a new Science framework to provide guidance for the state's public school science classrooms. In that document, advice is given to teachers about how to handle students who approach them with reservations about the theory of evolution:

> At times some students may insist that certain conclusions of science cannot be true because of certain religious or philosophical beliefs they hold. . . . It is appropriate for the teacher to express in this regard, "I understand that you may have personal reservations about accepting this scientific evidence, but it is scientific knowledge about which there is no reasonable doubt among scientists in their field, and it is my responsibility to teach it because it is part of our common intellectual heritage."[1]

---

1   Cited in Mark Hartwig and P. A. Nelson, *Invitation to Conflict* (Colorado Springs: Access Research Network, 1992), 20.

The real importance of this statement lies not in its promotion of evolution over creation, though that is no small matter in its own right. No, the real danger in the framework's advice resides in the picture of knowledge it presupposes: The only knowledge we can have about reality, and thus, the only claims that deserve the backing of public institutions, is empirical knowledge gained by the hard sciences.

Nonempirical claims—those that can't be tested with the five senses—outside the hard sciences, such as those at the core of ethics, political theory, and religion, are not items of knowledge but, rather, matters of private feeling. Note carefully the words associated with science: *conclusions, evidence, knowledge, no reasonable doubt, intellectual heritage.* These deeply cognitive terms express the view that science and science alone exercises the intellectual right (and responsibility) of defining reality. By contrast, religious claims are described in distinctively non-cognitive language: *beliefs, personal reservations.*

In such a culture we now live and move and have our being. Currently, a three-way worldview struggle rages in our culture among ethical monotheism (especially Christianity), postmodernism, and scientific naturalism. I cannot undertake here a detailed characterization of scientific naturalism, but I want to say a word about its role in shaping the crisis of the West.

Scientific naturalism takes the view that the physical cosmos studied by science is all there is. Scientific naturalism has two central components: a view of reality and a view of how we know things. Regarding reality, scientific naturalism asserts that everything that exists is composed of matter or emerges out of matter when it achieves a suitable complexity. There is no spiritual world, no God, no angels or demons, no life after death, no moral absolutes, no objective purpose to life, no such thing as the kingdom of God. And scientific naturalism claims that physical science is the only, or at least a vastly superior, way of gaining knowledge. Since competence in life depends on knowledge (you can't be competent at selling insurance if you don't know anything about it!), this implies that there just is no such thing as learning to live life competently in the kingdom of God. Thus, spiritual competence which depends on knowledge, including experiential knowledge, is a silly idea, since there is no spiritual or theological knowledge on which to base and develop spiritual competence.

Partly out of a reaction to naturalism, a second worldview—postmodernism—has come on the scene. Like a magnet, it's attracting more and more people, especially those in the arts and the humanities and the leaders of pop culture, by its mesmerizing power into its field of force. Postmodernism is a loose coalition of diverse thinkers from several different academic disciplines, so it is difficult to characterize postmodernism in a way that would be fair to this diversity. Still, it is possible to provide a fairly accurate characterization of postmodernism in general, since its friends and foes understand it well enough to debate its strengths and weaknesses.[2]

As a philosophical standpoint, postmodernism is primarily a reinterpretation of what knowledge is and what counts as knowledge. More broadly, it represents a form of cultural relativism about such things as reality, truth, reason, value, linguistic meaning, the self, and other notions. On a postmodernist view, there is no such thing as objective reality, truth, value, reason and meaning to life. All these are social constructions, creations of linguistic practices and, as such, are relative not to individuals, but to social groups that share a narrative. Roughly, a narrative is a perspective such as Marxism, atheism, or Christianity that is embedded in the group's social and linguistic practices. Nor can there be any such thing as knowledge or direct access to reality. In fact, according to many postmodernists, a claim to have knowledge about something is nothing more than an attempt to exert power over others who don't have that "knowledge."

Philosophical naturalism and postmodernism dominate the power centers of culture—the universities, government, news media, entertainment industry—and they shape the plausibility structure of our culture (the items people are willing to consider as possibly true). And while these two worldviews disagree about many things, they agree about one thing: *There is no such thing as knowledge outside the hard sciences. In particular, ethics, politics, and religion are private matters of opinion and feeling in which no one has any idea whose opinion is right and whose is wrong. Indeed, the very idea that someone is right and someone is wrong in these areas of life is bigoted and intolerant.*

This cultural situation has produced a crisis of knowledge regarding Christianity and theology: Is Christianity a source of knowledge of reality or simply a source of mere true beliefs that must be accepted by a blind act of the will (i.e., faith according to its contemporary understanding)? Do the central teachings of Jesus and, more generally, of the Bible present us with genuine knowledge or not? For example, most people regard some of the central ideas of psychology to count as things we now know. But the main teachings from Scripture about dealing with anxiety and so

---

2 For a helpful introduction to postmodernism, see Joseph Natoli, *A Primer to Postmodernity* (Oxford: Blackwell, 1997).

forth, and growing to have a mature, flourishing life are taken to be mere expressions of faith for those who need that sort of thing.

Why does this matter? Because it is on the basis of knowledge, not mere true belief, that we give people the authority to act in public and to define an aspect of reality. If my dentist told me he had a set of deeply felt beliefs about cavities to which he was really committed, but he did not actually know these beliefs were true, he would lose his job. History teachers, mechanics, doctors, and so forth are given authority to speak and act in their areas of knowledge and to tell us what is real and true in those areas. *If Christianity continues to be viewed as a mere faith tradition and not a knowledge tradition—an attitude that even most Christians currently hold—it will continue to be marginalized and not taken seriously.*

This will happen if we allow the culture to be dominated by opinions and attitudes that reduce the way of Jesus to a mere privatized hobby for those who need that sort of thing. As the great evangelical scholar J. Gresham Machen warned nearly one hundred years ago, "False ideas are the greatest obstacles to the reception of the gospel. We may preach with all the fervor of a reformer and yet succeed only in winning a straggler here and there, if we permit the whole collective thought of the nation or of the world to be controlled by ideas which, by the resistless force of logic, prevent Christianity from being regarded as anything more than a harmless delusion."[3]

Thus, the central issue currently facing the church is not whether Christianity is true. I can speak on a secular campus and announce that I think Christianity is true. That is usually acceptable if I add that this is just my own feelings and private opinion. But if I claim that one can actually know that Christianity is true, saying this is like hitting a golf ball in the shower: It comes right back at you with a frightening force! *So, the central crisis is whether Christianity can be known to be true.* Again, is Christianity a knowledge tradition or a mere true belief tradition? By raising this question, we are forced to take a brief look at what knowledge is and is not. To this issue we now turn.

THE NATURE OF KNOWLEDGE

Given the magnitude of the role knowledge plays in life and discipleship, it is important to get clear on what knowledge is and is not. Much

---

3 Address delivered on September 20, 1912, at the opening of the 101st session of Princeton Theological Seminary. Reprinted in J. Gresham Machen, *What Is Christianity?* (Grand Rapids: Eerdmans, 1951), 162.

confusion abounds today about the nature of knowledge, a confusion that hurts people and prevents them from growing in Christ with the sort of confidence that is their birthright in the Way of Jesus.

A. Three Kinds of Knowledge

There are three kinds of knowledge:

1) **Knowledge by acquaintance**: This happens when we are directly aware of something, e.g., when I see an apple directly before me or pay attention to my inner feelings, I know these things by acquaintance. One does not need a concept of an apple or knowledge of how to use the word "apple" in English to have knowledge by acquaintance with an apple. A baby can see an apple without having the relevant concept or linguistic skills. *Knowledge by acquaintance is sometimes called "simple seeing," being directly aware of something.*

2) **Propositional knowledge**: This is knowledge that an entire proposition is true. For example, knowledge that "the object there is an apple" requires having a concept of an apple and knowing that the object under consideration satisfies the concept. *Propositional knowledge is justified true belief—it is believing something that is true on the basis of adequate grounds.*

3) **Know-how**: *This is the ability to do certain things*, e.g., to use apples for certain purposes. We may distinguish mere know-how from genuine know-how or skill. The latter is know-how based on knowledge and insight and is characteristic of skilled practitioners in some field. Mere know-how is the ability to engage in the correct behavioral movements, say by following the steps in a manual, with little or no knowledge of why one is performing these movements. Before I elaborate on these three sorts of knowledge, I want to place a general feature of knowledge before your mind.

B. Certainty, Confidence, and Simply Knowing

Knowledge does not require rational certainty. There is a difference between psychological and rational certainty. Psychological certainty means that one feels settled, unwavering, and does not pray, "Our Father who probably art in heaven!" Psychological certainty is to some extent a function of one's childhood, one's ability to attach to others, and the experiences one has had of God. Rational certainty is quite different. Indeed, one can be psychologically certain without being rationally certain.

Something is rationally certain if it is utterly impossible that one be mistaken about it. If one has rational certainty about something, say, "I exist," then the denial of that ("I do not exist") is a logical contradiction. But the statement that "Jesus was not raised from the dead," while wrong, is not a logical contradiction. Thus, one does not have rational certainty about the resurrection, but one could still know it happened since knowledge does not require certainty. Indeed, few things can be known with certainty. Among them are that I exist, that basic principles of math are true (2+2=4), and that the fundamental laws of logic are correct (something cannot be true and false at the same time in the same sense). That's about it. But knowledge does not require certainty as Paul's remark in Ephesians 5:5 makes clear (emphasis added): "For this you know *with certainty*, that immoral or impure person or covetous man, who is an idolater, has an inheritance in the kingdom of Christ and God."[4] If knowledge just is a sort of certainty, then "knowledge with certainty" would be redundant.

This is no small point. Among other things, it means that one's degree of knowledge can grow or diminish over time. It also means that one can know something and, at the same time, acknowledge that one might be wrong about it. Indeed, the presence of doubt, the awareness of disagreements among experts, or the acknowledgment of arguments and evidence contrary to one's view on something do not necessarily mean that one does not have knowledge of the thing in question. When we seek knowledge of God, specific biblical texts, morality, and a host of other things, we should not assume that our search requires reaching a state with no doubt, no plausible counterarguments, no possibility of being mistaken. When people believe that knowledge *requires* certainty, if they aren't completely certain about something, say the existence of God or that God answers prayer, they will think that they don't know these things. But an absence of knowledge does not follow from an absence of certainty. People can know something without being 100% certain they are correct! In turn, the idea that one does not know something unless he/she is certain will lead to a lack of confidence and courage regarding one's ability to count on the things one knows. I am not suggesting that certainty is a bad thing—not for a second. I'm merely noting that it is not required.

C. In Defense of Logic

We have seen that understanding the nature of knowledge is important for developing a Christian mind that constituted part of our discipleship

---

4 All Scripture translations are NASB unless otherwise noted.

unto the Lord Jesus. But it is also important to note that cultivating some basic skills in logic is also essential to developing a Christian mind. Logic comes from the very nature of God himself. Its employment need not be cold and impersonal; it can be expressed through story and narrative, as C. S. Lewis's works of fiction nicely illustrate, and Jesus used logic with "the common man" every bit as much as he did with the "wise and intelligent." In what follows, I shall unpack these assertions by doing two things: present a primer on logic and God, and explain and illustrate Jesus's skill in using logic.[5]

1. A Primer on God and Logic

The Universal Validity of the Laws of Logic. These fundamental laws are true principles governing reality and thought, and are assumed by Scripture. As noted above, some claim they are arbitrary Western constructions, but this is false. The basic laws of logic govern all of reality and thought and are known to be true for at least two reasons: (1) They are intuitively obvious and self-evident. Once one understands a basic law of logic (see below) one can simply see that it is true. (2) Those who deny them use these principles in their denial, demonstrating that those laws are unavoidable and it is self-refuting to deny them. I will support and illustrate this claim below when we look at the three fundamental laws of logic.

God and the Laws of Logic. The basic laws of logic are neither arbitrary inventions of God nor principles that exist completely outside God's being. Obviously, the laws of logic are not like the laws of nature. God may violate the latter (say, suspend gravity), but he cannot violate the former. Those laws are rooted in God's own nature and govern his own mind. Indeed, some scholars think that the passage "In the beginning was the Word (*logos*)" (John 1:1) is accurately translated "In the beginning was Logic (a divine, rational mind)." For example, even God cannot exist and not exist at the same time; he cannot both love and hate Jesus Christ; there cannot be one God, no God and many gods. And even God cannot validly believe that red is a color and red is not a color or that 2+2=73. Divine omniscience is defined as the idea that for all truths, God knows and believes each one, and for all falsehoods, God knows each is false and does not believe it.

---

5 For more on the insights to follow, see J. P. Moreland, *Love Your God with All Your Mind* (Colorado Springs: NavPress, 1997), ch. 5; idem., *Kingdom Triangle* (Grand Rapids: Zondervan, 2007), chs. 3 and 4.

When someone correctly says that God need not behave "logically," they are using the term in a loose sense to mean "the sensible thing from my point of view." Often, God does not act in ways that people understand or judge to be what they would do in the circumstances. But God never behaves illogically in the proper sense. He does not violate in his being or thought the fundamental laws of logic.

The Three "Laws of Thought." There are three fundamental laws of logic. Suppose P is any indicative sentence, say, "It is raining."

The law of identity: P is P.

The law of non-contradiction: P is not non-P.

The law of excluded middle: Either P or non-P.

The law of identity says that if a statement such as "It is raining" is true, then the statement is true. More generally, it says that the statement P is the same thing as itself and is different from everything else. Applied to all of reality, the law of identity says that everything is itself and not something else.

The law of noncontradiction says that a statement such as "It is raining" cannot be both true and false in the same sense. Of course, it could be raining in Missouri and not raining in Arizona, but the principle says that it cannot be raining and not raining at the same time in the same place.

The law of excluded middle says that a statement such as "It is raining" is either true or false. There is no other alternative. Let's apply our understanding of these laws of logic to the issue of their unavoidability (even for those who deny them) and the self-refuting nature of their rejection. For example, consider someone who says, "The laws of logic are arbitrary imperialistic Western constructions that should be rejected." For ease of exposition, let's call this statement "P." If someone asserts P, they assert P and not some other assertion, say Q. And they want their listeners/readers to grasp P as their assertion. Otherwise, why would they take the time to assert P?

While lecturing at Miami of Ohio, a student actually asserted P to me, and I responded by threatening to call the campus police on her because she was an animal torturer. With disbelief on her face, she asked where I got that idea. I said that since on her view, P is not P, then her P ("logic is arbitrary and should be rejected") was actually Q (not P) to me ("this woman tortures animals"). Her assertion was, well, her assertion! And it was not "P and non-P (i.e., Q)" at the same time! And her statement was either true or false (she clearly meant for it to be taken as true) but not both. This would have become evident if I had responded, "Good. I'm glad to see that you think it is false that logic is arbitrary and should be rejected (i.e., non-P)!

2. Jesus the Logician

In his masterful article "Jesus as Logician," Dallas Willard correctly notes that while Jesus did not teach a *theory* of logic or *explicitly* call attention to logical forms, his skill as a logician resides in his accurate, powerful and effective use of logic in his teaching and debates.[6] To see this, let's look at some examples.

Consider Matthew 22:23–33. Here Jesus has brought his disciples into what today would be comparable to a colloquium meeting of the Stanford and UC Berkeley graduate religious studies faculty and their graduate students. These professors disagree profoundly over the reality of life after death with the Pharisees accepting and the Sadducees rejecting that reality. They bring in Jesus—a man without an accredited graduate degree—to see if, at the very least, they can discover which side of the issue he is on and, hopefully, they can even make him look stupid so his followers will leave him and study under them. This is a high-tension university setting, and Jesus's presence there shows he was at home among intellectuals as well as among ordinary folk.

The Sadducees raise one version of a *reductio ad absurdum* argument—in this case, an indirect proof—against Jesus. In such an argument you grant for the sake of argument that a premise is true—in Matthew 22, it is the Sadducees' opponent's premise (the Pharisees' and, as it turns out, Jesus's view that there is such a thing as life after death), and show that if the premise is true, it generates a logical contradiction, and conclude that the granted premise is false (there is no life after death). Here is a formal statement of an indirect proof (where "P" and "Q" are complete, well-formed sentences):

Prove not-P

1. P (assumption for indirect proof)
2. .
3. .
4. .
5. Q

---

6 Dallas Willard, "Jesus as Logician," *Christian Scholar's Review* 28.4 (1999): 605–14.

6. not-Q
7. Therefore, not-P

By granting the truth of P, a contradiction is generated in lines 5 and 6 (when combined they give us Q and not-Q), and thus, P must be false (which is the same as saying that not-P is true).

The argument in Matthew 22 is also an example of a dilemma syllogism (see below)[7]: Formally, the Sadducees argue thusly:

1. P (there is life after death)
2. If P, then either Q (adultery is permissible in the afterlife) or R (polygamy is permissible in the afterlife).
3. Not-Q (adultery is not permissible, period) and not-R (polygamy is not permissible, period).
4. Therefore, not-P (there is no life after death).

Grasping the heart of this syllogism, Jesus skillfully notes that the either/or dilemma his opponents have placed on him (premise 2: either adultery or polygamy is permissible in the afterlife) both make an assumption: There is marriage in the afterlife. They argue: If there is marriage in the afterlife, then either there is adultery or polygamy. Jesus denies that there is marriage in the afterlife (Matt. 22:39), and in one simple step, he undermines the dilemma (either adultery or polygamy) they have raised against life after death. Because he recognized this form of argumentation, Jesus went directly for premise 2 and undermined it. The result? The Sadducees no longer had a cogent argument.

Here's one more example. In Mark 11:27–33, Jesus himself uses a dilemma syllogism. Put formally, such a syllogism goes like this:

1. If P, then Q.
2. If R, then S.
3. Either P or R.
4. Therefore, either Q or S.

In context, the religious leaders are challenging Jesus's authority, and he asks, "Was the baptism of John from heaven or from men?" His argument is this: (1) "If John's baptism is from heaven, then the critics ought to believe John's teaching about Jesus," and "If John's baptism is from men, then the critics are in danger from the people." (2) Either "John's

---

7 See Norman Geisler and Ronald Brooks, *Come Let Us Reason* (Grand Rapids: Baker, 1990), 68–73.

baptism is from heaven" or "John's baptism is from men." Then, (3) "The critics should either believe John's teaching or place themselves in danger from the people." Realizing that Jesus had successfully placed them on the horns of a nasty dilemma, they responded by saying "We don't know from where John's baptism came."

To my mind, Jesus was the greatest thinker who ever lived. And while he did not come to develop a theory about logic or to teach logic as a field of study, it is clear that he was adept at employing logical forms and laws in his thinking and reasoning. We who are his followers should go and do likewise.

3. Jesus and Knowledge

A major goal of the Christian life is not simply to believe what Jesus believed; rather, it is to come to know what Jesus knew. Remember, knowledge gives people confidence and authority that mere belief does not. And it is because Jesus knew (and not merely believed) what he was talking about that we ought to accept his teachings, and work on coming to know them for ourselves. Knowledge can come from many sources: logic, evidence, experience, the testimony of the Holy Spirit, special revelation. But whatever its source, knowledge itself was important to Jesus and should be to us.

Jesus and his disciples in imitation of him placed a great emphasis on having knowledge and not mere belief. Below is a table with a very brief sampling of their assertions (italics are mine):

The Evangelists	"Inasmuch as many have undertaken to compile an account of the things accomplished among us, just as they were handed down to us by those who from the beginning were eyewitnesses and servants of the word, it seemed fitting for me as well, having investigated everything carefully from the beginning, to write *it* out for you in consecutive order, most excellent Theophilus; so that you may *know* the exact truth about the things you have been taught." (Luke 1:1–4)
	"This is the disciple who is testifying to these things and wrote these things, and we *know* that his testimony is true." (John 21:24)

Statements by Jesus	"You will *know* them by their fruits." (Matt. 7:16)
	"'But so that you may *know* that the Son of Man has authority on earth to forgive sins'—then He said to the paralytic, 'Get up, pick up your bed and go home.'" (Matt. 9:6)
	"Jesus answered them, 'To you it has been granted to *know* the mysteries of the kingdom of heaven, but to them it has not been granted.'" (Matt. 13:11)
	". . . and you will *know* the truth, and the truth will make you free." (John 8:32)
	"To him the doorkeeper opens, and the sheep hear his voice, and he calls his own sheep by name and leads them out. When he puts forth all his own, he goes ahead of them, and the sheep follow him because they *know* his voice." (John 10:3–4)
	"If I do not do the works of My Father, do not believe Me; but if I do them, though you do not believe Me, believe the works, so that you may *know* and *understand* that the Father is in Me, and I in the Father." (John 10:37–38)
The Later New Testament	"We *know* that no one who is born of God sins; but He who was born of God keeps him, and the evil one does not touch him. We *know* that we are of God, and that the whole world lies in *the power of the evil one*. And we *know* that the Son of God has come, and has given us understanding so that we may *know* Him who is true; and we are in Him who is true, in His Son Jesus Christ. This is the true God and eternal life." (1 John 5:18–20)

Obviously, I could go on and on. But these texts are representative samples that demonstrate the importance of knowledge in Christianity. But what about faith? Isn't it crucial to Christianity? After all, Hebrews 11:6 says, "And without faith it is impossible to please Him, for he who comes to God must believe that He is and that He is a rewarder of those who seek Him." And aren't knowledge and faith polar opposites? If you have knowledge of something, you can't at the same time have faith in it. And if you have faith in something, you don't need knowledge.

This skewed view of faith is both harmful and widely embraced by the culture at large, and it is ubiquitous among Christians. This fact was made evident to me years ago when I was giving an evangelistic message on "Evidence That Christianity Is True" in a high school gym in Synecdoche, New York. There were around a thousand people there, and it was evident that a lot of unbelievers had come. After my talk, there were two microphones with a line of people leading up to them in order to ask me questions. From the nature of their questions, it was obvious that the first two individuals were unbelievers. The third person, a dear lady, was a Christian. She stepped up to the mike and said this: "Dr. Moreland, I am troubled by your message." Puzzled, I asked her why. She continued, "If you prove there is a God, there will be no room for faith." Even though I have heard this sort of thing numerous times, it still shocks me every time I hear it, and that evening was no exception. While I responded graciously and explained her confusion about faith, inside I was thinking, "Maybe we should pray that archaeologists and scientists will find all kinds of apparent inaccuracies and serious problems in the Bible so our faith will have a chance to grow even stronger!"

What was the problem here? My dear sister had adopted the contemporary view of faith, viz., faith is a choice of the will to believe something in the absence of reasonable considerations for or against that choice. On this view, faith is a bare act of the will that has nothing to do with reasoning. But there are two problems with this view. First, it is impossible. We do not have direct free will over what we believe, so we cannot simply choose to believe something on the spot, and it will happen. You could not right now choose to believe that a pink unicorn is flying over your head, that $2+2=47\frac{1}{2}$, that cats are the same thing as tomatoes, or that George Washington was a space alien and not the first president of the United States. Even if you had a huge incentive to believe these things right now (say, I offered you $10,000 if you could choose to believe one of these things), you still couldn't do it. We have indirect control over our beliefs. If I want to believe more strongly in prayer, I can't just choose to do that, and it happens on the spot. But I can undertake a regimen of reading on prayer, asking all my Christian friends if they have seen answers to prayer and how they handle unanswered prayer, experimenting with different forms of prayer, and so on. Eventually, I would find my faith in prayer becoming stronger. Here's the key point: *Faith and knowledge are not opposite ends of a line, such that as one grows the other must diminish.*

The second problem with this view of faith is this: *It is unbiblical and lacks common sense.* A better biblical definition of faith is that *it is a confidence or trust in something or someone based on what one knows about the object of faith.* This does not mean we can always figure out why God is asking us to do something or where he is leading in a situation—after all, God's ways are higher than ours!—and it doesn't mean that what God does or does not choose to do will always make sense to us. After all, our perspective is so limited compared to God's. But it does mean that when we step out in faith and take a risk for God, we are warranted in doing so because of the things we know about God already. Consider Abraham's intention to sacrifice Isaac (Gen. 22:1–18). Isaac was horribly confused and did not know why God was asking him to do this or what any of the situation meant for the future of Israel. But he was warranted in stepping out on faith, even though he did not know why or what was going to happen because he already knew enough about God to trust him even in a dark time. Indeed, Hebrews 11:19 says that Abraham knew that God could raise Isaac from the dead if necessary, and that this knowledge was part of why he could take such a risk.

Further, this second definition is just plain commonsense. Consider the experience of buying a car. A price is set, but you know absolutely nothing about the car and have no idea at all if it is worth the price. It would be both foolish and pretty hard simply to choose to have faith in the car and buy it. By contrast, the more you know about the car, the more you can have an appropriate trust or confidence in it in accordance with the car's worthiness to be trusted. In general, the more we know about something (or someone), the more we can place an appropriate faith in that thing (or person) in accordance with our knowledge of its trustworthiness. *So faith is built on knowledge; it is not a polar opposite of knowledge.*

FINAL REFLECTIONS

If you have damaged emotions or an addicted will, it will hinder your ability to grow in Christ unless you colabor with the Holy Spirit, using all the effort you can, to overcome these problems. Why don't we think this way about our minds? Surely, if we have an undeveloped mind, we can't think very clearly, and so on, this will impede our growth in Christ just as much as inadequacies in our other faculties. We are told explicitly to love God with our minds, to learn what we believe and why, to learn to think biblically and to know the things God wants us, not merely to believe, but to know. And we are to learn to tell the difference between a good and a bad argument.

Quite frankly, as a community, we are pathetic at this last point. Case in point: I attended a service once, in which a friend of mine spoke about condom distribution in the public schools. He was very informed about the issue. He made very clear that he was against this practice, but he offered a critique of a favorite evangelical argument against condom distribution that showed it was a bad argument for a good conclusion. Well, he practically got lynched. I stayed after the service and listened as person after person accused him of promoting condom distribution in the schools. These people could not love God with their minds as they should, because they could not make a simple distinction between being for something vs. showing that an argument for what you are for is a bad argument.

God help us. We evangelicals have substituted mere belief for knowledge and the result is that it is simply irrelevant to the Christian life that one learns to think well and to gain knowledge of various things central to Christianity. Consequently, we are a marginalized community. As Dallas Willard put it, "Belief cannot reliably govern life and action except in its proper connection with knowledge and with the truth and evidence knowledge involves."[8]

With this in mind, I want to offer a summary list of reasons you can use to persuade others (and maybe yourself!) that we are to cultivate as rational a Christian mind as possible. Remember, knowledge puffs up. But the solution is not ignorance—it's humility.

1. We are commanded by Jesus to love God with all we have, and he explicitly includes the mind in that command (Matt. 22:37–39). The Christian life is holistic and includes all we have and are. We can't leave out the mind because we are lazy or feel uneducated. Within our limits of ability and other commitments, we are to develop our Christian minds as best we can.
2. One reason we should follow and internalize the teachings of Jesus is that he *knew* what he was talking about. Jesus had a worldview he *knew* to be true, and as his followers, we are to *know* and, therefore, act with authority from that knowledge.
3. We are told that we have the privilege and responsibility to defend our faith (cf. I Peter 3:15; Jesus regularly told people to believe

---

8 Dallas Willard, *Knowing Christ Today* (New York: HarperOne, 2009), 3.

him because of the evidence of his works [miracles] and not just take his word for things). Apologetics is a ministry of caring for people by helping them with intellectual difficulties in coming to or growing in Christ. If we don't know why we believe, this crucial way of loving people will not be available to us.

4. Knowledge aids us in discerning the difference between truth and error. Of course, we start with biblical knowledge, but go beyond that. Philosophical and cultural knowledge are important in this respect. To illustrate the importance of philosophy, one could argue as follows: What does the New Testament teach about the proper duties God has given to the state? You can read the New Testament hundreds of times and not know the answer without a simple philosophical distinction between negative and positive rights. A negative right (e.g., to health care) is a right that places a duty on the state to protect me from harm or discrimination as I seek to get healthcare on my own. The government doesn't owe me anything but to protect me from inappropriate blockage. A positive right (e.g., to healthcare) means that the government has a duty to give it to me, to provide me with healthcare. Negative rights favor a minimal government, positive rights an expansive government. Armed with this distinction, when one looks at the key New Testament texts about government—especially Romans 13:1–7, 1 Timothy 2:1–2, and 1 Peter 2:13–14—it can be argued that they teach a minimalist view of government that is to protect negative rights and not to provide positive rights. Of course, others may offer counterarguments to this conclusion or reason that the issue of the New Testament view of government is too complex to be decided by brief comments is a small set of verses. Whatever the case, the philosophical distinction between positive and negative rights is very important in the dialogue.

5. Knowledge aids us in being better parents and grandparents. Because I had earnestly studied a Christian worldview and the cultural climate, when something came on the news, was presented in my children's public school classroom, or was embedded in television, music, or a movie, I was prepared to spot the error, ask my girls good questions, and have a nondefensive conversation with them about what they were "learning." To this day, my daughters (in their mid-thirties) have thanked me for this. Now I have five grandchildren, and we start the cycle all over again!

How does one grow a well-developed Christian mind? First, read, read, read. You have to find an hour two or three times a week to read, and when you do, read some books that stretch your thinking. Two especially good websites that have brief, downloadable helpful readings are Stand to Reason (www.str.org) and Reasonable Faith (www.reasonable-faith.org). Also, listen to various forms of audio information, especially while driving in your car. I recommend you don't listen to sermons because they are not usually very intellectually stimulating. I recommend you check out Mars Hill Audio (www.marshillaudio.org). Don't accept Christian slogans. Instead, ask questions, express your doubts, and get answers.

A lot more could be said here, but I have tried to honor Mike Wilkins by contending for a set of values he has embodied for several decades, and I hope that in some small measure I have succeeded.

CHAPTER 19

Follow Me: Discipleship and Soul Care

Judy Ten Elshof

When I interact with Talbot School of Theology students in the spiritual formation classes I teach, I interact with disciples of Jesus who have reaped all they could from the discipleship opportunities they took hold of in their churches. I see students with a heartfelt reverence for God's word and many students who have memorized large portions of Scripture and bring passages up as they respond to what I teach. I see those who have given themselves to seminary training because they want to equip the people in their ministries, so they in turn can minister to and evangelize others. These are people who want to make a difference for the kingdom.[1]

But so often these same students express confusion about the soul care content of my classes and about the need for intentional prayer, the telling of their stories, and the impact of their family history on their relational experiences. Truth be told, I am confused about how Christians can think about their own discipleship narrative without thinking about foundational pillars of soul care like the development of trust, power, and identity, and the internal world of one's emotions. In my mind, soul care and the discipleship growth attained by my students need to develop hand in hand and remain united if Christians truly desire to follow Jesus in an intimate and dynamic manner, becoming the "citizens of heaven" they are (Phil. 3:20).[2] When we choose to trust our Savior and let the Spirit lead us into the vulnerable places of our hearts, we participate in authentic discipleship; we can pray as David did when he prayed, "Search me, O God, and know my heart; test me and know my anxious thoughts. See if there is any offensive way in me, and lead me in the way everlasting" (Ps. 139:23–24, NIV). By authentic discipleship, I mean following Jesus wherever he chooses to take us and allowing our Teacher to transform us into the people he made us to be. Scripture shows us in John 21 that Jesus invited Peter into vulnerability as part of their discipleship relationship.

---

1 I would like to acknowledge Brandon Taylor, a graduate of the Institute for Spiritual Formation with a MA in Spiritual Formation and Soul Care, who did the research and editing of this chapter.

2 All Scripture translations are ESV unless otherwise noted.

We must choose to let Jesus, through the work of the Holy Spirit, take us into our internal world as well so we do not lapse into a shell of discipleship that lacks the intimacy and dynamism that is available to us.

WHAT IS SOUL CARE, AND WHY IS IT IMPORTANT FOR DISCIPLESHIP?

Unfortunately, many discipleship programs in evangelical churches leave Christians feeling relationally empty and alone. The evangelical church in the West approached discipleship in a new way in the mid-twentieth century with the advent of new communication technology and removed many of the distinctives of discipleship that made it organic and capable of character change. I am not saying that the classic discipleship programs of the twentieth century did not achieve what they set out to accomplish. Because orthodox beliefs became cornerstones of evangelical spirituality, many discipleship programs focused on the intellectual component of participants' faith.[3] Programs concentrated on disciplined Bible study and Scripture memorization to make basic training in gospel truths and evangelism available to the largest number of Christians. But the discipleship model that shaped these programs compromised engagements with participants' hearts in order to streamline the material and achieve measurable results by the end of the six-month or nine-month program.[4]

This is not the paradigm of discipleship that we see with Jesus and his followers in the Gospels. The discipleship the apostles experienced impacted every area of their lives and clarified the vocational call God had on each of their lives. And discipleship was a journey that persisted and continued to develop even after Jesus had ascended into heaven. Discipleship is packaged into a program in many churches but is not presented as it was to the apostles. It was not implied that the apostles had the freedom to step away from discipleship if they stopped participating in Jesus's lessons; nor was it implied that the end of a program marked one's certification as a disciple the way it is sometimes done in churches.[5] Discipleship was a lifelong journey for the people who followed Jesus during Jesus's ministry.

I grant that the connection between this vision of discipleship and my expertise in soul care is not readily apparent to most people who have engaged in deliberate discipleship. I have to overcome skepticism and suspicion from

---

3   Dallas Willard, "Discipleship," in *The Oxford Handbook of Evangelical Theology*, ed. G. R. McDermott (Oxford: Oxford University Press, 2010), 236–46, http://www.dwillard.org/articles/artview.asp?artID=134.
4   Bill Hull, *The Complete Book of Discipleship: On Being and Making Followers of Christ* (Colorado Springs: NavPress, 2006), 18.
5   Hull, *The Complete Book of Discipleship*, 36.

many of my students when I teach on soul care because they do not see soul care spelled out in the Bible. Therefore, I think it is worth explaining my terms here in order to minimize confusion throughout the rest of the chapter.

David Benner distills things very nicely in his book *Care of Souls,* and I am grateful for the way he connects soul care to Christianity's understanding of personhood. The foundational assertion that makes Benner's definitions so helpful for this discussion is that soul care addresses the nurturing and development of the whole person.[6] When I refer to soul care in this chapter, I am not addressing some ethereal segment of disciples' being that is detached from their jobs, the bills they have to pay, or the recreational activities they love. It is exactly the opposite. When I speak about caring for souls I am trying to get at the core of disciples so that the totality of their persons can thrive in Jesus's love and be conformed to his likeness. As Benner says, "soul care that is worthy of its name should always nurture and care for the person's inner psychospiritual life while attending to the ways in which this life is lived and influenced by physical and external realities."[7] Discipleship that maximizes soul care should make itself known through people who can describe the way Jesus meets them in the personal particularities of their daily life.

> The **soul** refers to the whole person, including the body, but with a particular focus on the inner world of thinking, feeling, and willing.[8]

> *Soul care* refers to the care of persons in their totality, with particular attention to their inner lives. This can never be accomplished by ignoring a person's physical existence or the external world of behavior. Properly understood, soul care nurtures the inner life and guides the expression of this inner life through the body of external behavior.[9]

> *The biblical nature of persons* emphasizes first and foremost their essential unity of being. The possibility of breaking a person down into component parts was alien to the ancient Hebrew mentality, which was concerned with grasping the totality. The basis of Old Testament psychology is that persons in their totality stand in relation to God and can only be understood in the light of this relationship.[10]

---

6 David G. Benner, *Care of Souls: Revisioning Christian Nurture and Counsel* (Grand Rapids: Baker, 1998), 22.
7 Benner, *Care of Souls*, 63.
8 Benner, *Care of Souls*, 22.
9 Benner, *Care of Souls*, 22.
10 Benner, *Care of Souls*, 52–53.

Noticing the small ways one experiences God's presence or developing one's ability to identify the ways one can follow Jesus in daily life are not the marks of a realized disciple—in fact, no one ever is a realized disciple. But disciples who are participating in a dynamic discipleship journey with Jesus by the Spirit often report these particularities because following Jesus pervades their entire life and being. The soul is the organizing factor that incorporates all the parts of the self, including the physical, moral, relational, emotional, and cognitive. Therefore, soul care maximizes discipleship because it unlocks the totality of a person's soul to God's work. Discipleship no longer triggers only the parts of Christians that enable growth in Bible knowledge or moral control while the disciple subconsciously keeps the other parts of their soul locked up and dormant. Growth in Christlikeness extends beyond one's outward behavior or command of Scripture for those who receive genuine soul care because the profound experience of God's presence at the core of their person changes them deeply.[11]

Soul care changes people by bringing healing to the places of one's internal world where one feels hurt, broken, and alone. God and his church care for souls by offering gifts of acceptance and compassion in the moments when souls are vulnerable and exposed for who they truly are. As you might have experienced when you feel exposed, these moments often feel threatening and are filled with worry and anxiety for those of us who need care. As such, it takes effort and deliberate participation in one's own soul care to really experience the healing God offers through the embodied companionship of Christian brothers and sisters. But this participation is not an optional part of discipleship. These obstacles must be overcome if we desire to grow and experience God's love in a deeper way. Psychologists Henry Cloud and John Townsend assert that large areas of growth are forfeited if we do not present all of ourselves to God and allow the vulnerable parts of our hearts to be exposed: "We need to experience all of our souls, whether good, bad or broken; otherwise what is not brought into the light of God's love and relationship cannot be matured, healed and integrated into the rest of our character."[12] This embodied participation in transformation is a foundational Christian tenant (2 Cor. 4:11). We cannot escape being conformed to the world or have our minds renewed if we do not present all of ourselves to God (Rom.

---

11   Hull, *The Complete Book of Discipleship,* 156.
12   Henry Cloud and John Townsend, *How People Grow: What the Bible Reveals about Personal Growth* (Grand Rapids: Zondervan, 2004), 151.

12:2). The trick is overcoming our fear of being exposed as failures or of being judged as filthy, because we will suppress those vulnerable parts of ourselves out of fear. That suppression will make us incapable of deliberately presenting our full selves to God.

THE HARD WORK OF SOUL CARE

According to theologian Bruce Demarest, other believers help us experience all of our souls.[13] Allowing a brother or sister to know us truly is hard work when we bump against the parts of ourselves that feel weak or perhaps unlovable. But that hard work can pay off in feelings of security and safety with another Christian when they love and accept us in our weakness and vulnerability. This compassionate response to our vulnerabilities, first from another brother or sister and then from ourselves, is the first step in seeing our weaknesses become strengths in Christ and testimonies to God's mercy and faithfulness.

Traditional evangelical discipleship may also have a strong interpersonal component to it in the form of teachers for Bible study and mentors. But Demarest is quick to contrast the aims of soul care and the discipleship [programs? approaches?] he saw in the late twentieth century.[14] A growing disciple in the mainstream evangelical tradition was one who was building up their knowledge of the Bible and their understanding of how to live as a Christian through committed study and listening to the wisdom and encouragement offered by mentors and accountability partners. They were doing good, honest work to construct a competent foundation for their Christian lives. But Demarest contrasts soul care and this approach to discipleship because there is a unique deconstructive element to soul care that seeks to break down detrimental ways of thinking and feeling that hinder one's growth in Jesus. It is not an attempt to teach and empower, as if that form of growth alone enables Christians to "power through" the areas of their spiritual life where they are stuck. Soul care is at its best when the Spirit of God, often through others, convicts us or uncovers the areas where we come up short in the Christian life so we can see that Jesus is still for us and accepts us:

> Soul-care searches out the hindrances to prayer, obstacles to
> intimacy with Christ, and responsiveness to the Spirit's leading.

---

13 Bruce Demarest, *Satisfy Your Soul: Restoring the Heart of Christian Spirituality* (Colorado Springs: NavPress, 1999), 199.
14 Demarest, *Satisfy Your Soul*, 190.

> Spiritual helpers allow the life of Christ in them to flow into other Christians to bless, empower, and release the good seed of faith and love. Some discipleship programs strive to form the Christian from the "outside in." Soul-care, on the other hand, seeks to form the life from the "inside out." . . . Soul-care deals with foundational issues of the heart, recognizing that dysfunction at the core negatively affects everything the disciple does.[15]

Forming life from the "outside in," as Demarest puts it, requires the disciples to hold still, face the pain and brokenness, to confess the ways they have failed, and then invites them in silence to notice these small movements of God that have come to the surface. With soul care, there is no outrunning our failures and brokenness with service or growth in biblical knowledge. When it comes down to it, soul care makes a priority out of stopping our activities so we can face and find redemption for our failures and vulnerabilities as Christians.

This is a definite departure from the familiar cultural script of developing our strengths but it's something that we desperately need as we all participate in the discipleship that is simply following Jesus where he is inviting us to go. Soul care and the strengths of traditional evangelical discipleship that build our foundation in biblical truth are a powerful combination in the hands of God. But we live and have grown up in a world that demands success and teaches us to depend on our strengths. Consequently, we are reticent to allow others to be present with us in our emotional vulnerability and pain because we feel that something incredibly private and embarrassing is being exposed. We tend to just shut down and resist the uncomfortable tension of facing our vulnerability on our own or through soul care. Thankfully, Christian discipleship does not conform to the world's race because the way of Jesus embraces our vulnerabilities and is tender with our failures.

Because our spontaneous instinct is to resist the discomfort that comes with facing our vulnerabilities, entering into such sensitive and sacred places with brothers and sisters in Christ takes practice and requires compassion from soul care providers who give out of the immense compassion they received in their own weakness. The saints who hold their brothers and sisters in their true vulnerabilities and accept them as beloved children of God know that soul care is slow and inefficient by its very nature. There is no rushing the work of God in someone's heart or

---

15　Demarest, *Satisfy Your Soul*, 196–97.

someone's development of trust and willingness to go to those places in their heart. But in patience and stillness we can see the beauty God has bestowed on each person:

> Soul-care follows no fixed formula (other than the rule of authoritative Scripture through the transforming work of the Holy Spirit). It respects the God-created uniqueness of each believer. Like a one-of-a-kind snowflake, each disciple is specially gifted, and each has a special calling from God on his life. We must minister to the disciple in his or her God-created uniqueness . . . [and] recognize that people of varying dispositions relate to God differently.[16]

I sincerely doubt whether the modern and widespread trends of evangelical discipleship place enough importance on our God-created uniqueness to personalize the discipleship training for each believer. If given the choice between slowly searching alongside an individual who is learning to find God in the hidden places of their heart and leading a discipleship program that offers growth in Bible knowledge to twenty or more adults, which would the typical evangelical pastor or theology student assume is better? According to the recent evangelical tradition, the pastor and seminary student would seldom choose discipling one over teaching many.

Before he ascended into heaven, the Lord Jesus "taught, trained and nurtured his twelve disciples according to their individual needs."[17] It becomes particularly apparent that individual attention was incredibly important to Jesus at the conclusion of John's Gospel, where we see that three of Jesus's four conversations after his resurrection are directed toward individuals—Mary Magdalene, Thomas, and Peter—and focus on meeting them in their internal turmoil and vulnerability. When Jesus has vanquished death and proven himself to be the Son of God, he does not charge ahead into the new covenant and force his friends to cheer up and run after him. The resurrected Jesus moves toward his hurting followers and cares for them. Jesus first appearance after the resurrection is made to comfort a weeping woman who was overcome by the prospect that his body has been taken (John 20:11–18). Then he offers to meet Thomas's individual, but rather disturbing, demand to stick his hands in Jesus wounds so that one disciple would believe (John 20:24–28) . And finally he turns his focus on Peter and specifically leads their conversation so

---

16 Demarest, *Satisfy Your Soul*, 197.
17 Demarest, *Satisfy Your Soul*, 197.

that it redeems Peter's threefold betrayal (John 21:1–23). These individuals are still weighed down by the feelings and the pain connected to Jesus's crucifixion when Jesus comes to them. And Jesus meets them there, especially in the cases of Peter and Thomas where he references their words and actions as he talks to them individually. But John 21 is worth an in-depth examination because Jesus perfectly weaves soul care and a call to discipleship together in one loving moment with Peter.

EXEMPLIFYING SOUL CARE: JESUS'S RESTORATION OF PETER IN JOHN 21

The interaction between Jesus and Peter at the end of John's Gospel is a passage we ruminate on quite frequently in my department at Talbot. There is a vivid tension in the passage between Jesus's love for and commitment to Peter and the stark reality of Peter's failure. It has really allowed many of us to take steps toward opening up to Jesus's embrace as we ponder an encounter with Jesus while worrying about our own failures. But as I have been preparing for this chapter, I have found that this passage has volumes to say about the presence of soul care in discipleship.

> After this Jesus revealed himself again to the disciples by the Sea of Tiberias, and he revealed himself in this way. Simon Peter, Thomas (called the Twin), Nathanael of Cana in Galilee, the sons of Zebedee, and two others of his disciples were together. Simon Peter said to them, "I am going fishing." They said to him, "We will go with you." They went out and got into the boat, but that night they caught nothing.

> Just as day was breaking, Jesus stood on the shore; yet the disciples did not know that it was Jesus. Jesus said to them, "Children, do you have any fish?" They answered him, "No." He said to them, "Cast the net on the right side of the boat, and you will find some." So they cast it, and now they were not able to haul it in, because of the quantity of fish. That disciple whom Jesus loved therefore said to Peter, "It is the Lord!" When Simon Peter heard that it was the Lord, he put on his outer garment, for he was stripped for work, and threw himself into the sea. The other disciples came in the boat, dragging the net full of fish, for they were not far from the land, but about a hundred yards off.

When they got out on land, they saw a charcoal fire in place, with fish laid out on it, and bread. Jesus said to them, "Bring some of the fish that you have just caught." So Simon Peter went aboard and hauled the net ashore, full of large fish, 153 of them. And although there were so many, the net was not torn. Jesus said to them, "Come and have breakfast." Now none of the disciples dared ask him, "Who are you?" They knew it was the Lord. Jesus came and took the bread and gave it to them, and so with the fish. This was now the third time that Jesus was revealed to the disciples after he was raised from the dead.

When they had finished breakfast, Jesus said to Simon Peter, "Simon, son of John, do you love me more than these?" He said to him, "Yes, Lord; you know that I love you." He said to him, "Feed my lambs." He said to him a second time, "Simon, son of John, do you love me?" He said to him, "Yes, Lord; you know that I love you." He said to him, "Tend my sheep." He said to him the third time, "Simon, son of John, do you love me?" Peter was grieved because he said to him the third time, "Do you love me?" and he said to him, "Lord, you know everything; you know that I love you." Jesus said to him, "Feed my sheep. Truly, truly, I say to you, when you were young, you used to dress yourself and walk wherever you wanted, but when you are old, you will stretch out your hands, and another will dress you and carry you where you do not want to go." (This he said to show by what kind of death he was to glorify God.) And after saying this he said to him, "Follow me." (John 21:1–19)

From beginning to end, this final pericope in the Gospel is about discipleship, and about Jesus's discipling of Peter, particularly. The chapter starts off by focusing on Peter and his decision to return to fishing. But I want to draw our attention to that first moment when Peter learns that Jesus is present, because that is where we begin to see how the Teacher and disciple respond to each other. In verse 7, Peter abruptly jumps out of his boat and swims one hundred yards to shore without orders from anyone around him. At this point, Jesus has not said any words that are directed personally to Peter, and John's comment is more exclamation than anything else. But Peter completely drops his stated aim of fishing because his Master is present; he exemplifies the posture of abandonment to follow Jesus that is so often connected in the gospels with the cost of

discipleship. This is a strong indication that one of this pericope's aims is
to speak to discipleship in some way.

While Peter makes the physical effort to be closer with Jesus, his
strengths and competencies are evident. Many commentators mention
that Peter demonstrates great physical strength before all the disciples sit
down around the charcoal fire.[18] After Jesus calls to them, Peter swims
the equivalent of four laps in a pool while he is weighed down by his
clothes. Jesus asks the disciples a few minutes later to bring in some of
the catch for breakfast, and Peter is the only man named who hauled in
the nets with 153 fish.[19] I take Jesus's command for Peter to use his physical strength to be quite instructive in my understanding of discipleship,
because the command tells me Jesus sees and takes hold of every aspect
of his disciples' souls. Jesus did not disregard Peter's strengths and he will
not push aside our knowledge of the Bible or our skills either. These are
things Jesus is perfectly willing to embrace and even commands us to use.
It is correct for evangelical disciples to develop a deep understanding of
the Bible and to have competency in their Christian lives. In the name of
presenting ourselves to God, it is necessary for us to hold our strengths
with open hands before the Lord and use them in serving him. But we
cannot follow Jesus by exercising our strengths alone, because such a
"discipleship" would be a tacit denial that there is more in our hearts,
namely our vulnerabilities and weaknesses. Jesus knew that Peter needed
more than his own strengths to follow him as he intended, so he centers
the conversation on Peter after everyone has finished breakfast. Jesus re-
stores Peter among the apostles and actually clarifies Peter's discipleship
call by integrating principles that soul care providers use today to meet
people in their vulnerability.

The English translation indicates a shift in the text with a paragraph
break beginning at verse 15, and it is certainly a shift in posture for Peter.
He had leaned on his strengths up to this point; his headstrong claims
created many memorable moments in the apostles' walk with Jesus, and
he had just used his physical fitness to offer an appropriate response to
his Master's presence and requests. But then Jesus brings up something
that Peter's strength cannot change, because the emotional weight held
him captive. Clearly, the aim of Jesus's dialogue with Peter is to redeem
Peter's threefold betrayal by asking him if he loved Jesus three times.
Many commentators claim that this affects a restoration for Peter among

---

18 Craig S. Keener, *The Gospel of John: A Commentary* (Grand Rapids: Baker, 2003), 1231.
19 Keener, *The Gospel of John*, 1231.

the other apostles and even functions as an "almost 'official' sanction to his rightful place of leadership [in the church]."[20] But we cannot limit this conversation to a footnote in our mental biographies of Peter or to an interesting object of study in the Greek. In this conversation Jesus pushes Peter head on to confront a dysfunction in his heart and helps his disciple overcome an obstacle to intimacy with him. This conversation captures what the deconstructive element of soul care is about because Jesus helps Peter sit in his failure so that Peter can find healing by confessing his failure in the presence of a compassionate friend.

To really see the soul-care implications of the resurrected Master's conversation with his disciple, we need to understand what it would have been like to be in Peter's place in that moment. And it starts with imagining what it would be like to have your closest companions around you as Jesus pulls your failure to the surface. The text does not say that Peter and Jesus took privacy from the other apostles to have this conversation. The same men who heard Peter say that he would rather die than betray Jesus, and who know about his betrayal, are still huddled around as Jesus descends with Peter into his heart.[21] The words of Peter's premature promise to follow Jesus further than the other disciples may have burned in his mind during these very moments because Jesus may have intentionally alluded to Peter's prideful statement with Jesus's use of "more than these" language in his question (John 13:37, 21:15). The threefold affirmation is actually a fitting resolution to an arc for Peter. Just as he swore his allegiance publicly and denied his acquaintance with Jesus before witnesses, so now "his restoration to public ministry is effected in a similarly public environment."[22]

Even the setting of this conversation had the potential to unearth pain in Peter's heart. I have referred to the charcoal fire introduced in verse 9 in hopes that it helps us to imagine what this moment was like. But that fire is also a connection to Peter's betrayal, because that is where Peter was standing outside the courtyard when he denied knowing Jesus and became aware of his denial when the cock crowed (John 18:18, 25–27).[23] Therefore, this situation has the same potential to recall painful memories and feelings that other locations have for people who are injured or traumatized. I cringe when I drive through intersections where I have had

---

20 Leon Morris, *The Gospel according to John,* NICNT (Grand Rapids: Eerdmans, 1971), 767.
21 D. A. Carson, *The Gospel according to John,* PNTC (Leicester: IVP, 1991), 675.
22 Carson, *The Gospel according to John,* 676.
23 Gary M. Burge, *John,* NIVAC (Grand Rapids: Zondervan, 2000), 596.

fender benders or near misses with other cars. I can only imagine how vulnerable Peter felt and how many barbs seemed to be poking his heart when Jesus initiated this conversation in that social and spatial context.

Remember that Jesus has deliberately initiated this conversation. He intends to restore Peter's standing among the apostles and sanction him for a position of leadership in the burgeoning movement of the church. In order to accomplish this redemption and do what was best for Peter, Jesus needed to bring Peter into his heart to really address the wounds and shame left by Peter's betrayal. Peter's response, or better acceptance and surrender, to Jesus's lead in this conversation allows the mending to actually take place. He does not run from the conversation, nor does he turn to his stubbornness or strength to avoid really entering his failure. As a result of obeying Jesus in this moment, Peter is authentically present with his true, vulnerable self and can only explain his love for Jesus by appealing to Jesus's knowledge.[24] Essentially, this is less assertion and more of a confession by Peter. He is not asserting that he is strong enough; his confession of his love is made without comparing the strength of his love to that of others, as he did when he tried to elevate his willingness to follow Jesus above that of the other apostles.[25] Instead, Peter chooses the correct response for a disciple of Jesus. He recognizes that Jesus is at work in his heart and simply obeys Jesus's invitations into his weakness. That allows Peter to experience his own personal miracle, as Gary Burge puts it:

> [Peter] ran to the only one who could heal his memories, who could rewrite the terrible pictures and sounds of his recent past—the courtyard, that charcoal fire, the young woman. The miracle demonstrated that despite Peter's failings, Jesus was still on his side, cooking a good meal for friends, having fun filling nets with fish. Then the invitation to affirm his love three times drowned out the echoes of his betrayal that haunted him.[26]

This is a significant experience for Peter in his discipleship journey because the acceptance of Jesus's presence with him in his failure and vulnerability ultimately results in the clarification and specification of the discipleship call given to Peter. Notice that Jesus responds to Peter's answer with commands to feed his sheep. Peter does not know how being a shepherd translates into leadership roles in the church because he has

---

24 Carson, *The Gospel according to John*, 677.
25 Carson, *The Gospel according to John*, 677.
26 Burge, *John*, 596.

been a fisherman all his life. So this is an interesting move on Jesus's part, because his call to Peter changes in a way that clarifies what following Jesus will look like for Peter in the future. Jesus moved from commanding Peter to exercise his physical strength in an area of competency (fishing), to calling him into places of inexperience and physical weakness (shepherding and being led by the hand into death [21:18]). Therefore, Jesus needed to be with Peter in his vulnerability so Peter's capacity to trust would be prepared for this sort of simultaneous transition into leadership, on the one hand, and into dependence on Jesus in an area where he was as yet incompetent, on the other. This is the new and specific call in Peter's discipleship that grows out of the restoration of Peter's standing with the apostles, and most importantly, out of his restored intimacy with Christ.

Peter's engagement with his failure and Jesus's soul care were crucial for Peter's discipleship because that moment focused the way Peter, as an individual, was going to follow Jesus. And soul care can still help believers gain clarity in their individual call to follow Jesus today, because soul care offers acceptance and healing to a disciple's true self, thereby increasing their trust in and dependence on Jesus. I would think that many Christians would sign up for disciplines of soul care in an instant if healing and a growing trust in Jesus were the result. Sadly, I see many students resist soul-care disciplines like spiritual direction, implying that the contents of their soul are inconsequential or belongs to their own private domain. They have to be willing to trust another brother or sister who is offering to care for them and expose the truth of who they are to their soul-care provider. For many, the requirements of trust and bald authenticity seems too risky or too painful to pursue the benefits of soul care. That saddens me because there is no getting around an unwillingness to trust others in our growth as disciples. Bill Hull asserts that "trust is key" for disciples if they desire to grow into authentic Christlikeness, because our souls can only be positively impacted when we submit to others:

> Trust is key, because we only take in the truth we trust. And that trust has as much to do with the messenger as with the message. When you trust someone to the point you become vulnerable, you're giving that person permission to speak into your life. . . . Only in trusting relationships can we honestly deal with barriers to obedience and overwhelming sins that hold us back from spiritual growth.[27]

---

27 Hull, *The Complete Book of Discipleship,* 156.

As I have said before, this kind of vulnerability and submission to another in soul care is crucial for discipleship because it balances the activity and growth-emphasis of many contemporary discipleship programs. Allowing another to know us for who we truly are, including our failures and weakness, helps us to learn to accept our vulnerabilities and find healing for pains in our heart, because the person present with us embodies and mediates the full love and acceptance Jesus has for us. The aspect of soul care that invites us to trust others with our vulnerabilities also facilitates an authentic humility in disciples that is impossible to attain for the disciple who chooses to camp out in his or her strengths. Because a brother or sister embodies the love and care of Jesus for us in soul care, we are able to learn how to extend grace to ourselves and how to see ourselves more truthfully by watching how they respond to us and speak into our lives.

With all that I have already said about the need to trust, I feel obligated to say that trust cannot be generated in a moment by sheer force of will. Instead, the development of trust requires two experiences. First, one needs to know what it feels like to be in the presence of a trustworthy person; one needs to see that they can still feel safe, and still be known and loved, in both one's good and one's bad. Jesus exhibited this type of trustworthiness to Peter around the charcoal fire through his compassion and acceptance of Peter just as he was. Jesus's trustworthiness generated trust on the part of Peter as he accepted Jesus's invitation into Peter's vulnerability. Said another way, the way Jesus established relational safety and security for Peter to be honest and vulnerable in that moment inspired Peter's ability to trust. Jesus's decision to trust Peter for a proper response was validated when Peter followed Jesus into his heart and faced the pain of his betrayal. A disciple is empowered to let go of their shame and guilt when another has true knowledge of the disciple's sin and weakness and yet still chooses to trust them. The other person's choice to accept and forgive the sins and obstacles in our heart encourages us to do the same. Their act of love also gives us courage to move forward because that part of our heart is no longer off limits. As a consequence of being known and trusted by another, disciples can move forward to greater works of righteousness and integrity of character because more of their self and soul is unlocked. Peter experienced this when Jesus loved him in his weakness instead of condemning him. That love empowered and encouraged Peter to receive the specific discipleship call Jesus had for him and to become a shepherd in the church, even though it would eventually cost him his life.

CONCLUSION

Discipleship in the church today desperately needs the kind of soul care that helps congregants feel known and loved in the midst of their sin. That vulnerable moment is the pivotal point of change where disciples' souls can be impacted in a deep and lasting way. Peter had such a moment with Jesus and found that Jesus established the trajectory for the rest of his life in that conversation. But these conversations are not occurring in the lives of evangelicals who limit discipleship to church programs and developing Christian competencies. No amount of biblical knowledge or Christian morality can eradicate the pain in our hearts or neutralize that pain's effect on us. Only the healing touch of the Spirit of God, embodied by compassionate members of his church, can accomplish that task, because the aim of soul care is deconstructive.

I hope this chapter makes it evident that strengths and competencies are still gifts from the Lord intended for use and central to discipleship. Even so, I am convinced that it is absolutely vital for disciples to balance the use of strengths and virtues with the honesty and stillness of soul care so they become more intimate with God. It is not that the invitations of the Lord are only present in our brokenness and failures; God can meet his children in any and every circumstance. But the person God knows and invites into deeper intimacy is each of our true selves, not only the portion of ourselves that we are comfortable presenting to others. So the ultimate goal is learning how to accept the truth about ourselves and to respond to the Lord from that true self without fear of condemnation. That will allow us to obey Jesus's invitations to use our strengths and to follow him into vulnerability and humility.

The solid foundation of soul care is the belief that the work of Jesus's death and resurrection has accomplished full acceptance and unconditional love with God. That belief allows disciples to dive deep into their souls and to discover the unknown contents therein with hope and even comfort. Soul-care providers can embody that hope and offer comfort in those moments by accepting and forgiving the sins that Jesus has already paid for as his own. And in so doing, the spiritual disciplines of soul care can maximize the growth attained in discipleship by helping disciples release the burdens and overcome the obstacles that have impeded their development into Christlikeness. Disciplines like spiritual direction and prayers of examen that uncover our ability to trust God have the potential to bring legitimate fulfillment to the lives of Christians who deliberately participate in their discipleship. Like Peter, we only need to be willing to follow Jesus as he takes us into our heart and cares for our souls through the compassion and acceptance of our brothers and sisters in Christ. Even as we face our failure, we remain in the embrace of God who persistently invites us to repent and obey anew.

CHAPTER 20

A Good Beach Church: Discipleship and the Witnessing Power of Embodied Local Community

Tod E. Bolsinger

The scholar sitting in front of me at the diner gave me an answer I didn't expect. *"What we need to be is just a good beach church."*

While Mike Wilkins's reputation for being an avid surfer preceded him, I still blinked and sat for a moment dumbfounded. I had recently been named the new pastor of the church in question, and I had made a kind of pilgrimage from Hollywood down the busy I-5 freeway to the Biola University campus to meet Dr. Wilkins and to ask him to share his perspective on my community, the church he knew better than I did, and to offer his advice on my new calling.

For well over a decade Dr. Michael J. Wilkins, New Testament scholar, professor, and Dean of the Faculty for the Talbot School of Theology at Biola University, had taught an adult Bible class every Sunday morning at San Clemente Presbyterian Church. In every conversation that I'd had with the nominating committee as they were going through the discernment process for calling me to become the new senior pastor, his name had come up. No one was quoted more than him; no one's teaching had a greater impact. During a season of turmoil in the congregation, his class had been a haven away from conflict, pointing fretting church members back to their primary commitment as disciples of Jesus.

Disciples and discipleship. The themes of Mike's scholarship were also the focus of his church ministry. So, as we sat there—me, the new senior pastor who was in the final phases of my own dissertation at Fuller Theological Seminary on communal spiritual formation[1]; and Mike, also a Fuller alum, who had recently written a tour de force on discipleship—I assumed that the conversation would turn toward discipleship.

---

1 Tod E. Bolsinger, *It Takes a Church to Raise a Christian: How the Community of God Transforms Lives* (Grand Rapids: Baker, 2005).

To be sure, I was entering this new call with the hope that my dissertation would become a kind of blueprint for building a spiritually formative missional community. I hoped that Mike would become an ally and
counselor to me, offering me both local knowledge and biblical insight
for helping this congregation become a center of Christian discipleship
and communal formation. I had looked forward to a conversation about
discipleship strategies, contextual knowledge, and discerning first steps. I
thought the conversation would be about discipleship and *our* particular
congregation. But he wanted to talk about the *beach*? I thought we were
going to talk about discipleship. Or were we?

Yes, the opening illustration of his book, *Following the Master: A Biblical Model of Discipleship*, was about a conversation he had with a surfer,
but it didn't register with me at the time. When I heard his statement
about being a "good beach church," I assumed that he was speaking as
an insider and stakeholder trying to check a newcomer's enthusiasm for
bringing change. I thought—because I was a younger pastor (age thir-
ty-three) who had been trained at an older megachurch (Hollywood Presbyterian) in the great urban center that made most south Orange County
residents cringe (Los Angeles)—that Mike believed his task was to protect
me from coming into his beloved and embattled community of friends
and trying to refashion them into another generic big-box "worship center" that would try to compete with the seeker-driven churches that were
flourishing in the 1990s. And I thought that we would need to talk more
about discipleship another time.

But after some years of working together, more conversations, and
through my own reading of his writings, I now understand that when
Mike exhorted me to help San Clemente Presbyterian be a "good beach
church," he was indeed talking about the kind of discipleship that shows
up on beaches in the Gospels, and transforms communities and towns
in the Acts of the Apostles—that is, discipleship related to real people
in real communities. Or, to be even more specific, he was talking about
discipleship in a local community *in a local church*.

For Wilkins, writing on Jesus's charge to his disciples in Acts 1, the elements of discipleship in a post-Pentecost context are clearly about the way
that people who have believed the good news and experienced the power
of God's Spirit giving them new life, live out that life in a particular community in a very particular way.[2] This communal approach to discipleship

---

2 "Jesus did indeed call men and women into a deep personal relationship with himself, yet
if we focus exclusively on the individual in our growth in discipleship, we run the danger

is both a support and a corrective for the default individualism that frames a faith conviction for most western, particularly American, people.[3] And indeed, when Wilkins wrote *Following the Master* in the waning days of the twentieth century, the default mental model of "discipleship" was a focus on one-on-one relationships and "personal faith" in Jesus.

Wilkins, who admits his affinity for this personalized approach to faith, readily acknowledges the way in which discipleship often gets reduced to radically individualized ways of faith development. And he offers his reflections on the book of Acts as a corrective to a radically atomistic Christianity that often minimizes the deep need that humans—even Christians—have for each other.[4]

At the same time, he minimizes the *inherent* communal reality of discipleship as an expression of God's own life and Jesus's own personal embodiment as God incarnate.[5] Indeed, the communal, local, and missional aspects of Wilkins's model in *Following the Master* can be pushed further for a twenty-first-century world that has seen *personalization* in virtually every arena become an expectation of every product, process, or philosophy (including Christianity), and the deeper longing for connection that energizes the "social" in *social* media.[6] In other words, we can ask the

---

of separating the individual from the community of faith" (Michael J. Wilkins, *Following the Master: A Biblical Theology of Discipleship* [Grand Rapids: Zondervan, 1992], 244).

3 "We must have the community to support and correct our discipleship in the world. This seems so obvious, but our practice is so frequently individualistic. Christian discipleship is not for Lone Rangers (though in all fairness, even the masked man had Tonto as his sidekick). We must resist the individualism of our culture and cultivate deep and strong relationships with others" (David W. Gill, *The Opening of the Christian Mind: Taking Every Thought Captive to Christ* [Downers Grove, IL: InterVarsity Press, 1989], 135–36; cited in Wilkins, *Following the Master*, 244).

4 Note that for Wilkins, community is almost entirely a "support" for individual disciples in times of need. "But when challenges became so overwhelming that it was impossible to make it alone, our family community provided the strength, courage, and love necessary to endure the darkest moments of our existence. That is why individual disciples must function as a community, the family of God" (Wilkins, *Following the Master*, 247).

5 "Many pastors and lay leaders talk the right talk—about needing to be relational rather than programmatic—but they then get hopelessly lost in creating relational programs so that their collective of individual Christians will have a sense of connection to each other. However, *the fundamental reality of the church as an enduring, covenantal, irreducible, and Trinity-reflecting entity in and of itself is overlooked entirely*" (Bolsinger, *It Takes a Church to Raise a Christian*, 15 [emphasis added]).

6 See Rainie and Wellman's examination of how technology is shaping relationships in the twenty-first century: "the new social operating system we call 'networked individualism' [is] in contrast to the longstanding operating system formed around large hierarchical bureaucracies and small, densely knit groups such as households, communities, and workgroups. We call networked individualism an 'operating system' because it describes the ways in which people connect, communicate, and exchange information" (Lee Rainie and Barry Wellman, *Networked: The New Social Operating System* [Cambridge, MA: MIT Press, 2012], 6–7]).

question today like this: *In a day of social media and global movements, what does it mean to be followers of Jesus who "are members one of another" (Rom. 12:5) and participants in the very mission of God "in Jerusalem, in all Judea and Samaria [and in every local town, community, municipality, or city] and to the ends of the earth" (Acts 1:8)?*[7]

For Wilkins, discipleship after Pentecost is about the way that the Spirit of God works within the church to call and empower people to be disciples *without* the physical presence of Jesus. Because of both the Spirit and the church, disciples today, just like the disciples of the early church, are a continuation of Jesus's own discipling ministry.[8] A local church, therefore, is a gathering of a people who have believed the good news proclaimed, united themselves to each other through baptism, to learn and live out the teachings of Jesus—in order to reveal the presence of God's reign and rule in a *particular location* (Luke 8:39). Disciples, called and gathered as a local church, are to be the answer to Jesus's prayer, "Your kingdom come, Your will be done, *on earth* . . ." (Matt. 6:10, emphasis added), and in so doing to witness to the availability of that kingdom now for the blessing of that place and for the witness to the world.[9]

To do so, the particular *actions* of discipleship that are *inspired* by faith in Jesus are *enacted and embedded* in the life of a community. For Wilkins, those actions, first revealed in Jesus's charge to his disciples immediately preceding his ascension, are the paradigm for post-Pentecostal following of Jesus today: *First, focus on the teachings of Jesus for living out the meaning of life (vv. 1–3). Second, actualize the unity of community brought by the Spirit (vv. 4–5). Third, be a witness to the good news of Jesus in the power of the Spirit (vv. 6–8). Fourth, let the absence of Jesus be an incentive to hopefulness until his return (vv. 9–11).*

In this essay, I will draw upon Wilkins description of post-Pentecost discipleship as a communal endeavor that furthers the ministry of Jesus in the absence of the physical presence of Jesus through the power of the Spirit in the community of believers.[10] I will describe a picture of

---

7 All Scripture translations are NRSV unless otherwise noted.

8 "[T]he true believer is one who, although he or she can now no longer physically follow Jesus around, focuses his or her belief on the reality of a risen Lord and Savior, exercises personal faith unto salvation, and is characterized by a lifestyle consistent with apostolic teaching concerning the Christian life. This is truly a continuation of the concept of discipleship that Jesus taught in his earthly ministry" (Wilkins, *Following the Master*, 295).

9 Cf. Matthew 10:5–7, 14, where Jesus sends his disciples to the towns of the "lost sheep of Israel" and Jesus's own lament over Jerusalem in Matthew 23:37–39.

10 "As Luke continues his story from the Gospel to the book of Acts, he allows us to see the crucial necessity of the community for discipleship. Jesus no longer was with his disciples physically, yet he promised to be with them always (Mt 28:20). Through the Spirit, the

discipleship that is inextricable from the local congregation and make suggestions to nudge Wilkins's own definition of discipleship toward a personal, even more local—and increasingly *networked*—embodiment of the life of Jesus for the sake of the world. Finally, I will demonstrate that biblical discipleship, particularly as seen in the book of Acts, is best understood as *embodying the teachings of Jesus within a community for the sake of missional witness in a particular place.* To do so, let's explore the elements of biblical discipleship in the life of the disciples of Jesus best understood as: embodiment, community, witness, and location.

EMBODIMENT

> To withhold our bodies from religion is to exclude religion from our lives.
>
> —Dallas Willard[11]

After the temptations in the wilderness, Jesus makes home in the seaside community of Capernaum. It is from that very particular place that Jesus's kingdom movement begins on the beach of the Sea of Galilee with two pairs of brothers, whom Jesus calls to leave their nets, their businesses, and their families to follow him and take on his ministry (Matt. 4:18–20), and that we begin to understand the particular way that Jesus reframes discipleship.

The English word *disciple* normally designates a "follower," "adherent" or "student" of a great master, religious leader, or teacher. Very early it was used as the standard nomenclature for delineating a follower or believer of Jesus. And for Wilkins, this is the key distinction.[12] Unlike disciples of Jewish rabbis or Roman philosophers who have committed to a teacher for one's own learning, the Christian disciple follows Jesus as a believer who surrenders one's life to Jesus as teacher and lord in both faith in and personal embodiment of Jesus's own mission.[13]

---

community would now provide the fellowship, encouragement, edification, and mutuality necessary for following the Master in the new era" (Wilkins, *Following the Master*, 247–48).

11 *The Spirit of the Disciplines: Understanding How God Changes Lives* (New York: HarperCollins, 1990), 31.

12 "The disciples were Jesus's true followers, true believers. The crowd was the basically neutral group that was the object of Jesus's saving ministry of preaching, teaching, and healing; but as a group the crowd did not exercise faith in him" (Wilkins, *Following the Master*, 179).

13 "As he walked by the Sea of Galilee, he saw two brothers, Simon, who is called Peter, and Andrew his brother, casting a net into the sea—for they were fishermen. And he said to them, 'Follow me, and I will make you fish for people'" (Matt. 4:18–19).

Indeed, the "making of disciples" became the core charge of Jesus in his post-resurrection "commission."

> Go therefore and make disciples of all nations, baptizing them in the name of the Father and of the Son and of the Holy Spirit, and teaching them to obey everything that I have commanded you. (Matt. 28:19–20)

In this definitive passage, discipleship requires both "baptizing" or bringing the new disciple into the larger community of believers, and "teaching." And indeed, without question, Jesus's teaching and the disciple's belief in and adherence to Jesus's teaching—through the apostles—was at the center of post-Pentecost discipleship[14] in the same way that it had been the center of Jesus's rabbinic activity with his disciples during his life.[15]

While we will look more closely at the role of the community, it is worth emphasizing again that the emphasis on teaching is more than communicating knowledge but engendering obedience. Indeed, at the core of Wilkins's definition of discipleship is the expectation that the follower of Jesus "exercises personal faith unto salvation, and is characterized by a lifestyle consistent with apostolic teaching concerning the Christian life."[16]

While in many churches today teaching and discipleship ministries are the same ministry with different nomenclature, the differences between teaching for its own sake and discipleship in the manner of Jesus are most clearly seen in the end goal. While a teacher can assume that she has been successful with the transmission of content (usually demonstrated through an examination or report), discipleship demands that instruction must result in the transformation of behavior—in obedience.[17] Or, as Dallas Willard has written, "to believe something is to *act* as if it is so."[18]

Discipleship, therefore, is as much about the ethics, the activity, and indeed the very ministry actions of Jesus that the disciples joins as both a

---

14 "The expression 'devoted themselves to the apostles' teaching' (cf. Ac 2:42) indicated the means by which Jesus's teaching to them could be passed on to the new disciples of the church" (Wilkins, *Following the Master*, 261).

15 "Jesus's teachings are the foundation of the discipleship life of the new community" (Wilkins, *Following the Master*, 261).

16 Wilkins, *Following the Master*, 295. Cf. Matthew 28:20, "teaching them to obey everything that I have commanded you."

17 John 13:17, James 2:14–26, Matthew 28:20.

18 Dallas Willard, *The Divine Conspiracy: Rediscovering Our Hidden Life In God* (New York: HarperCollins, 1998), 319 (emphasis mine).

partner and supporter. When Jesus went through the countryside calling people to follow him, it was more like a candidate asking people to join his campaign and serve a movement, than a school-admissions counselor seeking to find new pupils to instruct.

For a disciple, the option of being an "adherent" or "believer" who assents to a set of dogmatic constructions, or even ecclesiastical confessions without any change in loyalty, life direction, or behavior is akin to the rich young ruler who asks the "Good Teacher" a most important question, but, refusing the required change of life, goes away both sad and unchanged (Matt. 19:16–22).

In this way, discipleship, is more akin to "adherence" and "apprenticeship" than to a course of study in an academy of learning.[19] Therefore, following the teachings of Jesus, that reveal both the "meaning of life" and the intentions of God revealed in the incarnation, requires believing the good news of the Creator God's restoration of creation through reestablishing God's loving and just rule (Matt. 4:17; Mark 1:15), *and* new embodied—and social—action.

COMMUNITY

> That the plural form [of "disciple"] is normally used expresses an important point: individual disciples are always seen in conjunction with the community of disciples, whether as Jesus's intimate companions or as the church. Hence, discipleship is a concept that normally occurs within the context of the community. With the inception of the church in Acts, that community is the church.[20]

Drawing on Acts 1:1–11, Wilkins describes the post-Pentecostal season as "the age of community." Believers in this age (which includes the present time!) are not inferior to the disciples who walked with Jesus through Palestine, but are less "privileged" because they didn't receive the gospel and the instruction in gospel-living directly from Jesus. The church—that is, the community that is created at Pentecost—continues

---

19 "But the divine co-action was to be true for Jesus trainees, or apprentices, also. After a time of instruction he sent them out to do what he did. As they went they were to heal the sick and announce that "the Kingdom of God has come upon you" (Luke 10:9). Even those who refused their ministry were to be informed that "the Kingdom" had come to them (v. 11)" (Willard, *The Divine Conspiracy*, 29).

20 Wilkins, *Following the Master*, 40.

the discipleship of Jesus by the Spirit, through the teaching of the apostles in the community.[21] The church, therefore, is the community where
the Spirit of God forms the lives of believers through the biblical teaching
that is passed down from the apostles to the church today[22] and is marked
by *unity that leads to conformity of life.*

For Wilkins, the spiritual unity of the believer with Christ is a blessed
fellowship between the believer and the ascended Christ that parallels
the original Twelve's relationship with the physical Jesus. But because
Jesus is not physically present after Pentecost, the unity of the community is then a sign and instrument *of the Spirit* for bringing conformity
of the believer to the life of Christ.[23] This spiritual unity leads to the
conformity of the believer's life to Christ's in both moral character and
missional capacity.[24] Again, this unity is not just the unity of souls that
imputes salvation, but of actual bodies and embodied actions that are
carried on by the Spirit, through the community of God's people for the
mission of God in the world.

In John 17, Jesus pushes the themes of embodiment and unity even
further than the spiritual unity of his followers with him. Indeed, the very
purpose of the life-conforming spiritual unity is not conformity for conformity's sake, but for the sake of mission and witness. The spiritual unity

---

21 "One of the most significant features for us to recognize is that the word *disciples* is used
in the book of Acts to describe the post-Easter believers intimately associated together as the
new community of faith, the church" (Wilkins, *Following the Master*, 256).

22 Wilkins, *Following the Master,* 256. See also Bolsinger, *It Takes a Church to Raise a Christian*,
17: "The church is God's incarnation today. The church is Jesus's body on earth. The church is
the temple of the Spirit. The church is not a helpful thing for my individual spiritual journey.
The church is the journey. The church is not a collection of 'soul-winners' all seeking to tell
unbelievers 'the Way' to God. The church is the Way. To be part of the church is to be part
of God, to be part of God's Communion and to be part of God's ministry. To belong to the
people of God is to enjoy relationship with God and live out the purposes of God."

23 "[T]he Spirit causes a transition to be made from the kind of discipleship relationship the
disciples had with the earthly Jesus to a discipleship relationship with the ascended Jesus. To
anticipate Paul's metaphor of the body, the church is now the community of disciples who are
brought together by the Spirit as Christ's body (1 Cor. 12:12–13), enjoying an unhindered,
loving fellowship with him through the Spirit (Eph. 1:22–23; 5:23–32)" (Wilkins, *Following
the Master*, 267).

24 "Analogous to other master-disciple relationships, Jesus's disciples would become like
him and carry out the same ministry as he did. But Jesus's disciples would become like him in
a unique way. The spiritual unity that would be established between Jesus and his disciples—
Jesus in them and they in Jesus (cf. John 17:13–26)—guaranteed a likeness quite unknown
in any other kind of discipleship relationship. This spiritual unity looks ahead to the kind
of "likeness" that Paul will eventually address, where his greatest desire is to be like Christ,
where the ultimate goal of the believer's life is to be conformed to the image of Christ (Ro
8:29)" (Wilkins, *Following the Master*, 132).

of the disciples with Jesus must be expressed and embodied in the actual physical unity of a shared, corporate life of discipleship and mission if the world is to know of the reality of God's redeeming mission in the Son.

> I ask not only on behalf of these, but also on behalf of those who will believe in me through their word, that they may all be one. As you, Father, are in me and I am in you, may they also be in us, so that the world may believe that you have sent me. The glory that you have given me I have given them, so that they may be one, as we are one, I in them and you in me, that they may become completely one, so that the world may know that you have sent me and have loved them even as you have loved me. (John 17:20–23)

The embodied spiritual unity of the ascended Jesus with his disciples by the power of the indwelling Spirit becomes the primary mode of witness to the ongoing presence of God's kingdom through the actual corporate life of the people of God. As C. Norman Kraus wrote, "The authentic community is the authentic witness."[25]

WITNESS

Since the time of the publication of *Following the Master*, the conversation about discipleship has been shaped by the language of the missional church. Indeed, for Darrell Guder, the entire enterprise of discipleship in a post-Christendom context is nothing more nor less than the forming of people for taking their place in the mission of God in the world. Churches as "communities of witness" are formed by God to demonstrate that God's project of redeeming the world through Israel was continuing and expanding through the church, the people of God in the present age.[26]

Very often today, the discussion of communities of witness, or what is often called "missional communities" becomes shaped as a reaction to "traditional" or "attractional" church. New creative missional endeavors that are rooted in neighborhoods or marketplace groups, in coffee shops, or public houses, are becoming alternatives to sanctuaries with steeples and pews and a cross on top. These alternative witnessing communities

---

25 C. Norman Kraus, *The Authentic Witness* (Grand Rapids, Eerdmans, 1979), 20.

26 Darrel L. Guder, "Walking Worthily: Missional Leadership after Christendom," *Princeton Seminary Bulletin* 28.3 (2007): 251–91.

are to be commended for their engagement with public life, their outward and neighborhood-focused emphasis, and their intentional design toward reaching and discipling the unchurched.

At the same time, however, there is a kind of reaction to traditional and ecclesiological models of church and worshipful life that leaves some wondering if in the name of "witness" and "mission" the very values of the church or community are being diminished or overlooked.

Recently on a trip to Auckland, New Zealand, I visited an innovative witnessing community that is led by a cadre of seminary-trained clergy, business leaders, and artists. As a church, they are both small and intense, numbering only twenty or so members, but insisting that members have a high commitment to the shared witness in the neighborhood. Their presence in their locality is much greater than their number. They host public events; they sponsor spirituality and religious-themed art exhibits; they convene discussions around topics; and they run a restaurant and coffee shop that are the heart of the neighborhood. They unabashedly and with great depth of thinking hold to a mission statement that is rooted in their understanding of what it means to love God and neighbor with a particular kind of exilic expression of "seeking the welfare of the city" (Jer. 29:7), seeking intentionally to make their specific neighborhood "a better place to live."

When I asked denominational leaders in the local area what they thought about this creative venture, all agreed that they were inspiring lots of similar ventures, but worried that in the name of "witness," "discipleship" was getting lost. Said one leader, "This is a Baptist initiative and I am worried that I don't see many people being baptized."

At a moment when the church needs more—not less—missional witness and more—not less—creative and innovative initiatives, it seems necessary to recapture the disciple-making imperative both at the heart of a witnessing community and at the center of the gospel commission that started from one particular location (Jerusalem) and has been led to churches throughout the world in very particular locations.

LOCATION

The intention of discipleship in the local church is to create a context—a very specific context—for the Spirit to move in the lives of people and shape the life of a follower of Jesus. This witness and this formation are both the results of embodied practices within a particular set of relationships and shaped by the issues of its social location. Paul's letters to Corinth—instructing believers in the way of Jesus—are profoundly different from his instructions to Galatia or to the encyclical letters that very likely became the book of Ephesians. Paul's sermon on Mars Hill is very different from when he taught in a synagogue or witnessed before the magistrate as a Roman citizen who had appealed to Caesar (Acts 17, 25).

Discipleship also takes seriously that the Spirit is always deeply incarnational, working through a specific people, in specific places, facing specific challenges *in order to* reveal God's saving work to all of creation. The gospel does not come and homogenize cultures, locations, and peoples in order to see people saved; it saves them within and for the places that they are sent. The end-goal of discipleship is not to build the church as generic franchises of cultural or denominational institutions. Nor does genuine embodied discipleship lend itself to models and approaches to church life that appropriate one community for another in the name of "best practices" or as a successful "model." In the same way that the Pharisee Saul of Tarsus had to be discipled into faith with a different path (Gal. 1:13–24) than the Gentile convert Timothy (2 Tim. 1; Acts 16:1–5), congregations that are being discipled for missional witness will have different characteristics and practices, and will be shaped uniquely. And the changing context of our rapidly changing world will shape our lives of discipleship also.

As Wilkins was writing *Following the Master*, the megachurch movement was hitting its zenith, making many nervous that the local character of community congregations was being lost to a "big-box" approach to faith formation. As the twenty-first century dawned, and advances in technology began to rapidly change the way media became increasingly "social," a thoughtful reflection of both local community and a deeper understanding and appropriate utilization of technology in an increasingly networked world seems even more urgent.

While there is considerable debate and even concern about the negative effects of technology on relationships,[27] younger generations often see their technological devices as a means to enhancing, furthering, and deepening *face-to-face* relationships.[28] While the debate (and the

---

27 See for example, "Is Technology Making People Less Sociable?" *The Wall Street Journal*, May 10, 2015, https://www.wsj.com/articles/is-technology-making-people-less-sociable-1431093491 (accessed December 2, 2017).

28 Tod Bolsinger, "Blog as Microwave Community", in *The New Media Frontier: Blogging, Vlogging, and Podcasting for Christ*, eds. J. M. Reynolds and R. Overton (Wheaton, IL: Crossway, 2008), 113–24, at 115–16.

necessary and to-be-welcomed studies) will continue, one clear impact of social media is the way that technology has changed the way *individuals* relate to and identify with *groups*.

> In incorporating gadgets into their lives, people have changed the ways they interact with each other. They have become increasingly networked as individuals, rather than embedded in groups. In the world of networked individuals, it is the person who is the focus: not the family, not the work unit, not the neighborhood, and not the social group.[29]

This insight should cause us to pause. In the gospel, the community *as a people* and as *a social location* are both intrinsic to the incarnation, and the establishment of the church. Discipleship for the sake of missional witness takes seriously both a people and their location—even the local geography—of place. As Willie Jennings has written in his commentary on the book of Acts regarding Jesus's command to the disciples to first wait for the Spirit of God and then "be witnesses" (Acts 1:8):

> Geography matters. Place matters to God. From a specific place the disciples will move forward into the world. To go from place to place is to go from people to people and to go from an old identity to a new one. Jesus prepares them for the journey of their lives by holding them in a place where the Spirit will be given to them in that place, and from that place they will be changed.[30]

So, what then do discipleship and location mean in a world of social networks? Articulating an "ecological model of spiritual formation" within the world of higher education and spiritual formation, Stephen and Mary Lowe optimistically remind us that "human connectivity is at the heart of community formation" and that drive to human connectivity can be utilized and even cultivated in an online space as it is in other ecologies or cultures.[31] Therefore, in an increasingly networked world, one of the many "uttermost places" of the world that requires the making of disciples includes the digital and online "spaces" that we inhabit both at home and at work, in social settings and in social media.

---

29 Rainie and Wellman, *Networked*, 6; cf. "The hallmark of networked individualism is that people function more as connected individuals and less as embedded group members" (12).
30 Willie James Jennings, *Acts: A Theological Commentary on the Bible*, Belief (Louisville: Westminster John Knox, 2017), 16.
31 Stephen D. Lowe and Mary E. Lowe, "Spiritual Formation in Theological Distance Education: An Ecosystems Model," *Christian Education Journal* 7.1 (2010): 84–102, at 85.

Discipleship in the twenty-first century that follows Jesus into the Sunday school room also requires following Jesus into the classroom and the courtroom, at kitchen tables and conference tables, in gardens and on gaming sites, in parks and on Pinterest, in meetings and in social media. Christian reflection on technology and discipleship will charge us to be a faithful presence in our globally connected networks, *and* in our local, geophysical context, to the end that "networked individuals" will become a people who are both *networked* and *embedded*, disciples who embody the gospel to their neighbors and their social networks equally.

DISCIPLESHIP AND A GOOD BEACH CHURCH

So, let me take you back to the diner and my discussion with Mike Wilkins about the congregation that both of us would serve and consider our own community of faith. I believe that when Mike was exhorting me to make the aim of my ministry at San Clemente Presbyterian Church to be a "good beach church," he was taking seriously both the high calling of discipleship for the sake of missional witness in this town that he loved and in which I was going to be living ("good"), and the critical element and reality of our particular location ("beach")—as opposed to some other particular location or some generic non-localized, even mass-produced, church.

Whether he intended to or not, his words resonated with me. I could not bring what I had learned in a church that was five times larger, in an urban setting, and featuring classical worship and a choir with paid soloists, and expect to export it to this laid-back small town, where the beauty of the ocean and a southwest swell seriously affected church attendance. I had to take seriously both the Scriptures and our local context. I had to be as focused on the teachings of Jesus as I was on the time that we found ourselves ministering.

So, what does faithful discipleship look like in the twenty-first century? It is a life that takes seriously the teachings of the Scriptures and the challenges of a rapidly changing, increasingly global, and pervasively networked age. It is a life that expresses the unchanging grace of the Spirit's presence and the ever-changing realities of our world. It is the life of a follower of Jesus Christ that is *empowered by the Spirit, embodies the teachings of Jesus, embedded within a local community, and expressed as missional witness in a particular place (or places) that we inhabit.*

A few years into my pastorate at San Clemente Presbyterian, Mike stepped down from his position as our adult Bible teacher to attend to a growing speaking ministry and to join his extended family at another congregation where they could all worship together. While we missed Mike and Lynne as active members in our congregation, Mike was eager to help by filling the pulpit or teaching a series whenever we needed him. Some years of this good arrangement went by, and then one day I spied Lynne and Mike in worship a couple of weeks in a row. I was thrilled to see them back with us more regularly and told them as much, hopeful that we may get a chance to connect and catch up at a local lunch spot soon.

Later that same week, a newer member of my children's ministry staff told me how excited she was about a couple who had just joined the preschool Sunday school team. This couple volunteered to teach the four-year-old class because their grandchildren were in the class—and, my staff member reported, "He really knows the Bible."

When I asked their names, she told me that her brand-new preschool Sunday school teacher was none other than the Distinguished Professor of New Testament and former Dean of the Faculty at Talbot School of Theology. Of course, she, not knowing who they were, just called them "Mike and Lynne."

I smiled, thinking of Dr. Michael J. Wilkins on the floor with a group of preschoolers telling Bible stories. I imagined him illustrating the lessons with surfing stories and asking them questions that they could then take home and talk about with their moms and dads. I imagined those children growing up in our congregation, going through confirmation, confessing their faith in Christ. I imagined them going off to college or entering the workplace and facing the challenges of the world that awaits them. I imagined them raising their own children, looking back on their own childhood, and remembering a Bible story told by a smiling, older surfer on the floor of a Sunday school room and then perhaps volunteering to do the same for another group of children yet to be born.

My mind raced back to that lunch at the diner. "Just a good beach church," the professor had said. Indeed.

Scripture Index

Person Index